# Where Girls Come First

Jeremy P. Tarcher/Penguin
a member of Penguin Group (USA) Inc.    New York

# Where Girls Come First

*The Rise, Fall, and Surprising*
*Revival of Girls' Schools*

ILANA DeBARE

Credits and permissions for photos are listed on page 381.

Most Tarcher/Penguin books are available at special quantity discounts for bulk purchase for sales promotions, premiums, fund-raising, and educational needs. Special books or book excerpts also can be created to fit specific needs. For details, write Penguin Group (USA) Inc. Special Markets, 375 Hudson Street, New York, NY 10014.

Jeremy P. Tarcher/Penguin
a member of
Penguin Group (USA) Inc.
375 Hudson Street
New York, NY 10014
www.penguin.com

Library of Congress Cataloging-in-Publication Data

DeBare, Ilana, date.
Where girls come first : the rise, fall, and surprising revival of girls' schools / Ilana DeBare.
p.   cm.
Includes bibliographical references and index.
ISBN 1-58542-289-4
1. Women—Education—United States—History.   2. Single-sex schools— United States—History.   I. Title.
LC1752.D43       2004              2003066266
371.822—dc22

Printed in the United States of America
1   3   5   7   9   10   8   6   4   2

This book is printed on acid-free paper. ∞

BOOK DESIGN BY KATE NICHOLS

*Where girls come first, and boys come after three.*

—Girls' school slogan of the 1990s

DEDICATED TO

NANCY SKUTCH DEBARE AND REBECCA NAN SCHUCHAT

# Contents

# Introduction: The Laptop and the Maypole

It was a drizzly gray afternoon, that time near the end of the school day when kids seem inevitably to start yawning and staring out the window, but inside the eighth-grade science classroom everyone was exhilarated. Eighteen students knelt in small clusters around race cars they had just built out of wood and glue and construction paper, with battery-operated propellers and paper sails and shiny silver CDs for the wheels. They lined the cars up and raced them against one another to a cacophony of shouts and cheers. "We should rip the seats out, they're adding too much weight!" one student called out. "Try turning the sail the other way!" another shouted. "Clear the starting line if you're not racing!" yelled a third who was sprawled on the floor. The sense of joyful chaos was somewhat enhanced by the students' appearance. They were all wearing pajamas as part of the school's annual Spirit Week, and some had on fuzzy slippers as well. There were plaid pajamas, moon-and-star pajamas, polar bear pajamas. One student wore pineapple-covered pajamas and had built a car named the Happy Pineapple. Its propeller fell off, but someone gave it a shove across the finish line anyway. "Try tilting your sails and see if it makes a difference," suggested science teacher Jennie Brotman. "Tonight you're going to read about Newton's third law. Think about it, and why your cars run differently if you tilt the sails or change the direction of the propeller."

There were several remarkable things about this scene—the pajamas, certainly, and the engaging, hands-on approach to teaching physics. But perhaps the most unusual was the composition of the class. All eighteen students were girls—girls building the cars, girls shouting out directions, girls sprawling across the floor to demarcate the finish line. The age of the school was also unusual. This was the third year of existence for the Julia Morgan School for Girls, and the first year that the school had included an eighth grade or had taught eighth-grade physics. This particular group of girls had made up Julia Morgan's opening class of sixth-grade students; they grew as the school grew; and soon, when the time came to head off to high school, they would be the stars of the school's first graduation.

The Julia Morgan School in Oakland, California, is part of a new wave of all-girl schools that opened their doors in the 1990s and early 2000s. Twenty years ago, girls' schools seemed headed for extinction, a minor footnote in the broad story of American education. Today they are experiencing a dramatic revival. More than thirty new girls' schools opened their doors between 1991 and 2001 around the country—not just in the old northeastern cities that had been strongholds of single-sex education, but in booming high-tech centers like Atlanta and Seattle. Enrollment at existing girls' schools grew by 15 percent, faster than the 12 percent growth rate estimated for all schools. More than six of every ten girls' schools ended the decade at full enrollment—up from 24 percent at the start of the '90s.

In New York City, the Board of Education opened the first new all-girls' public school in more than a century. In Boston, a group of nuns turned an old welfare office into a bustling school for poor and immigrant girls of color. In Silicon Valley, a former Apple Computer executive opened a girls' middle school focused on math, science, and technology. Across the country, coed public schools started experimenting with all-girl math and science classes. Instead of archaic holdovers from another era, girls' schools were suddenly being viewed as cutting edge—even trendy.

I was involved in a small part of this process as one of the founders of the Julia Morgan School for Girls. I was an unlikely founder: Before getting involved with Julia Morgan, I had never even set foot in a girls' school. My own education had been entirely coed, and quite happy. I loved school, did well academically, and had good friends of both genders. As a teenager I thought of girls' schools—when I thought of them at all, which was rarely—as stuffy and snooty and old-fashioned. If my parents had tried to send me to one, I would have kicked and screamed.

But as an adult, I became acutely aware of the barriers that women often face in society. When my reporting career led me to cover Silicon Valley, I wondered why all the engineers and CEOs were men. The answer wasn't just discrimination—it was also that very few young women were coming out of college with the technical knowledge needed for success in the high-tech world. I started thinking about girls' education, and ways to encourage girls to pursue math and science. Suddenly I remembered moments in my own schooling in a new light—how my eleventh-grade physics teacher made the girls leave the classroom so he could tell off-color jokes to the boys, how I scored 800 on my math SAT yet no one ever suggested that I take calculus or pursue math in college. How would my own life have been different if I had been encouraged to explore math and science-related careers?

When I had my daughter, Rebecca, I started reading books about girls' development. One of those books, the best-seller *Reviving Ophelia,* by psychologist Mary Pipher, was particularly disturbing. Pipher painted a scary picture of the heightened pressures facing adolescent girls today—pressures to be sexual, sophisticated, and skinny-as-a-supermodel at ever younger ages. One of her points particularly hit home with me. Many parents urge their daughters to stay true to their real selves—to keep playing sports and being smart, to stay away from diets and drugs—but parents are just about the last people that twelve- or thirteen-year-old girls want to hear from. "They model themselves after media stars, not parental ideals," Pipher wrote.

I began to wonder if it would be possible to create a school that would reinforce those parental messages of "be true to yourself," a school that would build girls' self-confidence and help them look critically at the expectations placed upon them by society. Other aspects of an all-girl school also intrigued me. I again thought about my own high school education, where boys and girls quietly drifted into stereotypical roles: Boys were the math whizzes and student government leaders, while girls ran the literary magazine and yearbook. Wouldn't it be great, I thought, to have a school where girls played all the roles—where the jocks, the nerds, the poets, the clowns, the leaders all were girls?

So in late 1996, I found myself sitting with about ten other parents in an Oakland living room to talk about starting an all-girl middle school. My own interest was relatively abstract, since my daughter hadn't even turned three. But the other parents felt an urgent need to get a school going *fast*: They had daughters who were in the third or fourth grade, and they feared that the smart, lively children they'd always known were starting to wither. Their daughters were coming home saying that they didn't like to play sports after school because the boys hogged the field. They were deprecating themselves as being bad at math. Or they were already starting to call themselves fat and talk about diets. These parents wanted a girls' school to help preserve the active, aspiring spirits they knew and loved—and they wanted that school *soon*.

So we started a process that, in retrospect, seems a little crazy. None of us were teachers or principals. None of us had huge amounts of money. None of us had ever started a school before. But we held countless meetings to hammer out an educational philosophy. We visited the Castilleja School, a century-old girls' school in Palo Alto, to make sure we really liked the idea of a girls' school. (We did.) We organized community gatherings in churches and libraries, and we ran around town taping up leaflets on telephone poles to let people know about the meetings. We drew up bylaws and other legal documents, and we spent months driving around looking for potential school sites. Eventually chance brought us together with someone who could turn our visions into reality—an educator named

Ann Clarke who had nearly thirty years of teaching experience, who had recently been an administrator at a girls' school in San Francisco, and who had a magical ability to communicate with girls and understand their needs.

As we described our vision during all those community meetings, we radiated confidence and energy. People were impressed with how well organized we seemed. But deep inside, I had a number of questions about what we were doing. I kept remembering my childhood stereotype of girls' schools—stuffy institutions that made you wear little plaid uniforms, that tried to mold you into being a "lady," that were run by grim-faced old biddies who didn't know how to have fun. I was pretty sure that girls' schools didn't make their students wear white gloves or serve tea anymore, but that picture still lingered.

Our 1990s vision for the Julia Morgan School seemed 180 degrees away from those old images. Instead of spooning sugar into tea, we wanted our students to measure chemical compounds into glass beakers. Instead of white gloves, we envisioned them running around in muddy soccer cleats. What was the connection, I wondered, between the old stereotypes and our new vision? What had girls' schools really been like in the past? Had they played a progressive role of opening broad new doors for young women, or did they play a more conservative role of channeling them into narrow, traditionally feminine niches? Had they helped girls, or held girls back? Underneath these questions lay an even bigger one: *Were we doing the right thing by trying to start a single-sex school in the 1990s?*

As Julia Morgan inched closer to opening, I found myself thinking more about these questions than about any of the articles I was writing for my job as a newspaper reporter. This book is the result of my search for answers. I visited dozens of schools, from the 180-year-old Emma Willard School in Troy, New York, to the brand-new Atlanta Girls' School, which opened a year after Julia Morgan did. I met with scores of teachers, students, administrators, and "heads of school," as headmistresses and headmasters are known in today's gender-free jargon. I spoke with over two hundred alumnae from the 1920s through the '90s. I read diaries of students at female seminaries in the mid-1800s, amazed at how similar they sounded to the words of girls today.

What I found was a rich history of girls' schools that had largely been overlooked and underappreciated. Contrary to the white-glove stereotype, girls' schools had radical roots. They were the first institutions in America to take women's minds seriously and to insist that girls could learn anything that boys could. They broke down countless educational barriers for young women—teaching "male" subjects like geometry and Greek, cultivating girls' physical and athletic selves, and preparing young women for college when that was still seen as a strange and dangerous idea. Their founders and headmistresses were models of smart, independent, and powerful women—women who today would be CEOs or college presidents. At the same time, there was a thick thread of conservatism running through the history of girls' schools. Parents often chose girls' schools to shelter their daughters rather than to challenge them. Catering to wealthy families, most independent girls' schools prided themselves for a long time on their social exclusivity—no Jews, Catholics, or girls of color need apply. They channeled their students into traditional roles of wife, mother, hostess, and volunteer. They gave girls a superb education but told them to use it only as polite ladies.

The late 1960s and 1970s turned out to be a watershed for girls' schools, a near-death experience from which they emerged with a renewed sense of purpose. The social ferment and student rebellions of that era challenged the complacent, cloistered tradition of many girls' schools. And the spread of coeducation forced many schools to question the very reason for their existence. One after another, the country's most prestigious male schools and colleges started admitting women—creating both an admissions crisis and an identity crisis for girls' schools. If girls could go to Andover and Exeter, was there still a need for a Miss Porter's or a Miss Hall's? If the local Jesuit high school started accepting girls, was there still a need for a Catholic girls' high school? Scores of girls' schools went coed or closed their doors. By the 1980s, the number of all-girl high schools had fallen from a peak of 1,132 to about 500. The number of girls' elementary schools had fallen from 399 to less than 200. There were only two public girls' schools left in the entire United States, the Philadelphia High School for Girls and Western High School in Baltimore.

Those schools that survived ended up redefining themselves in ways that brought them closer to their radical roots than they'd been in decades. Schools set their sights on preparing girls to be leaders—to be astronauts, senators, CEOs. They incorporated new research on girls' development by people like feminist psychologist Carol Gilligan. They developed curricula to help girls understand their own bodies and sexuality, and they focused on areas like math and science where coed schools seemed to be failing girls. Schools that used to discourage girls from attending college started vying to get their seniors into Harvard and Yale. Schools that were once all-white, all-Protestant enclaves boasted about the diversity of their student bodies. Schools that used to limit their curriculum to "feminine" subjects like English, French, and art history spent millions of dollars on new computer labs and science centers.

From New England boarding schools to California Catholic schools, the mantra of "etiquette" was replaced with "entrepreneurship."

No one "finished" girls anymore. They now "empowered" girls.

Meanwhile, in the 1990s, American society suddenly plunged into the biggest debate over girls' education and development in more than a century. The American Association of University Women issued a high-profile report charging that coed public schools were "shortchanging" girls. *Reviving Ophelia* spawned a whole genre of books analyzing the psychological challenges facing adolescent girls. By then, girls' schools were ready to go on the offensive and promote themselves as a positive alternative—even a national model—for helping young women grow and learn.

Girls' schools started drawing more applicants, and new kinds of applicants. Families had long chosen girls' schools for reasons of tradition—Mother, Grandmother, and Great-Grandmother had all gone to the same school. But now families were applying who had no tradition of single-sex schooling or even of private schooling. Our founding group at Julia Morgan was a case in point. None of us had a family history of attending girls' schools; most of us had grown up completely in the public school system. But we believed that a girls' school would be the best thing for our daughters, and we were willing to put in the time and energy to make it happen.

Girls' schools today have attracted some unlikely bedfellows as supporters. Backers of girls' schools include staunch conservatives—traditionalists who see single-sex education as a way to shelter their daughters from boys, sexuality, and general rebelliousness. They also include left-leaning feminists who see girls' schools as consciousness-raising institutions, places to help girls gain the self-confidence and skills to stand up for themselves in the larger world. Diane Ravitch, the former Republican assistant secretary of education, is an advocate of girls' schools. So is Susan Estrich, the campaign manager for former Democratic presidential candidate Michael Dukakis. And Republican Senator Kay Bailey Hutchison teamed up with none other than Hillary Rodham Clinton in 2001 to sponsor federal legislation allowing the creation of new public single-sex schools.

Girls' schools also have some unlikely opponents. In a battle that left many feminists shaking their heads, the National Organization of Women filed a sex-discrimination complaint against the new public girls' school that opened in Harlem in the mid-'90s. Meanwhile, some liberals fear that endorsing single-sex schools will indirectly undermine public education, by giving ammunition to voucher advocates who want the government to subsidize private-school attendance for poor families. The American Association of University Women is perhaps the most visible example of the liberal, feminist opposition to girls' schools. The AAUW helped fuel today's demand for girls' schools with its landmark 1992 report on sex bias in coed classrooms. But—fearful of the political implications of endorsing single-sex public schools—the AAUW issued another report in 1998 slamming single-sex education as no better for girls than coeducation. "Separating by sex is not the solution to gender inequity in education," said Maggie Ford, president of the AAUW Educational Foundation.

The political debate over girls' schools is mirrored by a debate among academic researchers. Some prominent scholars claim that single-sex education is better for girls, but others say it isn't. And what is "better," when it comes to schooling? Do you measure a good education by looking at students' test scores? By the number of Ivy League acceptances? The number of graduates who are prominent enough to be listed in *Who's Who*? Or by less empirical criteria—such as graduates' self-esteem, creativity, or happiness?

As I talked with girls' school alumnae around the country, I heard stories of pain from women who had been trapped in rigid schools that gave them no room to spread their wings. I also heard stories of deep gratitude for teachers who gave girls a passion for Shakespeare or geometry, and for schools that gave girls a lifelong sense that they could master any challenge. I found instances of great change, where schools that once taught girls how to curtsey now teach them AP calculus. I also found things that stayed the same, such as cultures that encourage friendship rather than rivalry among women.

One of my trips took me to Chattanooga, Tennessee, home of Girls Preparatory School, a nearly one-hundred-year-old private school with 750 girls in grades six through twelve. GPS is in many ways the embodiment of the modern, well-off suburban private school. It has a large, grassy campus on a hill overlooking the Tennessee River and downtown Chattanooga. It has two gyms, a pool, a 28,000-book library, and a 3,000-square-foot weight-training center. On a typical day, you would find twelfth-graders engrossed in AP physics and chemistry classes, and seventh-graders toting wireless laptop computers from class to class.

But May 3, 2000, when I visited, was not a typical day. At 8:55 A.M., florist vans started arriving and unloading elaborate bouquets of flowers. Teachers taped up brown butcher paper over the doors and windows of one corridor to create a secluded dressing area. Senior girls crowded inside carrying long bridesmaid-style pastel gowns. Their mothers bustled around, styling hair and applying makeup, and arranging the bouquets—by now more than a hundred of them, their fragrance overwhelming—in alphabetical order in a small conference room.

Parents and grandparents and siblings and boyfriends arrived and filled the folding chairs that had been set up in the grassy quadrangle. They wore visors saying "May Day 2000," and waved paper fans with a "May Day" logo against the humid, overcast, 80-degree heat. The ceremony began around 2 o'clock. To a slow, trumpet-filled processional, the seniors filed into the quad with their long dresses and bouquets. They stopped at the top of a small flight of stairs; each girl was introduced as Miss ———, then as the crowd applauded she walked slowly down the stairs, her head erect and gaze forward, circled the quad, and took her place among several rows of chairs. Girl after girl made the rounds; then came the May Day Committee; then the secretary of May Day; then the May Day Court—a crown bearer, a scepter bearer, and a maid of honor in a light aqua dress with an aqua ribbon in her hair. Finally the entire crowd rose as the May Queen herself made her entrance in a white gown with a train that stretched for about twelve feet, carried by two train bearers. The queen was presented with her crown and scepter; the other seniors all curtseyed to her, and she sat down. All in all, the procession into the quad took about thirty-five minutes. Then the queen and the other seniors and the audience watched as the younger GPS girls performed a series of dances, from a modern one with eighth-graders dressed as laptops and computer viruses to a more traditional one in which tenth-graders in white tunics and braids dipped and twirled around Maypoles holding pink and yellow and light blue ribbons.

This was May Day at a modern girls' school—a nineteenth-century ritual carried on by twenty-first-century young women, a strand of Victorian fantasy amidst the AP classes and track meets and college application pressures. Eighty years ago, May Day ceremonies were common at girls' schools and women's colleges throughout the country. Today GPS is almost alone in continuing the full-blown ritual with poles, dancers, a May Queen, and her court.

May Day at GPS is not without critics. Some teachers—especially the men, and newcomers from the north—feel that its focus on traditional feminine demeanor and appearance is undercutting their efforts to raise strong, independent young women. "It's another example of how we give two messages—be smart and competitive, but be submissive," said Keith Sanders, a chemistry teacher. "I was appalled by May Day when I first came here," said Jessica Good, a northerner who heads the English Department. "The girls turn to us to see what's important. And we put many more hours into May Day preparation than we do into AP preparation at the final hours."

But the girls themselves love May Day. In fact, most say that if they could invite a friend or relative to attend one event at the school, they would choose May Day over their own graduation. To them, May Day is a chance for each senior to be in the spotlight—all of them, not just the star athletes or Student Council leaders or National Merit finalists. It's also just plain fun. "You get to play dress-up. It's Queen for a Day," said student Mary Cady Exum. "It's a celebration of the seniors and what we've been through," said Rebecca Steele, a member of the May Day Court.

With its laptops and its Maypoles, GPS embodies the rich but contradictory history of girls' schools in America. There were times like the early 1800s when girls' schools played a leading role in shaping and broadening society's expectations of women. There were other times when girls' schools were mostly reactive and simply reflected whatever society thought women should be doing—whether that was learning needlepoint, preparing for college, or preparing to marry a successful businessman. Today, women's roles are in flux. Women can enter almost any profession and compete in almost any arena. We have female bankers, female engineers, and female surgeons. Yet women are still expected to be responsible for homemaking and child rearing, and are often left with wrenching private choices between family and career. Girls' roles are in flux, too. Girls are told that they can be anything from a scientist to a soccer star— yet pressures to be sexy and attractive descend upon them at younger and younger ages.

Girls' schools today are trying to sift through these mixed messages and give girls a coherent, affirming vision of themselves and their future. The women's movement of the 1960s nearly killed girls' schools by opening up male schools and colleges, but it also gave girls' schools a new lease on life by drawing public attention to the barriers and challenges confronting girls and women. Girls' schools today face their biggest opportunity since those pioneering days of the early 1800s. As single-sex institutions, they can focus resources and attention on the developmental issues of girls in a way that would be difficult for individual parents or coeducational schools. They can be laboratories for helping girls grow in this era of flux and transition.

Some schools today are confronting these issues of girls' growth in conscious and creative ways through leadership-training programs, "life studies" curricula, or other such initiatives. Others are flying more on autopilot, counting on school traditions or the simple fact of an all-female environment to help girls become healthy women. This book focuses on the commonalities among girls' schools, but it's important to remember that there are also big differences. There are good schools and bad schools among girls' schools, like anywhere else; there are innovative schools and traditional schools. Different schools pay different amounts of attention to the single-sex part of their mission.

GPS students cherish their May Day ritual. At Julia Morgan, our little group of founders would have jumped off the Bay Bridge sooner than have students parade around in expensive dresses and elect a May Queen. Despite their differences, what GPS and Julia Morgan have in common is a commitment to put girls first in a world that still, all too often, puts them second. That's an unusual and precious commodity. It's a real gift for our daughters. This book recounts what it was like for us trying to start a girls' school from scratch in the 1990s. And it explores the gifts that other girls' schools—the forerunners of our brand-new Julia Morgan School— have provided to young women over the past two hundred years.

# I

# Radical Roots

## SOMETHING FROM NOTHING

*Starting Julia Morgan was like one of those magic tricks where the conjurer makes something appear from nothing: "Ladies and gentlemen, the Great Palumbo with a flick of his wand will now make an elephant appear from THIN AIR!"*

*We started with nothing—no money, no school building, no teachers, no curriculum, no experience in the nuts and bolts of running a school. My daughter, Rebecca, was just two years old, and I had been casually chatting with her day-care provider about the idea of single-sex education for girls. It turned out that she knew someone, who knew someone else, who knew a couple of other parents who were interested in actually starting a girls' school . . . and so about ten of us ended up sitting in a circle and introducing ourselves in a small wood-paneled living room. I was intrigued. Until that point, starting a girls' school had seemed like a pipe dream, an occasional late-at-night fantasy that would evaporate as airily as teenage thoughts of becoming a rock star. But ten people? Ten other people who had the same idea? That was entering the realm of reality.*

*Even more than our group, the founders of the earliest girls' schools in America faced the challenge of creating something from nothing. As we worked on setting up the school over the next three years, our group would sometimes run into painful criticism from friends and relatives who opposed the idea of single-sex education. But when the first girls' schools opened up in America in the late 1700s and early 1800s, the question wasn't whether girls should go to school with boys or separately—the question was whether girls should be educated at all. Like us, those pioneer educators had to conjure up schoolhouses and lesson plans out of nothing. But they also had to create something much bigger—an understanding that girls could be educated, that girls could learn geography or math or science just as well as boys could.*

*As I looked around that living room, I was impressed by some of the other participants. There was a lawyer. There was a woman who had taught gender-equity workshops at schools. There were two particularly well-dressed women who seemed to have money. One was married to a contractor—a big plus if we'd need to renovate a building! Another talked about how much she had loved her own childhood experience at a private girls' school. To me, who had never even visited an actual girls' school, her words were like water in a desert. I felt more than intrigued. I felt inspired.*

*We started going around the circle, talking about what each of us envisioned in this school we hoped to create. One person described a school that would encourage creativity, another a school that would push girls to pursue math and science. Then one woman stated emphatically that it was really, really important that the school avoid using live animals in science experiments. Never, she said, she could never send her daughter to a school that required students to dissect frogs. A friend of hers emphatically agreed. The discussion spiraled into a debate about animal rights.* Wasn't dissecting frogs an essential part of studying science? Shouldn't decisions about the science curriculum be left up to the science teachers? What if instead of live animals, we used a computer program that simulated frog dissection? What about making dissection optional and allowing individual girls to make the decision for themselves? *As frogs took over the meeting, I watched the two wealthy-looking women shut down and withdraw into themselves. They sat there politely for the rest of the evening, but they never came back. I wasn't sure that I myself wanted to come back. We had no building, no teachers, no money, no educational philosophy, we didn't even know what grades this school should serve, and people wanted to sit there and argue about dissecting frogs? But give it a chance, I figured. At least we—unlike our predecessors two hundred years earlier—didn't have to prove to the world that girls could be educated. And a group of eight might not be as strong as ten, but it was still better than a one-person pipe dream.*

*As long as the frogs didn't take things over entirely.*

E very autumn, Rebecca Fox, the recent head of the Bryn Mawr School, would do a Powerpoint slide show for the first grade about how the school was started. Standing in the midst of about thirty little girls in sky blue jumpers and sneakers, Fox described a time when women wore floor-length skirts and corsets and lace blouses. She showed them black-and-white portraits of five young women friends who got the radical notion of opening a college-preparatory school for girls in conservative, southern Baltimore of the 1880s. She showed them a photograph of the grand staircase that connected the five floors of the original school building, and explained that a prominent local doctor advised parents not to send their daughters to Bryn Mawr because they would ruin their health climbing all those stairs.

The little girls would giggle and whisper. "What!" one of them usually exclaimed. "That's so silly! I could run up and down that a hundred times."

Today it's hard for anyone, much less a first-grader, to picture the daily routine of going to school as daring or controversial. Studying geometry as an act of rebellion? Writing term papers as a step toward revolution? But girls' schools have their roots in a radical struggle to educate women that goes back two hundred years. Girls' schools got their start at a time when educating women was a gutsy act. They took women's intellect seriously long before it became fashionable to do so—when most people still greeted the idea of an educated woman with scorn. "All a young lady needs to know is how to weave clothes for her family and how to paint a daisy in water colors," scoffed a Georgia legislator when someone proposed opening a school to train female teachers in his state in the 1830s. "I had rather my daughters would go to school and sit down and do nothing, than to study philosophy, etc.," said the *Connecticut Courant* in an 1829 editorial. "These branches [subjects] fill young Misses with *vanity* to the degree that they are above attending to the more useful parts of an education."

Pictures of nineteenth-century girls' school students and teachers—in their floor-length skirts and ruffled blouses—initially seemed to me like quaint relics from a distant era. But as I learned more about these first girls' schools, I felt a greater and greater kinship with some of their founders. Like those of us who were organizing the Julia Morgan School, these women believed passionately in the power of girls' minds. Like us, they were dedicated to helping girls transcend the limits placed upon them by society. I came to feel that if one of these pioneering girls' school founders were to walk in on a Julia Morgan planning session, she wouldn't bat an eye. She'd reach into the folds of her long woolen skirt, pull out a Palm Pilot, and jump right into the mix.

E ducation in colonial America had its roots in European traditions that offered little formal schooling to girls. Wealthy European families might hire a governess or send their daughters to a convent school to learn reading, writing, and a smattering of a foreign language. Middle-class families spent their limited funds on sons' education. Poor families couldn't afford to educate either their sons or daughters. Samuel Johnson, the English writer and lexicographer, summed up the conventional wisdom when he noted that "man is, in general, better pleased when he has a good dinner on his table than when his wife talks Greek."

The kind of education available to girls in colonial America depended on their race, class, and region. In the South, where sprawling plantations made it hard to set up schools, wealthy white families generally hired private tutors to educate their sons. If they were lucky, girls were allowed to sit in on their brothers' lessons. Meanwhile, African-American slave girls and their brothers were often prohibited by law from receiving any education at all.

In Pennsylvania, the Quaker and Moravian religious communities were early supporters of the idea of educating both genders. They set up a handful of schools for girls in the mid-1700s, including Linden Hall, a Moravian school in Lititz, Pennsylvania, that still exists today. In colonial New England, Puritan religious beliefs encouraged families to teach girls how to read. Women as well as men were supposed to read the Bible for themselves. However, girls weren't necessarily encouraged to learn writing along with reading: One historian concluded that just 42 percent of women could sign their own names on legal deeds in the mid-1600s, compared with 89 percent of men.

Young boys and girls in New England both attended "dame schools," which were a combination of what today would be considered family day care and early elementary school. A widow might take in a half dozen children, aged four to seven, and keep an eye on them in her home while going about her daily tasks and giving them some lessons in their ABCs and numbers. After a dame school, New England boys usually had the option of moving on to a one-room school organized by their town. Many towns had schools that offered the equivalent of elementary education. A few also offered what was called a Latin grammar school, intended to prepare a small number of select boys for college.

Girls, however, were generally barred from attending any kind of town school. One scholar who looked at the records of two hundred New England towns found only seven that explicitly voted to let girls into their schools, and five that gave implied permission. A 1656 court ruling in an estate case showed the typical expectations for boys' and girls' learning: "The sons shall have learning to write plainly and read distinctly in the Bible, and the daughters to read and sew sufficiently for the making of their linens."

Interest in girls' education first started to grow in the 1700s, as

American towns grew in size and prosperity. Wealthy men could afford to free their wives and daughters from time-consuming tasks like spinning and weaving all the family's clothing and linens. That left more time for activities like music, reading, or education. With the spread of factory-made cloth in the early 1800s, women and girls from middle-class households also found themselves with more free time than before. "As we have had much leisure time this winter, the girls have employed themselves chiefly in reading writing and studying French Latin and Greek," one woman wrote in 1816.

The demand for girls' education was filled initially by what were called "adventure schools"—one-person entrepreneurial ventures with no set curriculum or course of study. An adventure-school teacher would typically place an ad in the local paper to drum up students. He or she would teach whatever subjects were popular that year, students would attend for a few months, and then the school might fold after a year or two.

Adventure schools often focused on things like music, dancing, and needlework—"accomplishments" that were considered fashionable for wealthy young women in genteel society—rather than more academic subjects like mathematics or grammar. A Philadelphia magazine in 1792 took a father sharply to task for relying on the spotty education offered by such schools:

> You boast of having given your daughters an education which will enable them to "shine in the first circles." . . . They sing indifferently; they play the harpsichord indifferently; they are mistresses of every common game at cards . . . ; they . . . have just as much knowledge of dress as to deform their persons by an awkward imitation of every new fashion which appears. . . . Placed in a situation of difficulty, they have neither a head to dictate, nor a hand to help in any domestic concern.

By the end of the 1700s, a small but growing number of Americans were voicing similar complaints about the poor education offered to girls. This was part of a broader surge of general interest in education in the wake of the American Revolution. Leaders of the new country were worried by European predictions that their grand democratic experiment was doomed to fail. They believed that the republic's future rested on having an informed and patriotic population. They felt there was a pressing need to mold future generations of civic leaders and good citizens—and they saw schools as the way to do that.

New secondary schools called "academies" began springing up throughout the country. Phillips Academy at Andover and Phillips Exeter Academy—two of today's most elite boarding schools—were founded in 1778 and 1783, respectively. Most of the early academies, including Andover and Exeter, were for boys alone. Some were coed, including one run briefly by Noah Webster in Connecticut in 1781. Other academies were targeted at girls, and sometimes called "seminaries" to distinguish them from male schools or colleges.

In Philadelphia, a Young Ladies Academy opened in 1787 and offered subjects including reading, spelling, writing, arithmetic, and geography. By 1788, it had more than 100 students from places as distant as Virginia, Nova Scotia, and the West Indies. In Litchfield, Connecticut, Sarah Pierce opened a school in her dining room in 1792 with just one student. By 1802, she had nearly 70 girls attending for some portion of the year, and by 1816 she had 157. "Female academies are every where [sic] establishing, and right pleasant is the appellation to my ear," wrote Judith Sargent Murray, an essayist and supporter of women's education in the early 1790s.

The new female academies were plagued by some of the same problems as their predecessors, the adventure schools. Most academies didn't require girls to attend for any fixed amount of time or course of studies. Girls would come for a few months or a semester, then return home or perhaps try a different school. There was no stable source of funding for such schools from month to month— and many vanished as suddenly as they appeared. A woman named Sarah Callister, for instance, opened a school in Maryland in 1783. She had nine girls who came for two quarters, ten who came for the full school year of three quarters, and twelve who stayed only a month. She went out of business fairly quickly. "I have done every thing my small abilities would allow for a livelihood, & O painfull!"

[*sic*] Callister wrote in 1788. "Affliction, caprice, has rendered my endeavors vain!"

The curriculum at these early academies depended largely on the interests or background of the owner, who was often the sole instructor. Some schools taught little more than music, drawing, and French conversation. Even where academic subjects were taught, there was often a lack of coherence. Schools promised instruction in dozens of different subjects in order to attract students, and ended up delivering a hodgepodge of information. "I left school with a head full of something, tumbled in without order or connection," wrote Eliza Southgate, who attended a Boston academy run by a former British stage actress in the late 1790s. Parents were also responsible for the disjointed nature of the curriculum at some early academies and seminaries. An 1853 women's magazine printed this satire of parental expectations:

I HAVE BROUGHT MY DAUGHTER TO YOU
TO BE TAUGHT EVERYTHING

Dear Madam, I've called for the purpose
Of placing my daughter at school;
She's only thirteen, I assure you,
And remarkably easy to rule.
I'd have her learn painting and music,
Gymnastics and dancing, pray do,
Philosophy, grammar and logic,
You'll teach her to read, of course, too.

I wish her to learn every study
Mathematics are down on my plan,
But of figures she scarce has an inkling
Pray instruct her in those, if you can.
I'd have her taught Spanish and Latin,
Including the language of France;
Never mind her very bad English,
Teach her that when you find a good chance.

On the harp she must be proficient
And play the guitar pretty soon,
And sing the last opera music
Even though she can't turn a right tune.
You must see that her manners are finished,
That she moves with a Hebe-like grace;
For, though she is lame and one-sided,
That's nothing to do with the case.

Now to you I resign this young jewel
And my words I would have you obey;
In six months return her, dear Madam,
Shining bright as an unclouded day.
She's no aptness, I grant you for learning
And her memory oft seems to halt;
But remember, if she's not accomplished
It will certainly be your fault.

For teachers who aspired to provide real education, the situation could be frustrating. Catherine Beecher, the sister of Harriet Beecher Stowe, opened a girls' school with a friend in Hartford, Connecticut, in 1823. Feeling that they needed to offer the usual wide panoply of subjects, the two women taught ten to twelve subjects each day in a single schoolroom. Their enrollment grew from fifteen to seventy girls with a wide range of ages and abilities, forcing them to create even more classes. Pretty soon Beecher found herself careening through a school day with just eight or ten minutes for each separate subject.

"Thus, to the distracting duty of keeping in order and quietness so large a collection of youth . . . was added the labor of hearing a succession of classes at the average rate of one for every ten minutes," Beecher wrote later. "No time could be allowed to explain or illustrate. . . . All was perpetual haste, imperfection, irregularity, and the merely mechanical commitment of words to memory, without any chance for imparting clear and connected ideas in a single branch of knowledge."

## Emma Willard Writes a Manifesto

A handful of visionary teachers wanted something better for girls—an education that was as good as boys were getting. The best known of these was Mary Lyons, who started a seminary that later became Mount Holyoke College. But the real foremother of today's girls' schools was Emma Willard, founder of the Troy Female Seminary.

Willard was the most prominent advocate of girls' education in her day. She published a manifesto for girls' education that won endorsements from Presidents Adams, Jefferson, and Monroe. She wrote some of the best-selling textbooks of her time and pioneered the use of maps in studying geography. She founded a boarding school that educated twelve thousand young women during her lifetime, served as a model for hundreds of other schools, and continues to thrive today.

She was also a bundle of contradictions. Willard corresponded with presidents and European diplomats, while insisting that women's proper place remained inside the domestic sphere. She denounced the suffrage movement for most of her life, yet educated future suffrage leaders like Elizabeth Cady Stanton. She penned compelling speeches and then delivered them sitting down, so she could claim she was simply conversing rather than trespassing into the "male" realm of public speaking. She preached wifely subservience yet divorced her second husband—a difficult and scandalous process in that era—when it became clear he had married her for her money. Better than anyone, Willard personifies the radical roots of American girls' schools in the early and mid-1800s.

Willard's own education began in her family's Connecticut farmhouse, where her father was unusually encouraging of her intellect. "He was fifty years my senior," she recalled, "yet would he often call me when at the age of fourteen from household duties by my mother's side to enjoy with him some passage of an author which pleased him, or to read over to me some essay which he had amused himself in writing." Willard was strong willed and something of a feminist from her childhood. "The enterprizing [*sic*] turn of mind that has actuated Emma from her early youth, has been a source of considerable anxiety in my mind," her father wrote in a candid 1809 letter about Emma to Dr. John Willard, the man who would become her husband. "I was not without fears that her uncommon boldness and confidence in her own abilities would precipitate her into some extravagances that might terminate in disgrace, if not infamy. . . . Her liberal sentiments respecting religion; and high notions of female dignity & the rights of women, I was sensible would render her obnoxious to bigoted religionists. . . ."

Willard attended the local one-room primary school and, at fifteen, a new academy for girls that had been opened by a recent Yale graduate. At seventeen, she took over as teacher in her old primary school. At twenty, with a growing reputation, she took on the task of reviving and running a shuttered girls' academy in Middlebury, Vermont.

She started in Middlebury with thirty-seven students in one large room with a small fireplace at one end. By the end of the year, she had sixty students but was still working in fairly primitive conditions. "When it was so cold that we could live no longer," she recalled, "I called all my girls on to the floor, and arranged them two and two in a long row for a country dance; and while those who could sing would strike up some stirring tune, I with one of the girls for a partner, would lead down the dance, and soon have them all in rapid motion. After which we went to our school exercises again."

It was in Vermont that Willard first directly confronted the limits placed on girls' education. She asked all-male Middlebury College if her students could sit in on some college classes and was refused. She later asked if she could attend some of the college's public examinations to become familiar with collegiate standards and methods, but was told that attendance by a woman would not be "becoming."

Determined to offer a high-quality education, Willard added a new subject to her curriculum each term. There were no experienced teachers available, so she kept herself one step ahead of her students. Willard taught herself geometry from textbooks that her nephew was using at Middlebury College. She also began drafting a plan to improve women's education, telling no one except her husband, John. "I knew that I should be regarded as visionary, almost to insanity, should I utter the expectations which I secretly entertained," Willard later explained. The result was a thirty-seven-page manifesto called a "Plan for Improving Female Education"—the most forceful and thorough argument of that era for the education of American women.

Willard was well aware of the depths of opposition to women's education. Trying to preempt such opposition, she began by dissociating herself from the idea of creating a college for women. Instead she proposed a kind of school called a "seminary" and promised it would be very different from a men's institution. "The absurdity of sending ladies to college, may at first thought, strike every one to whom this subject shall be proposed," Willard wrote. "I therefore hasten to observe, that the seminary here recommended, will be as different from those appropriated to the other sex, as the female character and duties are from the male."

Willard did not challenge the common belief of her day that women and men were different creatures destined to live in very different worlds—men in a male sphere of business and politics, women in a female sphere of family, religion, and culture. Instead, she argued that education would enable women to do a better job within their uniquely female world. Educated girls would prove to be better mothers, Willard said, and would thus elevate the character of the whole nation. "Would we rear the human plant to its perfection, we must first fertilize the soil which produces it," she wrote.

Moreover, Willard said, educating women was particularly important in a young democracy like the United States. She wrote:

> In those great republics, which have fallen of themselves, the loss of republican manners and virtues, has been the invariable precursor, of their loss of the republican form of government. But is it not in the power of our sex to give society its tone, both as to manners and morals? . . . And who knows how great and good a race of men, may yet arise from the forming hand of mothers, enlightened by the bounty of that beloved country,—to defend her liberties,—to plan her future improvement,—and to raise her to unparalleled glory?

Willard's arguments that educating women would strengthen the republic weren't unique. Similar ideas had been voiced by Benjamin Rush, Judith Sargent Murray, and other advocates of women's education. These arguments all drew upon the early-nineteenth-century ideology that historians have labeled "republican motherhood"—the idea that women's calling was to strengthen their country by raising enlightened, high-minded citizens.

*Emma Willard, founder of the Troy Female Seminary, in 1830*

What set Willard's plan apart from other similar arguments for women's education was her insistence on state financial support for girls' schools. She called on state lawmakers to provide funds for female seminaries, just as they did for male academies and colleges. And she penned an incisive analysis of the structural defects of the privately run adventure schools and early girls' academies:

> Institutions for young gentlemen are founded by public authority, and are permanent; they are endowed with funds, and their instructors and overseers, are invested with authority to make such laws as they shall deem most salutary. . . . With their funds they procure libraries, philosophical [scientific] apparatus, and other advantages. . . . They regulate their qualifications for entrance, the kind and order of their studies, and the period of their remaining at the seminary.
>
> Female schools present the reverse of this. Wanting permanency, and dependent on individual patronage, had they the wisdom to make salutary regulations, they could neither enforce

nor purchase compliance. . . . [They] cannot afford to provide suitable accommodations . . . neither can they afford libraries, and other apparatus. . . .

Legislatures, undervaluing the importance of women in society, neglect to provide for their education, and suffer it to become the sport of adventurers for fortune, who may be both ignorant and vicious.

Some of Willard's Middlebury boarding students were from prominent families in upstate New York. When she was finally ready to show her plan to outsiders, she gave it to the father of one of her students, who passed it on to New York's Governor DeWitt Clinton.

Clinton responded with enthusiasm and asked the legislature to take steps to improve women's education. The Willards traveled to Albany to lobby for the plan. Emma paid to have a thousand copies printed up and read it several times to groups of legislators. The legislature agreed to incorporate a female school at nearby Waterford and to place it on a list of schools eligible for state funding. A legislative committee approved an endowment of $5,000. Encouraged, Willard moved her school—followed by most of her students—to Waterford in 1819.

But Willard's proposal then ran into numerous delays and partisan maneuvers. Conservatives ridiculed the idea of educating girls. Despite the committee's initial approval, the full legislature ended up denying her the $5,000 endowment. State education officials also determined that none of their annual budget for schools should go to Willard's project.

Willard was despondent. She had been counting on state aid. Without that $5,000—a small amount today but an enormous sum in 1819—the school in Waterford was a money-losing proposition. She wrote:

> To have had it decently rejected, would have given me comparatively little pain, but its consideration was delayed and delayed, till finally the session passed away. The malice of open enemies,

the advice of false friends, and the neglect of others, placed me in a situation, mortifying in the extreme.

It was by the loss of respect for others, that I gained tranquility for myself. Once I was fond of speaking of the legislature as the "fathers of the state". . . . That winter served to disenchant me. My present impression is that my cause is better rested with the people than with their rulers. . . . When the people shall have become convinced of the justice and expedience of placing the sexes more nearly on an equality, with respect to privileges of education, then legislators will find it their interest to make the proper provision.

## The Troy Female Seminary

Downtown Troy, New York, in the 1990s was a depressingly classic picture of urban decay—a northeastern industrial city where the industries died and were never really replaced by anything. Check-cashing outfits and liquor stores dotted the narrow streets a few blocks from the Hudson River. Efforts to create a downtown arts district among the beautiful old brownstone buildings hadn't yet begun to show results. It was hard to imagine Troy as the center of anything in American intellectual or economic life.

But in 1821, Troy was a booming young metropolis—the kind of city that today would be aggressively courting a pro football team and dubbing itself "Silicon River." It housed a wide range of industries such as cotton mills, a nail factory, soap factory, and tanneries and potteries. It was also a big commercial center, its harbor filled with sailing ships and steam-powered paddle wheelers carrying goods and people up and down the Hudson.

Troy's early civic leaders were farsighted and ambitious. Their biggest coup was convincing the government to build an east-west canal nearby—none other than the famous Erie Canal, which opened in the 1820s and made Troy a key way station in trade and travel to the growing American West. Troy's early leaders backed other smaller civic projects, too, including a lyceum of natural history and a scientific school that eventually became Rensselaer Polytechnic Institute. When Emma Willard's plan for a state-supported school in Waterford came crashing down, they offered her $4,000 to come open a girls' school in Troy.

Some of the Troy businessmen doubtless pursued Willard out of self-interest: Three of the eight initial trustees had daughters in the opening class. They were probably quite pleased to be able to keep their girls in town, rather than sending them miles away to a boarding school. But their motivation may also have been broader—a hunch that Willard's school would bring their town prestige, visitors, and business. Their gamble paid off. Over the next few decades, governors and cabinet secretaries sent their daughters to the Troy Female Seminary. France's General Lafayette came to visit the school. By 1830, nearly 250 students a year were coming to Troy from around the country to attend the seminary.

Today, with the nail factories and tanneries long gone, the Troy economy is kept alive by three nonprofit educational institutions. One of them is Rensselaer Polytechnic Institute. The other is Russell Sage College, created in the late 1800s by a wealthy widow who had been one of Willard's students. The other is, of course, the Troy Female Seminary, which changed its name in the twentieth century to the Emma Willard School.

## Life at "The Sem"

Students at the Troy Female Seminary in the 1820s typically traveled several days by horse-drawn carriage or a week by canal boat to get there. They found the school located in a three-story wooden building that used to be a coffee warehouse, across a small park from the Troy courthouse. The top two floors of the school were divided into forty lodging and study rooms, with two girls sharing each room. The rooms each had a low-post double bed (girls shared a bed), a painted bureau, two chairs, and a wood stove. Students lit their fires from a pan of coals in the hall; they filled their water pitchers from a pump in the yard. The first floor included a dining room that doubled as a dancing hall, a kitchen, laundry, lecture room, several small music rooms, and a room for lessons in making pastry. The second floor included a chapel, a large examination room, and the Willard family quarters.

A typical day at the seminary—"the Sem," as the girls called it—began with the wake-up bell at 6:30 A.M. in the summer and 7 in the winter. There was a half hour of study and a half hour of exercise, then breakfast at 8 and classes until dinner at noon. The afternoon saw more classes until 4, when school was dismissed with a prayer led by Willard, and then free time until 6. The students had supper at 6, dancing for an hour, then more study time. On Saturdays, Willard lectured the girls on religion and on the duties of the female sex. On Sundays, girls were required to attend the church of their parents' choice.

In some ways, student life at Troy and other nineteenth-century girls' seminaries was similar to that of a modern boarding school or to the more common experience of summer camp. The school established rules, which the girls tried to circumvent as best they could. ("Never forget our oyster stew . . . when we had stewed oysters in the washbowl!" Frannie Tabor wrote to a classmate in 1865.) Close friendships formed and broke up. Girls covertly waved handkerchiefs at boys who passed by their supposedly shuttered dormitory windows. Students wrote home begging for packages of food—cakes, pies, fruit, even pickles. "I have been in great want of something to eat," moaned Emma Cornelia Clark in a letter to her mother in 1823. "We have enough to eat at our meals, but it is so long between them I get most starved sometimes before I go to bed, after studying until ten o'clock. If you get an opportunity I want you to bake me something. I want you should take a box and bake a pie on a square tin and put it in the bottom of the box and fill it up with everything good, some apples too for we never get any. . . . P.S. I don't care for petticoats or anything else. If you will only send me something to eat."

In other ways, however, Troy and other nineteenth-century seminaries would seem quite alien to a modern teenager. Classes relied heavily on memorization and recitation, like virtually all schools of that period. Students' ages varied widely since seminaries were the

only educational option available for young women. The average age
at Troy was seventeen, but some students were as young as ten while
others were in their mid-twenties. Seminaries were also rocked by
the waves of evangelical Christian revival that swept America in the
early nineteenth century. Revivals were popular everywhere, but they
were particularly powerful in these tight communities of adolescent
girls. Scores of girls would declare themselves reborn as Christians;
others anguished over whether they had the ability to open their
hearts like their friends and accept Jesus. The peer pressure to un-
dergo a "conversion" was intense. Teachers and headmistresses also
encouraged girls' participation in revivals as a way to help them become good Christian women.

Caroline Eliza Willis, a Troy student from Pennsylvania, wrote
about how the sudden death of a schoolmate heightened the revival
fervor in 1840, when she was twenty-two:

> "Truly in the midst of life we are in death." It was a painful sight
> to look upon the lifeless remains of one so young, to be laid in
> the cold and silent grave, never to be beheld again until the res-
> urrection morn. How anxious should our onward course be in
> the way of holiness, that we may finally be made partakers of that
> rest which remains for the people of God. You have no doubt
> heard by the papers of revivals in different churches and cities.
> Our city has been visited lately with the outpouring of the spirit,
> and our Seminary has not been passed by.
>
> Many of our thoughtless number have felt much, and been
> resolved upon a new course of life, and we sincerely hope it may
> continue.

## "Enamored of Mental Arithmetic"

Despite Willard's semantic effort to distinguish her project from a male
college, the subjects taught at Troy mirrored those studied at men's
colleges. The curriculum included Latin, chemistry, natural philoso-

phy (the precursor to physics), and moral philosophy (a nineteenth-century combination of philosophy, psychology, and ethics).

Willard offered classes in geometry, something that had rarely been taught to girls before. She sliced up potatoes and turnips with a penknife to illustrate solid geometry. When she held a public examination of her geometry students at the end of the term—a common nineteenth-century practice in all kinds of schools—it caused a bit of a scandal. Skeptical townspeople muttered that the girls must be cheating or parroting answers without real understanding. "Some said it was all a work of memory, for no woman ever did, or could, understand geometry," wrote Willard's biographer Henry Fowler.

Willard collaborated with Amos Eaton, a professor at Rensselaer, to introduce some science courses that were even ahead of the men's colleges. Her sister Almira Lincoln Phelps, who for a time was assistant principal, wrote a botany textbook that sold ten thousand copies in four years. Willard herself coauthored a best-selling geography textbook, one of the first texts to teach geography with maps rather than through abstract memorization of countries and cities.

The Troy curriculum included "ornamental" subjects like music and drawing, but they were neither central nor mandatory: Students had to pay extra for them. Although plain and fancy needlework classes remained a staple at many girls' schools in the early and mid-1800s, Willard purposefully excluded needlework from the curriculum. She never even considered teaching "velvet painting," a dubious art form common at the less academic girls' schools of the period.

Willard made a point of including physical exercise for the girls—a cutting-edge idea for its time. However, exercise classes were hampered by girls' heavy, floor-length skirts and were generally limited to walking, dancing, and slow rhythmic exercises with weights. Team sports had not yet become common even at boys' schools. "The exercise in the gymnasium I am perfectly carried away with," wrote Emily Smith to a friend in 1865. "On Monday I am to take up dum bells. We have fun practising [sic] different positions of the hands, feet, head and body. I am getting quite limber. Every movement we make is in waltz time, some person playing on the piano all the time.

My shoulders are growing very broad, and I am getting so fat that I can only get two of my dresses together. . . . Sunday I go to church with my dresses unhooked at the bottom. You won't know me when I get home."

The Troy seminary placed a heavy emphasis on writing skills, requiring girls to turn in a composition every Wednesday. Most nineteenth-century girls' schools including Troy encouraged students to write sentimental and clichéd pieces on topics like "Springtime," "Hope," or "Friendship." A few went beyond that, though. Harriet Beecher Stowe attended Miss Pierce's school in Litchfield, Connecticut, and was inspired to a life of writing by a teacher who saw essays as a way to convey serious ideas. Stowe recalled:

> Mr. Brace exceeded all teachers I ever knew in the faculty of teaching composition. The constant excitement in which he kept the minds of his pupils . . . formed a preparation for teaching composition, the main requisite for which, whatever people may think, is to have something which one feels interested to say. . . .
>
> The first week the subject of composition chosen by the class was "The Difference between the Natural and Moral Sublime." One may smile at this for a child of nine years of age, but it is the best account I can give of his manner of teaching to say that the discussion which he held in the class not only made me understand the subject as thoroughly as I do now, but so excited me that I felt sure I had something to say upon it; and that first composition, though I believe half the words were misspelled, amused him greatly.

Some seminary students chafed at the challenges of traditionally male subjects, but many embraced them eagerly. One student at Abbot Academy in Massachusetts wrote in 1840 that her teacher had "taught me to love geometry above my natural food." Another Abbot student, Harriet Woods, noted that "I became enamored of mental arithmetic, and carried my Colburn's Sequel [textbook] back and forth from school, trying to puzzle my father and brothers over the examples I had conquered."

Caroline Chester, a student at Miss Pierce's School in 1816, struggled with math and then finally triumphed with a joy and sense of accomplishment that could be a model for any school today:

> Mr. Brace gave us a *very* difficult sum in *Multiplication* and said we were all capable of doing it & should stay (were it till morning) till we did—I thought I should stay all night and often told Mr. B. it was impossible for me to do it, but about sun-down to my great joy I finished it never shall I forget as long as memory holds her seat in my breast this day or what occurred, I shall for the future *try* before I say, what Mr. B. does hate so very much to hear *I CAN'T*.

## Preaching Separate Spheres

While taking the radical step of teaching "male" subjects, Troy and other seminaries remained distinctively female institutions. They completely accepted the common idea of separate spheres—the male world of business and politics, the female world of home and family. So while boys' schools taught subjects like geometry with the understanding that students would use them in future professions, the seminaries taught them primarily as a way to instill mental discipline. "Females, by having their understandings cultivated, their reasoning powers developed and strengthened, may be expected to act more from the dictates of reason, and less from those of fashion and caprice," Willard wrote in her plan.

Willard also placed the radical introduction of "male" subjects in a conservative context of enhancing women's continued role as mothers. Studying psychology could help mothers understand the way their children were developing, Willard claimed. Science classes could help them explain natural phenomenon to their young charges. "From the bursting of an egg buried in the fire, I have heard an intelligent mother, lead her prattling inquirer, to understand the cause of the earthquake," she noted.

Willard and others saw certain subjects as uniquely suited to girls

because of the nineteenth-century view of women's delicate nature. Seminaries that dared not teach physics were quite happy to teach botany. Even the most conservative townsfolk would smile at the sight of a group of well-dressed young ladies gathering wildflowers. Almira Lincoln Phelps's botany text noted that the subject "seem[ed] peculiarly adapted to females" because "the objects of investigation [were] beautiful and delicate."

Many of the rules in place at seminaries were designed to keep women within domestic, subservient roles. Girls were prohibited from delivering public speeches at Troy since that would seem immodest. They couldn't even read their own compositions aloud in class: Another student would read their work for them. Students were also warned to stay out of politics—some

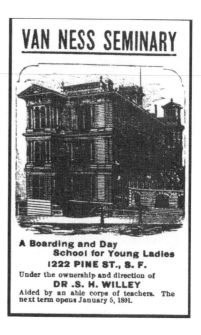

**VAN NESS SEMINARY**

**A Boarding and Day
School for Young Ladies
1222 PINE ST., S. F.**
Under the ownership and direction of
**DR .S. H. WILLEY**
Aided by an able corps of teachers. The next term opens January 5, 1891.

*Three nineteenth-century ads for girls' schools—Albany Female Academy (1883), which later became Albany Academy for Girls, Ward's Seminary (mid-1870s), which later became the Harpeth Hall School in Nashville, and the Van Ness Seminary (1890), which later became the Hamlin School in San Francisco*

girls who held a secret meeting with campaign speeches during the Adams/Jackson presidential campaign were reprimanded—although patriotic displays like unfurling flags on the Fourth of July were encouraged. "To be a political partisan, I deem derogatory to the delicacy of the female character; to be a patriot, its highest glory," Willard wrote in an 1816 letter.

Willard staunchly upheld contemporary ideals of female modesty.

She was appalled when she visited Paris and found statues of naked figures in the Tuileries. "No—my dear girls, I shall not take you to examine those statues," she wrote to her students. "I would leave you sitting on these shaded benches . . . and bid you depart for our own America, where the eye of modesty is not publicly affronted; and where virgin delicacy can walk abroad without a blush. . . ."

Willard continually cautioned the girls in her Saturday lectures and other classes that their role remained within the sphere of domestic duties. She warned them that education must not place them above the responsibilities of housekeeping, and recited cautionary tales of "literary" ladies who ruined their marriages through domestic ineptitude. "Shame on the woman, who marries and then says she has no talents for house-keeping!" Willard wrote in a women's magazine. "Let her learn—though she drop, for a season, every visiting acquaintance, close every book, rise early, and sit up late, and devote not only her hands but her head to her employments—let her learn her indispensable duty."

## "A Profound Self-Respect"

At the same time, however, Willard insisted that students and their families take girls' academic performance and attendance seriously—something that not all girls' schools did. "Must you keep Harriet at home quite as long as a week?" she wrote in an 1823 letter to one father. "Please do recollect that she belongs to a class who are girls of fine talents and noble ambitions as well as herself—that they will be going on with their studies, and that if she gets behind them she will not be contented till she overtakes them, and this overtaking will come on just about the time we begin to review for examination."

Willard herself also provided a dramatic model of a powerful woman who did much more than manage a household and raise children. She was one of Troy's best-known personages, corresponding with presidents, writing for national magazines, and visiting with international dignitaries such as Lafayette. She had an amazingly egalitarian relationship with her first husband, Dr. John Willard, an older man who essentially abandoned a career in politics and followed her from Vermont to New York to support her dream of a school. (He ended up serving as the school's doctor and business manager.) When she remarried after his death to a man who turned out to be abusive, she took the then-scandalous step of suing for divorce. By the time Willard traveled to France in 1830, her textbooks were generating a large amount of income and she was quite wealthy. Her quarters in Troy were filled with artwork collected in Europe. She had French clothes, servants, and horses and carriages—a far cry from the seventeen-year-old girl teaching in a one-room schoolhouse. "She was always robed—one must use the word 'robed,' so majestic was her bearing—in rich black silk or satin, and her head was crowned with a large white mull turban," wrote suffragist Elizabeth Cady Stanton, who attended the Troy seminary in the early 1830s. "She had a finely developed figure, well-shaped head, classic features, most genial manners and a profound self-respect (a rare quality in woman) that gave her a dignity truly regal."

Willard's personal example spread far beyond the relatively small world of the school. Her visible success may have helped inspire other women to become involved in social causes ranging from temperance to feminism. "Let it be borne in mind, that it [Troy Female Seminary] was founded by female enterprize [sic], and has been wholly sustained by female talent," noted a women's magazine in 1833. "Its improvements have been effected by female perseverance, and . . . it is now the most flourishing school of its kind in the Republic. . . ."

Perhaps most significantly, Willard opened up a whole new set of life options for many of her students by encouraging them to become teachers.

The teaching profession remained dominated by men in the early 1800s, but it was still more open to women than any other profession. And as the American West began to grow in the early 1800s, so did demand for teachers—creating significant job opportunities for young women. Willard considered teaching a noble profession, and one uniquely suited for women, an extension of their natural role as mothers. She wrote this earnest poem to one student who was leaving to run a female seminary:

Go, in the name of God
Prosper, and prove a pillar in the cause
Of Woman. Lend thy aid to waken her
From the long trance of ages. Make her feel
She too hath God's own image.

Willard structured her school to provide an unofficial kind of teacher training in an era before there were any "normal schools," as teacher-training schools were called in the nineteenth century. Top students often became assistant teachers at Troy and then went out into the world as teachers or schoolmistresses. Willard offered to defer tuition payments for poor girls who wanted to go into teaching, asking them to pay her back over time as they earned income from their work. So while her school attracted daughters of the elite, it also included many middle-class or poor girls who were hoping to teach. At one point, Willard had over $10,000 in outstanding tuition loans to students—about half of which was eventually repaid.

Historians estimate that Troy alumnae opened about two hundred schools modeled on Willard's. More than seven hundred Troy students went to work as teachers, although they often stopped teaching when they married. At Troy, students saw firsthand evidence that women could live independent lives based on their intellect. Every graduate who went into teaching and wrote letters back to the seminary was inspiration for another girl to do so. "When I first came here I roomed with a young lady in the fourth hall," Ellen Jay Thomson wrote to a friend at home in Granville, New York, in 1841. "Her name was Caroline Taylor. She was a native of New-hampshire [sic] she had been here two years—a very interesting young lady. She has gone to North Carolina to teach in a family. She has a salary of four hundred dollars a year." It's easy to imagine Thomson mulling this information over and considering what it would mean to have a four-hundred-dollar income. Thomson, in fact, went on to become a governess in Alabama when she graduated, then a teacher in a southern academy for two years, and then a teacher at Troy for seven years before marrying in 1854.

## Shifting Toward Suffrage

Willard's own views of women's place changed slowly over time. Through the 1830s, she was a staunch opponent of women's suffrage. Part of her opposition was ideological. "The only natural government on earth is that of a family—the only natural sovereign, the husband and father," she wrote in an 1829 letter to Catherine Beecher. Part of her opposition may also have been pragmatic. In that letter to Beecher, Willard warned that endorsing the nascent women's rights movement could jeopardize their progress in the educational arena. She warned that critics might say that " 'the studies which you pursue have inflated and bewildered you; you are the worse for your knowledge; return to your ignorance.'

"Such a sentence as this, my dear madam," she wrote, "you and I, as guardians of the interests of our sex's education, are alike desirous to avoid . . ."

By the end of her life, however, Willard's views had mellowed. Perhaps it was simply changing with the times, or watching the success of her students in the world. Perhaps it was the trauma of her own disastrous second marriage, in which her husband treated her with contempt while wantonly spending the money she had accumulated over the years. But in any case, in 1869 Willard wrote approvingly to her former secretary, Celia Burleigh, who had become a speaker for suffrage. "My first feeling when I heard you had become a public lecturer was one of regret," Willard wrote, "but now that I know your reasons for doing so, and that you have your husband's approval, I cannot withhold mine. After all, you have only entered now upon a work that I took up more than half a century ago—pleading the cause of my sex. I did it in my way, you are doing it in yours, and as I have reason to believe that God blessed me in my efforts, I pray that he will bless you in yours."

Willard wrote again to Burleigh in 1870, barely a month before her death. In that letter she indicated even more clearly that she saw suffrage as an extension of her work on behalf of women's education.

"I see frequent references to you in the papers, and I read with interest all that relates to you and your work," Willard wrote to her friend. "I am more and more convinced that it is a good work and one that will lead to good. As for me my days of toil are over and I must soon go to my rest; but I am glad to think that what I began alone and in the face of much opposition will be carried forward by able workers, and lead to great results and that the State will by-and-by, like the family, be controlled by the united wisdom of men and women."

By the time of Willard's death in 1870, secondary education for girls was no longer a controversial oddity in America. Female academies and seminaries had spread throughout the country. Coed public high schools were also spreading and enrolling even larger numbers of girls. Vassar College had just opened and was promising to offer a more advanced level of education for women. Early girls' schools like Troy played a key role in making all this happen, by proving to the world that girls were indeed capable of learning more than "how to weave clothes for her family and how to paint a daisy in water colors."

And what about their students? How did attending a nineteenth-century seminary like Troy affect the course of girls' lives? Historian Anne Firor Scott compiled data on 3,500 Troy graduates from the mid-1800s and found that Troy students tended to marry in much smaller numbers and have significantly fewer children than other New York State women of similar ages. Twenty-two percent of Troy alumnac stayed single, compared with 6 to 8 percent of other women. One out of five Troy alums had just one child, compared with one out of ten other women.

The numbers don't tell us whether these Troy alumnae were single by choice or by circumstance. Some, happy with their independence, may have made a conscious decision not to marry. In other cases, time may have quietly slipped by as these young women studied and taught, until one day they found themselves at the unmarriageable age of thirty or thirty-five. But in either case a Troy education gave these women the ability to support themselves respectably outside of marriage—a rare gift that allowed them an uncommon level of choice and freedom in their lives.

In 1893, two decades after Willard's death, Troy alumnae held their first reunion in the Woman's Building of the World Columbian Exposition in Chicago. The keynote speech was delivered by Susan B. Anthony on behalf of her friend Cady Stanton. She offered up a heaping dose of reunion hyperbole but also a kernel of truth: "To none of the heroes of the past do we owe such a debt of gratitude, as to the pioneers in the great battle for the education of women, and among these the name of Emma Hart Willard must ever stand first in the list. . . . We have not her difficulties to overcome, her trials to endure; but the imperative duty is laid on each of us to finish the work she so successfully began. Schools and colleges of a high order are now everywhere open to women; public sentiment welcomes them to whatever career they may desire . . . The most fitting monument we can rear to Emma Willard is a generation of thoroughly educated women."

# 2

# Elite Enclaves

## THE MONEY HUNT

*Shortly after our group started meeting, I called my cousin Mark, who had helped start a new private elementary school in Los Angeles. He told me that his group had spent $500,000 just to renovate space for the school, and that a synagogue near him had recently spent $12 million opening a high school. Mark also referred us to a consultant who specialized in helping start independent schools, who met with us and warned us we would need to come up with between $500,000 and $15 million to start a school. Our eyes glazed over. Our founding group included two therapists, an artist, a journalist, a social worker, an environmental consultant, a lawyer, and a woman who worked at a nonprofit that turned trash into art. We were not exactly the kind of people who could buy buildings or set up endowments. Some of us even had trouble finding $6 for a sandwich lunch. Where were we going to come up with $500,000 to $15 million?*

*The question of funding was complicated by our ambivalence about money and our fear of creating an elitist institution. Private girls' schools had a history of serving the rich. Although schools like Emma Willard's started out teaching daughters of farmers and shopkeepers as well as more wealthy girls, by the early twentieth century they had narrowed their range and were catering primarily to an elite WASP clientele. For much of the century most independent girls' schools discreetly closed their doors to Jews, and didn't even consider admitting girls of color. Headmistresses kept copies of the* Social Register *on their desks for easy reference about applicant families. Girls brought their own horses with them to boarding school and took cruise ships to Europe in the summers. Entire classes of girls made the rounds of debutante balls together and were routinely written up on the "society" pages of their local papers.*

*This was all far from what we envisioned for the school we were starting. We wanted a school that would mirror the diverse community of Oakland, a liberal multiethnic city with a big African-American middle class. We wanted to create a culture that would be welcoming to families from a wide range of economic backgrounds, as well as families of color and families with gay or lesbian parents. Some members of our group worried that if we let anybody with money onto our board, the school would turn into a snooty rich-girls' school. Others of us—myself included—feared that unless we got some wealthy people involved, we'd never be able to open any kind of school. The debate over wealth and class never really came out into the open. It festered along, with some people making snide comments about families from rich neighborhoods, and others stewing in quiet resentment.*

*The fears of elitism went hand in hand with an ambivalence about raising money. Some people were happy to spend hours arguing about educational philosophy, but were unwilling to put any time into fund-raising. Others were willing but felt too shy or embarrassed to ask people for money. Here, without knowing it, we were following in a long but dubious girls' school tradition. For much of the twentieth century, many girls' schools had looked down on fund-raising as distastefully unladylike—an outgrowth of the Victorian-era belief that gentlewomen don't talk about money. Only in the 1960s did many girls' schools start fund-raising in earnest. One consequence was that even to-*

*day most girls' schools are still playing financial catch-up, with their endowments and facilities trailing far behind onetime boys' schools that had no similar compunctions about asking their graduates for million-dollar gifts.*

*In our case, we initially dealt with fund-raising by ignoring it. We pretended we'd never heard the experts' warnings about needing $500,000 to $15 million to open a school, and we plunged ahead with drawing up our legal documents and drafting a mission statement. Gradually, of course, financial needs made themselves known. When the time came to file our articles of incorporation, we had to pay fees of $600 but barely even had a bank account. Each founder agreed to chip in $60, but some wanted to hold a yard sale to cover their share of the costs. A* yard sale! *We needed to raise hundreds of thousands of dollars, and people were still thinking in terms of yard sales? I took on the unofficial role of Fund-Raising Noodge. I asked my husband, an experienced nonprofit administrator, to give everyone a pep talk on how to look for money. He suggested that each of us start by compiling a list of fifty people—our relatives, neighbors, college friends, co-workers—and ask each of them for funds, even if it were only $20. But people demurred: They didn't know anyone with any money. Or they didn't feel comfortable asking their friends for money. Or their friends had sons and didn't support the idea of a girls' school. And so on . . .*

*Later I thought about the women who founded and ran elite girls' schools during the Gilded Age, the economic boom years of the late 1800s. They were rarely wealthy themselves, but through charisma and perseverance they managed to win support from rich and powerful people like Andrew Carnegie. I often lay in bed at night wondering how we could find our own modern-day Andrew Carnegie—say, a dot-com angel who could write a million-dollar check. But we had no Carnegie. We had no angel. We didn't even know where to look for such a person. And if we'd found one, we probably would have alienated him or her with our suspicions and ambivalence about wealth.*

*Then slowly things started to turn around. We held an informational evening at someone's home and raised several hundred dollars. We received a $2,000 grant from a local foundation to write a business* *plan, which allowed us to make our case more persuasively to other foundations. One founding family donated $1,000. My mother-in-law mailed me a completely unexpected check for $10,000. A man from Colorado who was interested in the school for his Oakland granddaughter sent in another unexpected $10,000.*

*For every step forward, there seemed to be a misstep. We held an inspiring meeting with women from high-tech companies, got them all jazzed up about the school, and then we let them go home and forgot to ask them for money. We were assured by the administrator of one foundation that we would get a $50,000 grant, only to have the grant rejected at the last minute by her board of directors. But by the time the school opened in September 1999, we had managed to raise a total of $144,000. Just as amazingly, some of our most stubborn footdraggers had become star fund-raisers. Our starving-artist member who claimed she "didn't know anyone with money" ultimately connected us with a fabulous donor who agreed to sponsor a low-income girl on scholarship for three years. Another "I-can't-fund-raise" complainer ended up organizing a work-a-thon where girls solicited pledges for their time cleaning up a local creek, which raised about $10,000 for the school. We weren't financially secure, and we certainly were far from that $500,000-to-$15-million benchmark. Our director would lose sleep for much of the first three years worrying about whether we'd be able to cover all our expenses. But we had moved beyond yard sales. We had raised enough money to open a school.*

A bbot Academy began its life in the early 1800s as a mostly local institution, a school aimed at serving daughters of families in the small town of Andover, Massachusetts. Andover boys had the option of attending Phillips Academy, a local academy that later evolved into one of the country's most prestigious boarding schools, graduating luminaries such as President George W. Bush and John F. Kennedy, Jr. But Andover girls didn't have any such opportunity. So in 1828, five community leaders—two ministers, two deacons, and a lawyer who was treasurer of Phillips—got together and posted a notice in town seeking "persons who feel favorably disposed toward the establishment of a FEMALE HIGH SCHOOL in the South Parish of Andover."

At first, only about a third of Abbot's students were boarders from out of town. The rest were local girls—middle-class daughters of farmers and craftsmen, as well as wealthy girls. Tuition was just $5 a term, a modest sum that could be earned through a week's work at one of the cotton mills that were cropping up in nearby towns. But then, in the 1850s, Abbot's character started to change.

A local benefactor left the town of Andover $50,000 to build a free coeducational high school. In 1856, the new high school opened and promptly started siphoning away many of the middle-class girls who had attended Abbot, according to Abbot historian Susan McIntosh Lloyd. The number of local students dropped from ninety-four girls in 1853 to twenty-seven in 1865—from 56 percent to 27 percent of the school. Abbot responded by seeking to increase its boarding population, building a new dorm in 1854 to attract out-of-

*Students celebrate the end of the Civil War*
*on the roof of Abbot Academy (Mass.), 1865.*

towners. With the shift toward boarding students, Abbot also began drawing on a more wealthy population. Along with its increased reliance on wealthy students went a certain genteel snobbery. Jews, Catholics, and recent immigrants were not admitted. One girl felt a need to explain in an 1887 writing exercise that her great-grandfather was "an Irishman but a gentleman." Emily Means, an alumna of Abbot who served as headmistress in the early 1900s, looked for long family trees when choosing both students and teachers. "Blood tells, blood counts, doesn't it?" she remarked to a trustee while discussing a prospective teacher.

Abbot's evolution is a small example of what was a broad change among girls' schools in the late 1800s, from middle-class to elite institutions. While the early seminaries were never free of charge, they often served middle-class girls along with wealthy ones—like at Troy Female Seminary, where Emma Willard made tuition loans to girls who planned to become teachers. But by the twentieth century, private girls' schools had largely become enclaves of the wealthy and privileged.

The transformation of private girls' schools into elite institutions really came to fruition between 1880 and 1915. In many ways, those years were a golden era for girls' schools. A large number of today's independent girls' schools were founded in this period—the Brearley School in New York in 1884, the Marlborough School in Los Angeles in 1888, and the National Cathedral School in Washington, D.C., in 1899, to name a few among dozens. They were run by a generation of powerful, entrepreneurial headmistresses who built their schools into small empires with wealthy donors, permanent buildings, and organized alumnae groups. But in terms of sheer numbers, girls' schools had become marginal. The vast majority of American girls would get their education at coed public schools. Unless they were Catholic, they wouldn't ever think about attending a single-sex school. Girls' schools filled a prestigious niche, but it was still just a niche. It would be half a century before private girls' schools started to repudiate the snobbery and prejudice that came with being an elite enclave. It would be nearly a whole century before they began to reclaim a role in educating a wide range of American girls, not just the elite.*

## The Spread of Coeducation

The transformation of private girls' schools into elite institutions was connected to broad changes in the world of American education—in particular, the growth of public school systems that were largely coeducational.

Today we take for granted that every community has a public high school, just as it has a firehouse and a police station. But for much of the 1800s, that was not the case. Educational reformers like Horace Mann spent much of the nineteenth century trying to establish the idea of free public schooling for all. By 1860, their efforts were paying off and a majority of states had set up public school systems. After the Civil War, public education began to spread to the secondary as well as primary level. There were only about 40 public high schools in the whole country in the 1860s, but by 1880 the number rose to 800. By 1890, public high schools outnumbered private ones 2,526 to 1,632. By 1920, there were 14,326 public high schools and only 2,093 private ones.

One big question about all these new public high schools was whether they would be mixed sex or single sex. Town councils debated the issue; educators argued it in journals; teachers' associations took positions on it. Most of the arguments in favor of coeducation would sound familiar to people today. Feminists claimed that keeping

---

*Today educators typically use the term *independent school* to refer to nonpublic schools with an independent governing board. However, many of the girls' schools in this category were started as individual ventures and did not develop a nonprofit board structure until later in their history. They came into existence before anyone had even thought of the term *independent school*. In this book, I use the terms *private school* and *independent school* interchangeably to refer to nonpublic, non-Catholic schools.

girls and boys separate would doom girls to an inferior education. When Susan B. Anthony and Elizabeth Cady Stanton launched the suffrage movement at Seneca Falls in 1848, they included a call for coeducation in public schools. And in fact, all-girl public schools usually were poor sisters to their male counterparts. Historians David Tyack and Elizabeth Hansot point out that in Louisville, Kentucky, per-pupil spending at the white girls' high school in 1902 was the same as that of the coeducational school for blacks—58 percent of the amount spent on the academic high school for white boys. "Only by having the schools and universities coeducational can we assure the girls of the world of receiving a thoroughly good education," said M. Carey Thomas, a nineteenth-century advocate of women's equality who was president of all-women Bryn Mawr College.

Meanwhile, many teachers and principals said that having girls in the classroom made it easier to control the boys—that both sexes, in fact, behaved better when kept together. "The rudeness and *abandon* [*sic*] which prevails among boys when separate, at once gives place to self-restraint in the presence of girls," wrote William Torrey Harris, a strong advocate of coeducation who started as school superintendent in St. Louis and later became U.S. commissioner of education. "The prurient sentimentality, engendered by educating girls apart from boys,—it is manifested by a frivolous and silly bearing when such girls are brought into the company of the opposite sex—this disappears almost entirely in mixed schools. In its place a quiet self-possession reigns."

On the other side of the debate, opponents of coeducation made some arguments that would also sound familiar today—not far removed from claims by modern girls' schools that they teach girls "in the ways that girls learn best." Nineteenth-century opponents of coeducation argued that it was easier to teach girls and boys separately since you could use methods of teaching and discipline that were geared to each sex. Many nineteenth-century teachers felt they needed to use whippings or canings to keep boys in line, but that such kinds of corporal punishment were unnecessary and offensive for girls. Gender differences are "radical and fundamental . . . progress is impossible without accepting and respecting in education this difference of sex," wrote Boston school superintendent John D. Philbrick in 1880.

Mostly, however, opponents argued that coeducation would corrupt girls—an argument that was based on Victorian ideas of female delicacy and invariably took on class and ethnic overtones. The San Francisco superintendent of schools said in 1868 that separate girls' schools were needed because "parents have objections to placing delicate and refined daughters in the same class with rude and depraved boys." The principal of Girls' High and Latin Schools in Boston warned that girls would be corrupted by the "coarse natures" found in schools that weren't "homogeneous"—in other words, schools that included working-class Irish and other immigrants. Coeducation might work in small towns, he wrote, "for there the conditions approach in simplicity the conditions of family or neighborhood life. In large cities, however, the case is different. The population is not homogeneous, the families represented in the school are not known to one another, the numbers brought together in a single school are much larger, and the proportion of coarse natures among the pupils is apt to be somewhat larger."

Although the coeducation debate continued through the late nineteenth century, gradually the supporters of mixed classrooms won the day. Money was a large part of the reason. Small cities found it cheaper to open one coed high school than two separate ones for boys and girls. Public attitudes also helped tilt the scales. People had grown used to the idea of coeducation in public elementary schools; why not continue that in the upper grades? "As God made us male and female to be in each other's society, in the family, the church, and all other social circles, so he would not have us separated in school," wrote a Cincinnati high school principal in 1854. By 1882, single-sex public high schools could be found in only 19 of 196 cities surveyed by the federal government. By 1900, the proportion was even smaller—just 12 of 628 cities surveyed had a single-sex public high school. Coeducation had become the norm in public high schools across America.

## The Single-Sex Alternative

Faced with competition from the new public high schools, some academies and seminaries went out of business or merged with their local public school system. Others tried to differentiate themselves, offering parents something they wouldn't be able to get at a public school.

Some distinguished themselves from the public schools by offering a religious education. Others like Abbot Academy became boarding schools. A number of boys' academies differentiated themselves by becoming college-preparatory schools. A few girls' schools defined themselves that way too: Girls Preparatory School in Chattanooga, for instance, was started in 1906 by a public school teacher who was frustrated with her district's refusal to prepare girls for college.

A single-sex environment was one of the strongest selling points of private schools. Boys' schools promised to teach manly virtues and a "muscular Christianity." Girls' schools promised to instill feminine virtues. Some schools that had been coed converted to single-sex during this period: In 1902 Frank Boyden took over Deerfield Academy, a struggling coed school that had primarily served townsfolk in western Massachusetts, and turned it into a nationally known college preparatory school for boys. The share of private secondary schools that were single-sex rose from 44 percent in 1899–1900 to 53 percent in 1919–1920—a sharp contrast from the nearly universal coeducation found in public schools.

Whether their focus was religious education or same-sex education, private schools found themselves catering to an increasingly wealthy clientele. Wealthy people were the ones who could afford to bypass the local public high school if they didn't like it. And in the 1880s and 1890s, there were more wealthy people with more money to spend on their children's schooling than ever before. This was the Gilded Age—the era after the Civil War when industrialization spread across America and men made immense fortunes in fields like steel, railroads, oil, and banking. Rockefeller, Carnegie, Morgan, and Frick started dynasties of wealth. Barons of industry built huge mansions on Fifth Avenue and transported their households each summer in private train cars to resorts like Newport and Saratoga. In the 1840s there were fewer than twenty people throughout the United States who could call themselves millionaires; by 1892, there were more than four thousand.

Old-money families sent their children to private schools because that was what their circle had always done. Meanwhile, new-money families sought out private schools as a way to establish themselves and their children in old-money society. This was an extremely status-conscious era—the era that saw the creation of the first *Social Register* listings and the first country clubs. And establishing a proper social status for daughters was even more important than for sons. A boy, after all, could make a fortune for himself in the business world. But a girl's prospects depended almost entirely upon marriage—and to marry well, a girl had to be part of "society." *Harper's Bazar* [*sic*] in 1900 advised mothers to consider social status in choosing a school for their teenage daughters. "In choosing a school for the young girl of this age, regard must be had for her future social companionships," the magazine said. "Friendships are often formed for life in the girls' school, and it is wise for her parents to place her among her social equals, and where she may develop among those of her own station."

Marietta Jackson Scurry Ransone, who graduated from the Hockaday School in Dallas in 1926, recalled classmates whose fathers had recently made fortunes as ranchers and oil-patch wildcatters. "Often these men had been roughnecks who became successful oilmen and married the local town beauty," she said. "Now they had elaborate homes in Houston and Midland—and bulging billfolds. They too came to Dallas to shop at Neiman's, visit the State Fair, see the bright lights, and raise a little hell. They envisioned something beyond the convertibles and fur coats for their daughters; that something was to be had at Hockaday."

## Miss Spence Wows Andrew Carnegie

The women who ran girls' schools around the turn of the century occupied an unusual place on the American social ladder. Although they were educating the daughters of the elite, they were usually from modest backgrounds themselves. They entered teaching as a way to support themselves or to help impoverished family members. But their ambitious or entrepreneurial character led them to start their own schools. And as headmistresses of successful private schools, they became near-peers of those titans of industry whose daughters they were teaching. They worked hand in glove with bank presidents and businessmen to acquire land or finance new school buildings, and were able to talk business in a way that few women could. They were gatekeepers for the social elite, determining whose daughters would be allowed to enter the coveted sanctum of their schools. They built their careers on knowing what was considered respectable and instilling it in their girls. Yet they themselves sometimes broke with convention in quiet but dramatic ways—espousing Fabian socialism, adopting children while remaining single, even leading the occasional grave-digging expedition.

Clara Spence, founder of the Spence School in New York, was one such figure. Spence grew up far from luxury and power. Born in Albany, New York, in 1862, she was the thirteenth and only surviving child of a Scottish couple who had lost six children in one week to a scarlet fever epidemic. She went to a public high school, Boston University, and then studied Shakespeare in London, where she supported herself by performing in evening entertainments. Spence flirted with an acting career but was discouraged by her mother, who did not consider it respectable. She took up tutoring instead and, when her brother died, took on additional teaching jobs to support his wife and children.

Spence was tutoring the daughters of the wealthy Shepard family when one day, she fainted from hunger and exhaustion on her daily walk across the Brooklyn Bridge to their Manhattan home. The Shepards were touched when they realized her situation and sent

*Clara Spence, founder of the Spence School (N.Y.), at the age of thirty-four*

her south for six weeks with their daughters to restore her health. The girls became close with Spence. One daughter tried to pawn her own diamond ring to get money to help Spence start a school. Her mother found out and halted the pawnshop plan in its tracks, but then offered to advance the rent for one year for Spence to start her school.

Spence was thirty. She lived at the school—a narrow four-floor brownstone just off Fifth Avenue on Forty-eighth Street, in what was then the heart of fashionable New York—with ten teachers and ten boarders during its first year. The faculty slept on small folding beds that were put away in closets during the day. Some teachers slept four to a room. Girls and teachers alike were limited to one bath a week, unless they got up early to light the water heater. The school offered thirty-nine subjects, including literature, Greek and Roman mythology, French, American history, botany, chemistry, psychology, and art history. By the end of the year, the school was doing well enough that Spence repaid the loan from the Shepards and leased another nearby house. By 1894, she had fifteen boarders and more than fifty day students. One of the families that was drawn to Spence's school was that of Andrew Carnegie. The steel magnate developed a rapport with Clara Spence and sent his daughter Margaret there. Later Carnegie's wife sold the school a plot of land next to the Carnegie family mansion on Fifth Avenue and Ninety-first Street—a prime piece of Upper East Side real estate. Carnegie's son-in-law led a fund-raising campaign to develop the site, which remains the Spence School's home to this day.

Clara Spence emphasized the classic Victorian values with her students. She spoke of the three Ds that a lady did not discuss—Disease, Dress, and Domestics. She didn't let boarding students leave the building for the slightest errand unless they had a hat, gloves, and chaperone. Tea was served daily in the dining room after the day students left, and boarders bowed as they said good night to the teacher. But Spence herself went outside Victorian conventions by building her own family of adopted children—a "single mother by choice" long before there was the vocabulary for such a thing.

Spence and a friend had taken two orphans into the Brooklyn boardinghouse where they lived before Spence started her school. In 1897, Spence was approached by a young woman named Charlotte Baker, the aunt of a former student, who was trying to find a home for a girl whose mother was dying of tuberculosis. Miss Spence adopted the girl, who went on to graduate from Spence and Wellesley, get a master's degree and a law degree, and raise a family of her own. Charlotte Baker in turn became close to Spence—becoming the school's art teacher, then associate principal, and ultimately head of the school after Spence's death. When the school added a new residential building on Fifty-fifth street in 1900, Spence and Baker shared a two-bedroom apartment on the fifth floor. Both Spence and Baker adopted several additional children—two girls and two boys altogether. For a while, the school added a nursery school but disbanded it when Spence and Baker's children outgrew it. Both families lived in the school's boarding facility for a number of years, with the little children getting piggyback rides and other attention from the big schoolgirls. The two women then moved to a Park Avenue apartment with their families, where six to eight people gathered around the dinner table each night. Spence carried her personal experience with adoption into a social project and started working with some prominent pediatricians to find homes for orphans. Altogether she and Miss Baker placed more than eighty orphans in homes. The Spence Alumnae Society picked up the ball and opened an adoption service and nursery for orphans.

If she were alive today, Clara Spence's drive and ability would probably make her a college president or a CEO. In her day, she was limited to presiding over the smaller fiefdom of a school but nevertheless won the respect of some of New York's top businessmen. At her death in 1923, Spence's eulogists included steel magnate Charles Schwab, who had served on various charitable boards with her. "Industry and finance have missed a great character in our beloved Miss Spence," Schwab said. "If she had been in such affairs, no one would have been more eagerly sought by the industries or by the business which I control. I valued her judgment . . . because her motive was so whole-souled and unprejudiced and so for the good of the organizations. She was a noble woman. She was a splendid woman."

## Miss Madeira Serves Up Tea and Social Conscience

Lucy Madeira was part of Clara Spence's generation of institution builders, and she shared Spence's humble roots. Madeira's father was a Civil War veteran whose health was broken by his stay in a Confederate prisoner-of-war camp. Plagued with tuberculosis and cirrhosis, he became an invalid when she was twelve. Her mother moved the family to Washington, D.C., and started taking in boarders. Madeira was an eager student who had good teachers in her local public schools. She enrolled at Vassar as the first recipient of a scholarship by the Washington organization of Vassar alumnae—not a grant, but an interest-free loan of $200 a year for four years. She wore hand-me-down clothes at college, wrote down every single expenditure, and managed to limit her spending to $40 in her first eight months. After college, she was prepared to teach Latin in her old high school when the job was taken by a male classmate with a letter of reference from President Cleveland. She taught temporarily in a poorly run girls' school in Maryland—the school had a ballroom with four tiers of boxes, yet paid Madeira just $150 a year, required her to share a room and bed with the music teacher, and provided no closet or dresser for her clothes, which she kept in a suitcase under the shared bed. She then moved to the much more reputable Sidwell Friends School. Even there, though, the poor salaries paid to teachers weren't enough to support Madeira's increasingly needy family.

Like Clara Spence, Madeira saw running her own school as a strategy for economic survival.

Madeira borrowed $6,000 from family friends to start the school, opening near Dupont Circle with fifteen day students and thirteen boarders. She kept costs down by hiring married women who only wanted to teach for two periods a day. She gave herself a salary but plowed all the profits back into the school. "I began the first year with four hundred dollars in cash and my room and board," she recalled. "I have always thought that a school should be a spiritual place—as much so as a church is, and that it should not make any personal profits. I have never taken any."

Madeira's school did well and soon became one of the places that Washington society sent their daughters. Among her students was Katharine Meyer Graham, whose father, *Washington Post* owner Eugene Meyer, was one of Madeira's strongest supporters. Meyer loaned the school $300,000 in 1929 to move to a bucolic woodsy campus in Virginia with a stunning view of the upper

*Lucy Madeira, founder of the Madeira School, at the school's former site in Washington, D.C.*

Potomac River. Later he gave the school 178 acres of property ad-joining its initial purchase.

Lucy Madeira married in 1917 and surprised some observers by continuing as headmistress; traditionally, women teachers and head-mistresses stopped working when they married. But the school still met all the upper-class social requirements of its time. A set of 1939 rules for table manners told girls not to argue with each other dur-ing meals: "The talk at the table should be lively, gay, high-spirited. . . . Amiability should prevail in all social intercourse." Miss Madeira insisted that adults be addressed formally with "Good morning, Miss So-and-so" and not with casual language such as "Hi." Julia Camp McLean, an alumna from 1934, recalls an inno-cent freshman running into Miss Madeira in the school post office and offering a friendly "Hi." "Miss Madeira FROZE and said 'WHAT DID YOU SAY TO ME?'" McLean recalled. "The poor girl was so frightened she couldn't remember what she had said."

Maid service and table service in the Madeira School dining room stopped in World War II, as they did at many girls' boarding schools, when the housekeeping staff left for better-paying defense jobs. But other niceties of elite WASP life continued. Girls continued to drink tea on the terrace and wear white or pastel dresses at dinner through the 1950s. Well into the 1960s, mothers were invited to meet the faculty over tea while fathers were invited for an annual re-ception with whiskey and gin. "One thing I appreciated and still do, is the dignified, well-appointed atmosphere of the school," recalled alumna Anne Conyers Bryan Wilkins, who graduated in 1941. "Things were well done—the serving of tea, the nice colored maids, the good food, the silver etc. all [sic] small things, but they rub off on the girls."

But Madeira also tried to instill a social conscience in her girls. She herself was a Fabian socialist and a strong supporter of Franklin D. Roosevelt, even though the New Deal was anathema to most of her students' wealthy families: In a 1940 straw poll, 139 girls voted for Wendell Wilkie while only 24 voted for Roosevelt and 6 for socialist Norman Thomas. "You should have heard the swearing and the screaming and the plans for assassinating Roosevelt" on the morning after Election Day, one girl wrote to her father. "Everyone was saying that they would now have to go back to the village high school, or they couldn't buy a new hat or get a car and so on and so forth!"

Madeira herself taught the school's public affairs and Bible classes—Bible classes that were defined loosely enough to include issues such as poverty and Swedish socialism. She read from a little gray book that began, "Poverty is less than it was and more than it should be." She liked to stir up debate and provoke the girls whose families were reflexively anti-FDR. "She told us directly and by metaphor that we were young women of privilege and thus had greater responsibility," said Mary Alice White Kimball, an alumna from 1937 who became a psychology professor at Teachers College. "Were we going to light one candle or curse the darkness? I took the pledge, however poorly kept. I heard a call to something noble at a time when I needed to hear such a call, and it has never stopped calling."

Lucy Madeira had two watchwords that were repeated so often that many alumnae say they will remember them 'til the day they die: "Function in disaster," and "Finish in style." "Function in disaster" came from her husband, David Wing, who advised her that "the time to judge a school is not when everything is going well. See how it functions in disaster." "Finish in style" came from Madeira's mother, who told her, "Lucy Madeira, you mark my words, unless you learn to finish what you start and to finish it in style, you will never amount to anything."

Lucy Madeira, while training girls to function in society as well as in disaster, was herself a quiet feminist. She set up a student government at the school in the 1910s, before women had the vote in the outside world. Katharine Graham recalls that Madeira also believed God was a woman. She refused to water down the school's high intellectual standards. Brooke Astor, who became one of New York's leading philanthropists, enrolled at Madeira as a girl in the 1910s, but was quickly pulled out because the school insisted that she take college-preparatory courses. As Astor recounted in her autobiography:

> "Imagine," [Astor's mother] said later to Granny, "this ridiculous young teacher insisted that they could not enroll Brooke . . . un-

less she took a lot of, to my mind, perfectly absurd subjects, so that she could pass a college-board examination."

"College," said Granny. "Goodness me, what does Brooke want to go to college for?"

"Well, that's just it, Mama [pronounced ma*ma*]," said Mother. "Naturally I don't want Brooke to go to college. Madeira's has really become very highhanded. I was absolutely furious, so what do you suppose I did?"

"What?" said Granny.

"What?" I echoed.

"Well," said Mother triumphantly, "I took a cab right up to Holton-Arms and had a most delightful talk with Mrs. Holton, and she is going to take Brooke there."

"Oh, no!" I cried. "Why did you do that?"

Mother looked at me and smiled. "Because I am not going to be bullied by some whippersnapper of a schoolmistress. We discussed what subjects Brooke should take and decided on English literature and history, history of art, French, Latin, and music; not any more, as Brooke's eyes aren't strong."

"Law," said Granny, "it seems quite a lot to me."

As time passed, Lucy Madeira's standards came to be the norm and Granny's became outdated. Madeira lived until 1960, and would often tell students how much the world had changed since her youth with the arrival of telephones, automobiles, airplanes, movies, and television. Technology wasn't all that had changed. In a 1945 speech to seniors, Madeira noted that "I think that girls are more interesting every year, and the reason I think that is that girls are no longer 'la Femme'—they are people. I think we still have a long way to go before women are free of all shackles of being women, but the advance in my lifetime is almost beyond belief."

# Miss Charlotte Teaches Riding,
# Drill, and Southern Charm

Miss Spence and Miss Madeira would never have brooked a student referring to them by their first names, but Charlotte Haxall Noland insisted that the girls at her Foxcroft School call her "Miss Charlotte." An unregenerate tomboy with a passion for horses and military drill, Noland spent much of her time as headmistress decked out in boots and riding clothes. Yet Foxcroft, located in rural Virginia hunt country, was heavily sought after by many of America's most elite families. "Well-to-do families from the north and west think they find here a flavor of southern aristocracy," noted a 1935 guidebook to private schools.

Noland herself disliked school as a child and never went to college. Raised in an old Virginia family and named after an aunt who was married to Robert E. Lee, Jr., she was educated by a tutor and spent much of her early childhood out of doors. "The greatest fun we used to have was with ponies," she recalled. It came as a shock when her family moved into Washington, D.C., and she was stuck in a classroom behind a desk. She started to dream of creating a more congenial school—more fun, more active, more outdoors, more *happy*.

Noland studied physical education with the world-renowned Dudley Sargent at Harvard, won a fellowship to study and teach at a German gymnasium, and returned to start her own gymnasium in Baltimore. As the first step toward a school, she opened a summer camp in the Virginia countryside—riding in the morning, swimming and tennis in the afternoon—and in some ways the feel of a summer camp never left Foxcroft. Even today, the girls spend four years as members of the Fox or Hound teams in a kind of perpetual color war, and they rowdily bang their cups in the dining hall while belting out camp-style songs: "I go to Foxcroft School so pity me, there's not a boy in the vicinity. . . ."

Riding and hunting were Miss Charlotte's passions, and they be-

*Charlotte Haxall Noland, founder of the Foxcroft School (Va.), leads a
military drill with her students.*

came Foxcroft's passions—to a point where school officials wondered in the 1970s and '80s if they would ever overcome their reputation as a stable with a school attached. The alumnae house, built
in 1921, was called the Spur and Spoon. The school's annual Christ-
mas cards showed Miss Charlotte in riding gear, and riding lessons
were included in the tuition. At one point, Miss Charlotte promised
a pony to each alumna who had a fourth child. Every October she
led the girls on a nighttime raccoon hunt. The girls bundled themselves up in blue jeans, sweaters, and woolly pom-pom hats and carried flashlights. They followed two huntsmen with dogs who sniffed
out raccoons. "When they hit the trail of a coon the girls ran struggling through the briers and over fences and splashing through
creeks until the baying of the dogs indicated a treed coon," an alumna
recalled. The night always ended with the girls sitting around a fire,
eating gallons of mulligan stew. Not exactly the finishing-school stereo-

type of needlepoint and dancing lessons—but equally in demand in certain wealthy circles.

Miss Charlotte took the best riders out on the Middleburg Hunt each spring, which some townspeople criticized as inappropriate for young ladies. She responded that hunting required quick decision making, a useful skill for girls. "It is the ideal training for the one thing most lacking in women—decision," she said. Miss Charlotte herself served as president of the Middleburg Hunt, the first woman to do so. She joked that her academic credential was an M.F.H.—Master of Foxhounds.

Foxcroft offered classes in dancing and decorum in its early years—how to enter a room, curtsey, and sit properly. But those lessons seemed geared for some distant time in life after school was done. While at school, the more common scenario was one recalled by alumnae from 1935: Miss Charlotte bursting into study hall, flinging the door open, and crying out, "Girls! Off with your shoes, jackets, even skirts! It's a race down Brick House lawn and pick the daffodils!"

Miss Charlotte told her students wild ghost stories and taught some of them how to shoot pistols. During World War II, she replaced calisthenics with West Point–style military drill, which continued all the way until 1968. There was one time in the late 1930s or early 1940s when Miss Charlotte led her genteel young charges on a grave-digging expedition. The main house on the Foxcroft property dated back to colonial times, and had allegedly been inhabited by Mrs. Kyle, a madwoman who was locked in the attic when her husband was away from home. Mrs. Kyle was supposed to have died by falling down the stairs, but rumor had it that she was actually shot while trying to escape her confinement and had transformed into a ghost who still haunted the estate. Miss Charlotte determined to test out the rumors and took six top students to dig in a field where the old landholders were buried. They made three holes but found nothing. The next day, each girl brought a friend and they dug some more. They found a man's femur, figured that was Mr. Kyle, and determined to dig on his left side "as wives always were." The next day, Miss Charlotte let all the girls come along and they set up a table of tea nearby. They dug some more. One girl fell in and got pulled out. Finally they hit some ribs, small leg bones, and a skull—which plainly had a bullet hole through the middle of it. Miss Charlotte sent the skull to the Smithsonian Museum's ballistics department, telling them it had been found in a plowed field since grave digging was illegal in Virginia. The experts confirmed that it was a pre-Revolutionary bullet. Miss Charlotte had the girls collect Mrs. Kyle's bones, put them in a big stone pickle jar, and bury them at the end of the orchard with a brass marker—presumably ending the ghost's wanderings. Again, not your standard finishing-school tea party.

Foxcroft was not an academic stronghold in its early years. In 1922, only one girl from the graduating class went to college, and Miss Charlotte was happy to hire teachers without any college education as late as the 1940s. But Miss Charlotte set other kinds of high standards. "O my girls," she said in a 1937 sermon, "after the thought, the work, and the prayers I've had for you, you MUST be fine women. Women who are going to count in the world; women who do not lose themselves. . . . Remember—and this is a work that will keep you on your feet—your life is an *entrustment*. It is not an accident. You were born for a purpose and you must find out what that purpose is and fulfill it."

One alumna recalled never having seen Miss Charlotte walk her horse—she was always galloping somewhere. When a riding injury forced her to stop hunting, she took up fishing and won an award for landing a sixty-eight-pound marlin. When a doctor told her to stop jumping fences, she jumped gates, which were higher. Through her seventies, she talked about wishing to be one of the people who would someday go to the moon. "She was always a 'doer' herself," an alumna from 1946 recalled. "I know she always asked after I got out of Foxcroft 'what I was doing with my life' and how terribly inadequate I would feel if I replied 'nothing.'"

## "Selfishness Is a Hedious Sin"

The feelings of that Foxcroft alumna were not unusual. Schools like Foxcroft catered to America's elite, but they also promoted a set of values that could seem surprisingly at odds with upper-class life. "There is this essential irony about our education of the *jeune fille* who is one day to become the *grande dame*," wrote *Fortune* magazine in 1931 in an arch guide to the top girls' boarding schools of that era, "that in preparing her for a life of sophistication, the almost universal emphasis should lie on simplicity and the Biblical virtues."

Schools tried to instill values such as responsibility, simplicity, and kindness. They were essentially trying to inoculate their girls against the pettiness and gaudy materialism of wealthy society, even as they were preparing their girls to enter the top tiers of that society. "We were encouraged to have a full life, and a full life meant taking responsibility not only for yourself but for others," said Rachel Hammond Breck, a granddaughter of Commodore Vanderbilt who graduated from Miss Porter's in 1925.

Headmistresses were quick to chastise girls who they felt were failing to uphold their school's values. Once Sarah Porter was disappointed to find the older girls forming cliques and snubbing the newer arrivals. She called the whole school together and rebuked the snobs, waving her finger at them, "You cannot afford to be so self-centered. Selfishness is a *hedious* [*sic*] sin, and it will *make you hedious*." Miss Porter's also developed an institution called Little Meeting, a kind of spiritual version of student government, in which students would present talks on various Christian or moral topics. "We were full of noble thoughts—we used to write about courage, strength, character," said Hellie Stowell, who was head of Little Meeting at age sixteen in 1930. Girls' schools encouraged their students to maintain these values after graduation. Many schools developed alumnae associations that took on a range of charitable projects, from knitting clothes for the poor to sponsoring weeklong country vacations for working-class young women.

Girls' boarding schools reinforced their emphasis on character through their relatively spartan surroundings. Most did provide maid service. But girls typically had to share small rooms and keep their own clothes and possessions tidy. Many schools limited the frequency of baths. At the Foxcroft School, girls slept on open-air "sleeping porches"—going to bed in flannel pajamas, wool socks, wool gloves, and balaclavas to keep themselves warm. For girls from wealthy homes, such living conditions could be a bit of a shock. "Farmington had miserable little bathtubs," recalled Emily Ridgway, who graduated from Miss Porter's in 1929. "I don't think you were even allowed to have a bath every night, which of course horrified me."

Schools also imposed strict limits on the kinds of clothes and jewelry that girls could bring to school. They purposely allowed little room for competition over dress. Foxcroft's founder, Charlotte Haxall Noland, once met a student who showed up at the train station with eight trunks and a maid. Noland asked which trunk held undergarments. She then loaded that one into the wagon for school and sent the maid and the other seven trunks home. That instance may have been extreme, but it was not unique. "If any arrived with elaborate clothes or jewelry—they were requested not to wear them," wrote Julia Manierre Mann, who attended Miss Porter's in 1899–1900. "One girl who came while I was there brought with her full sets of rubbies [sic], sapphires to match her various gowns etc. which, needless to say, she was obliged to return at once to her mother."

There was a political aspect as well as a moral one to girls' schools efforts to instill an ethic of simplicity. By the late nineteenth century, class differences were becoming more pronounced than ever before in U.S. history. Workers were trying to organize in unions; anarchists and socialists had led revolts in Europe. America's elite saw public education as a way to keep their own working class in line. At the same time, they saw private education as a way to discourage the kind of ruling-class excesses that spark rebellion. "Now, at this stage of the world's progress, every . . . girl, whether she will or not, has in her keeping a great responsibility," one teacher wrote in 1901. "Around her are the discontented masses, watching to see what the rich ladies and gentlemen will do next. What will the rich lady do? By her sumptuous living, and her pleasure-seeking, and her extravagance . . . will she throw her influence in the wrong way? Or will she bring a trained intelligence, a wise self-sacrifice, and a consecrated womanly tact, to aid in the social task of the time?"

## Anti-Semitism and Ethnic Exclusion

For all their efforts to transcend gaudiness and materialism, private girls' schools did not challenge the values of wealthy society in one important area—its elitism and social exclusivity. Too often, girls' schools subscribed to the anti-Semitism, racism, and snobbery that characterized wealthy America for much of the twentieth century.

Schools and their families prided themselves on being the "right sort of people"—which meant excluding Jews, blacks, and recent immigrant groups like Irish and Italians. In 1915, a Boston teacher named Porter Sargent published the nation's first guide to private schools, a progenitor of today's entire genre of prep school guides, college guides, graduate school guides, and summer camp guides. Sargent spent fifty-eight pages on 354 girls' schools, including 29 in Manhattan and 18 in Philadelphia alone. His descriptions of various girls' schools give a sense of the social exclusivity valued by many parents and promoted by many schools:

> Miss Winsor's School in Boston: "has long enjoyed the highest social prestige so that it is patronized by the most exclusive Boston families and those who appreciate the social advantages of membership in the school."
>
> The Misses Masters School in Dobbs Ferry, N.Y.: "is a school of the highest social prestige which zealously maintains an exclusive atmosphere, so that admission is eagerly sought."
>
> St. Timothy's School for Girls in Maryland is "one of the most exclusive girls' schools of the country, with the patronage of conservative families of New York, Philadelphia, and the South . . . The atmosphere of the school is simple and old-fashioned and gives evidence of breeding."

At the time Sargent published his guide, tuition for the best-known private girls' boarding schools ranged from $600 to $1,200—the equivalent of $10,000 to $20,000 in today's terms. Day school tuition cost the equivalent of $2,500 to $5,000. Schools didn't have any kind of organized financial aid program or make any systematic effort to serve non-elite families. The only kind of financial assistance occurred on an individual basis, when headmistresses would sometimes offer reduced fees to daughters of poorly paid church employees like ministers or to students from elite families that had suffered a sudden reversal of fortune.

Nor did schools try to cultivate a diverse student population—quite the contrary. Most private girls' schools didn't admit Jews or Catholics until the mid–twentieth century. The only Irish on their premises were the cooks in the kitchen, and the only blacks were the janitors or groundskeepers. Anti-Semitism and ethnic exclusion were so taken for granted that Porter Sargent, in his 1935–36 guidebook, included a separate listing of "Schools for Jewish Girls" and a listing of "Schools Accepting Jewish Students." The latter was not very long, naming only ten institutions.

Social exclusivity characterized both the least academic finishing schools and the most rigorous college-preparatory schools. Brearley, which opened in 1884 as the first college-preparatory school for girls in New York, admitted Jewish students from the start. But until the 1930s, admission decisions were nonetheless made by a committee of mothers who gave heavy weight to applicants' social prominence and connections. Similarly, getting into the Spence School in New York required more than good grades. Elizabeth Crawford Wilkin, an alumna from the class of 1918, recalled having to present letters of recommendation from two "socially prominent matrons," her minister, her doctor, her former headmistress, and the family bank. Then there was a personal interview with Miss Spence, which focused only tangentially on academic abilities. "What did matter was how I walked across the room, how I held my hands, my head, and what I did with my feet during the process," Wilkin recalled.

Baltimore's Bryn Mawr School was considered radical for offering college-preparatory classes to girls in the 1880s, but it was as racist and elitist as other private schools in its early years. The school employed two African-American maintenance men named Lee Taylor and James Mills, but the students never bothered to learn their names and so referred to them interchangeably as Lee-James or James-Lee. Bryn Mawr declined to rent its gymnasium to outside groups in 1911 because of fears that lower classes using the bathroom might bring "syphilitic diseases or other skin diseases to the school." Bryn Mawr also declined to admit or hire Jews. It faced a minor scandal in 1890 when a reporter from the local *Jewish Exponent* visited the school in the guise of a rabbi seeking a slot for his daughter, and was told that "we took a certain number of Jewish girls, but that our number was filled." When the incident became public, the school's headmistress claimed that the board of trustees had told her to respond that way; the board in turn tried to scapegoat the headmistress.

These kinds of racism and snobbery were a dark cloud that—to modern eyes—overshadows much of the good work that girls' schools did in the early part of the twentieth century. They persisted at some schools for decades: Miss Porter's headmaster Hollis French kept a copy of the *Social Register* on his desk through the 1950s. My stepmother, Mary DeBare, spent three years as one of the only Jewish students at the Masters School in the 1940s. When she arrived, she overheard another girl say that "if her mother knew there was a Jew in the school, she'd be taken out."

But as the civil rights movement forced white Americans to question their prejudices, girls' schools also began to open up. Judith Palfrey, now a professor of pediatrics at Harvard Medical School, was an eleventh-grader at the Bryn Mawr School in 1961 when she wrote a letter to the school's board of managers urging them to admit girls of color. "The Bryn Mawr School is seventy-six years old and it is surely now time to throw off all prejudices, and solely fulfill the task of making possible to any private family an outstanding education for their daughter," Palfrey wrote in a carefully typed two-page letter. "I realize that Bryn Mawr is a private institution. However it is a school and not an exclusive country club. To me the fact that Bryn Mawr is private is in order that it may give more individualized training and personal care, not that it may exclude capable children. . . . I feel that

Bryn Mawr is not only cheating itself by not opening its doors to any-one who is capable of passing the entrance examination; but it is also cheating the public by not educating every qualified girl, who wishes to avail herself of a fine, private education." Over thirty years later, Palfrey learned that her letter had played a key role in convincing the board to integrate the school in the early 1960s. "That was the hap-piest day of my life," she recalled.

Often it took the initiative of a courageous and liberal-minded headmistress to prod the board and parent community into opening their doors. "People will accept things for their sons which they won't accept for their daughters," one headmistress complained in 1963, referring to integration. At Abbot Academy, headmistress Marguerite Hearsey decided the school was ready for black students shortly after World War II, according to Abbot historian Susan McIntosh Lloyd. Hearsey started by writing a respected Abbot fa-ther in Georgia for his opinion. He advised against it and threatened to withdraw his daughter if blacks were admitted. "The negro, with many fine qualities, has other qualities which are very undesirable, and are apparently not affected by education or circumstances," he wrote. "Accordingly, I believe that social intermingling should be avoided, since I think it will lead to intermarriage. . . ." Hearsey then wrote to the headmistress of the Emma Willard School to ask how their one Negro girl was doing. The Emma Willard head reported back that their student was doing fine, and had tactfully kept poten-tial black boyfriends away. (When one young African-American man did visit, he was seated at the faculty table in the dining room.)

Most of Abbot's board supported Hearsey's initiative to inte-grate the school, but one longtime board member who was married to a southerner refused. Then, in the early 1950s, he died. Hearsey called a southern friend who knew some of Atlanta's black elite and found two black girls who were willing to apply. In spring 1953, she informed the school that they had been accepted. By midsummer, three white families had withdrawn their daughters. But the black girls enrolled and made friends. With two African-American stu-dents, Abbot was far from representative of a cross-section of Amer-ican girlhood. But it was a start.

# 3

# Finishing and Fitting

## RIGOROUS OR CHALLENGING?

*While I worried about fund-raising, other members of our group were working on drafting a mission satement and brochure that would outline the curriculum of our as-yet-unnamed school. They held countless meetings and sent even more e-mails, often arguing at length over a particular word or phrase. The debate sometimes seemed niggling, but it got at some very big questions: What kind of school were we going to start? Being a single-sex school defined one part of our identity, but not all of it. Were we going to focus on science and math, or on the arts? Were we mainly trying to promote our students' intellectual growth, or were we also interested in their emotional growth? What role should we give to sports and physical education? In an era of increasing emphasis on standardized exams, how much should we "teach to the tests"? Should we have letter grades? Should we have uniforms?*

*People threw a lot of educational buzzwords around, but the question came down to* What should girls learn? *We were all acutely aware that girls had traditionally lagged behind boys in math and science, while excelling in languages and arts. Some of us felt that the school should focus on math, science, and technology, to make sure girls had a strong base in these increasingly important subjects. Others in the group were passionately committed to the arts and felt that art should be an integral part of the curriculum, not an "enrichment" activity with second-class status.*

*Other differences within our group emerged on the balance between intellectual and emotional learning, and between individual and group work. Some people felt that middle-school-aged girls would learn best in an environment that acknowledged and valued their feelings and relationships. Others worried that if we became too "touchy-feely" we would be doing girls a disservice by not teaching them how to succeed in an individualistic, competitive world. One woman kept inserting the word* rigorous *into drafts of our mission statement, since it conveyed to her that our students would be pushed hard academically. Another woman kept taking* rigorous *out and substituting the word* challenging *because she felt* rigorous *sounded too rigid and strict.*

*Our disputes over what girls should learn weren't completely new. As I researched girls' schools of the late nineteenth century, I learned about a long-running national debate over whether young women could withstand the physical stress of a high school or college education. That debate gave root to a division among girls' schools, between schools that believed in preparing girls for college and "finishing schools" that promoted themselves as a less demanding and more feminine alternative to college. Girls at early preparatory schools studied intense courses of Latin and algebra; girls at finishing schools were able to pick and choose from a broader menu of subjects like literature, art history, and music, with a dollop of etiquette thrown in. We in Oakland certainly didn't think of ourselves as a finishing school—we wanted our girls to be strong and independent, to have careers and be leaders. We weren't about to teach girls which fork to use when dining with royalty. But as I learned more about the two traditions within girls' schools, I saw that we had things in common with each. Like the early prep schools, we wanted to ensure that our girls had the intellectual skills to succeed in traditionally male endeavors. Like the finishing schools, we also wanted to educate the whole girl—to feed her heart and spirit as well as her mind.*

*As we moved forward, the "whole girl" approach gradually won out over a more narrow academic focus. Ann Clarke, the woman we hired as our founding director, believed in an integrated curriculum where art and music would go hand in glove with other subjects like science and math. She envisioned an intimate, caring atmosphere where teachers were called by their first names and where even the corridor walls reflected girls' values and creativity. At the same time, Ann made clear that she believed girls grew through facing challenges, not through being coddled. We also made a strong commitment to technology. We had no money to buy hardware or software, but the first teacher we hired was a full-time technology director who drafted a 100-page plan for how to integrate computers into the curriculum.*

*The debates over the mission of the school continued in a slightly different form when it was time to choose a name. We thought about names based on nature—the North Star School, the Madrona School, the Briones School, the Polaris School, the Estero School. We thought about names based on mythology, like the Atalanta School. We also thought about names based on local women who had made history— women such as Isadora Duncan, Gertrude Stein, and Julia Morgan, the architect who designed Hearst Castle. But the committee was deadlocked. Some people liked Independent Girls' Middle School, but others felt that was too bland. I liked the Estero School—*estero *is the Spanish word for estuary, a body of water like San Francisco Bay where salt water meets fresh water. Middle school was like an estuary, I argued—not quite child or teenager, a unique habitat where wonderful things can happen. But other people worried that* estero *sounded too much like es-*trogen. *Above all else, we wanted a name that would be impervious to teasing. It would be tough enough for girls to tell their friends they were going to a single-sex school, without it being dubbed the "estrogen school." So that fell by the wayside.*

*The Julia Morgan School for Girls ended up winning by default: No one hated it enough to veto it. "What a way to name a school!" our secretary wrote in the minutes. But it turned out to be a wonderful fit. We researched Morgan's life and the more we learned about her, the more we loved her. Morgan was a true pioneer—the first woman to graduate from U.C. Berkeley in engineering, the first woman to study architecture at the Ecole des Beaux Arts in Paris, the first licensed woman ar-*

*chitect in California. She designed public and private buildings, modest bungalows and mansions. Her career blended art and science, creativity and community involvement, in a way that perfectly expressed our multidisciplinary vision for the school. Several months later, we met Morgan's goddaughter, who assured us that our namesake would have been thrilled with the idea of the school. Morgan had enjoyed having children visit her office, she told us, and often gave them treats. Those treats weren't candy or cookies—they were pencils for drawing.*

M. Burch Ford, the head of Miss Porter's School, is a tall, smart woman with a dry wit. During her time at the school, she has presided over construction of a new multimillion-dollar library that rises from the grassy lawn behind the school's small nineteenth-century white clapboard buildings. She started a summer program for middle-school girls in math, science, and technology. She beefed up school sports so that students now play to win rather than simply for a lark. The school offers AP classes in nineteen subjects including calculus, computer science, and physics. Like many other heads of top schools, Ford worries about whether her girls are overloading themselves with classes and activities and turning themselves into premature grown-ups.

When Ford got a call in the spring of 2000 from a local TV station, though, it wasn't about girls' athletics or the rigors of college placement or the emotional stresses on high-achieving teens. The reporter wanted to know about etiquette. Had society today lost its respect for etiquette and polite manners? And what manners would it be necessary to know in the twenty-first century? Ford laughs about the episode, but it struck a nerve that is equally sensitive in many other principals of girls' schools. Here she is, in the era of AP exams and computer labs, still fighting off the old stereotype of a finishing school.

*Finishing school.* The very term brings rolled eyes and exasperated sighs from many heads of longstanding girls' schools. "The media is primarily where I hear it," said Mary Lou Leipheimer, head of the Foxcroft School. "I get questions like 'Isn't it unusual for a national chair of a group like the SSAT [Secondary School Admission Test] to come from a finishing school?' One tries to stay reasonably calm, and indicate 'What rock did they climb out from under?' graciously."

Almost everyone is familiar with the stereotype of the finishing school—a place that focused on teaching etiquette rather than academics, that trained girls to be well-dressed debutantes and society ladies, that valued the superficial and the ornamental. These schools "finished" their students with a glossy sheen of culture, much as a carpenter would finish a mahogany coffee table. Alumnae were to be as decorative as that table, and just about as outspoken.

The reality of girls' schools at the start of the twentieth century, however, was more complex than the finishing school stereotype. Some schools saw themselves as genteel and feminine alternatives to college, the final stage or "finish" of their students' formal education. Others took the radical step of preparing girls for college. Over the course of the century, finishing schools gradually died out and virtually all private girls' schools became college-preparatory schools. But even in their heyday, finishing schools were not as frivolous as the stereotype implies. Many of them sought to build character in girls who might otherwise have been raised as spoiled pets. And they offered a broad liberal arts education that looks surprisingly like the curriculum at top high schools today.

At the same time, both finishing schools and some of their college-prep counterparts put a heavy emphasis on social education and the etiquette of being "ladies." Many schools gave girls a message that it was more important to be polite than smart, more important to dress properly for dinner than to understand the laws of physics. They discouraged girls from imagining lives beyond the traditional feminine world of family, social engagements, and volunteer work. Even today, many girls' schools struggle to overcome an ambivalence about competition that is a legacy of the finishing-school era. Many have also struggled to improve weak math and science programs, another legacy of that era. Many still have to remind themselves that girls don't always need to be "nice"—that it's not the end of the world if girls shout in the halls, argue with each other, or turn in messy homework.

## Finishing or Fitting?

Until the 1870s, virtually all private girls' schools were finishing schools—in the sense that they were the end, or finish, of a girl's education. College education for women did not yet exist on any significant level. So the term *finishing school* was used nonjudgmentally to describe any kind of private secondary education for girls. In 1866, an English churchman who was visiting the United States observed that nearly all wealthy northeastern families sent their children to private schools—"finishing schools for young ladies . . . and private day or boarding schools for boys."

That all changed with the rise of women's colleges in the late 1800s. Vassar was founded in 1861—the first institution set up explicitly as a female version of schools like Harvard, Yale, and Princeton. Wellesley and Smith were founded in 1870 and 1871, respectively, followed by Bryn Mawr and Radcliffe. The creation of women's colleges forced girls' schools to define themselves. Were they going to become colleges, too? Were they going to become feeder schools for the new women's colleges? Or were they an alternative to college—a different kind of education that was more appropriate for young women than the male-modeled curricula of the colleges?

Some girls' schools went the route of turning into full-blown colleges. The Mount Holyoke Female Seminary became Mount Holyoke College in 1893. Bradford Academy and Wheaton Female Seminary, both in Massachusetts, also became colleges. Other schools positioned themselves as an alternative to college, creating what we think of today as the classic finishing school. Miss Porter's was perhaps the best-known example of a finishing school in America—the Connecticut boarding school that turned out the country's most elegant First Lady, Jacqueline Bouvier Kennedy.

Miss Porter's actually predated the rise of women's colleges and of finishing schools as an alternative to college. The school was founded

*Classroom at the Buffalo Female Seminary, 1880s*

in 1843 by Sarah Porter, a thirty-four-year-old minister's daughter from the Connecticut village of Farmington. Porter worked as a teacher in various towns, such as Buffalo and Springfield, then returned home to Farmington and opened her own school in an effort to be financially independent of her parents.

Porter herself was a deeply religious woman, influenced by the revivals of the early nineteenth century. She was also deeply committed to her work. One of her journal entries from 1853 gives a sense of both passions:

December 16, 1853. Between two and three A.M. I have been making out term bills, after taking coffee to wake myself. . . . Yesterday morning I had a not very pleasant talk with Miss Merrill about Mr. Basch's coming to give drawing lessons. She was wrong, but my temper towards her is not altogether right. After hearing her, there came over me a feeling of the eye of my Savior bent over me in gentle reproof. Would that I would ever live under that eye. Let me. Sat in my school room and caught from time to time sight of the sky. It was grey with clouds until 10; then the tops began to glow, then turned transparent, and finally melted and revealed the blue sky. Thus, thought I, Oh, that the dross of my nature might pass away, preceded by the grace of Christ.

Porter saw her job as educating women to fill the traditional role of Christian wife and mother—a view she continued to hold even in old age, after suffrage and women's rights had become popular causes. Unlike Emma Willard, she opposed the idea of women voting to the end of her life. Porter wrote to a female friend in 1894:

As to the woman question, I suppose no one can deny God's appointment, she is designed to be, and must be, wife and mother—that she must administer the home. And just as plainly that the man must provide for it. . . . I do not believe we can revolutionize what God has so implanted in us as the relations of man and woman in this world.

As women's colleges began to spread, Porter took a stance firmly in opposition. She discouraged her students from attending college. She refused to hire college-educated teachers. "I do *not* want *one* college trained woman—they are *narrow,* arrogant—and do not infuse the spirit which I want," Porter wrote to her nephew in 1883.

Porter's disdain for college filtered down to her Farmington students. In the 1890s, girls made up a school song that poked fun at their collegiate counterparts:

> The Wellesley girl is out of joint.
> The Vassar joker has lost her point.
> The Farmington girl is all the go.
> The Farmington girl is never slow.
> To College. To College
> We'll never go there, anymore!

## Dr. Edward Clarke Creates
## a Gloomy Specter

In today's world, where college is the natural next step after high school, it can be hard to understand the onetime appeal of finishing schools. It's tempting to write off parents who chose finishing schools as dinosaurs—backward and shallow people who didn't value their daughters' minds. But the rise of finishing schools should be seen in the light of a furious debate that raged for several decades in the late nineteenth century over whether college education would harm a girl's health.

The brouhaha began rather unexpectedly. Edward H. Clarke was a respected doctor and professor at Harvard who had made a name for himself in women's rights circles in 1869 when he denounced some male medical students in Philadelphia who had driven female students out of the classroom by hurling tobacco quids and tinfoil at them. In 1872, suffragist Julia Ward Howe invited him to speak to the New England Women's Club of Boston about higher education for women. Clarke informed the group that he felt women had the right to train to become physicians if they were capable of doing so. However, he added, he did not believe that women *were* physically capable of studying medicine or other advanced subjects.

It's hard to imagine who was more surprised—the Women's Club members, who had expected to hear words of encouragement from an apparent ally, or Clarke, who found his expert pronouncements greeted with fierce hostility. Spurred by what he called the "unexpected amount of dissension," Clarke turned his speech into a book called *Sex in Education; or, A Fair Chance for the Girls.* Published in 1873, it was an immediate sensation. In Ann Arbor, home of the newly coed University of Michigan, two hundred copies were sold in one day. A second edition was printed just a little more than a week after the first. In thirteen years, the book went through a total of seventeen printings.

Clarke essentially argued that a woman's body could only handle a limited number of developmental tasks at one time—that girls who spent too much energy developing their minds during puberty would end up with undeveloped or diseased reproductive systems. Clarke insisted that his conclusions were the results of scientific research, not mere opinion or moral judgment. He couched them in the language of recent developments in physics—saying that all physical systems were subject to laws of the conservation of energy, and women's physiology was no exception. He then cited a string of anonymous anecdotes to prove his point. One was an alleged "Miss G," who graduated first in her class from a western college. She never studied excessively or appeared weak in college but—her tragic error, in Clarke's view—she didn't tailor her academic schedule around her menstrual cycle. Clarke wrote:

> Not a great while after graduation, she began to show signs of failure, and some years later died under the writer's care. A post-mortem examination was made, which disclosed no disease in any part of the body, except in the brain, where the microscope revealed commencing degeneration. This was called an instance of death from overwork. . . . She was unable to make a good brain, that could stand the wear and tear of life, and a good reproductive system that should serve the race, at the same time that she was continuously spending her force in intellectual labor. Nature asked her for a periodical remission, and did not get it.

While Clarke's arguments might seem absurd today, they carried great weight during his time. They were endorsed by other prominent doctors. They fit in with Victorian cultural ideas about the delicacy and fragility of women. They were couched in the impressive-sounding language of the emerging fields of medicine and physics. Perhaps most important, they played off people's deep-seated fears about what would happen if women went to college, entered professions, or won the vote. They were also echoed by other prominent doctors. Gynecologist Thomas Emmet wrote in 1879 that "the young girls in the better classes of society should pass the year before puberty and some two years afterwards free from all exciting influences . . . She should be kept a child as long as possible, and made to associate with children . . . Her mind should be occupied by a very moderate amount of study, with frequent intervals of a few moments each, passed when possible in the recumbent position, until her system becomes accustomed to the new order of life."

Some teachers and feminists lashed back at Clarke and his colleagues with books of their own. Julia Ward Howe, who had sparked the entire debate with her speaking invitation to Clarke, published a rebuttal in 1874 that included essays by the wife of Horace Mann and by the resident physician at Vassar College. Educator Anna Brackett published a similar collection of anti-Clarke pieces including one by Sarah Dix Hamlin, a student at the University of Michigan who went on to found the Hamlin School for girls in San Francisco.

Hamlin researched the health of recent graduates of Michigan, which had been coed for four years, and concluded that there were no more incidents of illness among women than men. Her survey, although informal, was in fact more systematic than any evidence cited by Clarke. "It is a fact that thus far the women of Michigan University have demonstrated . . . that brain-work is good for the health," Hamlin wrote. "If the seeds of future disease have been in some mysterious manner implanted in their systems, it is in no sense apparent except to the imaginations of those who are least acquainted with our girls."

Clarke's dire warnings didn't stop the spread of coeducational public high schools or the entrance of women into colleges. He certainly scared many parents and girls, though. Some of those families turned to finishing schools—places where girls would get an education, but a decidedly feminine education that would not stress their young bodies or give them any wild ideas about going to college. Some girls' schools adopted Clarke's ideas lock, stock, and barrel. The student newspaper at Tilden Ladies' Seminary in New Hampshire published a long article quoting Clarke approvingly in 1873, and using his writings to make a case against suffrage, for women remaining in "women's sphere," and for single-sex schools. "No one dares deny that the best colleges for men in the nation, are for *men only*," the Tilden students wrote, "and it is equally true that the best seminaries and colleges for our daughters, are for *ladies only*. . . . in their own Seminaries and Colleges, they can reach any grade of learning and culture which they desire, with special adaptation to their wants as women, and special choice of studies suited to the womanly sphere of life they are to occupy."

At other girls' schools, the main effect of the Clarke debate seems to have been a heightened sensitivity to girls' physical health. That sensitivity took varied, often contradictory, forms. Some schools instituted systematic programs of physical fitness to ensure that girls maintained their health. Others bent over backwards to excuse girls from classwork at the least complaint of illness or fatigue. Even Brearley, which prided itself from the start on high academic standards and a college preparatory program, noted in its 1892–93 catalogue that "studies will be remitted or lightened in case of delicate health." One schoolteacher complained in a 1900 magazine article that girls often used health complaints to get out of difficult work, and their parents were too happy to support them in this:

> Girls seem to me to have too many imaginary ills, or rather they succumb to the smallest ache; a slight headache is enough to make them give up every duty of the day. . . . I think that more than 90 percent of the girls that come to us could do a reasonable amount of work if they had the ambition, but as they do not wish to go to school to study, their parents have them excused from one thing or another on the plea of nervousness. . . . I think there is more laziness than ill health in the world.

## All Out for Brains

Despite the warnings of Clarke and other conservatives, a handful of pioneering schools took on the controversial mission of preparing girls to enter college in the 1880s and 1890s. Some of these schools were started at the request of women's college presidents, who were dismayed at the low caliber of students they were getting. When

Wellesley opened in 1875, only 30 of its 314 initial students were able to pass a test aimed at assessing their readiness for college courses. Wellesley tried running its own preparatory division briefly but then asked two faculty members to open the Dana Hall School. Other schools started at the request of college administrators included the Baldwin School, founded to prepare girls for Bryn Mawr College, and the Castilleja School, founded to prepare girls for Stanford. In other cases, college-prep schools were started at the initiative of teachers or parents. Sarah Dix Hamlin—who had written that University of Michigan study rebutting Clarke—bought an old San Francisco finishing school called the Van Ness Seminary in 1896 and turned it into a college-preparatory school. The Brearley School was born when a wealthy mother convinced Harvard graduate Samuel Brearley to open a school for her daughters by arguing that "there are many good schools for boys, but none for girls."

In their early years, college-preparatory schools for girls sometimes faced an uphill battle to recruit students. Perhaps the steepest climb was that of the Bryn Mawr School in Baltimore, which was founded in 1885 by a group of five wealthy young women. Baltimore in the 1880s was a large but still very conservative city. There were twenty-nine private schools in the city, but those for girls were small and limited. Run out of private homes by expatriate southern women who had moved to the city after the Civil War, none offered Latin, Greek, or laboratory science. Johns Hopkins College had recently opened but was not particularly welcoming toward women. When M. Carey Thomas tried to do postgraduate study there after graduating from Cornell, she was allowed in classes only if she concealed herself behind a screen. Nor were the new northeastern women's colleges considered socially acceptable for Baltimore girls of the 1880s. One young woman who enrolled in college was so embarrassed when she came home to visit that she would cross the street to avoid seeing old friends.

Thomas and four of her friends felt differently, and decided to create a model girls' college preparatory school in Baltimore. The women were unusually well placed to make it happen. Thomas had impressive educational credentials including a doctorate from Germany; Mary

Garrett was heiress to the B&O Railroad fortune; Mamie Gwinn was the daughter of Maryland's attorney general and granddaughter of a U.S. senator. Four of the five had fathers who were Hopkins trustees.

They wanted to ensure a stream of qualified applicants for newly formed Bryn Mawr College—thus the name, the Bryn Mawr School. From the beginning, they aimed to provide an education that was identical to the best boys' schooling. They rejected the idea of educating women for the domestic sphere: BMS graduates were to go on to college and then professional lives. The women insisted that all students study five years of Latin, as well as either Greek or German; they also had to study math from geometry through algebra. They required every student—whether college bound or not—to take the Bryn Mawr College entrance examination in order to graduate, and Garrett offered scholarships to Bryn Mawr College to the two top graduates each year. They hired a genuine scholar to run the school, classicist Edith Hamilton, whose books *Mythology* and *The Greek Way* continue to be read today. The school intentionally excluded "ornamental" subjects that were the staple of less rigorous girls' schools. It would be nice to have a piano for graduation ceremonies, Gwinn acknowledged to Garrett in 1895, but "we'll never consent to teaching music!"

Even the physical setting conveyed a message of high expectations. When the school opened its own building in 1889, it was filled with imposing replicas of great art that Garrett had brought back from Europe, including a giant marble frieze of the Parthenon in the central study hall. "The winged Victory supervised our lunch-counter and the Elgin Marbles paraded around the study hall walls," recalled Mary Cadwalader, an early alumna. She continued:

> No child could walk through that heavy, iron-studded front door (which closed with a sombre slick-swuush!) without sensing that the building Stood For Something. Solid and spacious, it was furnished not for comfort or charm but for serious study—and it had Status. Among the city's private schools, we knew simply and without question that Bryn Mawr was the *best*. Others could be

finishing schools . . . or country-style boarding schools; they could teach manners, art, piano, horsemanship; we were all out for brains. Other schools might believe in being bright, colorful, attractive, warm; Bryn Mawr believed in being Important. Bryn Mawr School girls went to college, or if they didn't, no matter; they were educated as though they were going—and going straight through with flying banners to an A.B.

Being "all out for brains" didn't exactly go over big, however, in nineteenth-century Baltimore. Wealthy families stayed away, and so most of the first students were daughters of Johns Hopkins professors—not fertile ground for fund-raising. At one point, a leading Baltimore gynecologist warned that studying Latin would undermine girls' health, and some parents withdrew their daughters from the school. BMS had trouble filling its rolls and often offered free or reduced tuition. It ran deficits every year except three between 1902 and World War I. Edith Hamilton put it bluntly in a 1915 letter to Thomas: "The school is offering the people of Baltimore what they do not want: a first class college preparatory education for girls; she is utterly disregarding the popular demand." But the BMS founders refused to give up. Mary Garrett repeatedly dipped into her personal fortune to pay the school's debts. To defuse parents' health fears, BMS instituted a state-of-the-art physical-culture program with a school physician, a gym designed by Harvard's Dudley Sargent, exercise machines, an indoor running track and swimming pool, and newfangled devices called "needle baths," which today are commonly known as showers. And the school stuck by its tough academic standards. "Don't allow these soft Baltimore mothers to weaken their daughters by insisting they drop Latin!" Thomas insisted to Hamilton.

## The Surprisingly Modern
## Finishing School

The curricula at girls' prep schools and finishing schools were quite different from each other. The early girls' prep schools modeled themselves on boys' prep schools of the late 1800s, which had very narrow curricula that were oriented to the classics. Students typically were required to study Latin, Greek, algebra—and little else. Finishing schools, meanwhile, had few required classes and offered a wide number of subjects ranging from French and science to music and drawing. Miss Porter's, for instance, had no required classes in the late 1800s but offered English, Latin, math, French, German, science, art history, studio art, and music. The Baldwin School in Philadelphia offered two separate tracks—a finishing track and a college-preparatory track—that give a good view of the different curricula. Girls in the college-preparatory track in the early 1900s were required to take algebra, English, Latin, French, and either German or Greek in their junior year. The girls in the finishing track were re-

*Students performing* As You Like It *at Rosemary Hall (Conn.), 1898*

quired to take just geometry, English, and American history—and then had a choice of Latin, French, German, biblical history, history of art, zoology, drawing, and music.

Art history was one of the strongest subjects at finishing schools, an outgrowth of the nineteenth-century belief that women's sphere included the world of art and culture. Seventy years after they graduated, alumnae from the 1920s and 1930s still pour forth praise of teachers who made da Vinci or Giotto come alive for them. The impact of art history courses was heightened, of course, by the fact that many finishing school graduates were wealthy enough to follow up their classes with visits to Europe, where they saw firsthand the works they had studied. Some girls went with their families or on chaperoned tours; others attended international finishing schools in Switzerland or Italy for a year. Betty Merck, who attended Miss Porter's from 1935 through 1938, went on to an even more elite boarding school in Lausanne, where her classmates included the daughters of Haile Selassie, Gertrude Lawrence, and Marlene Dietrich. She skied a lot, spoke French every day, studied gourmet cooking and home economics, and went home after a year to make her debut in society. She is one of those who still speaks with awe of her art history teacher at Miss Porter's. "You had to keep up, there was no laziness about it," Merck said. "She had a very strict program, looking at slide after slide after slide. She just loved the whole progress of art—which is of course the most important part. You wanted to go see the things you studied with her."

Critics never had a hard time finding things to ridicule academically at finishing schools. While motivated girls could find extremely bright teachers who pushed them to think, others were able to coast through with just a smattering of art or French. "You know, really what I learned at Farmington was to ride horseback," wrote Grace Hoadley Dodge, who attended Miss Porter's in 1873 and went on to found Teachers College in New York. "We did a little history, learned how to be good girls, and then rode horseback all over these hills."

Such criticisms were sometimes on the mark. But ironically, American education evolved in such a way that the curriculum at today's top high schools has a lot more in common with finishing schools than it does with college-preparatory schools of the nineteenth century. It wasn't that boys' schools or coed schools set out consciously to imitate finishing schools. It was more of a gradual, unnoticed convergence as American educators increasingly came to view their goal as turning out well-rounded human beings rather than classics scholars.

By the 1890s, educational leaders were starting to question the single-minded classical curriculum of boys' prep schools as too narrow and too focused on college entrance exams. Boys' schools gradually broadened their curricula to include subjects like modern languages, science, and the arts. They dropped or downplayed the teaching of Greek and Latin. They added some electives, at least for their oldest students.

Today parents of both boys and girls aggressively seek out schools that offer many of the same liberal arts courses that the old finishing schools did—classes in music, drama, studio arts, and modern languages. Subjects that were once viewed as feminine "fluff" have now become an essential part of the top-quality school. Today's high school looks a lot more like the finishing track at Baldwin than the college-prep track. Finishing schools died out, but their founders may be smiling discreetly from beyond the grave as prep schools like Andover and Exeter offer dozens of courses in music, art, and drama. All that's missing, really, is the instruction in manners.

## Court Curtseys and Gentle Voices

The stereotype of the finishing school conjures up images of girls pouring tea, practicing curtsies, and learning to host elegant dinner parties. And that part of the stereotype isn't all wrong. In the late nineteenth and early twentieth centuries, many finishing schools offered explicit instruction in ladylike manners.

A Bryn Mawr College professor named Samuel King made the rounds of various northeastern girls' schools in the 1910s and '20s teaching elocution. He zeroed in on girls from the Midwest and tried to rid them of their "twang." "Dr. King felt very strongly about the evils of slurred syllables and growling rrs," recalled Lydia Chapin Kirk, who wrote a witty memoir about her time at Miss Porter's School in 1911–13. "He also claimed that many a young girl's future had been ruined because her tongue protruded between her teeth as she pronounced the word 'the' and he made us hold a hand glass and repeat 'Through the throng' until he was sure our tongue would remain discreetly against our teeth."

Meanwhile, an Englishwoman named Miss Palliser made the rounds of girls' schools teaching deportment and etiquette. This was not just good manners; it was *aristocratic* good manners. Kirk recalled:

> Miss Palliser marshaled us in long lines and then, in turn, called us to walk across the room, bowing gracefully to friends on the way.
>
> "Don't peck. You look more like a hungry hen than a lady. Bow, bow from the waist."
>
> And Miss Palliser would pounce upon an unfortunate victim, seize the sixteen-year-old waist and bend it forward.
>
> "Now girls. You, Lydia, will be the Duchess of Westminster. You are receiving in your drawing room. You, Hilda, are Lady Smith Ponsonby. You are pouring tea. You, Jane are Sir Henry Hamilton. You are calling on the Duchess and you Catherine are the Earl of Oxford. You also are calling and must be introduced to the other guests. Proceed, please.
>
> "Sit down properly. Please do not cross your knees. No lady should do more than cross her ankles. . . ."
>
> The spectacle of Hilda from Buffalo, Jane from Youngstown, Ohio, Catherine from Boston, Mass., and Lydia from Erie, Pennsylvania aping the British peerage, solemnly pretending to pour tea in their gym suits, must have been very comic indeed. But Miss Palliser took it all very seriously and drilled us week after week. . . .

Just twenty-seven years later, when I was really presented at court and bowed before another King George I thought of Miss Palliser. I'm sure she would not have approved of my curtsey, but to this day, when picking up an object from the floor I place one leg behind the other and bend both knees.

"Don't double up like a jumping jack, keep your spine straight, your head up, flex the knees."

Etiquette instruction wasn't limited to finishing schools, however. Many schools that were preparing girls for college also offered guidance in feminine manners. The Hathaway Brown School in Cleveland and the Springside School in Philadelphia both engraved the same Shakespearean quote on their walls: "Her voice was ever soft, gentle, and low, an excellent thing in woman." The headmistress of the Agnes Irwin School in Philadelphia instructed her charges in 1905 that "horses sweat, men perspire, and ladies glow." The Columbus School for Girls held chapel talks in the 1920s that included tips such as:

Ladies do not drink from a drinking fountain.
Ladies do not eat on the street.
Ladies do not cross their knees in public.
Ladies *never* wear red shoes.
No lady ever writes a letter on tinted paper.
Ladies never chew gum in public.

The etiquette classes and lectures were aimed at helping girls move seamlessly into adult lives as upper-class wives. As trivial as they may sound today, knowing how to serve tea or write formal invitations were essential skills for women charged with keeping their families well placed in elite society. But while the "social curriculum" of schools helped prepare girls for life, it was a very limited sort of life. "They wanted us to be leaders, but in those days, leaders consisted in their minds of being good wives of future presidents," said Rachel Hammond Breck, who graduated from Miss Porter's in 1925.

*May Day ceremony with the May Queen and her court
at Ferry Hall (Illinois), 1920s*

*May Day ceremony at Chatham Hall in Virginia, 1931*

*Senior Tea at the High School of the Sacred Heart, San Francisco*

Explicit instruction in proper feminine behavior was reinforced by rituals like May Day. Starting in the 1800s, many girls' schools and women's colleges instituted annual May Day celebrations that involved an elaborate pageant with gowns and flowers, and the selection of a May Queen and her court. These rituals celebrated spring, but they also celebrated and promoted the Victorian ideal of woman as delicate, graceful, pure, and virtuous. "The queen was usually elected by the students on the basis of 'sweetness' and beauty," wrote historian Christie Anne Farnham, "although the father's status often played a role."

As time went on, girls' schools gradually replaced the explicit teaching of manners with an atmosphere in which proper upper-class behavior was conveyed by example. Social events often took the shape of formal teas—mother-daughter teas, junior-senior teas, tea with the headmistress or the dorm advisor. Many boarding schools had nightly sit-down dinners with white tablecloths, nice dresses, and assigned tables. At Miss Porter's in the 1920s, girls often wore black velvet skirts and ropes of pearls to dinner. "We weren't supposed to giggle at meals, we were *never* supposed to put our elbows on the table, and if we raised our voices, everyone would say 'Ssssh!' " recalled Rachel Breck. "We were taught good manners in the sense of being quiet, listening to our elders, and always opening the door for other people. It was sort of a subtle training. You watched other people do it, and so you did it yourself. I don't remember anyone ever saying, 'You must do this.' But if the Old Girls did it, and you were a New Girl, you did it too."

While elite girls' schools paid close attention to feminine manners, they did not jump onto the bandwagon of home economics. Home ec entered coed public schools in the 1910s and '20s—partly as an attempt to "Americanize" the great numbers of new immigrants, partly as the female version of vocational classes for boys. Catholic girls' schools that served working-class communities often added home ec to their curriculum. And some elite girls' schools also offered a limited amount of domestic education: The Marlborough School in Los Angeles started cooking lessons in 1919, as part of which each girl had to invite two teachers to dinner. Abbot Academy added a domestic science course in 1913, saying it would "help girls realize the importance of the home as a unit of national life and the influence of a scientifically conducted house on the welfare of the state."

But home economics courses never took hold as a permanent feature of private girls' schools the way they did in public schools. That was partly because the schools' wealthy clientele didn't see a real need for their daughters to learn the rudiments of cooking and sewing: That work, after all, was supposed to be done by the servants. But it was also because some headmistresses took a strong stand against watering down their academic program with courses in housewifery. In 1923, the Headmistresses Association of the East was addressed by a professor who urged them to add home ec to their schools. Some headmistresses, including Caroline Ruutz-Rees of Rosemary Hall, a Connecticut boarding school that later merged with Choate, objected strenuously. "One of my general observations is that college girls do seem to be great marryers," Ruutz-Rees countered. "The college girls do most beautifully all these household arts without any training. Their little houses and apartments are charming, and the American girl probably has better taste than any one else; she acquires it out of the air probably,—but I don't believe she does it because she has been studying home-aesthetics. Housekeeping seems to be most admirably done by college-girls without any special training. . . ."

## The Legacy of the Social Curriculum

Many girls' schools hedged their bets by offering both a finishing track and a college-preparatory track in the early part of the twentieth century. But as the idea of collegiate education for women became more acceptable, college prep won the day. By the 1950s, virtually all girls' schools had become college-preparatory schools, although that meant different things at different schools. Some girls' schools pushed their graduates toward academically elite Seven Sister colleges, such as Wellesley and Radcliffe, while others were content to send them off to two-year junior colleges.

The social curriculum lingered on even after the end of the finishing school. Most schools stopped holding formal dinners and afternoon teas during the cultural upheavals of the 1960s. But here and there, schools continued to offer instruction in ladylike deportment. At Westover in the late 1960s, girls were given candy in homeroom as a prize for sitting with the best posture. As late as 1967, a Columbus School for Girls trustee advised seniors in their commencement ceremony, "You are a woman by birth. Be a lady by choice." Girls were still being taught to curtsey at Chapin in the early 1970s and at the Hewitt School in New York in the 1980s. When Jessica Good arrived as a teacher at Girls Preparatory School in 1976, women faculty were still not allowed to smoke during breaks. "I whipped out a cigarette and another teacher pulled me aside and said, 'Only men get to smoke in the cafeteria,'" Good recalled.

Susan Erba attended fourth through seventh grades at the Hutchison School, a day school in Memphis, in the late 1960s. She recalls that the school was "very big on teaching us manners." Erba and her classmates were required to take ballroom dancing in seventh grade. Each Saturday night, they would put on dresses and white gloves and learn the foxtrot and waltz with coat-and-tie-clad students from a nearby boys' school. "We had a class trip to New Orleans," she said, "where part of the trip was to take us out to the fanciest restaurants and have us know how to eat. We had a whole lesson on which fork to use and what to talk about. We had a seven-course meal in a private dining room at Antoine's. It was not just to show us New Orleans, but to make sure we knew how to eat in places like that. . . . In many ways, I felt like I was being educated to be a great wife of an executive."

In today's girls' schools, salad forks and handwritten invitations have completely vanished from the radar screen. The typical girls' school dining room looks like any other school cafeteria—jostling lines, noisy tables, kids waving sandwiches in the air and tossing empty potato chip bags into trash cans. School dances feature hip-hop music and DJs, not waltzes and receiving lines. The only gloves that anyone wears are warm woolly ones in the winter.

But more subtle legacies remain from the finishing-school and fitting-school era. One such legacy was a historic neglect of "male" subjects like math and science. A rare study of private girls' school curricula in 1932 concluded that girls' schools required significantly less science than other schools: Girls' schools required an average of 0.4 units of science to graduate, for instance, compared to 2.2 units in coed public schools. And only 2.4 percent of private girls' schools required their students to take biology, compared to 26 percent of public schools. At Abbot Academy, one alumna from the early twentieth century recalled the science department chairwoman as "dry, quiet, and unstimulating." Another said that taking physics at Abbot was like "taking castor oil." Ellen Reeder recalled a benign neglect of science at Garrison Forest School in the early 1960s. "I got the sense that science was a 'sigh'—everyone sighed having to do it," recalled Reeder, who became director of the National Museum of Women in the Arts in Washington, D.C. "The poor science teacher tried, but everyone looked on it as the death knell to have to take biology or chemistry." It wasn't until the 1980s and '90s that many schools realized they had a math and science problem, and started renovating labs or beefing up their math and science faculties.

Girls' schools also received a legacy of ambivalence about competition, which extended to both sports and academics. Some schools had always embraced competition with joy and fervor. At the Agnes Irwin School in the 1880s, teachers used competition to encourage academic achievement: The top students of the month had their names written on the blackboard for the following four weeks, prizes were awarded at commencement, and the most accomplished poems and essays were written into a special Red Book kept by Miss Arnold, the English teacher.

Other schools, however, saw competition as unladylike. They frowned upon "emulation," the nineteenth-century phrase for academic competition. They refused to give out academic awards and declined to let their students play sports against other schools. The Hathaway Brown School did away with its honor roll in 1890 "to avert the injurious spirit of emulation." Miss Porter told a student in 1896 that she was opposed to replacing the school's grass tennis courts with dirt courts because the new courts might foster competitive playing:

> We do still quite positively object to giving them [the grass courts] up. Their prettiness and neatness are for their decided advantage over the dirt courts. We like to see the skill and grace with which you and your friends play and would leave no obstacles in your way which we could reasonably remove, but we have no desire that any of you should become or be known as *accomplished* tennis players. We desire that you should enjoy playing as an entertainment. We are glad for the physical agility and strength which it promotes, but it does not directly bless the soul as country walks in the early summer. Then, we *utterly disapprove* of any competition—any emulation entering into it. I see notices in newspapers of competing, playing in the women's and girls' colleges, and the names of the best players. I think this is wholly disagreeable—injurious to manners and to character. And if com-

*Basketball team at the Agnes Irwin School (Pa.), 1912*

petition for the highest place is to enter into your little tournaments, I should wish to forbid them. . . .

Even today, some girls' schools refrain from fostering academic competition between students. The Holton-Arms School in Bethesda, Maryland, deliberately doesn't have an honor roll or academic ranking. The Laurel School in Cleveland didn't enter regional science competitions until the late 1990s. "We were very reticent about competing and saying 'This kid is outstanding' until several years ago," said Helen Marter, head of Laurel.

Other schools are trying to overcome decades of hostility to athletic competition. At the Nightingale-Bamford School in New York, the physical-education director helped start a girls' sports league in the 1970s but called it an "association" since "league" sounded too male. "You never used to be taught to compete," recalled Linda Sicher, who was captain of the volleyball and basketball teams at Nightingale-Bamford in the early 1960s, "You learned to play and to lose or win—gracefully."

At Miss Porter's in the 1980s, the school finished last in the local sports league so often that it dropped out entirely. Burch Ford pushed Miss Porter's toward athletic competitiveness in the 1990s, and Farmington today is producing top-level athletes who are recruited by colleges like Dartmouth and Villanova. But teachers continue to disagree about how hard student athletes should be pushed. "There seems to be some residual fear that by turning the girls into winners, we are going to rob them of their femininity," Ford said.

Without intending to, Ford put her finger on a broader legacy of the finishing-or-fitting era—an ambivalence about the assertive, aggressive side of girls' characters. Society as a whole continues to give out mixed messages about female assertiveness. And people dealing with girls often unthinkingly promote what psychologists have called the "tyranny of niceness"—an expectation that young women should naturally be neat, quiet, and accomodating.

Girls' schools traditionally reinforced that emphasis on "niceness," in a lingering legacy of the fitting-or-finishing era. When former headmistress Joan McMenamin first arrived at Nightingale-Bamford in the late 1950s, girls were not allowed to interrupt each other. "A kind of comfortable courtesy suffused the whole building," she recalled. Some graduates of girls' schools found themselves unprepared for an adult world that was not particularly nice or even polite. "I was not prepared in graduate school for a serious hard debate where the debater felt strong enough that there was an edge to her voice," said Ellen Reeder, who graduated from the Garrison Forest School in Maryland in 1965.

Today schools have started to look more critically at their expectations of girls' behavior and give girls more room to be noisy, messy, or brash. When Helen Marter arrived at the Laurel School in Cleveland in 1992, she found a focus on educating "good little girls" and "keeping the noise down." Some colleagues initially told Marter that

*Field Day at the Chapin School (N.Y.), 1917*

she should insulate the doors to her office because she laughed too loud. "But this is a school, not a mausoleum," Marter countered. And at Garrison Forest today, headmaster Peter O'Neill lets students know that there are appropriate times to be nice—and also appropriate times *not* to be nice. During an interscholastic field hockey game one day, O'Neill watched in bemusement as a Garrison player left her defensive position to pick up and return a hockey stick that had been dropped by an opposing player. It was a polite gesture that would have won the approval of Sarah Porter, but not today's girls' school leadership. "'Never give it back when the ball is at our end of the field!'" O'Neill recalled hearing the Garrison Forest coach tell his polite hockey player. "'Turn the ball around. Then you can give it back to her when the ball is at the other end.'"

# 4

# "God Give Us Girls": Single-Sex Schools for Girls of Color

## LOVE US, HATE US

*Our efforts to organize a girls' school met with dramatically different responses from different people. My own family supported Julia Morgan mostly because it was my project—Ilana's latest crusade, a little strange and eclectic perhaps, but close to my heart and thus close to their hearts. But others in our group faced painful and unexpected criticism from their families. Irene Yen, an epidemiologist who didn't have a daughter of her own but wanted to help girls make a positive transition to womanhood, had sent a fund-raising letter to her sister. Irene expected a friendly and affirmative response. Instead she was stunned to receive a three-page single-spaced letter detailing all the reasons why her sister disapproved of the idea of Julia Morgan. "She felt that coeducation was the real world, it was important for everyone to have that experience, and that secluding girls was artificial," Irene said. "She was also opposed in principle to private schools because she felt they took away resources from public schools. . . . At first I thought about responding, but then I realized I wasn't going to be able to turn her around. She was coming from such a different place that it would have been too much to bridge."*

We had assumed that starting a school would be a pretty noncontroversial project: Wasn't education as all-American as apple pie? Who could oppose adding one more small option for girls' education? We weren't going to force anybody to attend Julia Morgan, after all. But starting a single-sex school brought out some of people's deep fears about gender and society. Some women like Irene's sister feared that single-sex schooling would deprive girls of tools that had been essential for their own survival in a hostile world. Some parents of boys feared that we were going to "steal" all the girls and leave their sons without any female classmates. Our project also brought up people's fears about the future of the public school system. Some people saw any support for private schools as a sign of betrayal, abandoning the leaky ship of public education rather than trying to patch the holes. Others questioned why we were putting so much time into a single private school when there were so many bigger problems facing the world—poverty, hunger, global warming, you name it.

But Julia Morgan also evoked positive responses that were as visceral as the negative ones, and those in the end outnumbered the negative ones. I was struck over time by how many adult professional women wanted to do something to help girls—to ensure that the next generation had an easier time growing up than they themselves did. Many women recalled junior high as a time of social insecurity and misery, and were thrilled at the idea of improving that experience. Others felt their own careers had been a struggle—to enter male-dominated fields, to gain skills that were not traditionally taught to girls, to develop the self-confidence necessary for success. They wanted to teach girls the things they wished someone had taught them.

Jackie Kleinman, a financial planner in San Francisco, got involved with Julia Morgan shortly after we opened the school. Jackie had no children and never wanted children. But she did want to do something for girls—a conviction that grew out of her own life experience. When Jackie grew up in the 1960s, the only career option that she and her friends knew about was teaching. She didn't want to teach but *didn't know of any other options—so since her brother was a dentist, she became a dental hygienist. That didn't fit. But by the time she discovered her aptitude for financial planning and got the necessary credentials, she was in her late forties. "I want to help these girls become strong women and achieve what they want to do earlier than age fifty," she said.*

*Jackie found a niche in helping create a financial literacy program at Julia Morgan. During the school's first year, financial literacy was just a short unit within the sixth-grade math program. Since then, the teachers have expanded it to a comprehensive three-year curriculum that includes everything from stock market investing to household budgeting and international economics. Jackie comes in a couple of times a year to explain topics like compound interest and investment strategy. She helps the girls learn what goes into a business plan; the girls then draft their own business plans for imaginary companies. Jackie also joined the Julia Morgan board and became our treasurer. "I love that all the girls recognize me and know I'm the financial person," Jackie said. "I love when they come up to me and tell me how they've put my information to use. Visiting the school takes me back to where I was at that age, and makes me wish I'd had the decision-making capabilities these girls are being given."*

Lucy Madeira or Clara Spence might have felt a stunning slap of vertigo if, on a visit to the exclusive turn-of-the-century winter resort of Daytona Beach, Florida, they had somehow wandered into the local school for girls. Just as at Miss Madeira's or Miss Spence's schools, students would have been dressed neatly in floor-length skirts and stiffly ironed white blouses. They might have been working intently on an arithmetic problem or perhaps studying a Bible passage. But there the similarities ended. The Daytona girls would also have been learning to do laundry, clean houses, and make brooms. They would have been raising chickens and producing syrup from sugar cane. Not least of all, the Daytona girls would all have been black.

The Daytona Educational and Industrial Training School for Negro Girls was founded in 1904 by Mary McLeod Bethune, a daughter of slaves who went on to be one of the most prominent African-American leaders of her time and an official in Franklin Roosevelt's administration. Daytona was an unusual mix of cultures. It espoused Booker T. Washington's philosophy of vocational education for blacks, but it also offered the academic and moral training of Victorian-era seminaries for white girls. It placed a uniquely African-American spin on seminary culture: Girls were getting an education not just to improve themselves or their families, but to help lift their race up from poverty and prejudice. The future of blacks in America, Bethune wrote in a 1926 essay, "rests upon the type of education which the Negro woman will receive."

Daytona was part of an uneven history of single-sex education for girls of color in the nineteenth and early twentieth centuries. African-Americans and other girls of color were typically barred from attending white girls' schools or seminaries. When schooling *was* available for girls of color, it was usually in a segregated coed setting with girls and boys facing the same hurdles of meager funding and inadequate facilities. Here and there, however, single-sex schools for girls of color did crop up. Some were started by church groups, others by idealistic individual teachers. These schools were often short-lived and left little behind in the way of historical records or documents. The few that survived did so by turning into colleges, such as Spelman College, Barber-Scotia College, and Bethune-Cookman College. But what the early African-American girls' schools lacked in numbers or longevity they made up for in passion and dedication. Emma Willard may have faced ridicule for proposing to educate white girls, but Prudence Crandall went to jail for teaching black girls. Lucy Madeira may have had to endure low pay and a shared bed at her first job, but Alice White had her schoolhouse burned to the ground—twice. While white families in Victorian America worried whether education would undermine their daughters' delicate constitutions, black families grabbed onto schooling like a life raft. They were willing to make great sacrifices and face great risks to educate their daughters.

## Prudence Crandall's Battle

Prudence Crandall started out running a typical early nineteenth-century New England girls' school. An unmarried white Quaker, Crandall grew up in the small Connecticut town of Canterbury and attended a Quaker boarding school in Rhode Island. She was twenty-seven years old and teaching in another Connecticut town when, in 1830, some of Canterbury's most prominent men asked if she would return home and set up a school for their daughters. The men helped Crandall buy a house at the center of town, and for about a year she quietly operated a small but well-regarded girls' boarding school.

Connecticut had started to gradually abolish slavery in 1784, and at the time Crandall started her school, there were about a dozen free African-American families living in the Canterbury area. Crandall employed a young black household helper named Mariah Davis, whose fiancé subscribed to *The Liberator,* a radical abolitionist newspaper published in Boston by William Lloyd Garrison. As a Quaker, Crandall was already more disposed to see African-Americans as equals than many other whites. She started borrowing Davis's copies of *The Liberator* and became increasingly disturbed by its accounts of American racism and slavery. "My feelings began to awaken," Crandall later recalled. "I saw the prejudice of the whites against color was deep and inveterate. In my humble opinion it was the strongest, if not the only chain that bound those heavy burdens on the wretched slaves. . . . I contemplated for a while, the manner in which I might best serve the people of color. As wealth was not mine, I saw no means of benefiting them, than by imparting to those of my own sex that were anxious to learn, all the instruction I might be able to give however small the amount."

Meanwhile, the seventeen-year-old sister of Davis's fiancé approached Crandall and asked if she could enroll in classes. Sarah Harris had gone as far as she could at the rudimentary district school—studying alongside white girls and boys—and wanted to learn more so she could become a teacher. Crandall considered her request and, in January 1833, allowed Sarah Harris to enroll as a day student.

Harris was from a respectable and moderately well-off family of color—her father was a farmer who had immigrated from the West Indies. With a mix of black, white, and Indian ancestors, she was also quite light-skinned. But the white families in Crandall's school had an immediate and negative reaction. They threatened to withdraw their daughters if Harris continued in the school. Crandall stood her ground, and the white students all left.

That might have been the end of the affair. Another woman would have shut her school doors and returned to her parents' home, or looked for work as a teacher elsewhere. But Crandall's resolve just deepened: If white parents were going to shun her for teaching black girls, then she darn well *was* going to educate black girls! Crandall wrote to Garrison, the leading abolitionist voice of the day, and asked if he thought she could find twenty to twenty-five students of color. She travelled clandestinely to Boston to meet with Garrison, and then on to Providence to recruit students. On March 2, 1833, Garrison ran an ad in *The Liberator* announcing that Crandall would start classes the following month for "young Ladies and little Misses of color." On April 1, Crandall reopened her school with fifteen black girls from Philadelphia, New York, Boston, Providence, and Connecticut.

The white residents of Canterbury went berserk. People accused Crandall of everything from threatening property values to fomenting a radical plot to mix the races. They held an emergency town meeting that drew a thousand people and passed a resolution protesting the "injurious effects and incalculable evils" that the school would bring. Leading the opposition was Andrew T. Judson, a lawyer with ambitions to become governor and, not coincidentally, the next-door neighbor to Crandall's school. "We are not merely opposed to the establishment of that school in Canterbury," Judson thundered.

"We mean there shall not be such a school set up anywhere in our State. The colored people can never rise from their menial condition in our country; they ought not to be permitted to rise here. They are an inferior race of beings, and never can or ought to be recognized as the equals of whites. Africa is the place for them. . . . Let them be sent back there, or kept as they are here."

Crandall had a few valiant local supporters, including Unitarian minister Samuel Joseph May and the young abolitionist William H. Burleigh. But most of the town opposed her. The village doctor refused to treat Crandall's students; the druggist wouldn't provide medicines; the milkman wouldn't deliver milk. Vandals smashed the windows of her house and threw manure in her well. When Crandall would lead her girls on a daily exercise walk, townspeople would pelt them with rotten eggs, manure, dead cats, and chicken heads. The *Norwich Republican* newspaper charged that the school was intended to "break down the barriers which God has placed between blacks and whites—to manufacture '*Young Ladies of color*,' and to foist upon the community a new species of gentility, in the shape of sable belles." Crandall and her supporters intend, the newspaper continued, "by softening down the rough features of the African mind, in these wenches, to cook up a palatable morsel for our white bachelors. After the precious concoction is completed, they are then to be taken by the hand, introduced into the best society, and made to aspire to the first matrimonial connections in the country. In a word, they hope to force the two races to amalgamate!"

Not content with hurling words and dead cats, Crandall's opponents got the Connecticut legislature to pass a law directly targeted at her school—the infamous "Black Law" prohibiting people from teaching out-of-state "colored persons" without consent of town officials. On June 17, Crandall was arrested. She asked her friends not to post bond, and spent one symbolic night in a jail cell that had previously been occupied by a notorious wife murderer. Crandall became an international cause celebre within the abolition movement. *The Liberator* carried regular headlines about each new development in her case; abolitionists set up a local newspaper edited by William

Burleigh to plead the cause of her school; female sympathizers sent money and gifts to Crandall from as far away as England and Scotland.

Crandall's prosecution ended in a hung jury. Her case was re-tried, and she was found guilty. Her defenders appealed, and the guilty verdict was thrown out on a technicality. Through it all, her pupils courageously continued to study. Crandall offered the range of subjects common at seminaries for white girls—reading, writing, arithmetic, geography, history, natural and moral philosophy, chemistry, astronomy, drawing and painting, piano, and French. Students put on evening entertainments for themselves, including one skit that reworked Gilbert and Sullivan lyrics to poke fun at their persecutors. But the emotional toll on these girls must have been immense. "The Canterburians are *savage*—they will not sell Miss Crandall an article at their shops," one student wrote shortly after the state passed the Black Law. "My ride from Hartford to Brooklyn [Connecticut, near Canterbury] was very unpleasant, being made up of blackguards. I came on foot here from Brooklyn. But the happiness I enjoy here pays me for all. The place is delightful; all that is wanting to complete the scene is civilized men. Last evening the news reached us that the new law had passed. The bell rang, and a cannon was fired for half an hour. Where is justice? In the midst of all this Miss Crandall is unmoved. When we walk out, horns are blown and pistols fired."

Although Crandall's supporters had gotten the legal case against her dismissed, the Black Law remained on the books. Crandall's school existed in a kind of legal limbo. Her opponents grew increasingly violent. One night someone threw a two-pound rock through a bedroom window, just missing a student. An arsonist set the school on fire, and authorities tried to scapegoat a black tradesman who had been fixing a clock there and had in fact helped douse the fire. Finally, at midnight on September 9, 1834, a group of white men surrounded the house, yelling and beating on the doors and walls with lead pipes and heavy clubs. They smashed a number of windows, including one where students were sleeping, then entered the house and overturned much of the furniture on the first floor.

This was the end for Crandall. She gave in, dismissed her students, put the house up for sale, and left Canterbury forever. A month earlier, she had married a widowed Baptist minister who had been attracted by her notoriety. Now she moved to upstate New York with her new husband. The marriage was an unhappy one, but Crandall refused to return to Connecticut and instead spent her later years living alone on the Illinois and Kansas frontier.

Several years after Crandall shut down her school, Connecticut repealed the Black Law. In 1885, four years before Crandall's death, friends of hers in Connecticut began organizing a campaign to right the wrongs done to her. They ultimately got the state legislature to approve a pension for Crandall—$400 a year for the rest of her life. One of those who campaigned on Crandall's behalf was Mark Twain, although she didn't learn about this until after the fact. Crandall wrote Twain a thank-you note, asking humbly for a photo of him and a copy of *Innocents Abroad*, "that I may be able to finish the book and loan it to others who are not able to purchase it that they too may learn from you to describe the most trivial thing in such beautiful language as they can there find." More than a century later in 1991, Crandall's schoolhouse was declared a national historic landmark and the state of Connecticut turned it into a museum. In 1995, the state went a step further and offically declared Prudence Crandall "Connecticut's State Heroine."

## Crandall's Sisters

Possibly inspired by Crandall, some white women in other northeastern cities started their own small schools for African-American girls. Around the time of Crandall's battle, abolitionists announced the opening of "A New School for Colored Females" in Boston. A woman named Rebecca Buffum opened a school in Philadelphia in 1834 that promised to "receive young females without regard to their complexion, for instruction in all the useful branches of an English education."

Some African-American educators were also directly influenced by Crandall. Sarah Mapps Douglass, born into a well-off free black Philadelphia family, was in her mid-twenties and teaching in a coed black school in her hometown when Crandall was under siege. Douglass—a frequent contributor to abolitionist newspapers—wrote a commentary on the Crandall affair. "Alas, for the inconsistency of American Christians," she wrote. "While they are sending missionaries and Bibles to Greece, to enlighten and instruct her females; they shut out every ray of knowledge from their own darker sisters. . . . Our enemies know that education will elevate us to an equality with themselves." Shortly afterwards, Douglass moved to New York City to work in a black girls' school run by the Manumission Society—a move that her biographer, Marie Lindhorst, suggests may have been inspired by Crandall, and that took a fair amount of courage because of racial tensions and antiblack riots in New York. Douglass returned to Philadelphia about a year later and opened a girls' school that lasted until 1853, when she merged it with the Institute for Colored Youth, one of the earliest institutions of higher education for young black men. Douglass—a close friend of the abolitionist Grimke sisters—won recognition for progressive teaching methods that went beyond the rote memorization that was common at many schools. Douglass had a well-stocked cabinet of nature specimens, such as shells and minerals, which she would use as fodder for student writing assignments. "She evidently treats her pupils as intellectual, moral and immortal beings," one visitor wrote. "She has relieved them from the thralldom of grammar rules and spelling book columns without an idea connected with either, and introduces them to a knowledge of things, and with them, connects both grammar and spelling, to some practical purpose, which I am sorry to be compelled to believe is a very rare thing in schools."

Another early school for African-American girls predated Prudence Crandall's effort and sprang from completely different roots. Maryland had been the center of Catholic life in the British colonies, and after the French Revolution a number of both white and colored Catholics fled to Baltimore from the French West Indies. Two black West Indian women, Elizabeth Lange and Marie Magdalene Balas, ran an informal girls' school in their home but were unable to make a living at it. Meanwhile, a French priest was charged with teaching catechism to local Catholic children of color but found many of them unable to read. "I wondered then if it would not be possible to establish a school, mainly for colored girls, in order to teach them to read so that they might be able to recite their catechism lesson," he wrote. "This, I felt would be a work most useful and pleasing to God." In 1828, the priest convinced Lange and Balas to form a religious order focused on teaching—the Oblate Sisters of Providence, the first African-American religious order in the United States. They began with eleven boarding students and nine day students, including some poor girls who were allowed to attend for free. By 1835, the school was teaching such staples as reading, writing, French, English, arithmetic, sewing, embroidery, beadwork, geography, and music. But unlike most seminaries for white girls, it also taught washing and ironing and had as one of its goals training students to be domestic servants. "The object of this institution is one of great importance," a school prospectus said. "These girls will either become mothers of families or domestic servants. In the first case the solid virtues, the religious and moral principles which will have been acquired in the school will be carefully transferred as a legacy to their children . . . As to such as are to be employed as servants they will be entrusted with domestic concerns and the care of young children. How important, therefore, that these girls shall have imbibed religious principles and have been trained up in habits of modesty, honesty, and integrity."

Schools like those of the Oblates or of Sarah Mapps Douglass were the exception rather than the rule. In the South, the small amount of schooling that had been available to blacks dwindled away in the 1830s and '40s as one state after another responded to the spread of abolitionist literature by making it illegal to teach African-Americans to read. In the antebellum North, blacks struggled to provide the most basic primary schooling for boys and girls—let alone secondary schooling geared to one gender or the other. African-Americans could only look on with envy as seminaries became a common option for young white women. "When we hear you talk of female seminaries and of sending your daughters to them, we weep to think that our daughters are deprived of such advantages. Not a single high school or female seminary in the land is open to our daughters," a black minister told an abolitionist convention in 1837. "We as much need good seminaries for girls as for boys," the *Colored American* newspaper wrote in 1839. "The culture of their minds requires more care and attention and it should not be neglected. We expect our females to be educated and refined; to possess all the attributes which constitute the lady yet we fail to provide the means whereby they can acquire an education which shall fit them to become the wives of an enlightened mechanic, a storekeeper or clerk."

The *Colored American*'s wish that black girls could "possess all the attributes which constitute the lady" gives a hint of what girls' education meant to nineteenth-century blacks who were fighting for equality—and to those whites who opposed them. There was much less dissension among African-Americans than among whites over whether girls should be educated. While there were certainly black critics of female education, none had sway among black families the way that Dr. Edward Clarke did among whites. Nineteenth-century blacks shared a belief that education was a key to "uplifting" their race—and every individual with an education, whether male or female, represented a step forward.

Young black women flocked to coed institutes of higher learning such as Oberlin and Fisk. But the kind of education provided by seminaries and other all-girl schools carried special meaning both to blacks and whites. Slavery had tarred black women with a stereotype of being immoral and promiscuous—a bitter, blame-the-victim inversion of historical reality, since the truth was that slave women and girls were commonly raped and sexually exploited by their male owners. African-American women aspired to be "ladies" and to cast off those old degrading stereotypes. They wanted to show the white world that they too could be cultured, poised beacons of Christian virtue. They wanted to play the same inspirational role in black families that white women were expected to play in theirs. Seminaries and girls' schools claimed to be the path to refined and cultured womanhood, and so African-Americans like the author of that *Colored American* article dreamed of seminaries for black girls. At the same time, many whites would have laughed out loud in derision at the idea of seminaries for young black women. Whites might tolerate and even help pay for teaching black girls how to read and write, or how to do useful domestic tasks like sewing or washing. But teach them to be *ladies?* That would have been unimaginable, and an insult to the name of real—meaning, white—ladies. That was most likely the thinking among the town fathers of Canterbury, who had no objection to Sarah Harris attending primary school with their daughters but refused to allow her into Prudence Crandall's more advanced school for older girls.

## White Teachers, Black Girls

The end of slavery sparked the educational equivalent of the Gold Rush among African-Americans—an avalanche of individuals, male and female, hurrying to get some of the schooling they had so long been denied. "It was a whole race trying to go to school," Booker T. Washington said. "Few were too young, and none too old, to make the attempt to learn."

There was no public education system in the South for either whites or blacks, so thousands of schools had to be created from scratch. Some of the first schools for former slaves were started by African-Americans themselves. But the vast majority were funded and overseen by white northerners—typically through the federal Freedmen's Bureau or through church groups such as the American Missionary Association. In 1866, northern relief organizations were supporting 975 schools with 1,405 teachers in the South. By 1870, they were supporting 2,039 schools with 2,560 teachers.

Northern white donors and southern black families were equally enthusiastic about education, but they often approached it from different angles. The freed slaves saw education as the first step to becoming full equals in American life—a step toward prosperity, power, and respect. Some of the missionary groups, however, took a more patronizing view of education as a way to "civilize" blacks and instill values such as humility, hard work, thrift, and temperance. "To these groups," wrote historian Ronald Butchart, "freedmen were a menace, a dangerous mass to be controlled and neutralized."

Most of the schools set up by the Freedmen's Bureau and northern church groups were coed, including the hundreds of primitive one-room schoolhouses serving rural black children. But a few schools were created specifically for young women of color. Scotia Seminary was founded in 1867 by the Presbyterian church in Concord, North Carolina. The Atlanta Baptist Female Seminary—which later became Spelman College—was started in 1881 by two northern white teachers with support from the Woman's American Baptist Home Mission Society. In 1886, two other northern women founded the Montgomery Industrial School for Girls in Alabama, whose graduates eventually included Rosa Parks.

These schools offered black girls a profoundly mixed experience. On the one hand, these white teachers were offering girls the very precious gift of education, sometimes at great personal risk. Rosa Parks recounts that Alice White, who founded the Montgomery Industrial School for Girls, was ostracized by local whites to the point that she had to attend black churches. Hostile townspeople burned the school down twice in its early years. Along with academic skills, the Montgomery School gave students a sense of self-confidence and dignity. "What I learned best at Miss White's school was that I was a person with dignity and self-respect, and I should not set my sights lower than anybody else just because I was black," Parks wrote in her autobiography. "We were taught to be ambitious and to believe that we could do what we wanted in life. This was not something I learned just at Miss White's school. I had learned it from my grandparents and my mother too. But what I had learned at home was reinforced by the teachers I had at Miss White's school."

On the other hand, some white-run schools treated girls of color with a kind of demeaning condescension even while they were offering the gift of learning. Myrtilla Miner's school in Washington, D.C., began a little earlier than some of these others, but is still a good example. Miner was a northerner who had gotten a job in 1848 teaching at a school for white girls in Mississippi, where she was appalled by the reality of slavery. "Nothing in all I have seen of the 'blessings of slavery' has been able to abate my suffering on account of it one iota," she wrote. Miner left the Deep South and moved to Washington, D.C., where in 1851 she opened a school to train black girls to be teachers. Miner faced skepticism from friends because of the harsh attitudes of Washington whites toward blacks. Frederick Douglass called her plan "reckless, almost to the point of madness." But Miner persevered and opened a school with six girls in a fourteen-square-foot room, quickly growing to fourteen students, then forty. She faced the same kind of hostility that had greeted Prudence Crandall. People threatened to burn down the school or attack it with a mob; some gathered each night to throw stones at the school building. A white lawyer who lived next door to the school threatened Miner's landlady to the point that the school had to move. "We are not going to have you Northern Abolitionists coming down here to teach our niggers," the lawyer told Miner. "We know better what to do with them than you do." But Miner persevered. She taught the range of subjects that white seminary girls were studying—history, math, philosophy, zoology, grammar. She personally helped pay for several of her graduates to attend Oberlin. Her students clearly appreciated her commitment to them. "Miss Miner if you had never come to Washington, I'm afraid that we would not have had the aspirations and feelings, that we now have," her student Matilda Jones wrote in 1858. "We can scarcely be grateful enough to you, & the strengthening Power that supported you through the obstacles & trials, that you have to surmount & endure in teaching us the only true way to escape from this galling bondage, that is to get knowledge, & use it."

However, Miner also apparently treated students with a condescending superiority that gave a bitter aftertaste to the sweetness of learning. Emma V. Brown was one of Miner's star pupils, filling in as an instructor when Miner was out of town, attending Oberlin with Miner's help, and eventually becoming the first teacher hired when Washington, D.C., established public schooling for blacks. Yet Brown stated quite vehemently that she would never work at her alma mater while Miner was still running it. "I have thought of your suggestion about my applying to the trustees for Miss Miner's school," Brown wrote to her close friend Emily Howland in 1860. "I do not like or respect Miss M. I know this is wrong, but I cannot help feeling so, or explain my feelings. . . . I shall never teach there while she has anything to do with it. I suppose there will be openings elsewhere." Another student reminisced about Miner being "severe in her kindness." Miner was "perfectly intolerant of bad odors because [of] the result of generations of unwashed bodies," she wrote, and "perfectly indifferent to the luxurious meals often prepared for her, because of the untidiness of the homes where these tables were spread." These words conjure up a painful image of black mothers cooking for days to present a fitting meal to honor their daughters' teacher, while all the teacher could see was a "primitive," "ignorant" family.

A similar sense of racist condescension comes across in records of some nineteenth-century white schools for Native American girls. The Ramona School for Indian Girls opened in Santa Fe in 1885 with support from the American Missionary Association. A school newsletter from 1887 described Ramona's students as "literally children of the wilds, with no home but the tepee, no ethics but that of plunder and the scalping-knife. . . ." It noted that, while the Native American girls were naturally good at handicrafts, they were deficient at intellectual reasoning. "The reflective faculties . . . are not so well developed in the Apache children as in the whites," it said. "It will probably require the education of several successive generations to bring them up to the same standard, or even near it." The newsletter credited the school with civilizing these girls in record time. "It only seems necessary to attire them in civilized garb and dress their hair *à la Américaine,* to convert them into at least the semblance of civilized beings who present as good a general appearance as the average children of the masses of any race. . . ."

## Black Teachers, Black Girls

The start of the twentieth century saw the emergence of a number of industrial schools for African-American girls, offering instruction

*Mary McLeod Bethune, founder*
*of the Daytona Educational and*
*Industrial Training School*
*for Negro Girls in Florida*

in low-paid, traditionally female fields like cooking and cleaning. These schools were part of a nationwide surge of interest in vocational education for white students as well as blacks. But there was also an aspect of these industrial schools that was uniquely African-American. Black leaders and educators were divided over the kind of schooling their young people should be getting. One camp led by Booker T. Washington argued that black education should focus on manual training for the kinds of menial jobs that were traditionally open to blacks. Another camp, led by W. E. B. DuBois, argued that black schools and colleges should provide a challenging academic curriculum that would prepare African-Americans for leadership and equality. White donors and government officials typically favored Washington's industrial model. So a number of schools cropped up teaching blacks useful skills for "their place" in society—washing, cooking, and sewing for girls; farming and carpentry for boys.

Two extraordinary girls' schools opened their doors during this period that, while offering industrial training, also managed to transcend the limits of that model. One was Mary McLeod Bethune's school in Daytona Beach, Florida. The other was the National Training School for Girls and Women, run by Nannie Burroughs in Washington, D.C. Both schools were founded and run by strong African-American women who provided black girls with the same kind of inspirational role model that an Emma Willard or Lucy Madeira offered to her white students. But unlike most white headmistresses of the era, Burroughs and Bethune moved beyond the world of education into the world of politics. Both were leaders in black women's organizations and vocal advocates of racial equality. Both their schools gave girls explicit messages about African-American dignity and activism. Unlike many vocational schools, Daytona and the National Training School also maintained strong academic programs. And both further strengthened their academic programs as time passed, adding college classes or instruction in subjects like business and nursing.

Bethune was the better known of the two, rising to become head of the Division of Negro Affairs in Roosevelt's National Youth Administration and a representative of African-Americans at the founding of the United Nations. But she was proud of her own humble roots. Bethune was born in 1875 in South Carolina, the fifteenth of seventeen children and the first in her family to be born in freedom. Her mother's breast bore a scar where she was burned with hot soap for refusing to meet her master's sexual demands. Bethune picked cotton with the rest of her family as a child and outworked many adults, picking up to 250 pounds a day when the average was 100.

Bethune's drive to teach was sparked when, as a young child, she visited the home of the former plantation owner. The owner's granddaughter invited her into a beautiful playhouse, but when Bethune picked up a book she told her, "Put that down, you can't read!" "Something happened in my heart and in my mind," Bethune recalled. "My little eyes sparkled and I said to myself, 'If I cannot now read, I will someday.' It was a challenge . . . I think I picked more cotton the next day than I had ever picked. . . . I determined not only to read myself, but to teach as many others as I could."

Bethune's first schooling was from a black teacher who had returned from Scotia Seminary to open a Presbyterian mission school for black children. Bethune walked ten miles round-trip to and from school each day. After three years, she had learned everything she could from that teacher and was offered a scholarship to attend Scotia herself. Scotia Seminary had been founded as a Presbyterian school for the daughters of ex-slaves. Although Scotia was headed by men, virtually all the teachers were women—white alumnae of northern girls' schools like the Troy Female Seminary or black women who themselves had been educated at Scotia. "My contact with the fine young Negro teachers gave me the confidence in the ability of Negro women to be cultured, gave me the incentive and made me feel that if they could do it, I could, too," Bethune recalled.

Scotia's northern white teachers brought along the Victorian view that education should help women become a moral, uplifting presence in the home. However—unlike most northern seminaries for white girls—Scotia taught utilitarian domestic skills such as laundering, sewing, and hat making alongside academics and Christian values. As unbelievable as it would sound today, it was considered a high honor when Bethune was given the task of doing laundry for the family of the man who ran the school. "I was the prize winner in making breads and cakes; and a fine scrubber," Bethune recalled. "I worked in the kitchen in the morning, getting in the coal and starting the fires. Nothing was too menial or too hard for me to find joy in doing, for the appreciation of having a chance."

Bethune brought Scotia's emphasis on "head, heart and hand" with her when, some years later, she moved to Daytona Beach and started a school in a rented shack in the heart of the black community. She opened her doors to five girls, aged six through twelve, and charged 50 cents a week. If families couldn't afford the tuition, they provided eggs, chicken, or vegetables. Conditions were daunting, to say the least. "We burned logs and used charred splinters as pencils, and mashed elderberries for ink," Bethune recalled. "I begged strangers for a broom, a lamp, a bit of cretonne to put around the packing case which served as my desk. I haunted the city dump and trash piles behind hotels, retrieving discarded linen and kitchenware, cracked dishes, broken chairs, pieces of old lumber. Everything was scoured and mended. This was part of the training—to salvage, to reconstruct, to make bricks without straw." The school quickly took off. Within three months, enrollment had tripled. Bethune soon found herself buying land for a permanent site, with a down payment of $5 that she had raised by selling homemade ice cream and

*Mary McLeod Bethune and her students in Daytona, circa 1905*

sweet-potato pies. Local black construction workers donated their labor to construct the first building, Faith Hall.

Bethune carefully cultivated financial supporters among the wealthy whites who spent winter vacations at Daytona Beach. She would peruse the social column of the local newspaper to see which new industrialists had arrived in town; then she would visit them and extend an invitation to tour the school. She built a board of trustees with prominent whites and blacks, and an advisory board made up of the wives of wealthy winter residents. With her white patrons, Bethune talked about teaching values such as cleanliness, moral living, and hard work—qualities that many whites presumed were lacking in African-Americans. But beyond appealing to white donors, Bethune herself genuinely believed in the value of teaching manual skills such as housework. In its early years Daytona offered classes in sewing, cooking, handicrafts, poultry raising, rug weaving, caning, and broom making along with reading, writing, and math. Students and teachers did virtually all the work on the farm associated with the school, producing 250 gallons of sugar-cane syrup, 80 bushels of corn, 250 crates of tomatoes, and four tons of hay in one typical year. "Girls who came to us three years ago unable to earn one dollar and fifty cents per week can now, because of the training received here, earn five dollars a week," Bethune said in 1912.

However, Bethune went beyond simple manual training. She gradually moved into teacher training and business classes like stenography and accounting, and in 1911 she added a hospital and nursing classes. She stood up to her white board members when they wanted to limit students' academic horizons: In 1911, she wanted to add a high school but was told by one white board member that "eight grades are good enough for black girls." "I called you in here to assist me, not to tie my hands," Bethune responded. "In my estimation, my people need just what in your estimation your people need. If you're going to tie my hands, I'll start over." School walls were decorated with maxims aimed at inspiring both individual achievement and a commitment to helping uplift the race. Some signs instructed girls, "Enter to learn and depart to serve," while others showed a woman in a collegiate cap and gown and stated, "Is this your aspiration? Study!" Outside her own office, Bethune hung a sign that read, "self-respect, self-reliance, race-pride." Her vision for her students was strikingly modern and empowering, as embodied in a poem that she would recite:

> God give us girls—the times demand strong girls, good girls,
>      true girls with willing hands;
> Girls whom the world's gold cannot buy
> Girls who possess opinions and a will;
> Girls who have honor and will not lie
> Girls who can stand before the motley crowd and down its
>      treacherous flatteries without winking.
> Tall girls, sun-crowned girls whose voices cry aloud
> And give a challenge to the whole world's thinking.

Bethune's instructions about character hit home with her students as deeply as did similar teachings by white headmistresses like Sarah Porter or Charlotte Noland. "With Mrs. Bethune, there were just no short cuts," recalled alumna Lucy Miller Mitchell some sixty years years later in 1977. "Over and over you would find, 'Whatever you do, do it to the best of your ability.' And so this feeling about thoroughness—to this day, any kind of sloppiness disturbs me greatly. . . . She wove into the warp and woof of our personality and character her philosophy of life, her inspiration, her deep religious fervor; it was all there. . . . she drilled into her students our obligation to help the less fortunate of our people." By 1915, Daytona was providing a full high school education, and in 1923 it merged with the Cookman Institute for Boys to become Bethune-Cookman College.

Halfway up the Atlantic seaboard, Nannie Helen Burroughs was spearheading a similar project with the National Training School for Girls and Women. Like Bethune, Burroughs was the daughter of former slaves. She was raised by her mother in Washington, D.C., where she attended Dunbar High School, an excellent black public school. She applied for a job as a public school teacher but lost out to a woman with lighter skin and more social connections. Burroughs was crushed and resolved to open a school where "politics had nothing to do with [it], and that would give all sorts of girls a fair chance, without political pull, to help them overcome whatever handicaps they might have." Burroughs eventually found work with the National Baptist Convention, the leading group of black Baptists, and in 1909 the Women's Auxiliary of the NBC authorized her to start a vocational school for girls.

Burroughs's school was unique in that she relied almost entirely on African-Americans for financial support, purposefully avoiding the dependence on white philanthropists that marked schools like Tuskegee or Spelman. Burroughs also managed to maintain a fair amount of independence from her Baptist supporters, insisting on a school that would be open to girls from all Christian denominations.

Burroughs found a site in the southeast section of Washington, in an undeveloped area without water, telephone lines, or electricity. She nicknamed her school "The School of the Three Bs" for the Bible, the bathtub, and the broom—symbols of spiritual cleanliness, physical cleanliness, and industriousness. But like Bethune's, Burroughs's educational approach went beyond narrow training for subservient roles. Every student who attended the National Training School was required to take a course on African-American history—the only school of its time with such a requirement. Burroughs herself gave girls a strong message of racial pride. Carnegia Gordon, a boarding student in the late 1920s, remembers Burroughs telling girls to walk with their heads up like "they were the Queen of Ethiopia." She urged her students to value their own appearance instead of mimicking white standards of beauty: "What every woman who bleaches and straights out [her hair] needs, is not her appearance changed, but her mind," she said. A 1925–26 brochure noted that NTS was not just trying to educate homemakers and domestic workers, but "to prepare leaders by emphasizing honor, orderliness, precision, promptness, courage." As time went on, the school expanded its offerings and by 1926 had two divisions, a trade school and a more academic school. The trade school offered classes in business, homemaking, home nursing, interior decorating, printing, waitressing, music, sewing, and salvaging (finding ways to use castoff items). The "seminary" offered a more academic program starting at grade seven, and continuing through a teacher-training course and two years of junior college.

Burroughs expressed a commitment to single-sex education that was surprisingly modern—closer to today's rationales for girls' schools than to nineteenth-century rationales that were based on assumptions about separate spheres or about women's delicate constitutions. "For [girls'] proper training and development, courses closely adjusted to their special and particular needs are best," a school brochure from 1925–26 said. "Careful investigation shows that the women who are rendering the most effective service in slum, social settlement, reformatory and missionary work were trained in separate schools. The normal adolescent girl quickly 'finds herself' if she is given three or four years in a girls' school."

Unlike most white headmistresses of their era, Burroughs and Bethune both assumed roles of political activism that went far beyond the walls of their schools. White headmistresses often had strong political opinions—for instance, Lucy Madeira's Fabian socialism—and sometimes played a prominent role in local charitable groups. Some even joined in suffrage marches. But Bethune and Burroughs were unabashed political organizers on the national level. Burroughs was the catalyst behind the growth of the Baptist Women's Convention to about a million members, and led the group in opposing segregation and lynching. When women won the vote in 1920, Burroughs helped set up a National League of Republican Colored Women. She also helped start a short-lived group called the International Council of Women of the Darker Races, which promoted education about women of color in other countries. Bethune, meanwhile, became president of the National Association of Colored Women and then founder of the National Council of Negro Women, as well as vice president of the NAACP. As a Roosevelt appointee from 1936 through 1943, she helped create an unofficial advisory group of African-Americans in the administration that was called the "black cabinet."

The struggle against racism was the common denominator linking Burroughs's and Bethune's political lives with their lives as educators. Both saw their schools as more than vehicles to educate individuals—they were tools to help uplift the race. Other African-American leaders saw Burroughs's and Bethune's schools that way, too. In 1926, when a fire damaged the National Training School, one of the people who rallied to support the rebuilding effort was Carter Woodson, the pioneering African-American historian who launched the tradition of Black History Week. Woodson, who sent his niece to the National Training School, wrote an article in which he recounted meeting several impressive women—a café owner, a secretary, a printing shop owner. They were all from different states but each had attended Burroughs's school. "Woodson said that if Burroughs only turned out one student a year like the ones he had met, the public was repaid for its contributions," said Burroughs' biographer Opal Easter. "He gave the school $100 and urged others to do the same."

Despite Bethune's and Burroughs's commitment to educating young women, their schools grew in ways that ultimately took them away from their initial single-sex mission. Seeking a more stable financial base, Bethune's school merged with the Cookman Institute, an all-boys Methodist school, and became a coed college. The National Training School became a preschool in 1967 and, more recently, a coed elementary school that bears Nannie Helen Burroughs's name. African-Americans continued to make education a central priority throughout the twentieth century—but for most of that time, their attention was focused on ending segregation rather than on questions of gender in education. Only in the last few decades did single-sex schooling reemerge as a significant issue in the African-American landscape. In the late 1980s and '90s, some black educators started proposing the creation of single-sex public high schools designed for African-American boys. These all-male academies were aimed at providing positive role models for young black men, along with a sense of racial pride and responsibility. As historian Audrey McCluskey points out, their goals were strikingly similar to those of Bethune and Burroughs. Bethune and Burroughs were fighting a racist stereotype of black girls as loose and immoral; the new proponents of Afrocentric boys' academies were fighting a stereotype of black boys as gangsters and criminals. Each generation hoped to marshal the tools of a single-sex environment, same-gender role models, and racial pride to overcome the challenges facing black youth. But while Bethune and Burroughs focused their efforts on girls, their successors a hundred years later were hoping to bring the magic of a single-sex education to the benefit of African-American boys.

# 5

# Smashes, Crushes, and Female Friendships

## TERRIFYING AT THE TOP

*The committee working on our mission statement and philosophy was made up of about a half dozen volunteers, including a woman who had recently been an administrator at the Hamlin School, a century-old girls' school in San Francisco. Ann Clarke wasn't one of our core members—she hadn't been around for that first dubious meeting about frog dissection, and she was busy with a number of other projects in her life. But her ideas and experience were invaluable in drafting the school's mission and in starting to define our curriculum. One day, she casually mentioned to the other committee members that she was a finalist for the head's job at a well-established local independent school. They were* stunned: Ann was going to be a head? Wait a minute . . . Ann could be *our* head! *It was like the moment in a romantic comedy where you realize that the boy next door, who's always been your buddy and pal, is really the passionate love of your life. And he's in his tuxedo on the way to church to marry someone else!*

*We were in no way ready to hire a head. We were still eighteen months away from our planned opening date. We hadn't raised enough money to pay a head. We hadn't started thinking about where to look for a head. We hadn't even talked about the qualities we wanted in a head. But the perfect head was sitting right among us—and she had a job offer somewhere else. That would mean losing her for good. She wouldn't even be able to continue volunteering with us, since she would be at the helm of a competing institution.*

*We called an emergency meeting and drafted a job description and a list of interview questions. We phoned Ann and invited her to an impromptu job interview, where for two hours we grilled her on every aspect of her educational philosophy and experience. We huddled, decided we desperately wanted her, and then we made her an offer. It was a highly unorthodox offer. We had no funds to speak of, so we proposed a kind of conditional salary—a relatively low base salary that would start six months in the future, when she would officially come on board, with additional pay if we reached certain enrollment and fund-raising targets. Shortly afterwards, Ann was offered the head's job at that other school. She had to choose. On the one hand was the attractive possibility of a six-figure salary at a well-established, well-regarded school. On the other hand was our offer of money we had not yet raised, to run a school that did not yet exist.*

*The decision made Ann dizzy. It felt like jumping off a cliff into a void. She liked working with us, and she loved the idea of creating a school from the ground up—no dysfunctional traditions, no frustrating legacy of other people's bad decisions. Instead you could create the school of your dreams. But she had no idea whether our motley group was capable of making Julia Morgan happen. She herself had never started a school from scratch before. She wondered what would happen to her professional reputation and her career prospects if the venture flopped. "What if I jump off this cliff, tell people I'm doing this, and it doesn't happen? I'd feel like a complete failure," she thought. She talked about the choice with her friends, her husband, and her mother. One friend told her to imagine herself ten years in the future. Would she wish she'd taken the job at the established school? Or would she wish she'd helped start Julia Morgan? "Then it was so easy," Ann said. "I knew there would always be a seed of regret if someone else started it and I wasn't part of it."*

For the year and a half until Julia Morgan opened, Ann herself was essentially the school—there was no building, no staff, no student body, just Ann and our little volunteer corps. We had an impressive-looking letterhead, but the address on it was actually a Mail Boxes Etc. storefront. When Ann spoke with funders or prospective parents on the phone, they had no idea she was sitting in a narrow closet in her house that she had converted into the school's "office." For a long time, the most tangible evidence of the school's existence was a canvas tote bag embroidered with JULIA MORGAN SCHOOL FOR GIRLS that Ann's daughter had bought for her as a gift.

Ann leveraged her personal connections in the education world to help us get off the ground. Her husband was head of another local independent school, and was unfailingly generous with advice. Ann's own experience running schools was also critical. She knew how to do things that the rest of us didn't even know needed to be done—logistical things like emergency contact forms for each child or fingerprinting the staff to screen out felons. We didn't need to reinvent the wheel when it came to operating the school. As a result, Julia Morgan ran astonishingly smoothly from day one. Sure, there were aspects of the school that developed slowly or with friction. But we had an employee handbook from the start. We had successful audits from our very first year of operations. We never lost a child's application form or misplaced anybody's tuition checks—the kind of disaster story that we would hear sometimes from other start-up schools.

The job of running a private school requires a Renaissance individual under the best of circumstances. A good head must provide vision for the school's general direction, oversee the curriculum, inspire the faculty, placate angry parents, shmooze potential donors, manage the school's facilities, track its business operations, and serve as an ambassador for the school with the general public, the school's neighbors, the media, and alumnae. At a start-up school like Julia Morgan, the head's tasks range even further afield. Ann was our chief scavenger, stopping by the dump on weekends to look for useful stuff or driving a U-Haul to the warehouse of a high-tech firm that offered to give us some of their extra furniture. She drove around Oakland, looking at bread factories and old office buildings, in search of a site for Julia Morgan. Once we found *our site, she brought in vases of flowers from her own garden to decorate it. When the flower box in front of the school started to look run-down, she spent her weekend pulling out the old dead plants and putting in new ones.*

*Above all, Ann sold the school. As we moved toward our opening date, parents had no way to judge Julia Morgan—there were no classrooms to observe, no teachers to meet, no campus to tour, no current families to quiz. There was only Ann and her embroidered tote bag. But that was enough. Ann's words and vision were sufficiently compelling to enroll thirty-five families by the fall of 1999. She inspired these families enough to entrust their children to a completely untested school. She inspired confidence in the rest of us, too.*

*At the same time, Ann's own feelings of terror never completely went away. Her worst moment was September 1998, one year before our planned opening date, when she returned from her summer family vacation and officially started work for Julia Morgan. Her husband and her educator friends all went back to school. Ann went into her little closet "office." Her days were wide open. She had no road map, no daily structure of meetings or classes, no colleagues, and no resources. The stress was so intense that she came down with shingles. "It had been adventurous when I finally made the decision, but then everyone started back to work and there I was," Ann said. "I'd been so used to being part of institutions, of having people around to bounce ideas off of. Everyone I knew was back in a school. I felt utterly alone."*

W hen Susan Klaus turned fifty, she found herself thinking a lot about the "outdoor lunch bunch"—eight girls who ate lunch outside every day because they hated the hot, noisy underground cafeteria at St. Catherine's School in Richmond, Virginia. They weren't her closest friends and they didn't stay in very regular touch, but she'd known them for forty-five years and that seemed like something to celebrate. Klaus, an urban historian whose most recent book was on Frederick Law Olmsted, Jr., started organizing a weekend get-together without spouses, kids, or dogs. It took her two years. Finally the group gathered at a bed-and-breakfast for what Klaus thought would be a casual weekend of chatting, shopping, and hanging out. But the unexpected happened. The women sat down together outside the bed-and-breakfast around 10:30 on Saturday morning, started talking, and kept going until dinnertime. They did it again the next day, and the next. "Something just happened," Klaus recalled. "One person started talking, and we just listened. Nobody tried to fix anything, nobody tried to give advice. Some people talked about where they were now, others about the last forty years. We knew right away something was happening. We didn't even get up for lunch, because we knew it would break the mood. . . . I had thought we'd get together for a fun weekend. We'd giggle, shop, have a good time. It never occurred to me we'd talk for three solid days."

That group of St. Catherine's grads has met for these talking weekends four times now, every two years. When Klaus felt stuck trying to complete her book on Olmsted, she thought of those women. Every time she saw them, it gave her a charge of energy. "This book was a very painful experience, which hung over me for ten years," she said. "Writing can be very lonely. I don't think I'd have finished it without them and their jolt of love and support. I could *feel* the positive energy . . . We all know we are there for each other in a very powerful way. If I got [a life-threatening illness like] cancer now, they would be the first people I'd turn to."

Klaus's story shows how deep and enduring the ties can be among women who grew up together at a girls' school. Many alumnae whom I interviewed used the metaphor of family—in specific, *sisters*—to describe the level of trust and love they felt for their school friends. "I still feel a lot of these people are like my sisters, like a big extended family," said Elizabeth "Beppie" Huidekoper, who transferred to the Westover School in Connecticut from a public high school in tenth grade and graduated in 1970. "If I see someone from my previous school, there's no bond there. I can scarcely mention a friend from growing up. But my Westover friends—we'll be the people going to each other's funerals."

Certainly alumnae of girls' schools have no monopoly on close school friendships. Countless men and women stay in touch with their best friends from high school or elementary school; many college roommates remain each other's closest confidants until the day they die. But the single-sex environment adds a twist to girls' relationships that can increase their intensity. That intensity can be either good or bad—there is nothing better than the feeling of sisterhood that Beppie Huidekoper described, but there is little worse than being fourteen years old and feeling that everyone else is in a sisterhood and you are somehow excluded.

Girls' schools have handled these intense relationships in different ways during different eras. More than one hundred years ago, headmistresses looked on with benign tolerance as girls entered into wild, passionate crushes and romances with each other. Later, schools sought to bury the romantic side of these relationships for fear of lesbianism—even while many headmistresses and teachers led closeted lives as lesbians themselves. Girls' schools have long encouraged student friendships through traditions such as "big sisters," who were assigned to befriend new or younger students. More recently, schools have started paying attention to the dark side of girls' relationships, too, experimenting with "clique-busting" curricula and acknowledging that within a classroom of attentive smiles, some very nasty things can be going on.

## The Era of Smashes

Elizabeth Failing Conner was in love. She felt "gusts" of affection for her beloved that carried her outside of herself in a way she had never known before. She felt as if they had known each other for five years, even though they had just met recently. The two of them spent late nights alone together in Conner's dorm room, fighting at 11 P.M. and making up by 1 A.M. Conner was alternately exhilarated and miserable. In class, her mind wandered away from a history lesson on Benedict Arnold to her relationship with her beloved. "I feel perfectly desperate and have really nothing to make me so," Conner wrote in her journal. "Except that I love her dearly, and she loves me, and yet we are always bickering. . . ."

Conner's anguished journal entries could pass for those of any modern girl infatuated with a male classmate—except that the object of Conner's affection was a girl named Carita, a fellow student at Miss Porter's School in the late 1880s. There was nothing illicit or even terribly unusual about their passionate involvement with each other. It was, in fact, quite common in the late nineteenth century for young women at girls' schools and women's colleges to develop romantic relationships. Girls flirted with each other, idealized each other, felt jealous rages, sent each other flowers and candy, and

*Five friends at Miss Porter's School (Conn.), 1890s*

wrote schmaltzy but heartfelt love poetry to each other. They hugged and kissed. They took long, intimate walks together. Sometimes they snuggled together in bed. Same-sex infatuations were so commonplace at girls' schools and women's colleges that there were a number of different terms for them—crushes, smashes, mashes, or raves.

Girls used the language of romance to describe these friendships. They talked about each other as "lovers" and described one classmate as "making love to" another one. And they did this completely openly—in letters to each other, to their parents, even in school publications—without any apparent fear of social disapproval. "Hattie is *in love* dear father, most *dreadfully,* with one of my friends, so much so that you need not expect her home for some time yet," a girl named Bonnie Munroe wrote in a letter home from a Georgia school in 1851. "There seems to be an epidemic of crushes at Foxcroft this year, and every other year, too, so far as that goes," the student newspaper there noted in the late 1920s. "It is easy for a girl who has had a crush to understand how they do come on a person. But after the crush wears off it leaves a person feeling awfull [*sic*] silly, especially if you have done a lot of talking, and everyone has known about it and teased you a lot. . . ."

Today teenage girls who talked about being in love with each other—let alone shared beds and wrote each other love poems—would quickly be labeled as lesbians. But romantic relationships among girls in the nineteenth century carried no such sexual implications. Victorian culture assumed that women were pure, delicate creatures who were too moral and high-minded to feel lust the way that men did. And nineteenth-century society was brimming with intense relationships among women—mothers and daughters, cousins and friends, women who filled church pews together or worked together in the suffrage or temperance movements. Men and women of that era lived in such different worlds that they often had little in common beyond raising a family. Women's most intimate relationships, even after marriage, were frequently with other women.

Schoolgirl friendships were particularly intense. Anyone who recalls their teenage years can remember the emotional peaks and valleys—the blundering efforts to define yourself through others, the elation brought about by a favorable glance from an object of adoration, the complete despondency when the adored one rejects or simply ignores you. Teenage years are years of extreme emotional power and need. In the early 1800s, adolescent girls channeled much of this emotional energy into religious revivals. Today they typically channel it into relationships with boys. In the late 1800s, that energy went into same-sex crushes and romances.

Like Elizabeth Failing Conner, some girls detailed the Sturm und Drang of their infatuations in their diaries. Susan Duryee, a student at Miss Porter's in 1883 and 1884, didn't know anyone at the school when she first arrived with her sister, Lily. The two sisters shared a room and a bed and wondered whether they would ever make friends. "I can see ourselves the first term forlorn, homesick, lonely little things," Susan later wrote in her journal. But soon Susan embarked on a series of crushes that brought peaks of joy and valleys of anguish.

> I was very much gone over Kate Franchot then and used to send her oranges and flowers weekly. . . . In the winter term . . . I learned to know [Alice Carter] very well and during the first weeks was devoted to Cora Burt. But with Kate I had only wavered, and the old feeling was never lost. And every concert I gave her flowers, and we always walked together either Wednesdays or Saturdays. That term the loneliness came very seldom comparatively, and we were both, I think, very, very happy. I felt more sure of girls, and it was only when things were gotten up or there was any choosing of people that I sometimes felt left out. . . .

Susan's crush on Kate seems to have helped her overcome her homesickness and become part of the Miss Porter's community. Later that year, she developed a particularly close relationship with Alice, a girl who suffered from neuralgia. Sometimes when Alice couldn't sleep because of her illness, Susan would trade places with Alice's roommate and spend the night in Alice's bed, whispering and reading together until 4 A.M. But then Alice started developing a relationship with another girl named Jennie, and Susan was torn by intense jealousy.

> Alice and Jennie Hunt grew to know each other quite well, and one Sunday night Jennie came in after the lights were put out and talked to Alice. I could not help hearing a little—enough to make me wild and I cried for a long time. . . . They were extremely devoted, horribly so, and Alice used to "rile" me as she

*Miss Porter's students braided their hair together
to celebrate Halloween in 1896.*

*Girls from the Class of 1904 form a lighthearted conga line
at the Agnes Irwin School.*

would never allow its being a "mash." . . . I am so glad she was happy but oh, if I had but made her more so. Dear child, she does not love me. But I should not feel badly. I love her. . . .

M. Carey Thomas found that infatuations were common when she arrived in 1872 at the Howland School, a Quaker boarding school for girls in upstate New York. She soon became close with an older girl named Libbie Conkey, studying with Conkey and spending evenings talking together in the gallery of the gymnasium. "The girls said we 'smashed' on each other or 'made love,' I don't know," Thomas wrote in a journal entry at the end of her first year at Howland. "I only know it was elegant. She called me 'her boy,' her 'lieber Knabe,' and she was my 'Elsie.'"

Thomas ended up living a life that was unusually devoted to women. She never married and shared her Bryn Mawr College dean's residence for years with her close friends Mamie Gwinn and then Mary Garrett. Today, historians consider her a lesbian. But what is striking about her school days is that her crush was not an isolated or unusual affair: It was the norm among girls who went on to marry as well as those who didn't. Even Thomas's mother accepted the relationship as normal. "I guess thy feeling for Libbie is quite natural," Mary Thomas wrote her daughter. "I used to have the same romantic love for my friends. It is a *real* pleasure."

Some nineteenth-century school romances were shallow and of fleeting duration. Girls could list long strings of crushes, including some on their teachers. Yet other school romances lasted for years, long after the girls had left school. Take Molly and Helena, two young women described in a seminal 1975 article by Carroll Smith-Rosenberg that focused historians' attention on the whole topic of nineteenth-century women's intimate friendships. Molly Hallock Foote and her friend Helena met and became close while attending the Cooper Institute School of Design for Women in New York in 1868. The two women wrote each other tender and passionate letters long after they had left school. (Wallace Stegner used them as the model for the two women in his novel *Angle of Repose.*) More than five years after they first met, Molly wrote to Helena:

I wanted so to put my arms round my girl of all the girls in the world and tell her . . . I love her as wives do love their husbands, as *friends* who have taken each other for life—and believe in her as I believe in my God. . . . You can't get away from [my] love.

Molly and Helena continued to correspond after both women married. Twenty years after their schooldays, Molly still wrote from two thousand miles away in the west, "It isn't because you are good that I love you—but for the essence of you which is like perfume."

Was there a sexual element to girls' school crushes and romantic friendships like those of Molly and Helena? Did students do more than kiss and cuddle when they shared beds? Looking at it from a hundred years later, it's impossible to say. It's probably safe to assume that some of these romantic relationships were sexual. But it's likely that the vast majority were not. Most women didn't question Victorian taboos on sexuality; they valued their relationships with other women precisely because those relationships were untainted by lust. Girls were as besotted with each other as any lovestruck teenager today—but sex didn't enter into the picture.

Rachel Hammond Breck, who graduated from Miss Porter's in 1925, had a "terrific crush" on a senior girl who was sweet and pretty. She picked bunches of violets and hepaticas for her beloved in the springtime. But despite their intensity, her feelings had more in common with hero worship than with sexual desire. "You brought them little flowers. You waited for a thank-you note," recalled Breck, now in her nineties. "You asked them or they asked you to go to a play with you. It was ridiculous; I laugh when I even think of it now. It was very open, part of the whole system. She was a very, very pretty girl, with big brown eyes. I used to think she was wonderful. It was perfectly innocent, so innocent."

## The Shadow of Freud

School romances were generally accepted by headmistresses and teachers as normal behavior in the nineteenth century. They were

*An all-girl "sock hop" at Western High School in Baltimore, 1950s*

even seen as preferable to intimacy with young men, which was completely off-limits. Many schools reinforced this message by hosting formal dances to which only girls were invited. Girls filled up each other's dance cards; younger students hoped and dreamed about getting a dance with their older beloved. M. Carey Thomas's mother—like many parents of that era, seeking to shelter her daughter from men—urged Thomas to make sure that an upcoming school party was for girls only. "I hope the ball will be a ladies [*sic*] party only. *Do try*," she wrote.

As late as 1927, the Foxcroft School student newspaper included a tongue-in-cheek item about a popular student whose devotees got out of hand at an all-girl dance:

> Her innocent admirers, whose names we leave to the imagination or to the barn-door, nearly drove her mad and certainly made her mad, by cutting in on her every two-step. Their rivalry rose to such a pitch that they actually fought over her, but were disappointed, for the fair lady was rescued by a chivalrous and wise girl.

Some nineteenth-century educators frowned on crushes. The Association of College Alumnae was told in 1882 by Vassar astronomer Maria Mitchell, "What a pest the 'smashing' was to teachers there—how it kept the girls from studying, & sometimes made a girl drop behind in her class year after year." And Phebe McKeen, headmistress of Abbot Academy, wrote an 1872 novel called *Thornton Hall* that touched disparagingly on crushes:

> "Cousin Julia says that, at Lakeside, where she is, the girls have what they call 'smashes.' One girl falls in love with another and sends her flowers and confectionary, and all that, without making herself known. At last the smasher finds out the smashee, and either a flaming friendship comes of it or it fizzles out."
>
> "It is simply disgusting," said Grace with her looks, no less than her voice.
>
> "Absurd!" pronounced Belle.
>
> "You know that is a tremendously large school, with a great many city girls in it; it seems to me that they try to make up for the want of gentlemen's society and keep their hand in at flirtation by practicing on each other," said Helen.
>
> "Well, if I was going to fall in love, I would fall in love with a man," said Belle.

But the nineteenth-century criticism of crushes tended to be muted. Critics like Mitchell didn't see crushes as immoral or abnormal—they were more of an annoying distraction that kept girls from their schoolwork. More commonly, headmistresses viewed crushes as a normal part of life, and even a tool to help educate students. A nineteenth-century English headmistress could have spoken for some of her American counterparts when she wrote:

> Warm affection does naturally belong to the body as well as the mind, and between two women is naturally and innocently expressed by caresses. I have never therefore felt that I ought to warn any girl against the physical element in friendship, as such. The test I should probably suggest to them would be the same

as one would use for any other relation—was the friendship helping life as a whole, making them keener, kinder, more industrious, etc., or was it hindering it?

In the early twentieth century, attitudes toward schoolgirl romances began to change. Influenced by psychologists such as Krafft-Ebing, Havelock Ellis, and Freud, both teachers and girls began to see crushes and smashes as dangerously sexual.

## The Discovery of "Inversion"

Richard Krafft-Ebing and Havelock Ellis were early pioneers in the field of psychology who attempted to look at sexuality from a systematic and scientific perspective. They wrote detailed case studies of individuals with a variety of sexual histories, trying to catalogue sexual behaviors much as nineteenth-century biologists were cataloguing different species of animals and plants. They wrote in a matter-of-fact clinical style, but their works were seen as immoral and inflammatory in Victorian England and America. When Ellis published his *Studies in the Psychology of Sex* in England in 1897, his publisher was brought to trial on charges of printing "a wicked, bawdy, and scandalous, and obscene book."

Before the work of these early sex researchers, most Americans didn't look at same-gender friendships in a sexual light. Most had never even heard the word *lesbian*. "We had never, I am thankful to think, heard of Freud in those days and it had never occurred to us that there was anything morbid or indecorous about a crush," recalled Sarah Phelps Stokes, who attended Miss Porter's School in 1884.

Krafft-Ebing and Ellis placed a spotlight for the first time on the phenomena of homosexuality and lesbianism, or "inversion," as they called it. Both Krafft-Ebing and Ellis viewed homosexuality as abnormal, although they differed in whether it should be viewed as a disease or as a more benign kind of abnormality like left-handedness. Both researchers drew a line between women who were lesbians from birth and those who could be "cured." Ellis claimed that one sign of the congenital lesbian was a tendency to have girlhood crushes on other females. In fact, Ellis was so intrigued by girl-to-girl crushes that he devoted an entire appendix of his treatise *Sexual Inversions* to "The School-Friendships of Girls."

Ellis's and Krafft-Ebing's work had the effect of casting a shadow over the kinds of romantic female relationships that had been accepted as normal through most of the 1800s. Suddenly girls sending each other love notes was no longer seen as sweet devotion; it was a sign of potential deviance and perversion. By the 1920s, Sigmund Freud's writings had become widely popular in America and further deepened the shadow over same-sex relationships. Most people hadn't read Freud for themselves, but they picked up on the idea that sexual drives lurked under the surface of all relationships—including intimate female friendships. The result was that teachers at girls' schools became more wary of crushes.

The Headmistresses Association of the East, a voluntary membership group of private girls' schools, invited a Freudian psychologist to speak at their annual meeting in 1920. One of the first questions had to do with student crushes. "We all have to experience it, and I should like to know what is the best way to handle it," asked Charlotte Conant, head of the Walnut Hill School. The psychologist gave a fairly measured response, saying that crushes could be either beneficial or harmful. "A crush may mean just the result of a purely intellectual attachment," he said. "It may mean an attempt to find something in the other personality that the girl has somehow missed in the past . . . I don't think there need be any difficulty unless you are dealing with one who is homo-sexual. On the other hand, it may be used to great advantage."

Some girls were expelled from boarding schools—very quietly, of course—due to accusations of lesbianism. Eleanor Brewster, who graduated from Miss Porter's in 1913, recalled a student who suddenly vanished from the school. "Years afterward [a classmate] found out why it was . . . It's because she was a lesbian. If you had said that or explained it to me any way at that age, I wouldn't have known what you were talking about. I wouldn't have had the *vaguest* idea what you were talking about. . . . Apparently she had bothered her roommate and several other girls and she was sent home."

Meanwhile, girls themselves also began to be wary of crushes. Lois Poinier withdrew from Westover in the early 1930s in part because crushes were such a dominant part of school life. She recoiled at any suggestion that she herself might have a crush on a schoolmate. "I had a couple of friends who were a little older," Poinier recalled. "But as soon as someone said, 'Oh, you've got a crush on so-and-so,' that canned it. I wouldn't go near them. I wasn't of that ilk, and didn't want any part of it. It was very peculiar for any girl to do that to another girl. I wasn't about to send flowers to another girl, no way."

Freud and his associates weren't the only factor leading to a gradual decline in crushes and smashes in the early twentieth century. As Victorian beliefs about female modesty gave way to more casual attitudes, girls' schools became less hermetically sealed worlds. Boys and men became more of a presence in girls' lives. Boarding schools gradually provided more occasions for visits by male friends. Some organized coeducational social events such as concerts or dances with boys' schools. Students at the Agnes Irwin School in Philadelphia played a couple of baseball games against boys from a nearby school as early as 1907. Girls from the Holton-Arms School, then located in Washington, D.C., appeared in theatrical productions with boys as early as 1910. St. Catherine's School hosted its first senior dance in 1929, after making girls attend an etiquette class where they learned how to go through a receiving line. "When men came into my life, I never had crushes again," recalled Rachel Breck, the 1925 Miss Porter's graduate.

Meanwhile, new mass media such as movies brought attractive male figures into girls' lives in an abstract yet emotionally gripping way. "Today six of our clique went to Lynchburg to the dentist," wrote Hope Kiesewetter Medina, a boarding student at Chatham Hall School in Virginia in 1935. "There wasn't anything wrong with anyone's teeth, but it was our only legitimate excuse for going to town without a teacher. We shopped, smoked, ate, of course, and saw Clark Gable in *Office Hours*."

By the late 1930s, crushes and smashes had effectively vanished from many girls' schools—or gone underground, nurtured in private by girls who feared ridicule or condemnation if they showed their feelings. The change can be seen in the student newspaper of Girls Preparatory School in Chattanooga. In 1931, the paper was running a "Dear Hortense" advice column that included occasional questions about female crushes. "I am a very sweet little girl, and I have a crush on an older girl," one student wrote. "She is so sweet, and I bring her flowers lots of times. . . . What must I do to make her like me as I like her? Yours, Miss Fortune." By the late '30s, however, the GPS paper had shifted to a gossip column that was at one point called "Current He-Vents." Girls had no lack of crushes—but as the title suggests, the subject now was boys, and items included the likes of:

> "What cadet does Catherine Buffon hope to see every afternoon after school?"
> "Mary Ann Taber isn't doing so bad. Little Ed Campbell has fallen for her in a big way."
> "Love thy neighbor seems to be Alice Bogart's motto. In case you haven't heard it's Billy Cartinhour."

## Lesbianism: Myth and Reality

A school is a kind of small, self-contained society, and the idea of a society that doesn't include men is unnerving to many people. They find it hard to imagine that girls can feel complete without boys around—that they can have deep friendships, fun outings, fingernail-biting basketball tournaments, or crazy, laughing-till-you-pee moments without boys. Kids themselves can find it hard to imagine girls' social needs being met without boys around on a daily basis. So the taunt comes out: "Aww, that school is filled with a bunch of lezzies."

Since the days of Krafft-Ebing and Ellis, girls' schools have struggled with this specter of lesbianism. In communities where there is not a strong tradition of single-sex education, girls invariably have to face taunts about lesbianism if they decide to switch to a girls' school. Ivana Lebron enrolled in the new Young Women's Leadership School in Harlem for sixth grade and was teased by her old friends, "Oh, you're gonna like girls." In Charleston, South Carolina, Erin Stevens left a coed public school for Ashley Hall in eighth grade and friends told her, "There's a bunch of lesbians there, don't turn into a lesbian." The stereotype of girls' schools as hotbeds of homoesexuality exists among adults, too. I was flying home from a research trip back east, when I started talking with a woman who was checking out boarding schools for her daughter. She described visiting one girls' school in Connecticut but vehemently said she would never send her daughter there because "it was full of lesbians." I was familiar with the school and its head, and knew for a fact that it was not "full of lesbians." What had this woman actually seen? Maybe some girls with pierced noses and leather jackets, or maybe a poster announcing a meeting of a student Gay-Straight Alliance. She could have seen these things in any big-city coed high school and they would have just seemed like one small part of today's adolescent culture. But in the context of a girls' school? They signaled, to her, that the school was "full of lesbians."

In the late 1990s, homosexuality and lesbianism have become somewhat less taboo subjects in schools in general. Some schools—mostly in liberal, urban areas—have brought in speakers about gay rights or backed students and teachers who wanted to set up gay support groups. Girls' schools have been part of this movement, but not noticeably in the lead. The longstanding stereotype can make it scary for a girls' school to identify itself publicly with gay rights. In the mid-90s, the Masters School in Westchester, New York, had two young female faculty members who were running dormitories and became involved with each other. They approached Pamela Clarke, the school's head at that time, and said they were going to have a commitment ceremony and wanted to run a dorm together, like a heterosexual couple. Clarke said no, and offered them faculty housing that was not connected to a dorm. Part of it was that she didn't believe in putting brand-new couples—gay or straight—in the pressure-laden situation of running a dorm together. But part of it also was a concession to homophobia. "I just felt Masters wasn't ready for it," Clarke explained. "This was one or two years before we went coed. We were just hanging on as a girls' school, and I said to myself, 'This will confirm everyone's fears about us.'"

In fact, girls' schools have a long lesbian history that they have never fully acknowledged—that many, in fact, have covered up. Some of the most illustrious and accomplished founders of independent girls' schools in the late nineteenth century were in all likelihood lesbians. These were single women who often spent decades living with a female companion—who occasionally, like Clara Spence, even raised adopted children with their companions. Edith Hamilton, the Greek scholar who was headmistress of the Bryn Mawr School in the early 1900s, lived with a former student named Doris Fielding Reid for forty years. Hamilton dedicated her first published book to Reid. Reid wrote Hamilton's biography. Were Hamilton and Reid gay? Were other school founders like Clara Spence or Charlotte Noland gay? We don't know. The histories of their schools—usually written by loyal alumnae to celebrate a seventy-fifth or one hundreth anniversary—remain discreetly silent on the topic. But today's heads acknowledge that some of their predecessors probably were gay. "The founders of these schools were countercultural—many were lesbians, though no one said so at the time—they were very much *not* traditional women," said Fran Norris Scoble, head of the Westridge School in Pasadena. "Looking back at all those tall fabulous white-haired women who lived with companions—some of those people had to have been gay," said Pamela Clarke, the former Masters School head who now runs St. Paul Academy and Summit School in Minnesota.

As girls' schools matured and became stable institutions, they also became quiet havens for teachers who were lesbians. Until the 1960s, girls' schools relied almost entirely on women for their faculty. Some schools, especially boarding schools, expected their faculty to remain single. For a gay woman in the mid-twentieth century, a girls' school would have been less hostile than many other work-places—you could blend in, respected for your skill and intellect, as part of a community of independent and interesting women. Among the more worldly students, there was ongoing speculation and ru-mor about which teachers were "that way." "Some of the faculty and the headmistress, the word was they were gay," said Catherine Stern, who graduated from the Ethel Walker School in 1965. "At the time, it was just one of those things that people whispered about."

Until very recently, lesbianism remained something that was only talked about in whispers at girls' schools. Both teachers and girls had to stay in the closet if they wanted to survive. Teachers who were too open about loving women were quickly fired. For teenagers who were struggling with an emerging lesbian or bisexual identity, at-tending a girls' school was often a double-edged or bittersweet ex-perience. On the one hand, girls' schools were places where young women valued each other's friendship and became extremely close. On the other hand, there was often a paranoia about being perceived as gay. Girls asserted their heterosexuality by making nasty jokes about lesbians. Students who felt attracted to other girls walked a silent tightrope, fearful of that one false step that would expose them and turn them into outcasts.

Rebecca Fox, who graduated from St. Mary Academy in central New Jersey in 1996, found the school had a little lesbian clique who were "out" to their friends but not to others. "Everyone at St. Mary acted like lesbians—walking around holding hands, having deep friendships, writing each other notes," Fox said. "There was no way to tell who was lesbian because we all acted like that. You could spend your entire weekend with your girlfriend and not have anyone think anything different about you, since everyone was doing that . . . But there was also homophobia. Being called a lesbian wasn't a positive thing. It was also so important to have a boyfriend. Boys—who you were hooking up with—defined so much of who you were as a person. I think it came out of people feeling, 'I don't want to look like a lesbian.'"

Alison Cobb came out as a lesbian while in high school at Salem Academy in North Carolina, from which she graduated in 1990. "It was scary because it was such a small school and the tensions around lesbianism were high because it was a girls' school," she recalled. "There was a lot of intimacy, but at the same time a kind of joking and bravado: 'I'm sitting on your lap but I'm letting everyone know I'm not a lesbian because I'm making fun of them.'" Students had suspicions about who was straight and who was gay, but no one talked about it. Nor was there any discussion of sexual orientation by teachers or administrators. "It would have been easier to come out at a [coed] public school because of the number of people," Cobb said. "There you could get lost in the crowd or find a comfortable group of people. Here it was just really scary if you let the secret out."

There are other aspects of young women's lives that used to be talked about in whispers but now are explicitly addressed by girls' schools—things like eating disorders, date rape, and pregnancy. Like these other topics, homosexuality and lesbianism are gradually emerging from the shadows. The head of the Laurel School in Cleveland, Helen Marter, asked her board to include sexual orientation in the school's antidiscrimination policy when she was hired in 1992. "I can't be the CEO and know I might have to fire someone because of who they're sleeping with," she said. The next year, Marter proposed an antiharassment policy that included sexual orientation along with religion and race. "The bottom line for the school is if you call someone a nigger or a faggot, you get in as much trouble for one as for the other," she said. Several years ago, schools throughout Cleveland were shaken by news reports about a local boy who committed suicide after being ostracized as gay. At Laurel, Marter responded with several training sessions for faculty about the issues facing gay teens and a similar film and panel discussion for parents. She also showed the film to students whose parents gave them permission. The parents' night was quite controversial, and several families withdrew from the school over the issue. "But we gained many more families because of what we did," Marter said. "When kids had the option of seeing the movie, about ten weren't allowed. Everyone else did, and gave the panelists a standing ovation."

Society's growing openness about lesbianism and homosexuality provides an unprecedented opportunity for girls' schools. Like coed schools, girls' schools today have a chance to help students deal with some of the most charged issues of adolescence. They have a chance to help lesbian and bisexual students come to terms with their own identity without fear or stigma. They have a chance to help straight students understand and respect their gay peers. But—and this is different from most coed schools—today's more open environment also allows girls' schools to come to terms with those parts of their own history that have been kept in the shadows. Schools must start to recognize the complexity of the lives of their founders and early teachers—that perhaps they were not just the simple icon of the ever-so-proper spinster who devoted every waking breath to the school, but women with emotionally rich, sometimes frustrated, personal lives that they were forced to keep under wraps.

Destigmatizing homosexuality can help girls' schools by removing one of the main barriers to girls considering a single-sex school—the "they're all lezzies" taunt. That taunt loses its power when kids can say, "Some people are straight, some people are gay, I can have friends of all kinds and still be myself." Destigmatizing homosexuality can also remove some of the nervousness about female friendships. Students who are secure in their own sexual identities don't have to make those nervous jokes, those "I'm-sitting-on-your-lap-but-I'm-not-a-lesbian" comments. As society's paranoia about lesbianism fades, girls' schools should feel free to boast a little louder about one of their most precious attributes—their ability to foster strong female friendships that don't vanish in smoke when a boy enters the room.

Like girls' schools boasting about the strength of their math and science programs, this could have a ripple effect that benefits young women at coed schools, too. Often parents who are considering a girls' school pepper the admissions staff with anxious questions about boys: "Will my daughter know how to relate to boys when she goes on to college? What does your school do to help girls meet boys?" Perhaps someday soon parents who are looking at coed schools will pepper *those* admissions directors with questions about

girls and their friendships. . . . "What about my daughter's relationships with other girls? What does your school do to help girls become allies rather than rivals?"

## Cliques, Cattiness, and Other Pitfalls

The year 2002 saw the sudden emergence of a cottage industry centered on teenage female aggression. Three separate books were published about girls being cruel to each other, and the *New York Times*
ran a cover story in its Sunday magazine titled "Girls Just Want to Be
Mean." *News flash,* the media trumpeted: *Girls can be mean!*

Doubtless this was shocking to people who thought of girls as
sugar, spice, and everything nice, but teachers at girls' schools rolled
their eyes at what was to them old news. Of course girls could be
mean! They'd watched girls treating each other badly since the beginning of time, or at the very least since Sarah Porter had warned
her charges that selfishness was a "hedious" sin.

The "mean girls" books pointed out, correctly, that female aggression often gets overlooked because it takes a less obvious form
than male aggression. Teenage boys fight with punches or knives;
middle-class girls fight with words and withering glances. There are
cliques. There is gossip. There are girls who suddenly drop a lifelong
best friend and expose her deepest secrets to ridicule by the world.
Middle school—the period from sixth through eighth grades—is often the peak time for this kind of meanness. Girls are starting to
grow out of their childhood identities; they are trying on new roles
in the world and groping toward a sense of who they want to be as
adults. Some girls experiment with new social alliances like outfits in
a dressing room—dropping old friends, picking up new ones, dropping them in turn. They test the limits of their own power by hurt-
ing or ridiculing others. They try to give structure to their unsettled
world by creating cliques with strict rules about who is "in" and who
is "out."

Cliques and gossip can happen in any kind of school. The "mean
girls" books, for instance, were all written by women who had at-

tended coed high schools. But cliques can be especially painful in the emotionally intense world of a small girls' school. Lee Steadman, who graduated from the Brearley School in 1979, described the cliques within her class as "ferocious." "Eighth and ninth grades were terrible," Steadman said. "It was very clearly defined who were the 'in' girls and who were the 'out' girls. By tenth grade, we were a little more mature. We were able to have lunch with an 'out' girl." Merry Ross started eighth grade at the Baldwin School in the late 1970s and found a class sharply delineated into cliques. The dominant set was a small group of pretty, athletic girls who dressed in preppie-style clothing, dated the most popular boys, and determined through a constant whirring of gossip who was "in" and who was "out." Appearance played a large part in who was admitted into the group. Ross, who was chubby and a poor athlete, was an outsider for all of eighth grade. Then she went on a starvation diet at summer camp and lost twenty pounds in two months. "I came back really skinny," Ross recalled, "and the first day of school one of these girls came up and said, 'Let me see your schedule, do you want to sleep over at my house on Friday?' Now that I looked acceptable, I was acceptable in some way."

Wendy Walsh, who graduated from Providence High School in Burbank in the early 1970s, still feels ashamed at being part of a classic clique centered on one particularly charismatic girl. This girl would draw people in, make them feel special, and then abruptly drop them—while making sure that everyone else dropped them too. "They had no idea what they had done wrong—why no one would return their calls, and why all of a sudden they weren't invited to anything," she recalled. Walsh herself knew deep down that this behavior was wrong, but was afraid to stand up to the leader. Her teachers—liberal nuns who worked hard to instill a sense of social justice in their students—were oblivious to the entire drama. "This was a dynamic that was totally, completely under the radar screen of the administration," Walsh said.

Unlike Walsh's school, some girls' schools today have started taking active steps to confront and defuse the clique phenomenon. The absence of boys allows them to focus their attention on the quieter, less visible kinds of aggression common among girls. The Holton-Arms School in Bethesda, Maryland, developed a "clique bashing" curriculum for the fifth grade that comes after a unit on friendships in fourth grade. As part of it, students do role-plays about standing in a closed circle in the hallway at snacktime, and how it feels to be outside the circle. They keep a record of their own behavior and what is "inclusive" or "exclusive." "It's tricky," said Anna Puma, lower-school director. "You want them to understand that close friendships are a wonderful thing to have. But you need to talk about inclusive and exclusive behavior. Recently a group of sixth-graders came to us and said, 'We're worried that a clique is forming.' We can focus on the social issues that come up with girls and target those issues. In a coed situation, you'd be less likely to do that."

Even without such programs, many cliques dissolve on their own by the later years of high school. Some students find that taking boys out of the mix actually decreases the amount of cliquishness. "In my old school, you were 'in' because all the guys liked you," said Olivia Harris, a member of the founding seventh-grade class at the new Atlanta Girls' School. "Here there's no 'in-crowd' because there's no reason to be in an 'in-crowd' or 'out-crowd.'" Natasha Lal, another student at the Atlanta school, agreed. "If two girls fought at my old school, their clique would gang up on your clique," Lal said. "Here it's just them and you. . . . I know some of my friends here better than people I knew for four or five years. We're more open, more free to talk here."

## Template for Friendships

At their worst, girls' schools can be a fishbowl where cliques and gossip play out even more intensely than in coed schools. But at their best, they can give students a message that female friendships are important and that women can trust each other. That's something that sounds like a no-brainer, but many women without the experience of a single-sex school don't really understand it until their thirties or later.

As I talked with girls' school alumnae about their friendships, I was reminded of a moment in my own adolescence. When I was fifteen, I went to see *The Sting*, one of the biggest hit movies of the early 1970s. *The Sting* was a buddy movie with the irresistible team of Robert Redford and Paul Newman playing two down-on-their-luck con men who set out to fleece the biggest, meanest con man in New York City. I loved the movie and saw it twice, which was a lot for a kid who didn't go to movies much. But I left the theater afterwards with a vague, unspoken sense of envy. Redford and Newman had competed over a woman in the course of the movie but walked off together, buddies, at the end. The woman didn't come between them. Thinking about it later, I realized that my friendships didn't work that way. I had wonderful, fun girlfriends, but any one of them would sell the others down the river in a moment for the sake of a boy. We might have plans for a Saturday afternoon, but if a boy called—forget those plans. At fifteen, I didn't have the words to express any of this, let alone challenge it. All I had was a vague sense of regret that somehow, in my world, friends didn't stick together the way that Newman and Redford did.

From the nineteenth-century era of smashes and crushes through today, girls' schools have been places where Redford-and-Newman-style female friendships are unusually possible. Sometimes schools have used formal rituals and traditions to encourage the development of friendships. Many girls' schools have Big Sister–Little Sister traditions, in which older students are paired up with new arrivals. Many have ring ceremonies where senior girls hand out class rings to their counterparts in the junior class. But even without these kinds of formal rituals, there is the daily reality of an exclusively female environment—the feeling of openness described by Natasha Lal, the absence of boys as a source of rivalry or distraction. Milbry Polk, a 1971 graduate of Madeira, says the school taught her that "women could be my best friends." Tori Williams, a Miss Porter's grad from the early 1970s, remembers being struck by the way girls genuinely enjoyed each other's company. "Yeah, people had boyfriends but we had these really strong friendships that impressed me," Williams said. "There was a sense of loyalty to your friends and helping each other out that was really nice." Similarly, Susan Sweitzer remembers her friendships at Westover as "our whole focus." "It wasn't just a little distraction to have tea with a girlfriend," said Sweitzer, class of 1961. "We listened to each other. The friendships I have from there are perhaps more focused. We really know each other because we took the time."

Sometimes it took the transition to a coed college for students to appreciate the female friendships they made in high school. Marjo Talbott graduated from Hathaway Brown in Cleveland in 1972 and noticed at college that students from girls' schools were more comfortable spending time with other women. "Women from coed schools tended to look first for acceptance in the 'guy group,' not really wanting close intimate relationships [with other women]," Talbott said. "The girls' school grads were very comfortable in wanting the relationship of a group of girls going off together. On Friday night, spending it all with girls was fine. There was a sense of security, a sense that women were really interesting, too."

Tracy Gary, a graduate of Miss Porter's School, is one of the country's leading experts on women and philanthropy, and founder of a group called Resourceful Women that helps wealthy women learn to manage their money. Gary feels that her Farmington friendships were a kind of template for positive connections with women throughout her adult life. Like many girls' boarding schools, Miss Porter's had a tradition of assigning older girls to befriend newly arrived younger students. When Gary first arrived at school, she was given a date book by a senior. The first Friday night already had a name written in it—some gender-neutral name like 'Park.' Gary was thrilled that someone had set her up on an actual date with a boy. Then Friday came, and she was stunned to realize her date was a senior girl—part of the school's strategy to help new students feel at home. When the shock wore off, Gary had fun. "In a normal [high school] community, would you ever spend an evening out with someone three years older than you? It was fantastic," she said. Gary credits Miss Porter's with showing her what it meant to have and be a mentor, something she has used constantly in her career. It also taught her to value her relationships with women. "Where I am today is completely the result of the traditions I learned at Farmington," she said. "It gave me a commitment to mentorship, with older people who are much wiser and with younger people from whom I've learned all kinds of things. . . . It taught me to love and value women."

# 6

# "The World Was Breaking Open"

## LOCATION, LOCATION, LOCATION

*We had a name and a director but no site. We needed a safe, attractive, affordable location, but we were like a wild animal caught in brambles— every way we turned, there was a different thorny branch blocking our way. The available sites were too small, or they had just been bought up by a high-tech firm, or they were too expensive for our meager budget. If we looked in residential areas, we risked neighbors who would fight the noise and traffic of a school. If we looked in industrial areas, we risked ending up on a pile of toxic waste. Then there was the earthquake issue. A decade after the Loma Prieta quake of 1989, many East Bay buildings were still not safe for occupancy. Downtown Oakland had a number of beautiful vacant buildings, but there was no way we could afford hundreds of thousands of dollars worth of earthquake repairs.*

*A blond, doe-eyed psychotherapist named Laurel Hulley took on the site issue for us. Laurel had absolutely no background in real estate, and she had a gentle, ethereal manner that made me initially doubt her abilities. But she attacked the task with an almost monomaniacal* *focus. She called every church in central Oakland and Berkeley to see if they might have extra space to rent. She called local colleges. She set aside one morning each week just to drive around various neighborhoods, looking for buildings that could be potential schools. She met with a city councilman who referred her to a commercial real estate agent, who told her that we needed $100,000 in the bank and a formal business plan before we could get a lease. Laurel was so depressed after that meeting that she went into the coffee shop below his office and ate a maple scone and a slice of pecan pie. "It was either chew on a sweet or chew on my knuckles," she recalled.*

*Whenever there was a site that looked somewhat possible, Laurel called in our director, Ann, and our lawyer member, Barry Epstein. They looked at a former auto dealership. They looked at a boarded-up office equipment store. They considered subletting space from a biotech company. Laurel went through little flurries of excitement—"This is it!"— followed by long periods of feeling buried by the difficulties. Her family grew annoyed with the amount of time she was putting into the site search, time that was spent away from her therapy practice. "We're not a family that can afford you doing this," her husband told her. "Not another meeting!" her daughter would complain when Laurel left the house in the evening.*

*There were two sites that seemed perfect to us. One was Mills College, an all-women's liberal arts college in Oakland where students had occupied the administration buildings for two weeks in 1990 to stop trustees from turning the college coed. Mills was interested but unable to offer us any usable space. The other ideal site was the top two floors of the YWCA in downtown Oakland. The Y was housed in an original Julia Morgan building from 1915 with a beautiful interior courtyard, a theater, a dance studio, and a basement swimming pool. But the building had suffered extensive earthquake damage and the Y needed a buyer or tenant with deep pockets to cover the repair costs. We spent months going back and forth over the finances but, in the absence of a rich angel donor, we were unable to figure out how to make it happen. As our opening date grew nearer, we increasingly feared ending up in some dingy second-floor office over a dry-cleaning shop—or in someone's living room. At one point, we started to discuss whether the school could work if we opened in Barry's living room.*

*Then we got our lucky break. A supporter of ours who worked at Holy Names College mentioned that it had an empty, unused dormitory. Laurel had contacted Holy Names before to no avail, but this time something clicked. The college was eager to lease the space. And we saw wonderful possibilities there. The college sat high in the Oakland hills, with a panoramic view of the San Francisco Bay. Being on a college campus would give us amenities far beyond the means of most start-up schools—use of the college gymnasium and library, college students who could serve as tutors, college coaches who ended up helping out our fledgling basketball team. Most of all, the simple fact of being on a college campus would inspire our girls. We had some applicants from working-class families whose parents had not even finished high school. Being at Holy Names would make college something real for these girls, a natural step in their education rather than an alien, abstract idea.*

*Holy Names, it turned out, saw possibilities in us, too. Holy Names had been founded in 1868 as a girls' secondary school, serving the daughters of Bay Area Catholics who had stayed and prospered after the Gold Rush. The college itself was now coed, but the Sisters of the Holy Names of Jesus and Mary still operated an all-girl high school right across town in Oakland. They understood our mission. They liked the idea of seeing young girls on their campus again. And as they grappled with rising costs and declining enrollment, they needed the income we could provide. We signed a one-year lease for one floor of the dormitory. We had, at least temporarily, a home.*

J osie Merck grew up hearing wonderful stories about Miss Porter's School. Her mother had spent some of the best years of her life at Farmington in the 1930s. As a child, Josie would dreamily page through her mother's old yearbooks, looking at the pictures of the pretty girls in pearls and sweaters who would go on to marry handsome Yale men. She would interrogate her mother about the intricate rituals of school life—the wishing rings that were presented by seniors to younger girls, the Mink, Possum, and Squirrel teams named after the school's initials, the colors of clothing that New Girls and Old Girls were allowed to wear. Miss Porter's was glamorous. It was a ritual of passage. "My mother didn't talk about it a lot, but I got the sense it was hugely important to her," Merck recalled. "I got the picture pretty early—the die was cast. This was where I had come from, and where I was going to go." Jenepher Stowell, a friend of Merck's whose mother was also a Farmington alumna, agreed. "Most of us went there thinking it would be the best place on earth because our mothers thought so," Stowell said.

When Merck and Stowell arrived at Farmington in the early 1960s, however, they found a very different place than what they had imagined. It wasn't that Miss Porter's had changed since their mothers' day. It was that Miss Porter's had *not* changed, while the world had.

Some of the teachers who had taught their mothers thirty years earlier were still there. They no longer seemed dynamic and inspiring—they seemed old, humorless, and burned-out. The school's plethora of rules governing everything from room décor to skirt length seemed rigid and oppressive. School rituals that had seemed fun to Merck's mother now felt weird and meaningless. This was the '60s—with the Beatles taking America by storm, with freedom riders facing death to register southern black voters—and Miss Porter's still required girls to bring their male callers to tea with the headmaster on Saturday afternoons. Girls were still being told that the correct way to eat soup was to tip the bowl away from yourself. The list of required school clothing still included items like an "ice cream social dress." Josie went clothes shopping before heading off to Farmington, and discovered that none of the salespeople at the department stores had the slightest idea what an "ice cream social dress" was. "Traditions had been handed on but didn't seem to have substance anymore. They seemed too sweet and sentimental. They'd make us smirk," Merck recalled.

"We felt we were in a sort of bell jar, being there in the first half of the sixties," Stowell said. "The world was breaking open with the

Vietnam War, the free-speech movement, the pickets. It was all sort of thrilling and horrific and amazing, and we were locked in a little bell jar."

Although they never would have admitted it, many private girls' schools had calcified by the early 1960s. There were a variety of reasons for this. Their entrepreneurial founders had passed away, and they were being run by people who were more concerned with maintaining past successes than with trying new things. Most schools had been around long enough to have legions of loyal alumnae, who provided a useful base of support but also a strong lobby against change. With the baby boom and economic prosperity of postwar America, schools could pick and choose their students from a growing population of well-off families who didn't see anything wrong with doing things the way they'd always been done—who in fact often chose private schools precisely for their conservatism. Foxcroft was turning away four girls for every one it accepted in the late 1950s; Madeira was turning away three girls for every one it took.

Most private girls' schools had quietly lost sight of their radical roots by the 1950s and early 1960s. Rather than blazing new trails for women, they were following in the wake of society as a whole. Few schools challenged the dominant postwar assumption that women belonged at home—preferably a well-decorated suburban home—raising children, hosting dinner parties to help their husbands' careers, and volunteering with the local hospital board. "You were to be the best you could be, but you were to be a prize filly for some Exeter stallion," said Marny Hall, who attended the Emma Willard School in the late 1950s. Hollis French, the headmaster of Miss Porter's, put it bluntly in an interview with *Newsweek* in 1959: "The main point is to educate the girls, first and foremost to prepare them for what comes next: college, marriage, and a place in the community."

Some girls quietly wondered about the narrow scope of the future laid out before them. "I was being trained to be a 'leader,'" recalled Olivia Tsosie, who attended St. Mary's Hall in San Antonio in the 1940s. "I kept asking them who I was going to lead where. They looked confused and changed the subject. Later I realized they were talking about Lady Bountiful and the Junior League." Belinda Smith Walker, who graduated in 1963 from the Marlborough School in Los Angeles, wondered why a school that taught challenging works like *Julius Caesar* also spent time telling her how to get in and out of a sports car like a lady. "The expectation was that you went to college, got engaged, got married, and came back and did it all again," Walker recalled. "I remember being a senior and seeing some very young women dropping off their daughters for seventh grade and having it hit me: 'Omigod, they went all the way through it and are back here doing it again.' I wanted more than that."

Rules and traditions were a dominant feature of life at private girls' schools in the years after World War II. Most girls in the 1940s and '50s simply accepted them as part of life. Some even welcomed the sense of structure they provided. "There were lots of rules and regulations, and I loved that—it suited me," said Louisa Palmer, an Ernst & Young executive who attended the Westover School as a boarding student in the early '50s. She liked the strict uniform, since it allowed her to stop worrying about clothes. She liked that weekends were crammed with school club meetings and activities, and she didn't mind at all that she was allowed only one weekend off campus during her first year. "I didn't have to worry about which boys were going to call me on Saturday night. It gave me time to grow up in other ways," Palmer said.

The baby boomers who started arriving at high schools in the 1960s were different from earlier generations like Palmer's. They were more likely to question authority. They were more emotionally expressive and demanding. (Their grandparents might have described it more bluntly as "spoiled.") They grew up in a society that was saturated with mass media, where TV fostered a culture of immediate gratification but also connected kids with the broader world in a newly visceral way. Individuality was important to boomer girls as well as boys. Being part of the world was important to them, and as the decade went on, "relevance" became one of their battle cries.

Some girls felt a quiet sense of betrayal as they realized that the teaching at their highly regarded schools was crummy. They knew enough of their schools' histories to suspect that it hadn't always been that way. Louise Stevenson, a Farmington student who later became a historian, would stare at the portrait of Sarah Porter in the dining hall each night and wonder "if this was what she had in mind." When Josie Merck finally went to her father and told him that Farmington was not a very good school, he replied, "Well, it has a very good reputation."

Frances FitzGerald, the Pulitzer Prize–winning author of *Fire in the Lake,* attended Foxcroft in the late 1950s and was "bored out of my mind"—the only time in her life that she recalls being bored. Students were not allowed to leave campus until their senior year, and then only if they had good grades. Classes mainly involved rote memorization. In English, girls had to learn one poem by heart each week and remember them all by their third year of school. If they missed one word, they were sent to the bottom of the class. On the other hand, high achievers were rewarded with the dubious honor of dining with Miss Charlotte, the school's dynamic but aging founder. "Here were the five smartest girls in every class, endlessly going to dinner with Miss Charlotte, when it was the last thing any of these girls wanted to do," FitzGerald recalled. "I remember being absolutely shocked at one of these dinners when she produced a head and started talking about phrenology. She was clearly of another era, the nineteenth century."

Boomer girls chafed at the plethora of rules that were intended to regulate every aspect of their appearance or behavior. In the outside world, girls were starting to wear blue jeans and miniskirts. Inside most girls' schools, knee-length skirts and slips were still the order of the day. Many schools made girls kneel down each morning to see if their hems reached the floor. The Columbia School in Rochester, New York, levied fines for uniform infractions—five cents for a loose hem or ten cents for the wrong-color socks. At St. Timothy's School in Maryland, girls would line up by the dining hall and lift their skirts to show that they were wearing a slip. "I was always being sent back from the dining room because my hair was not neat enough," recalled Sally MacNichol, a 1969 graduate of St. Timothy's who was also a great-niece of the school's founders. "I felt like I was in a prison camp. It made me completely oppositional. More than anything, I came to understand what a punitive authoritarian environment was like."

School discipline often seemed arbitrary and cruel to girls of the increasingly free-spirited 1960s: The incorrect shoes might bring as severe a punishment as cheating on a test. Abbot Academy continued to limit girls to five-minute conversations with boys they passed in the street. The Ethel Walker School said that girls could keep only two items on top of their dressers. Mary-Sherman Geyelin Willis was suspended for a week from Madeira for doing a pirouette during chapel in 1969. "It was an April morning, a beautiful, beautiful day," she recalled. "I was suddenly struck by how beautiful it was—rays of sun shining through the glass, a sudden shaft of light—and I did a pirouette. The headmistress immediately shouted for everyone to be quiet, called me out, and told me to go to her office and wait for her. She was so terrifying and so ridiculous at the same time: 'Miss Geyelin, all I want to know is WHY.' I burst into incredulous giggles. She was outraged, and suspended me for the rest of the week."

The sexual revolution heightened many girls' sense that their schools were hopelessly out of date. In the outside world, young women were discovering the birth-control pill and listening to Mick Jagger sing "Let's Spend the Night Together." Inside schools, girls were still supposed to be young ladies who remained pure and virginal until after marriage. Foxcroft would show movies on Saturday nights but turn off the bulb in the projector during sexually suggestive scenes. Madeira required boarding students to have a chaperone with them if they received a male visitor. At St. Francis High School in Sacramento, Kath Kettmann's biology teacher would completely skip the textbook's chapter 13, which covered the reproductive system. (Kettmann and her friends struck back by sneaking into another classroom, reading chapter 13 together, and then when the teacher finally found them, innocently insisting that she had told them to gather in that room.)

Schools tried to provide "proper" occasions to meet boys, which felt increasingly stilted and oppressive to girls of the 1960s. Maisie Grace, who graduated from Foxcroft in 1974, recalls being bused to a dance at a boys' school and descending from the bus to walk through a double line of staring boys. "It was like being in a parade. Needless to say, I never did that again," she said. Amy Stone Glenn, who graduated from Emma Willard in 1971, remembers dances where girls were paired up with boys according to their height. "I never did it. I couldn't get off the bus," she said.

What seems particularly amazing in hindsight, given women's traditional role as nurturing caregivers, is the lack of emotional support that many private girls' schools provided their students in the early 1960s. Teachers often maintained distant, formal relationships with students. The dormitory staff at boarding schools were typically older single women who seemed clueless about how to relate to young girls. "They'd have teas," recalled Glenn, the Emma Willard grad. "You'd go sit with her [the house mother] and eat cookies and drink tea. It was ludicrous, really a throwback." Girls were struck by what went unsaid at many schools. While some schools offered current-events classes and brought in speakers about world affairs, others seemed determined to ignore the outside world. Miss Hall's initially refused to let its boarding students watch President Kennedy's funeral on television for fear it would make them hysterical, until their parents insisted they be allowed to watch. "We didn't talk about the Vietnam War, we didn't even talk about the Korean War that much," recalled Sharman Anderson, who graduated from the Kent Place School in New Jersey in 1967. "It was a pivotal point in history, and we never talked about that. We never talked about the assassination of President Kennedy. We never talked about Martin Luther King winning the Nobel Peace Prize. Newark burned during one of those summers, and no one even discussed it."

Schools also remained silent—and thus unresponsive—to problems within their own communities such as eating disorders. Society as a whole hadn't yet become aware of eating disorders in the early 1960s; most Americans had never even heard the terms *anorexia* or *bulimia*. But the problem should have been apparent to administrators at the tight, all-female communities that were girls' schools. Almost every school had girls who dieted to the point of illness. At some, bingeing and purging were common student practices. Students themselves were certainly aware of it and felt a sense of betrayal when the adults in charge pretended it wasn't going on.

At Brearley, Audrey Maynard recalls one anorexic classmate dwindling away before her eyes while the school said absolutely nothing. "I remember being in the bathroom, trying to convince this one particular girl that she was not fat, and feeling helpless and that the grown-ups were doing nothing," said Maynard, who graduated in 1973. "I was so upset about it. It made me feel extremely vulnerable. It was very scary to have someone walking around like a skeleton, to our eyes killing herself, and no explanation why."

At Miss Porter's, it was common practice among some groups of students to make themselves vomit after meals. Girls would get thinner and thinner and then vanish—presumably to the hospital. The school never said a word. "Some girls got thin and then disappeared," Josie Merck said. "People would talk about how they threw up at every meal. I just thought, 'That's the secret of their good looks, that's how they have two helpings of ice cream.' We had no idea this was a pathological event. No one talked to us about it."

## Rebels in Rolled Skirts

Like young people throughout the country, students at girls' schools rebelled against the restrictive conventions of their schools in both private and public ways. The most common form of rebellion had to do with school dress codes: You didn't have to be a flaming radical to yearn for the miniskirts, bell-bottoms, and halter tops that were showing up on college campuses and in fashion magazines.

There were a million little ways to circumvent a school's dress code. Instead of brown oxfords, girls wore brown clogs. On top of the required white blouse and pleated skirt, they might add a fringed hippie-style belt. Probably every girls' school in America has had students who rolled up their skirts at the waist to make them shorter. "They would make us kneel to make sure our skirts touched the floor," recalled Lorraine Harper, who graduated from the Columbia School in Rochester, New York, in 1966. "But then you'd stand up

*Long hair, mod fashions, and folk music at*
*Roland Park Country School (Md.), 1970*

and roll up the waist on your skirt and pull down your sweater to
cover it. You'd end up with a miniskirt, and a size eighty-eight waist
from rolling it up so much."

Rebellions were initially small, even silly. Lucinda Zeising and her
friends at Miss Hall's flouted the rules by sneaking food into their
rooms, playing music at night, peeing out the windows, and rolling
plastic cups down the hallways to make noise. "One time I went
down to the kitchen and raided the refrigerator, which felt like I had
done something really radical," she recalled. But these individual rebellions became more serious as the 1960s progressed and girls ven-
tured into the drugs and sex that were a growing part of the outside
youth culture. At Madeira, the school would bus girls into Washington, D.C., for what was supposed to be some nice ladylike shopping
on the weekends. The girls would jam into the department store
bathroom, change en masse into jeans, and head straight off to
countercultural Georgetown where they could find drugs and boys.
"The school didn't change much, while everything around it was
whirling," said Martha Dudman, who was expelled from Madeira in

1969 for rolling joints in a dorm. "I felt like I was in this nowhere zone, where no one 'got' anything. These were the 1960s. It felt like the beginning of everything. We were going to be-ins, with people painting their faces and wandering around—then we had to go to this very rigid place and follow the rules."

Like other schools and colleges, girls' schools had a harder and harder time keeping their students' behavior under control. For girls' schools, with their traditional emphasis on rearing virginal young ladies, the focus of this struggle often had to do with sexual mores. Katherine Matheson, a graduate of Foxcroft in 1972, had numerous friends who were expelled for illicit contacts with boys. "All my friends got thrown out by the droves when they were found in D.C. with strange boys. Then there was a summer-abroad program where some of the girls had to be sent home for doing nothing but make out with French boys. . . . The school tried to be hip and invited Indians to campus who were leading people in ceremonies, the headmaster was sort of spastically trying to dance like an Indian, they had a powwow in the gym, and the same thing happened—all the girls were out in the bushes making out with the Indians. My friend Susan was thrown out for making out in the bushes with an Indian. There was constantly a state of emergency in protecting everyone's virginity."

Girls' schools never faced the overwhelming kind of student protests that paralyzed many colleges in the '60s. Organized revolts tended to be relatively rare, dependent on a confluence of world events and the personalities of a particular class. But even a single organized uprising was more than most girls' schools had ever experienced before—certainly something that their nineteenth-century founders had never imagined.

Like individual rebellions, group revolts often centered on the dress code. Mary Pat Pfeil and her friends at Divine Savior High School in Milwaukee were angry when the nuns kept telling them to dress more properly, so one day they all wore formal gowns to school. They were sent home, and the student council had to cancel its meeting that day because so many members were gone. Ellen Rutt's class at Notre Dame Academy in Waterbury, Connecticut, rebelled against ankle socks by tying their socks in knots and hanging them all over the school. (They won permission to wear kneesocks.)

Group revolts also went beyond the dress code to touch on broader issues of how schools were run. At the Ethel Walker School in Connecticut, seniors pushed to overhaul the school's honor code in 1965 so it would focus on major rather than minor transgressions. "It was as if there was a crack in the fortress wall," said Catherine Stern, one of those seniors. Katherine Matheson was president of her Foxcroft class in 1969 when they decided it was time for some changes. The girls called the headmaster to come meet them in a room near the gym. They turned out the lights, put on Native American–style bandanas, and found a rickety Victrola to play the Beatles' "Revolution" really loudly. "We had a long conversation about changing the school, about going places and having speakers. Why couldn't we be taught more interesting things? Why couldn't we go into D.C.? It was very confrontational. To his credit, he stayed there and talked with us."

## Change in the Air

As America changed around them, girls' schools also began to change—sometimes incrementally, sometimes in broad sweeps that washed away decades of tradition. At boarding schools, elderly dormitory supervisors were replaced with "house parents"—young women or couples with small children, who provided a warmer, more familial atmosphere in dorms. Some schools added counselors to their staff, while others began hiring male teachers in significant numbers for the first time. Responding to calls for "relevance," schools revamped their curricula to include courses like Race in America or Women's Literature. To provide more opportunities for creative expression, they added electives in subjects like photography, ceramics, and yoga. At Abbot Academy, trustees hired a thirty-three-year-old headmaster named Donald Gordon in 1967, who set up an unprecedented "town meeting" form of governance in which each student and faculty member had one vote. The newly democratic school swiftly abolished its old five-minute limit on sidewalk conversations with boys, replaced the uniform with a more liberal rule that girls must look "neat and clean," eliminated daily chapel services, allowed students to leave campus on weekends, and officially invited boys from nearby Andover to visit after dinner.

The breadth of Gordon's changes at Abbot may have been unusual, but his hiring wasn't. Through the mid-'60s and early 1970s, private girls' schools embarked on a wave of hiring men as heads for the first time. The trustee boards that ran the schools may have felt that men could provide the leadership needed to make major changes and steer through those turbulent times. They also may have felt that men would be better at raising money, an increasingly important part of the job for heads of schools in that era. Dennis Collins, head of the Emma Willard School from 1970 until 1974, recalled that for much of his time there, all the top staff of the school was male—not just the head but the assistant head, the dean of faculty, the treasurer, and the director of development. It was ironic that—at precisely the time when careers in business and politics were starting to open up to women—many girls' schools abandoned their century-long tradition of women's leadership and rushed to put men at their helms. A 1974 article in the *Independent School Bulletin* put it bluntly in its title, "Where Have All the Headmistresses Gone?"

## Opening the Doors

The late '60s and early '70s brought one particularly historic change to the small world of elite girls' schools—integration. Spurred by the civil rights movement, many private schools started opening their doors for the first time to African-American boys and girls. In a number of big cities, nonprofit groups like A Better Chance sprang up to help private schools find and recruit inner-city kids. But before these organized outreach programs got going, the first steps toward integration often involved a discreet inquiry by the headmistress or headmaster to a few families they knew in the local black community. Kumea Shorter-Gooden, a psychology professor who graduated from

Madeira in 1970, found out about the school when headmistress Barbara Keyser approached her Washington, D.C., public school and "said she was looking for a black girl to integrate the school." "I had always done well academically, and it was because of that that we applied," Shorter-Gooden recalled. "The fact it was a girls' school wasn't significant, but my father saw it as a real opportunity for me academically. I don't remember having any say-so in the matter."

Black families like Shorter-Gooden's took the decision to enroll their daughters as seriously as the schools undertook the decision to integrate. Parents saw the tremendous academic opportunity represented by these schools, but wondered how the pressures of personally integrating a school would affect their child. In Shorter-Gooden's case, there was also the cultural divide between Washington, D.C., and Virginia. Madeira was only a few minutes' drive across the Potomac, but it was part of the South. Shorter-Gooden had driven through Virginia just once before enrolling in Madeira, and she remembered how the passersby had yelled epithets at her. "My dad took me to see his grandfather," she said. "It seemed what he wanted to do was get his permission. Black Washington knew of Madeira, knew it was a white-girls' school, and anyone who was thinking might ask, 'Why send a black girl to a racist white-girls' school?' I had a sense that he had to get his grandfather's blessing. I was aware there was something significant and momentous about this decision."

The first black students who entered private girls' schools rarely encountered the kind of overt hostility that marked integration at white public schools in places like Little Rock or Boston. Partly this was due to a kind of self-selection—those racist white families that opposed integration were free to withdraw and go elsewhere. Partly it was due to schools' culture of WASP politesse, where dissension was more likely to be voiced in whispers over cocktails than in shouting or name-calling. And certainly it was due to the modest nature of the first steps at integration—the admission of one or two handpicked black families did not seem likely to change the culture of a century-old private school. But it was also due to active leadership by the heads of these schools. They made a decision that integration was both morally right and legally inevitable, and they shepherded their communities along that path. "People were very careful and mindful," said Francene Young, an African-American who graduated from Westover in 1971 and today is a human-resources manager. "If you sat down and told somebody you didn't like something and why, they'd listen to you. I didn't feel any overt racism."

Some African-American girls of this generation had thoroughly wonderful experiences, both socially and academically. "I fell in love with the place because it was everything a girls' school offers—small, intimate, empowering, familylike, cozy," said Karen Lynn-Dyson, who was a day student at Miss Hall's School in the early 1970s. "I didn't have any sisters, so this was a chance to connect with all these girls. Miss Hall's was like one big home. I remember spending as much time as I could over there, with girls hanging out in their PJs, studying, in the TV room. I remember spending a lot of time in the smoker just goofing and playing backgammon." But for other girls of this generation, the school experience was decidedly mixed. They thrived on the rich academic program. But socially, they were never quite comfortable. These girls sometimes felt they were viewed as a curiosity—the first black person other than a housekeeper that their wealthy classmates had ever met. Ellen Pinderhughes, a psychology professor at Vanderbilt University, integrated the Winsor School in Boston as a ten-year-old girl in the mid-1960s. While she sat in a classroom taking the admissions exam, white students came by and whispered, "Look at the Negro girls taking the test!" "I instantly knew what it felt like to be in the zoo," Pinderhughes said. When she grew an Afro in high school, white girls would approach her just to touch it. "They wanted to know more about us, our lives, but they were doing it in a way that was like a bull in a china shop," Pinderhughes recalled.

Some girls felt accepted by their white classmates but not by their classmates' families. Trish Campbell Smith, who graduated from the Garrison Forest School in 1983, was sometimes quizzed by friends' parents who apparently doubted her academic abilities. "I was being asked to do third- and fourth-grade arithmetic at the dinner table," she said. "The shock for me was encountering people who were so poorly behaved. I felt like their parents were observing and watching me. I became very adept at excusing myself between dinner and dessert." Other times, girls of color were placed uncomfortably on the spot by white teachers who wanted to know "the black perspective" on a particular topic—in effect, asking a fourteen-year-old child to be a spokesperson for her entire race. Veda Howell, a 1973 graduate of Foxcroft, was asked by her American history teacher, "What month do you-all harvest tobacco?" Howell answered, "I don't know, why don't you ask your grandmother?" since the teacher had mentioned earlier that his grandmother worked in tobacco.

Economic differences added to the unease felt by some girls of color. Although some of the first black students were from professional families, they had nowhere near the wealth of their elite white classmates—they didn't vacation in Europe, or have housekeepers, or own houses with pools. At the same time, attending a private school could distance them from their old friends at home. "I got quite a bit of grief from other African-Americans," said Monica Simmons Hammonds, who graduated from Ashley Hall in Charleston, South Carolina, in 1976. "They'd say, 'Oh, you're one of THOSE, you must be this rich snotty person if you're going to that lily-white snobby rich-girls' school.'"

Some girls responded to this host of pressures by rallying around their racial identity and organizing a black student association. Their efforts helped push schools to admit more girls of color, seek out faculty of color, and reevaluate the curriculum. Other girls in this first generation responded by going full speed ahead academically but walling themselves off emotionally. School was their "job"—something they did to get ahead in life and to help their family—but home was the real center of their lives. Kumea Shorter-Gooden, the Madeira student from Washington, did well academically at school. She had friends and was a leader in extracurricular activities. But in other ways, she always felt apart. She felt silently ashamed by a history textbook that described Africans as primitive people; she was embarrassed by classmates' questions about her hair; she remained amazed by a world in which girls brought their own horses to school. Her social life remained rooted mainly in the black community. "There is a way in which I wasn't fully invested," she said. "I was partly there but not fully there. It's a kind of disengagement. In part it's a survival mechanism, but there's also a loss when you're not fully there."

## Coeducation Rising

Schools of all kinds—coed and single-sex, public and private—found themselves reeling a bit in the late 1960s and early '70s as their old ways of doing things were suddenly up for question and challenge. But girls' schools felt the ground beneath their feet become particularly shaky. They didn't just worry about pot-smoking students or recruitment of minorities—they began questioning their fundamental identity as single-sex institutions.

Coeducation seemed to be the wave of the future. More than at any time since the late 1800s, there were strong societal pressures to convert single-sex institutions into coeducational ones. Prestigious male colleges like Harvard, Yale, and Princeton were making headlines by going coed, offering not just coed classes but coed dormitories and even bathrooms. Young people wanted to be around members of the opposite sex. Women were starting to seek access to male arenas that had long been closed to them, demanding acceptance in traditionally male professions, sports, social clubs, and schools. Students were insisting that their colleges and schools become part of the "real world"—and the "real world" was decidedly not composed of a single gender. At the same time, young people were making more of the decisions when it came to their own education. Private schools had to market themselves not just to parents, but to teenagers. And teenagers—surprise!—wanted to be around members of the opposite sex.

The pressure to go coed typically hit boys' schools first. Boys' schools were often perceived as superior to nearby girls' schools, with good reason—they had bigger endowments, better-paid faculty, more spacious campuses, and vastly superior sports facilities. Trustees and administrators at private boys' schools started wondering whether it was fair to exclude girls. They also saw some pragmatic reasons to go coed. Not enough top-notch applicants? Opening yourself up to girls would automatically double the size of your applicant pool. And being coed would make you more attractive to potential male applicants, too.

As boys' schools started going coed, this created a major enrollment problem for girls' schools. With their greater prestige and superior financial resources, newly coed boys' schools started to attract the most promising female students—even if their mothers were girls' school alumnae with fond memories. "In the seventies and up through the eighties, you couldn't get women who'd been here in the fifties to send their kids," said Trudy Hanmer, assistant head at Emma Willard. "If an Emma Willard alumna married a man who went to Deerfield, the daughter went to Deerfield."

Concord Academy, a Massachusetts girls' boarding school founded in 1919, exemplified the pressures on girls' schools. The school had a history of fund-raising troubles: A 1950s campaign had set a goal of $1.5 million but reached only $799,000 by 1969. On top of the financial worries came enrollment worries as nearby boys' boarding schools like Groton, St. Paul's, and Exeter considered coeducation. "I thought we were going to be a second-rate institution if we didn't do anything," said David Aloian, who had been hired in 1963 as the school's first male head. "One option was to stay the way we were. But if we did, we would experience a slow deterioration. We would get fewer and fewer applicants; the quality would go down; and we would become a second-class school, when we had been—academically and in terms of support and quality of students—first-class." In 1970, consultants reported to the board that there would be a "heavy increase" in the school's annual deficit if it remained all girls. The board voted 17–4 for coeducation. One dissenting board member resigned. In 1971, the school became coed with a class of twenty-six boys and sixty-two girls.

Around the country, the number of single-sex schools dwindled. In 1965–66, there were 1,132 private girls' schools and 961 private boys' schools nationally. By 1978–79, that number had fallen by half—to 551 girls' schools and 499 boys' schools. Some girls' schools simply went out of business. Others took Concord Academy's path and admitted boys. But this was easier said than done. Boys and their families typically insisted on better sports facilities than were available at most girls' schools, so girls' schools had to commit themselves to a major capital investment in gyms and playing fields if they wanted to attract boys. But those girls' schools considering coeducation were often doing so because they were in shaky financial shape—not able to make that kind of multimillion-dollar investment. Presentation High School, a century-old Catholic girls' school in Berkeley, California, briefly considered and rejected admitting boys as a solution to its financial troubles in the mid-'70s. "Attracting boys to a school traditionally identified as a 'girls' school' appears to be far more difficult than attracting girls to a previously all-boys school," one Presentation report concluded. "Boys' schools'

*The last graduation at Ferry Hall in June 1974, just before its merger with all-boy Lake Forest Academy*

athletic traditions undoubtedly contribute to this factor, as does the more general problem of 'image.'"

Another alternative was merging with a boys' school. Through the late '60s and '70s, the independent school world saw a spate of hyphenated names and institutional marriages. In Minnesota, all-girls Summit School merged with nearby St. Paul Academy in 1969 to became St. Paul Academy and Summit School. In Indianapolis, Tudor Hall joined with the Park School for Boys in 1970 to become Park Tudor. Northfield Seminary in Massachusetts became North-field Mt. Hermon in 1971. Miss Beard's School in New Jersey be-came the Morristown-Beard School, while the Everglades School for Girls in Florida became Everglades Ransom . . . In fact, hyphenated names were only part of the picture. Many schools merged but kept only one name—typically the name of the boys' school. In the Chicago suburbs, a 105-year-old girls' school named Ferry Hall merged with the nearby boys' school in 1974 and became Lake Forest Academy. In Massachusetts, Abbot Academy became part of its much larger neighbor, Phillips Andover—or as some disgruntled Abbot alumnae put it, their school was "devoured" by Andover.

## Eating Abbot Academy

Abbot had enjoyed a siblinglike relationship with Andover from its start in 1828, when the treasurer of Andover was one of five citizens who got together to start a school for girls. However, by the 1960s, Andover's resources completely dwarfed Abbot's. Andover had a sprawling hilltop campus that covered 600 acres, compared to Ab-bot's approximately 45 acres. Andover had three times as many stu-dents as Abbot. And Andover's endowment of $64.7 million in 1972 was 28 times the size of Abbot's endowment.

Abbot's board chair—a man—had long wanted to see the two schools merge. When applications to Abbot dwindled to two appli-cants for every opening, the board initiated major changes at the school. It hired Donald Gordon, a thirty-three-year-old administra-tor who had recently taken a Kansas City girls' school coed, and told him that his job was to get Abbot ready for a merger. "You're going to merge yourself right out of a job," the board chair told Gordon, as reported by Susan McIntosh Lloyd in her very thorough history of Abbot.

Gordon instituted a variety of changes at the school that started to attract more applicants. Some faculty felt the school's fortunes were beginning to rebound. But the locomotive of coeducation was already steaming ahead. The dean of Andover expressed the view of a growing number of private-school educators when he said in 1970, "As the roles of men and women become less differentiated, differentiated education loses its validity. . . . The separation of the sexes in secondary boarding schools is a kind of hiatus in the normal process of growth . . . at odds with the experience of all but a tiny minority of the American population. . . ." In 1969, Abbot and Andover started allowing students to cross-register for classes, an arrangement known there and at other schools as "coordination." Students liked the arrangement: By 1971, 193 girls were taking classes up at Andover and 327 boys were enrolled in classes down the hill at Abbot. In 1972, Andover hired a new headmaster—former Harvard education school dean Theodore Sizer—who was a strong advocate of coeducation. And in 1973 trustees of the two schools agreed on a merger that ended Abbot's history as an institution. Abbot sold all its assets to Andover for $1. The combined school kept the Andover name and retained Sizer as its head. Three Abbot trustees were invited to join Andover's eighteen-member board. Most of the academic departments at the combined school were headed by Andover men. Male faculty outnumbered female by about five to one.

The merger was far from a marriage of equals. "Phillips Academy ATE Abbott," one alumna complained. "Merger it was not, rather a complete takeover, lock, stock, and barrel," wrote Abbot trustee Jane Baldwin, a member of the class of 1922. But Abbot had little choice. "The Board [*sic*] would accept it," wrote Susan McIntosh Lloyd, "because Abbot's five-year financial projections showed that the smaller school had only two alternatives: an ever-increasing deficit or an ever-increasing tuition. . . . If Abbot refused the Phillips terms and the larger school backed away from coordination to take in its own girls, the future looked grimmer still."

In the wake of coeducation, women faced some rocky years at Andover. Sizer, the headmaster, made genuine efforts to welcome girls into the school. But about one-third of the Abbot faculty were dismissed as part of the merger, while nearly all the Andover faculty were kept on. "It was a massacre, I don't care how much you gloss it over," said Stephanie Perrin, a former Abbot teacher who today is head of the coed Walnut Hill School. Boys initially outnumbered girls by about 70 percent to 30 percent. Girls had to struggle to gain equal access in areas like sports. A 1979 study by the New England Association of Schools and Colleges criticized the school for not taking into account the different needs of boys and girls: "Andover is still a boys' school with girls who are students," it said.

The school did take steps to keep a flicker of Abbot's history alive. It set up an internal foundation called the Abbot Academy Association to fund projects related to Abbot's traditions, such as student counseling, innovative teaching, and projects relating to female students. In 1999, the school held a symposium looking at twenty-five years of coeducation. In 1994, the school hired its first female head—Barbara Landis Chase, who came directly from the Bryn Mawr School, the pioneering girls' college preparatory school in Baltimore.

Today's coeducational Andover is a thriving institution. The number of girls now equals the number of boys. The total numbers of male and female faculty are also roughly equal—although if you limit your count to full-time teachers, there are still three men for every two women. For girls as well as boys, attending the school is an unparalleled academic opportunity, like being at a younger version of an Ivy League college. Students choose from some three hundred courses, including classes on Milton's *Paradise Lost,* James Joyce, Literature of the American Suburb, and Contemporary Caribbean Literature. They can study Chinese, French, German, Greek, Italian, Japanese, Latin, Russian, or Spanish. In their spare time they can work at the campus radio station, commune with nature at the sixty-five-acre bird sanctuary, visit the school's art gallery and its archeology museum, or stretch their muscles on one of the two hockey rinks, two swimming pools, eight squash courts, eighteen tennis courts, or eighteen playing fields. Not many American high schools can boast of a $455-million endowment, or a scholarship fund set up in honor of alumnus George Herbert Walker Bush with the help of a $500,000 contribution from a Saudi prince.

But today's Andover is not so different from other coeducational high schools—or from society in general—when it comes to the status of female students. Girls tend not to be chosen for top leadership positions: Just four of the past twenty-six student-body presidents have been girls. Boys' sporting events typically draw more attention and bigger crowds than do girls' events. There was a small brouhaha shortly before I visited Andover in the 2000–2001 school year when some male students commented on a campus radio show that girls only used the weight room to show off their spandex. There was another brouhaha that year when a female student wrote an opinion piece in the school newspaper about how younger girls were servicing older boys with oral sex in a misguided effort to be popular. The piece was titled "On Your Knees, Eleanor Roosevelts." "There is a discrepancy at this school between the way girls act during the week and they way they act on the weekends," student Elizabeth Edmonds wrote. "Be clever during the week, but be sexy and likeable on the weekends. Be assertive, but be congenial. . . . With all their talents, intelligence and capabilities, women at Andover should not have to resort to oral sex in order to receive attention and social eclat."

Barbara Chase, with her years of experience at the Bryn Mawr School, is more sensitive than many school heads to issues of sexism and bias against girls. She admits there is a problem with the lack of girls in leadership positions, but isn't sure what to do about it. Overall, Chase believes, coeducation has been an enormous success for both girls and boys at Andover. The occasional run-ins over sexist comments or behavior are just part of life in twenty-first-century America. "Disrespectful language on radio stations or in rap music— we fight it here, we talk about it, but it would be a miracle if it weren't here," Chase said.

## A Different Path

Dennis Collins arrived at the Emma Willard School under circumstances similar to Donald Gordon's at Abbot. Both schools were greatly in need of an overhaul to keep up with the changing culture of the 1960s. Both schools were seeing a dangerous dwindling of applicants. Both schools had chosen young men—Collins was just twenty-nine—to take their helm at this troubled time. And both instructed their new headmaster to take a look at coeducation as a solution. "I arrived, green green green in the spring of 1970, and the charge of the board was, 'Do something about this issue of coeducation,'" recalled Collins, a former college administrator who had never worked at a prep school until he came to Emma Willard. "Those who'd been thoughtful were aware that this [trend toward coeducation] was a significant event. It was complicated by the fact that for several decades prior, we had not been enjoying a bountiful supply of applications. No one was quite sure how it was all going to unfold, but they were aware that in education circles the mood and tone was coeducational. Single-sex was seen as a little peculiar. The question was, 'So what did this mean for Emma Willard?'"

Collins spent a lot of time visiting other campuses to see how they were handling the various roads to coeducation. He looked at the possibility of admitting boys to Emma Willard but was discouraged by the difficulties of formerly female colleges like Vassar in overcoming the image of a "women's school" and recruiting top male applicants. Collins also looked at a coordinate model, where nearby girls' and boys' schools adopted a system of cross-registration for classes and extracurricular activities. But that option was complicated by Emma Willard's location in Troy, New York—far away from the bulk of comparable boys' boarding schools in Connecticut and Massachusetts. "I remember my visit to Hotchkiss, where the head's wife was an Emma Willard alumna," Collins said. "The head waltzed me around the campus and said, 'This is where we would put Emma Willard.' I said, 'My God, I don't think anyone wants to board up our beautiful Gothic campus and be put in low-rise buildings.'"

Emma Willard's board of trustees set up a committee to consider coeducation in 1970. The group surveyed alumnae, teachers, students, parents, and potential applicants about their thoughts on the matter. The alumnae were divided, with younger alumnae more likely to favor coeducation. The faculty also seemed divided. Students and potential applicants, meanwhile, were overwhelmingly in favor of coeducation: Fewer than one in twenty potential applicants said they liked the idea of a single-sex school.

But the trustee committee also found that coeducation was not the main factor applicants considered when choosing a school. Most said their primary concern was finding a school that would help them get into college and give them a chance to choose their own courses. The experience of existing coeducational schools provided an additional counterbalance. The committee surveyed fifty-five coed schools and colleges and found that 90 percent of the student body presidents were boys, while more than 80 percent of the student body secretaries were girls.

In the end, the committee found itself divided into two camps based less on the data they'd gathered than on their philosophical views. "Some of us feel that coeducation will eventually come to Emma Willard whether we like it or not," the committee report said. "These same people and others feel that the advantages of coeducation outweigh the disadvantages . . . Others feel that there is a job to be done in educating women, that we have been committed to the task and that we should continue to be." The board chairman felt the school should go coed for marketing reasons. Collins was opposed and said that a decision to take the school coed would give him the right to reconsider his contract.

The board ultimately resolved things by agreeing that—whatever they felt about coeducation—this was not the right moment for Emma Willard to make such a momentous change. The school was just starting to implement a radical new curriculum; it was also grappling with how to integrate minority students and how to interact with the community of Troy. "Part of our considerations must be with the unfinished jobs that the School is now dealing with," the committee wrote. "This brings the coeducation proponents to the 'not now' position."

The board did recommend continuing to explore what it would take for the school to do a successful job in adding boys. And over the next few years, Emma Willard tried several exchange programs with boys' schools—one with the Thacher School in southern California and one with Deerfield Academy in Massachusetts. But both programs ended when the boys' schools decided to go fully coeducational by admitting their own girls. By the mid-'70s, Emma Willard had quietly moved past the question of coeducation and settled back into its traditional identity as an institution for girls. "These experiences [with Thacher and Deerfield] just solidified Emma Willard's hard-nosed position that we were destined to remain a women's institution," Collins said. "There was a very strong sense of history there, and a deeply seated feeling that we ought not abandon that. It was a courageous decision—it ran in the face of trends pointing the other way."

Over the next two decades, the school's sense of itself as a female institution grew even stronger. Emma Willard offered one of the country's first high school courses in women's studies in 1972. Emilia Benjamin, a member of the class of 1974, remembers being taken to New York City on an exhilarating kind of feminist field trip—the girls visited an abortion clinic, a women's theater company, a day-care center. "We ended up somehow talking to Puerto Rican separatists on a rooftop," Benjamin said. "I don't know if our teacher would have called it women's liberation, but the whole weekend was on women's issues."

The school began rediscovering its own important role in women's history. School officials erected a plaque in honor of alumna Elizabeth Cady Stanton and arranged to have the school placed on the Register of Historic Places. They collaborated with the city of Troy in rededicating a century-old statue of Emma Willard near the school's original downtown site. They gathered up copies of a nineteenth-century history of the school that had lain moldering in lounges, and built up a professional-quality archive. Marcie Easterling, an English teacher who arrived at Emma Willard in the late 1960s, remembers "being treated as a weirdo when I first came here, because I was really interested in the history of the school." But now, she said, "we celebrate it."

The school reached out to feminist psychologist Carol Gilligan in the early 1980s and convinced her to do a research project on its students that turned into a book, *Making Connections: The Relational World of Girls at the Emma Willard School.* The collaboration with Gilligan further strengthened the school's sense of itself. Teachers started suddenly understanding why girls acted in particular ways, and how their teaching styles could take gender into account. In the early 1990s, Emma Willard went out on a limb and purchased a series of feisty advertisements in the *New York Times* touting the benefits of an all-girls education. The ads shattered the long-standing reluctance among private girls' schools to publicly promote themselves. They set tongues wagging among the coed schools that were Emma Willard's rivals. They were one of the first blows in a battle for survival by girls' schools that ultimately helped create a new wave of interest across America in single-sex education.

# 7

# Revival

## SEEKING STUDENTS AND TEACHERS

*As we moved through the year before our opening, we spread word about Julia Morgan everywhere we thought we might find potential students. We continued to distribute flyers in places where girls congregated—elementary schools, soccer teams, ballet classes. We held informational meetings in libraries and churches in both rich and poor neighborhoods. Parents and girls peppered us with questions at these meetings:* Would we hire male teachers? Would we have a uniform? Would there be a student council? How would we keep boys from becoming 'forbidden fruit'? Would we be too insular and precious? Would we have an instrumental-music program? How much homework would there be? *A Berkeley fifth-grader named Clare Kelly came to one of our meetings with her mother and was intrigued.* "People sounded so excited about making the school, not like it was their job," *said Clare, who became part of our founding class.* "My mom has two sisters and our family is mainly women, so this kind of reminded me of that. . . . I was thinking about how nice it would be to go to a smaller school, really smaller. I got really excited."

Our outreach brought a call from a group called the I Have a Dream Foundation, which had "adopted" a class of inner-city elementary school children and promised to put them through college if they graduated from high school. That class was now about to enter sixth grade, and the foundation was worried that some of the kids wouldn't make it through the large, anonymous middle school in their neighborhood: Would we be willing to take a couple of their girls? We got another call from a science teacher in a mostly Latino public elementary school. She believed that Julia Morgan was just what some of her girls needed— believed it so much that she personally drove the girls to their admissions interviews, and filled out the application forms with them.

By the spring we had enrolled thirty girls, eight of whom needed financial aid. That was enough to open our doors, if we could raise some money for scholarships. Ann set to work trying to hire top-notch teachers with our shoestring budget. She convinced a sympathetic staffperson at a teacher-recruitment firm to let us use his service for free. As wife of the head of an established school, she gained free entrance into a national hiring conference where private schools look for teachers: She removed her "spouse" name tag, flipped it over, wrote "Director of the Julia Morgan School for Girls," and got busy recruiting. We all knew our teaching staff would be critical to the success of the school, more important even than the site. If we had great teachers, students would flourish even in a living room. If we had lousy or uninspired teachers, the nicest campus in the world wouldn't help.

The founding staff that Ann assembled was young, creative, passionate about the subjects they'd be teaching, and a bit unorthodox. Our technology director was Katie Topper, a thirty-four-year-old software marketing professional who was trying to switch careers into teaching. Our social studies/language arts teacher was Kristen Brookes, a twenty-nine-year-old drama therapist who had been a feminist as long as she could remember, writing term papers on Queen Hatshepsut in sixth grade and Willa Cather in ninth grade. Our art teacher was twenty-eight-year-old Michele Levesque, a sculptor who was teaching art one day a week and working in a fish market to pay the rent.

Hiring teachers for a school that didn't yet exist presented some challenges. Private schools often evaluate teacher candidates by having them visit and teach a class. But we had no existing students for them to teach. In Katie Topper's case, Ann arranged to observe her teaching a sample computer class at the Katherine Delmar Burke School, a girls' school in San Francisco. It was a somewhat weird situation for Katie—teaching a strange group of girls in a strange school in front of her potential boss, who was also a stranger to that school. At one point Katie noticed Ann scowling and assumed she wouldn't be hired. Much later, she learned that Ann had been scowling because she was looking at the rolling chairs in the computer lab and wondering how we could get chairs like that for Julia Morgan.

Ann didn't need to borrow somebody else's class to observe Kristen: She had watched her in action during admissions season. Kristen had been captivated by the idea of Julia Morgan and volunteered to help create an admissions process that would let us know our applicants on a deeper level than test scores or essay-writing skills. Together she and Ann developed a series of group activities based on Kristen's drama therapy work that were both fun and revealing. Girls formed a "circle of strength" in which each one was asked to name a personal strength she would bring to this new school—characteristics like honesty, friendship, or truthfulness. They sculpted each other's bodies into "statues" representing things that excited them. They were given brightly colored scarves to wear, and then told to think of their scarf as one of the qualities they dreamed of in this new school. The girls cited things such as friendship, beauty, safety, field trips, music, and honesty. Then Ann and Kristen laid the scarves down side by side into a long path. "We are starting something new, we are all pioneers, and these are the bricks we will need as we make this journey," they said.

Those activities became a permanent part of the Julia Morgan admissions process, along with more standard evaluation measures such as tests and teacher references. They helped define the culture of the school—this was a place where girls' values and inner thoughts were as important as grammar and math. The activities excited and inspired the girls, which was particularly important that first year when we had no classes for them to visit. They gave Ann a way to evaluate how girls handled group work, which would be a central part of the Julia Morgan experience. They also led to a teaching job for Kristen. "When I started to realize how magical our admissions process was, that's what I wanted for the school," Ann said. Kristen got married shortly before Julia Morgan started and spent her honeymoon in Italy cramming for her new job—reading books about teaching and about ancient civilizations, the social studies unit she would be teaching to our new sixth-graders.

Our math/science instructor was supposed to be that public school teacher who had helped her Latina students apply to Julia Morgan. Ann and her new staff gathered in August and hunkered down for the intense challenge of creating an entire sixth-grade program from scratch. But two days into their planning, the math/science teacher was offered a senior position in the public schools. She quit. It was August, one month until opening, and we had nobody to teach half of our curriculum.

This was one of those moments when Julia Morgan herself might have been looking down from heaven and sending us luck. The math/science teacher casually mentioned quitting her Julia Morgan job to one of her neighbors, a young woman named Teri Putnam, who was also a teacher and had worked at a girls' school in Hawaii. Teri mentioned that she might be interested in the job. Within one hour, she had a call from Ann. That same day, she was invited in for a group interview by Ann and the other teachers. Teri was underwhelmed, to say the least, by the physical setting. "It was a mess," she recalled. "There were all these file cabinets. It looked like a business office, a crappy business office with lousy furniture that had been donated. Part of me was laughing at them—You're going to start a school with this? Another part of me was saying, 'These women and their vision are amazing. I have to jump on this.'" The next day, Ann offered Teri the job and she accepted.

The founding team of teachers quickly gelled into tight friends and colleagues. Their brainstorming together made it possible to create a genuinely integrated curriculum. Many schools claim to help students see connections between subjects, but few actually do it. During that month of planning, our teachers created a sixth-grade curriculum in which girls would learn about ancient civilizations in social studies, read a novel about an archeologist's daughter in English, study geology in science, create their own cave paintings in art, and make primitive

*instruments out of rocks and gourds in music. It was an incredible cur-
riculum. The teachers were completely energized. Only later did it oc-
cur to Teri that, at age twenty-six, and with only four years of classroom
experience under her belt, she had more on-the-job experience than any
of the other founding teachers at Julia Morgan.*

The makers of M&M's candies and Mars bars were looking for a catchy way to promote their latest product, a candy bar called Twix with a cookies-and-cream flavor. They opted for a lighthearted good news/bad news approach. A TV commercial started airing in spring 1991 that showed a girl sitting behind a stairway railing that resembled prison bars, while a woman's voice said, "Honey, your dad and I think you should attend an all-girls school." "Bad news!" declared the narrator, who then went on to add that the good news was the cookies-and-cream flavor inside Twix.

M&M/Mars got a different kind of publicity than it had anticipated. Its ad triggered a protest campaign by a newly formed coalition of girls' schools. The group immediately shot off a telegram to Mars saying they "were deeply disturbed and disappointed . . . The image of the girl behind bars associates a girls' school with a prison. Obviously, you and your advertising agency are uninformed about girls' schools and the opportunities they afford young women." The group demanded that Mars executives pull the ad and visit a girls' school to talk with students and alumnae about the value of single-sex education. It also asked students and parents to boycott all M&M/Mars products until the ad was withdrawn. Some schools like the Agnes Irwin School in Philadelphia had their students start removing M&M and Mars candies from their cafeteria vending machines—an image that was bound to draw TV news cameras like bears to honey.

Mars's marketing people may have been caught unawares, but they weren't stupid. They realized that images of angry eleven-year-old girls throwing candy in the trash was not what they wanted to see on the evening news. Just hours after the coalition started its campaign, Mars dropped the commercial. The *Wall Street Journal* did a short feature story on the brouhaha that recycled some of the old stereotypes but also made the schools' clout clear to all. "Some day," the *Journal* piece began, "marketers will learn not to poke fun at groups that are tougher than they are—such as oh-so-proper private schools for girls."*

The Twix campaign was a baptism by fire for that new organization of girls' schools, called the National Coalition of Girls' Schools. NCGS had officially formed just a few months earlier—an attempt by schools to counter the negative images and outdated stereotypes that were making it harder and harder for them to fill their classrooms. The 1980s had been a tough decade for private girls' schools, many of which were suffering from a slump in applications. Part of the problem was demographic. America's postwar baby boom ended in the early 1960s, which meant that the total pool of high-school-aged kids in America started shrinking in 1976 and didn't begin growing again until 1991. Private schools of all kinds were competing for a smaller pot of kids each year. On top of this, girls' schools had to contend with the allure of coeducation—in particular, the allure of prestigious boys' schools that had recently started admitting girls. The problem was particularly severe for girls' boarding schools. Fewer parents wanted to send their kids away to school than in past decades, and fewer kids wanted to go. Pam Clarke felt the crunch personally when she was head of the all-girl Masters School in the 1990s. The school—a boarding and day school that once had an enrollment of 350—was down to 186 girls. It was losing $1 million a year on a budget of just $6 million. Clarke's admissions staff was

---

*Ironically, Mars's chief executive was a supporter of girls' schools. All of Forrest Mars's daughters had attended girls' schools, and one of them was even a trustee at Foxcroft at the time the commercial ran. The incident left Mary Lou Leipheimer, the head of Foxcroft and a founding member of the National Coalition of Girls' Schools, in a delicate position. But over time, the damage was repaired. In 1998, the Mars family donated $1 million to Foxcroft to create two merit scholarships, including one for science and math.

having trouble getting girls to consider the school, let alone choose it: Only 10 percent of girls taking the SSAT (Secondary School Admissions Test) said they would consider a single-sex school. "We were scrambling to get a market share of 10 percent of girls—that's just 5 percent of all students," Clarke recalled. "When I was a kid, all boarding schools were either for boys or girls. Now we were the odd man out. If you were a kid seeing your friends at the country club, you had to justify why you were going to a single-sex school. . . . We were certainly scraping the barrel, and anyone who tells you differently is lying." The Masters School couldn't afford to keep losing that kind of money indefinitely, and in 1996 made the dramatic decision to admit boys. "It always comes down to money," Clarke said. "We just didn't have enough money to get the school through the demographic slump of the 1980s."

Miss Porter's was another school that, like Masters, found itself struggling simply to get applicants' attention. Admissions staff constantly had to parry comments like "Oh, you don't have any boys here" or "Oh, you're not in touch with the real world." Applicants would visit Miss Porter's as the token girls' school on a list of a half dozen prestigious formerly male boarding schools. "They would go off to Choate, Hotchkiss, or Kent, and not really consider Miss Porter's," said Rachel Belash, head of Miss Porter's in the 1980s. "Girls' schools were at the bottom of the heap. It really made me annoyed. I don't like being on a losing team."

If Belash had little affinity for being on a losing team, she had even less interest in simply sitting around and passively complaining. A native of Wales who still has a clipped British accent, Belash had received a Ph.D. in Spanish literature and worked as a banking executive before becoming head of Miss Porter's in 1983. In 1987, she organized a group of about thirty girls' boarding schools to figure out a joint marketing strategy. The group hired consultants to do a comprehensive study of how girls' schools were viewed by potential applicants. Although some schools had done their own small marketing efforts, this was much larger and more thoroughly researched—and, at $40,000, more expensive. It was a dramatic departure for schools that, a few decades earlier, would have found it gauche even to take out a newspaper advertisement. "We [at girls' schools] all knew we were doing well educationally, but none of us would have ever thought about marketing or bragging," said Mary Lou Leipheimer, head of Foxcroft. "Educators are 'above' that—this is not supposed to be an 'industry.' And women traditionally have not talked about money. All of us were severely underenrolled, and none of us knew what to do."

The consultants surveyed about three hundred families enrolled in girls' boarding schools and another three hundred that had inquired about the schools but declined to apply. Their conclusions were not exactly unexpected, but they showcased the problem with stark clarity: Families with daughters attending girls' schools loved their schools, but outsiders viewed them through a negative, outdated lens.

"The myth out there was that girls *didn't* love their high schools— that these places were ivory towers of girls in white gloves serving tea," said Whitney Ransome, a former girls' school admissions director who was one of the consultants. "It was as much a misperception problem as anything else. The reality of how we'd changed was not as well documented as the image of double-strand pearls, riding horses, and pouring tea."

Ransome and her colleagues drew up a public-relations strategy to turn the schools' image around. Girls' boarding schools should emphasize the strength of their math and science programs, they said. They should beef up their athletic programs. Most importantly, though, they should stop trying to copy coed schools and instead show pride in the benefits of a single-sex education. "The tone . . . should be one of opportunity and optimism, of excitement and anticipation. It should reflect an air of active offense instead of passive defense," they wrote.

The boarding schools' efforts were being watched closely by headmistresses at girls' private day schools. They too formed an organization, and in 1991 the two groups merged to form the National Coalition of Girls' Schools. They hired Whitney Ransome and Meg Milne Moulton, another of the consultants from the boarding school study. They contracted with one of the most prestigious public-relations firms in New York, the Howard Rubenstein agency. When the Twix commercial appeared on TV that spring, the coalition was new, untested, but ready to spring into action.

## Transformations

NCGS's mission was to promote a new, updated image of girls' schools, but this was more than just a glossy coat of paint. Girls' schools genuinely *had* changed in the 1970s and 1980s.

Girls' schools started presenting their students with career role models before anyone thought of "Take Your Daughters to Work Day." They sank millions of dollars into new sports complexes and science buildings. They began developing curricula to address issues such as eating disorders, sexual pressures, and distorted media images of girls and women. They started gradually opening their doors to students of different racial and class backgrounds. They threw out—or, more often, gently ushered out—old traditions that no longer made sense. Perhaps most significantly, inspired by emerging research on girls' psychological growth, they developed a renewed sense of mission and confidence.

Career education was the first of these changes to emerge. Even back in the era of Emma Willard and Sarah Porter, schools had loved to show off successful alumnae to their students. But in the 1970s, working women began talking publicly about their need for mentors and role models. Girls' schools realized that their alumnae files offered a treasure trove of role models who could open students' eyes to new career options. "We had a constant stream of assembly speakers—women in careers, women in law, women in science," recalled Evy Halpert, who was head of Brearley from 1975 to 1997. "One out of every three special days was on women's careers. I started and ran an extracurricular course on careers in medicine. We also had our fair share of truly silly assembly speakers on deeply silly aspects of the women's movement, including one who came in and talked about how she'd changed her name from Cooperman to Cooperperson."

Along with career education, girls' schools began gradually revising their curricula in the 1970s and '80s to include the experience of women and minorities—adding writers like Toni Morrison to literature classes and making sure that history courses covered topics such as the suffrage movement and the life experience of slaves in the antebellum South. These changes usually started with a handful of young teachers whose own eyes had been opened by the women's movement. "I asked the hard questions and I never let up: 'You mean you are teaching this course and the writers are all men?'" recalled Deborah Dempsey, former head of the English department at the Springside School in Philadelphia. "You had to seduce, cajole, suggest—show people how much more fun it is to be exploring something rather than teaching everything the same way you were taught."

Including more women in the curriculum was hardly limited to girls' schools—schools and colleges around the country were opening up the canon during the 1970s and '80s to include women and minorities. But girls' schools often did it earlier and more passionately than coed schools. As all-female institutions, they were particularly sensitive to the presence or absence of women in the curriculum. That in turn made them receptive to including other underrepresented groups like ethnic minorities. "We talked a lot about questions of pedagogy, gender, balancing the curriculum," said Brendan Burns, a history teacher at Miss Porter's since 1975. "We tried to become more leading-edge in addressing questions of race, class, and gender. I gave some talks at conferences including one at Choate in the early 1990s, thinking this was old hat. But people came up to me like this was water in the desert, asking 'How did you get your school to let you do this?'"

Girls' schools also reevaluated their math and science programs in the wake of the women's movement. Up through the 1970s, many schools had let these subjects quietly languish while taking pride in their offerings in English or art. Schools sometimes required only a year or two of high school math; science labs were often outdated and hidden away in a basement. At Ashley Hall in Charleston, South Carolina, calculus wasn't even offered until 1981, although the school provided electives in typing, studio art, ceramics, music, sewing, and advancing sewing. "It was taken for granted that girls would do very well in French, Spanish, and Latin, and would take art history—all our best girls did splendidly in those subjects," said Springside's Deborah Dempsey. "If you found a kind of grimly determined girl who did a lot of science, you thought, 'Isn't that nice,' but it wasn't expected of them."

Shrugging off math and science became increasingly untenable in an era in which women were entering the ranks of engineers, doctors, and astronauts. Individual teachers at girls' schools began experimenting with ways to get their students jazzed up about math and science. Parents began seeking strong math and science programs for their daughters. Even the most conservative girls' schools couldn't ignore the glistening new chemistry labs and AP calculus courses that were being offered by the coed competition. Girls' schools jumped onto the math-and-science bandwagon with a vengeance and turned what had been a weakness into a strength.

The Westover School, a boarding school in Connecticut, is a good example of how girls' schools transformed their math and science programs. When a young calculus teacher named Ann Pollina arrived at Westover in 1972, she found that most girls stopped taking math after their sophomore year. Out of a student body of two hundred, there were only two girls signed up for calculus. Pollina embarked on a crusade to keep girls doing math. She experimented with new teaching methods—bringing in works of art and quilts to show geometrical ideas, giving the girls more hands-on activities, encouraging them to write essays and notes about the process of doing math problems. Gradually, the number of girls taking math started to rise. The school invested in a $3-million new math and science complex in the early 1980s. Pollina helped organize a national conference on math and science for girls that was sponsored by NCGS in June 1991. Today, Pollina is head of Westover and about 70 percent of her students take calculus—enough to fill three sections each year. "The math department was very deliberate about our teaching strategies and spent a lot of time talking about how we teach," Pollina said. "We adopted strategies that made math very accessible. Then, once it's accessible and girls feel they are successful at something hard, they

*Marymount (N.Y.) students and Sister Kathleen Fagan, head of the school, celebrate construction of a new science wing, 1994.*

get excited about it. Now our math program runs under its own weight. Students look at the kids two or three years ahead of them and see them taking calculus and assume that's what they'll do too. No one looks at them strangely and says, 'Calculus, huh?'"

Along with math and science, competitive sports also got a makeover in the '80s. Through much of the century, girls' schools had offered more opportunities for female athletes than did coed schools, typically fielding teams in sports such as basketball, field hockey, tennis, and swimming. But these sports often had a genteel sheen. Girls were encouraged to play for fun rather than pushed to win.

The passage of Title IX of the Education Amendments in 1972 was the beginning of a revolution in women's sports, both for girls' schools and nationally. As the women's movement spread in the late 1960s and early '70s, Congress came under pressure to adopt laws barring sex discrimination in education. Title IX was modeled on the Civil Rights Act of 1964, which had banned discrimination on the basis of race, color, and national origin. It promised that "no person in the United States shall, on the basis of sex, be excluded from participation in, be denied the benefits of, or be subjected to discrimination under any education program or activity receiving Federal financial assistance." In the area of sports, Title IX required public schools to take girls' athletics as seriously as boys'—to give girls equal time on the courts and fields, to provide them with comparable coaching and competitive opportunities. Gradually, coed public schools started fostering serious competitive female athletes. Colleges started offering athletic scholarships to young women as well as men. The total number of high school girls involved in sports rose from 300,000 in 1971 to 2.4 million in 1996—from 7.5 percent of all high school athletes to 39 percent.

In response to the surge of interest in women's sports, girls' schools beefed up their own athletic programs and facilities. In 1980, the Baldwin School in Philadelphia offered about two team sports per season with one coach per team. Today it offers five or six sports each season with two or three coaches per team, along with specialty coaches for things like pitching and catching. St. Catherine's School in Richmond used an old garage as its gym in the 1970s. Today it is building an $18-million sports facility with three basketball courts, an eight-lane pool, a 4,000-square-foot fitness center, and a hydrotherapy and training room. Joyce Rainwater arrived as a coach at the Hockaday School in Dallas in 1976 to find a mere skeleton of an interscholastic sports program. The school offered just a handful of sports—tennis, basketball, volleyball, and field hockey. The basket-

*Field hockey players at the Laurel School (Ohio), 1975*

ball team played about four games a year. Hockaday didn't have the position of an athletic director. "When I arrived, there was a self-image as losers," recalled Rainwater, who passed away in 2001. "There had never been a winning team. They didn't know what it was to be disciplined and push yourself to the highest level. But we went up to our tournament and beat a big basketball team. When we came back, the girls were so elated. From that point, volleyball picked up, field hockey picked up." Today Hockaday offers thirteen interscholastic sports—cross-country, fencing, golf, crew, lacrosse, and soccer, along with more traditional sports like basketball. There are thirteen full-time physical-education staff and another fifteen part-time coaches. The school has three basketball courts, two racquetball courts, three playing fields, ten tennis courts, a pool, track, and dance studio. Hockaday recently added a fitness center that would allow it to begin a weight-training program. In 2003, twelve members of the graduating class were recruited to play college athletics in nine different sports.

## Broadening Their Base

Along with the various curricular changes, girls' schools began opening their doors in the 1980s and '90s to a broader range of families than they had served before. This was part of a gradual change among independent schools in general—from a time in the 1930s and '40s when WASP exclusivity was part of the private school raison d'être, to today's era when nearly every school catalogue trumpets its diversity and features photos of brightly smiling children of different races with their arms around each other.

The trickle of minority students at private girls' schools in the 1960s grew to a small stream in the 1980s and '90s. Over time, schools came to realize that admitting students of color was just part of the story—they also had to ensure that they had a positive academic and social experience once they were enrolled. Often that meant recruiting a "critical mass" of minority students and faculty so students wouldn't feel isolated. Schools broadened their constituencies in ways other than race. They raised millions of dollars to expand their financial-aid programs and enroll low-income or moderate-income girls. (As private-school tuitions approached $20,000 per year in areas like New York City in the late 1990s, scholarships were needed not just for poor students but also for children of middle-class professionals like teachers and social workers.) Like the rest of society, girls' schools gradually became accustomed to families that didn't look like the Ozzie-and-Harriet mold. Some began acknowledging families headed by two gay parents. Elite schools found themselves serving girls with two working parents for the first time, and adding services such as after-school care that hadn't been necessary in the days when mothers were available to pick up kids promptly at 3 P.M.

This increased diversity and the broad changes in women's roles pushed schools to begin questioning whether their traditions met the needs of modern young women. One by one, they quietly dropped exclusionary practices such as holding school events at private country clubs or inviting mothers to tea-and-cookie meetings in the middle of the workday. At Ashley Hall in Charleston, headmistress Margaret McDonald put an end to the school's Annual Card Party—an event where alumnae would gather for bridge in the auditorium and, over lunch, watch a fashion show featuring little girls from the lower school. "They wanted children to leave class to wear a fancy dress and parade around! Now that's dumb," said McDonald. "What are we supposed to be doing here? Teaching school! They didn't want to have the card party at night, and I didn't want to have a fashion show during the day. There was a backlash, but enough people said, 'Oh, maybe we are delivering the wrong message here.'" Helen Marter, head of the Laurel School, ended a tradition of hosting classes for the local dancing school. Unaffiliated with Laurel, the dancing school was a private institution that prepared sons and daughters of the WASP elite for cotillions and charity balls. It was still holding Friday-afternoon classes in Laurel's dining room when Marter arrived in 1992. "I was thinking, 'Is this part of the mission of the school?'" Marter recalled. Soon after Marter's arrival, a Jewish student at Laurel applied to join the dancing class and was rejected. "We asked to see their admissions criteria. They said, 'It's who we know and like.' That was the end of it. They were gone at the end of the year," Marter said.

Not all the changes happened smoothly. At the Castilleja School, a Palo Alto girls' school that was founded in 1907 to prepare young women for Stanford, the main fund-raising event for years was the "Table Setting," in which people bought tickets to see fancy dinner tables decorated by local celebrities. In the early 1980s, that was replaced with a mother-daughter fashion show that completely preoccupied the school for two days each spring. The faculty hated it, feeling that its emphasis on female appearance completely contradicted Castilleja's goal of educating women to be thinkers and leaders. "I could hardly shut my mouth when I went to that event, there was such a disconnect between the event and what the faculty thought we were trying to do here," said Marsha Miller, the school's development director at the time. "We didn't want a fashion show to be the signature event of the school—and for everyone who came from the outside, it was. We had tables full of elementary school mothers, and this was the only time they ever came to Castilleja." School administrators finally managed to replace the fashion show with a fund-raising dinner and auction—but not without a lot of argument and a year's hiatus from all fund-raising events. "It was a hard thing to give up for a lot of people, and you still find some people who are sorry," Miller said.

## Carol Gilligan Redefines Girls' Development

While girls' schools were moving in fits and starts to modernize themselves, two things were happening in the broader world of education research that would ultimately change the entire image and mission of girls' schools. One was the increasingly well-known research on girls' psychological development by Carol Gilligan. The other was the media's sudden discovery of sex discrimination in coed schools, as documented by scholars like David and Myra Sadker and by the American Association of University Women.

Gilligan, a former Harvard education professor who now teaches at New York University, had received a Ph.D. in clinical psychology in the early 1960s before leaving academia for several years to raise three sons and work in the peace and civil-rights movements. Gilligan became a nationally known name in psychology in 1982 when she published a book called *In a Different Voice* arguing that girls experienced a very different process of emotional and psychological development than did boys. Like many scholars who were influenced by the women's movement of the 1970s, Gilligan began by taking a second look at the traditional canon—in her case, the canon of psychology. She realized that very few of the landmark studies of psychological development had included girls or women. The psychological idea of "normal" growth was based on what was normal for boys. For instance, traditional theory said that it was necessary for young people to separate themselves from parents and friends in order to become mature individuals. However, many women and girls seemed to value relationships more than forging a separate self—interdependence more than independence. Were these women abnormal and psychologically immature? Or was the problem with a definition of "normal" that had been based on studies of men?

Although similar questions about women's psychology were being raised by other feminist scholars, Gilligan's work was what caught the national spotlight. Gilligan was pronounced woman of the year by *Ms.* magazine in 1984. She was the focus of a seven-page profile in the *New York Times Magazine* in January 1990, and was deemed one of the twenty-five most influential people in America by *Time* magazine in 1996. Gilligan was awarded the prestigious Grawemeyer Award in Education and the Heinz Award for her contributions to understanding the "human condition."

Within the academic world, Gilligan caught flak from critics who felt that she didn't do the kind of quantitative research needed to back up her theories. Still, Gilligan's influence was tremendous. Gilligan forced psychologists to think about the role of gender in human development. She opened the door for feminists to consider the idea of innate psychological differences between men and women. Certainly, people had always talked about differences between men and women—think of the countless sandboxes across America where moms marvel at how Johnny turns his plastic shovel into a machine gun while Jenny makes a nice cradle for it and puts it to bed. But the women's movement of the 1960s and early '70s had looked on such differences skeptically, as a sign not of innate difference but of relentless socialization. Before Gilligan, someone venturing the opinion that men and women were fundamentally different on a psychological level would have been attacked as a sexist pig. Gilligan paved the way for a strain of feminism called "difference feminism" that supported and even celebrated the idea that women were deeply different from men—that women were more emotionally connected and compassionate.

## "A Recognition That We Had Something Here"

*In a Different Voice* had focused on how women and men responded differently to moral dilemmas. Next Gilligan turned her spotlight on the psychological development of adolescent girls—writing two books based on research at girls' schools, the Laurel School in Cleveland and the Emma Willard School.

Gilligan described a kind of existential crisis that hits girls at early adolescence. Up until the age of ten or eleven, she said, girls are self-confident, resilient creatures with a clear sense of their own values and abilities. But with the arrival of adolescence, they somehow lose their confidence and outspokenness. Their psychological need to maintain relationships clashes with their need to stay true to their own beliefs. In an effort to meet society's vision of being "nice," they silence themselves. They succumb to what Gilligan called "the tyranny of nice and kind." As their bodies change with puberty, girls also find the world comparing them to unattainable standards of airbrushed perfection. "Seeing themselves seen through the gaze of others, hearing themselves talked about in ways that imply they can be perfect, and that relationships can be free of conflict and bad feeling, they struggle between knowing what they know through experience and knowing what others want them to know and to feel and to think," Gilligan wrote in her book about girls at the Laurel School. Torn this way, girls silence their true thoughts. They lose their "voice."

Gilligan's writing struck faculty at girls' schools like a thunderbolt. Many longtime teachers found that Gilligan had put words to behaviors that they had observed in their students and daughters for years. "I don't know if it was the strongest research to date, but on an intuitive level it made complete sense to me," said Fran Norris Scoble, head of the Westridge School in Pasadena. "Prior to Gilligan, I always knew that an all-girls education worked, but she gave us the language to describe it," said Arlene Hogan, head of the Archer School for Girls in Los Angeles and former head of the Hamlin School.

Gilligan's work on gender differences in moral development opened a door for teachers to think about differences in boys' and girls' learning styles. As a calculus teacher at Westover, Ann Pollina had been experimenting with new ways to teach her subject but was reluctant to accept the idea that girls might learn differently from boys. "Now here was an analysis in the moral sphere that was similar to what we were talking about in math and science," said Pollina. "Seeing it in a totally different arena was very exciting because it made it clear it was more than an isolated phenomenon."

Deborah Dempsey found that Gilligan's theories validated her own participatory style of teaching. Dempsey didn't lecture; she let the girls talk. But she had never felt completely good about that, because of the common assumption that great teachers were people who stood in front of a class and captivated them with their eloquent delivery. "What Gilligan did was give us a theoretical underpinning for what we had been doing," Dempsey said. "She helped us believe in what we were doing."

In other places, teachers found that Gilligan's work challenged their old ways of relating to girls. At the Laurel School, teachers were shocked as they realized that they themselves had been encouraging girls to be docile and "nice." One teacher at Laurel recounted that:

> It was first with a sense of shock and then a deep, knowing sadness that we listened to the voices of the girls tell us that it was the adult *women* in their lives that provided the models for silencing themselves and behaving like "good little girls." Unless we, as grown women, were willing to give up all the "good little girl" things we continued to do, and give up our expectation that the girls in our charge would be as good as we were, we could not successfully empower young women to act on their own knowledge and feelings.

As head of San Francisco's Hamlin School, Arlene Hogan sent some of her teachers to a conference at Laurel about Gilligan's work.

They came back determined to let girls express a full range of emotions, including anger and conflict. "We decided that if two eighth-grade girls were going to yell at each other, within boundaries we would let them work it out," Hogan recalled. "We didn't allow obscenity. But we stopped saying, 'There, there, calm down'—which was difficult because it was your first reaction."

Gilligan's books and similar writings by other feminist psychologists gave girls' schools a renewed sense of purpose and mission. They weren't educating girls just as a way to keep them out of trouble with boys; nor were they doing it simply because it was a precious tradition that had been passed from mother to daughter. Gilligan sounded a clarion call that girls developed differently from boys—and that there were unique challenges in girls' growth that could best be handled by institutions that were focused on girls. "In the '80s, the school changed because enough of us on the faculty began to see that simply being a girls' school because we'd always been a girls' school wasn't enough," said Deborah Dempsey of Springside. "There was a recognition that we had something here—a growing understanding of how girls learn. We developed an enormous amount of confidence in our ability to do for girls what other people weren't doing."

## Uncovering Gender Bias

While girls' schools were rediscovering the unique nature of their mission, other educators were starting to challenge the conventional wisdom that coeducation was an automatic route to equality for girls.

Just as the women's movement led Gilligan to take a critical look at the canon of psychology, so it prompted other scholars to look critically at how gender was handled within the typical classroom. Through the 1970s and 1980s, a small but growing body of research focused on what became known as "gender equity"—whether girls and boys were being treated fairly and equally.

Two of the earliest researchers in this field were Myra and David Sadker, who stumbled into it nearly by accident. In the late 1960s, the Sadkers were a pair of young married graduate students—David in education, Myra in English. Then Myra got fed up with the "medieval" nature of her English studies and switched into education. The couple discovered that they were sitting in the same classrooms but having very different educational experiences. "Myra would often say something in class that wouldn't receive much attention and then a male would repeat it and get credit," David Sadker recalled. "We'd co-author a work and people would use shorthand to refer to it as mine, even though Myra was the better writer and often the first author." Myra wrote an editorial in the college newspaper about feeling invisible as a woman in academia. A professor saw it and asked her to turn it into a book. The term *sexism* hadn't even been coined yet. But the Sadkers started looking at how women fared in education—how women were barely mentioned in most textbooks, why most teachers were women but most principals were men, why girls did well on report cards but poorly on standardized tests.

The Sadkers received some grant money under Title IX and embarked on years of research about the treatment of women in classrooms and curricula. Gradually their ideas began entering the public arena. In 1985, *Psychology Today* featured a long article by the Sadkers on sexism in the classroom. Columnist Judy Mann wrote them up in the *Washington Post*. The Sadkers took their research to a level of detail that went far beyond simply counting the number of girls and boys in a classroom, or comparing their test scores. They videotaped classrooms and analyzed the interactions within them. They tracked which students raised their hands, which ones shouted out answers, which ones were called on by the teacher, and what kinds of responses students got from their teachers. They found that subtle sexism persisted even in the best coed classrooms. Teachers called on boys more often, gave more constructive criticism to boys, and praised boys more. When girls got feedback from teachers, it was often on their dress and appearance.

"On the surface, girls appear to be doing well," the Sadkers wrote in their 1994 book, *Failing at Fairness: How Our Schools Cheat Girls.* "They get better grades and receive fewer punishments than boys. Quieter and more conforming, they are the elementary school's ideal students . . . [However] the girls' good behavior frees the teacher to work with the more-difficult-to-manage boys. The result is that girls receive less time, less help, and fewer challenges. Reinforced for passivity, their independence and self-esteem suffer. As victims of benign neglect, girls are penalized for doing what they should and lose ground as they go through school."

## The AAUW Tidal Wave

While the Sadkers were well known in the world of educational research by the early 1990s, their ideas hadn't exactly become household words.

Then came the AAUW.

The American Association of University Women issued a report in 1992 called "How Schools Shortchange Girls" that hit the educational world like a tidal wave. The AAUW pulled together research done by the Sadkers and others into a broad denunciation of girls' second-class status in coed public schools. Doing their own polling, the AAUW discovered that girls' self-esteem drops dramatically during early adolescence. They combined that with a synthesis of research by others like the Sadkers, concluding that "there is clear evidence that the educational system is not meeting girls' needs."

"Girls and boys enter school roughly equal in measured ability," the AAUW Report, as it came to be known, began. "Twelve years later, girls have fallen behind their male classmates in key areas such as higher-level mathematics and measures of self-esteem."

The AAUW Report grew out of an effort by the century-old organization to refocus and revive itself. Founded in 1881 to advocate for women's higher education when that was still a radical thing, the AAUW had gradually broadened its focus over the years to a point where it had little impact on anything. Its membership dwindled as young professional women saw little reason to join. "When I was hired, our director of public policy said to me, 'I don't think it's right that we have seventy legislative priorities,'" recalled former executive director Anne Bryant, who was hired in 1986 with a mandate to revive the organization. "I said, 'Seven priorities?' He said, 'No, *seventy.*'"

The AAUW's leadership settled on educational equity for girls and women as the group's new central mission. They did some focus groups, and the idea played well; it was also nicely in keeping with the AAUW's original purpose. They issued an initial report based on their polling data; then they hired the Wellesley College Center for Research on Women to compile a larger report on girls in school. The AAUW did its P.R. homework in advance of releasing the report. AAUW staff started contacting the press six months before the report came out. They offered media training and talking points to their hundreds of chapters around the country. Before releasing the report, they convened a roundtable meeting of key players in educational policy to make sure that no one felt blindsided or threatened.

"I was worried that the message would be seen as blasting public schools," Bryant said. "I went and spoke with every single person at the roundtable. I wanted to hear the National Education Association, the National School Boards Association, what they thought of it. I went to see Keith Geiger at the NEA and I saw the report sitting there in his office, highlighted with paper clips and yellow stickies. He dropped it on the table and said, 'This report is dynamite.' I thought, 'Oh boy, dynamite-good or dynamite-bad?' He said, 'You may not know this but I taught math in Michigan for years. Every time I turned a page I wondered, 'Did I do this? Did I favor boys or girls?'"

The report received coverage that could have come from a publicist's dream. Hundreds of newspapers gave the story major play; some even took phrases right out of the press release. Because of the AAUW's careful politicking, reporters had trouble finding any critics. The group's phones began ringing off the hooks with calls from parents and teachers: The AAUW generated an initial mailing list of ten thousand people from the report and ended up adding sixty thousand new members. NBC-TV's *Dateline* followed up with a vivid report in which the camera documented a terrific, well-meaning teacher unconsciously doing all the things the AAUW and Sadkers said—

ignoring girls, focusing on boys. Even *Doonesbury* got on board with a series of cartoons in which Mike Doonesbury's young daughter vainly waved her hand in the air for her kindergarten teacher's attention and wondered, "Maybe if I wore brighter colors . . ."

The drumbeat of concern for girls continued in 1994 with the publication of a book called *Reviving Ophelia: Saving the Selves of Adolescent Girls*. A Nebraska psychologist named Mary Pipher argued that, despite the gains of the women's movement, girls in the '90s had a tougher time in adolescence than their mothers or grandmothers. Pipher wrote:

> At first blush, it seems things should be better now. After all, we have the women's movement. . . . Many of us are doing things our mothers never dreamed of doing.
>
> But girls today are much more oppressed. They are coming of age in a more dangerous, sexualized and media-saturated culture. They face incredible pressures to be beautiful and sophisticated, which in junior high means using chemicals and being sexual. As they navigate a more dangerous world, girls are less protected.

In one case study after another, Pipher described girls who tried to commit suicide, girls who burned themselves with cigarettes, girls who forced themselves to vomit twice a day. She echoed the AAUW's description of adolescence as a time of crisis for girls:

> Something dramatic happens to girls in early adolescence. Just as planes and ships disappear mysteriously in the Bermuda Triangle, so do the selves of girls go down in droves. They crash and burn in a social and developmental Bermuda Triangle. In early adolescence, studies show that girls' IQ scores drop and their math and science scores plummet. They lose their resiliency and optimism and become less curious and inclined to take risks. They lose their assertive, energetic and "tomboyish" personalities and become more deferential, self-critical and depressed. They report great unhappiness with their own bodies.

Pipher's book was entirely anecdotal and based on pseudony-
mous cases from her own private practice. But it was easy to read and
profoundly disturbing. It sold more than 1.5 million copies and
spent three years on the *New York Times* best-seller list. Together
with the AAUW report, it sparked a wave of concern among parents
about how, in this era of unprecedented freedom and opportunity,
their daughters really were doing.

## Girls' Schools Seize the Day

When the AAUW report was first released in 1992, the National
Coalition of Girls' Schools was young but geared for action. It was
quick to jump on the AAUW's coattails. The coalition had sponsored a national conference on math and science for girls just a few
months before the AAUW report came out; it followed up with similar conferences on teaching girls about technology and the physical
sciences. It cited the AAUW findings in its promotional materials.
Even now, it still includes those *Doonesbury* cartoons in its annual directory of girls' schools around the country. The AAUW's critique
of coed classrooms got parents throughout the country asking questions about their daughters' education; then NCGS stepped forward
with an answer to those questions. "We were smart and organized
enough so that when these studies came out, we could relate it to
what was right about girls' schools," Whitney Ransome said.

Individual girls' schools were also able to refer to work by people like the Sadkers and the AAUW in marketing themselves and
explaining why they were single sex. Between 1991 and 1994, the
Emma Willard School took the unusual step of purchasing a series of
"advertorials" on the opinion page of the *New York Times*—space
more typically purchased by powerful, deep-pocketed institutions
like oil companies. The Emma Willard ads spoke directly to parental
worries about the loss of girls' self-esteem and academic success during adolescence. "How to make certain your daughter connects with
the most important person she'll ever know. Herself," one headline
stated.

The Emma Willard ads took the themes identified by Gilligan, the Sadkers, and others—girls' loss of confidence during adolescence, the hidden double standard in coed classrooms—and melded them into a compelling argument for a girls' school. The most talked-about ad in the series, though, was one that delivered a slap in the face to the famous boys' boarding schools that had gone coed. "Why the St. Grottlesex education you enjoyed might not be the best idea for your daughter," read that headline. It continued:

> In the 1970s, many of the great boys' schools went coed. As the doors were flung open, in rushed the girls . . . [But] a growing body of research by psychologists at institutions such as Harvard, Michigan, and USC reveals that coeducation perpetuates sexual stereotyping and an academic environment in which boys dominate. . . . Even the brightest girls perceive that less is expected of them than of boys, that they are expected to play supporting roles and that they are traditionally not "as good" as boys in math and science.

St. Grottlesex was an old insiders' nickname for the coterie of elite northeastern boys' boarding schools, an amalgamation of St. Paul's, Groton, and Middlesex. The ad ruffled feathers in the boarding school world by violating an unspoken agreement among schools not to disparage each other. "I would go to independent school meetings where people would do presentations on marketing strategy, and they'd reference this 'untoward' behavior of the Emma Willard School," recalled Robin Robertson, head of Emma Willard at that time. But "untoward" or not, the Emma Willard ads worked. They energized the school's alumnae and gave a boost to the school's fund-raising. They caught the eye of parents and potential students— to a point where, within a few years, the school was no longer struggling to find qualified students.

The coalition's marketing efforts, the Emma Willard ads, the broad concern over girls' education sparked by the AAUW report and *Reviving Ophelia*—all these things worked together to create a new interest in single-sex schools among many parents of girls. The interesting thing was that these weren't families with a long tradition of mothers and grandmothers attending Miss Porter's or Miss Madeira's or Miss Hall's. In fact, many were families in which no one had ever attended any kind of private school. But they had daughters—they saw the AAUW findings firsthand in their daughters' lives—and they were willing to look at a private single-sex school if it would help their children grow up self-confident and strong.

## Modesty and Money

As girls' schools went on the offensive to boost their enrollment, they also began grappling with another institutional challenge—money. Historically, women's schools and colleges had raised less money than men's institutions. Girls' schools were underfunded and undercapitalized compared to their male counterparts. A 2002 survey of sixty-nine independent girls' schools showed an average endowment of $15.3 million, compared to an average of $17.5 million at fifty boys' schools. Some girls' schools today do have very large endowments—Hockaday in Dallas led the pack with $75 million in 2002, followed by Miss Porter's with $61 million and Brearley with $58 million. But they still don't come anywhere near the nest eggs of the most elite onetime boys' schools, like Phillips Exeter Academy with $532 million and Phillips Academy (Andover) with $455 million. The gender gap continues down the line to schools that are often seen as peers of each other and that compete for faculty or for students. In Baltimore, the Bryn Mawr School had an endowment of $14 million while the all-boys Gilman School, which is literally across the street, had $54 million. In Dallas, all-girls Ursuline Academy had $6 million while all-boys Jesuit College Preparatory School had $18 million, even though Ursuline is six decades older than Jesuit.

What has this gender gap in endowments meant for girls' schools? A lot. Schools with large endowments have more income to spend on programs and facilities—to buy boats so they can have a crew team, to keep the science labs up-to-date, to hire specialists, to defray the cost of a senior trip to Washington, D.C. They can pay for employee perks such as faculty housing that help attract the best teachers. They can offer more financial aid. They can use endowment income to help keep tuition lower than their competitors, giving them a better shot at recruiting the students they want. And they're not as dependent on tuition revenues for survival, thus making it easier to weather temporary downturns in enrollment or other financial crises. A 1959 *Newsweek* article noted that girls' schools typically charged $1,000 more in tuition than boys' schools because of smaller endowments and less financial support from alumnae.

Girls' schools started taking some thoughtful looks at their fundraising programs in the 1980s and '90s. They realized their alumnae were giving much less money than graduates of boys' schools, for a variety of economic and cultural reasons. On the most basic level, men had traditionally earned and controlled vastly greater amounts of money than women. But along with men's greater direct control of wealth, there was an additional layer of psychological control—of women ceding control of their own money or their family's money to men.

Most girls' school graduates—like well-off women everywhere—did not consider money a polite subject of discussion. Fund-raising was seen as a bit crass. Many alumnae were frightened by the whole idea of money and shied away from managing their own finances. If they were married, they left the big financial decisions to their husbands. When widowed, they passed the buck, literally, to a financial adviser who was typically a man. Even women with their own inherited wealth often deferred to their husbands' judgment in managing that wealth. "We run up against this whole thing of 'It's not my money, it's my husband's money,' even if it *is* her money," said Starr Snead, a former director of development for Ashley Hall.

The result was that few alumnae felt confident or informed enough to give sizable, significant donations—the kind of donations that could build a new science lab or endow a faculty position. Randy Tucker, head of Girls Preparatory School in Chattanooga, recalls visiting an alumna with a net worth of $75 million who was too worried about running out of money to make a $250,000 gift. Other school heads groan in frustration at devoted alumnae who write them $50 checks while their husbands give $5,000 or more to their own schools. Blair Jenkins, head of the Dana Hall School outside Boston, has alumnae who identify more with their husbands' schools than with their own. "We've got alumnae from the '50s who refer to 'our' class at Princeton," Jenkins said. "It's their husbands' class, but they do the secretarial support work. I couldn't figure out what this one alumna was talking about, because she was too old to have been at Princeton when it went coed. But Princeton had done such a good job in fund-raising that she considered herself part of the Princeton class. She couldn't give to her own school because she was giving to 'her' class at Princeton."

Through the 1980s and '90s, girls' schools started taking fund-raising more seriously. They had to begin by convincing themselves that fund-raising was not a dirty word—something that often went against decades of tradition. "Traditionally money wasn't something you talked about," said Marsha Miller, the Castilleja development director. "Heaven forbid you should have an idea of someone's net worth. It wasn't ladylike." Schools broadened their fund-raising drives to include all their parents and alumnae, rather than just a handful of board members. They learned to ask for specific amounts of money rather than making vague, open-ended requests for support. Like women's colleges, they also gradually realized that raising money from women was different than raising it from men. Competition worked as an incentive among most men—"John R. just gave $500,000, how'd you like to match that or even give $750,000?"—but it didn't work with women. Women were also less eager than men to have buildings named after them. Just as Carol Gilligan was calling attention to the importance of relationships to girls' identity, schools began realizing that relationships were the key to women's philanthropy. They started putting in the time—years, sometimes—to build personal connections with potential donors. "I've visited hundreds and hundreds of people that I've never asked for money," said Mary Lou Leipheimer, head of Foxcroft. "It's a long process. But it makes me feel cleaner and better. . . . Women don't give to competition; they give to connection. Why are we surprised by that? It's how they learn too."

Girls' schools also started seeing how their traditional modesty—*"Ladies don't boast about themselves"*—made it difficult to raise money. In order to inspire donors, they needed to feel proud of themselves, and show it. "What we needed to do was feel worthy," said Molly Hathaway, development director at Garrison Forest. "I hate the word 'empowered,' but once we felt truly worthy, we could ask our alumnae to elevate their thoughts about what they were doing for their alma mater."

## Revival

By the end of the 1990s, girls' schools were experiencing a full-blown revival. More families were asking for admissions information, and more were following up by mailing in application forms for their daughters. Applications to NCGS schools rose by 40 percent between 1991 and 2000. Enrollment rose by 29 percent. By 2000, 64 percent of NCGS members' schools were at full capacity, compared with just 24 percent in 1991.

There were a number of reasons for this turnaround. The number of school-age children was on the rise again as baby boomers raised their own families. The economy was booming through the second half of the decade, which meant more families could afford to send their kids to private school. But on top of these general trends affecting all schools, girls' schools were also benefiting from NCGS's marketing efforts and from the broad media attention throughout the '90s to girls' development. Schools no longer had to spend their time parrying questions about why there were no boys around. Prospective parents would walk in the door well aware of the arguments for a girls' school, which allowed schools to spend time talking about their music or science or community-service programs. "So many parents now say they've read the research—if they didn't read Carol Gilligan, they read Pipher, and if they didn't read Pipher, they saw something on TV," said Judy Minor Campbell, admissions director at the Marlborough School in Los Angeles, which saw applications rise 18 percent in the 2000–2001 school year.

While existing schools like Marlborough boomed, new girls' schools started to sprout up—something that even NCGS hadn't anticipated. In New York, city officials opened the first new public girls' school in almost a century. In Boston, several nuns turned an old welfare office into the Mother Caroline Academy for very poor and immigrant girls. In Atlanta, a high-powered group of parents managed to raise $4 million to open the city's first independent girls' school in a generation. By 2002, more than thirty new girls' schools had opened up across the United States. The significance wasn't so much in the exact number—thirty is hardly a drop in the ocean of America's more than one hundred thousand coeducational schools—but in the fact that, for the first time in decades, the number of girls' schools was rising rather than declining.

This revival created a kind of positive cycle around modesty and money for girls' schools. Schools increasingly saw themselves as national leaders in a battle to help girls grow up smart and strong. They were not just carrying on a pleasant tradition; they were fulfilling an urgent mission. This renewed sense of mission inspired their alumnae and donors to give more generously. Increased giving then helped the schools build a slew of new science labs, sports complexes, and libraries that further reinforced their identity as the best place for today's young women. School after school took advantage of the economic boom of the late 1990s to carry out unprecedentedly ambitious fund-raising campaigns. By 2001–2002, six girls' boarding schools and sixteen day schools within NCGS had undertaken capital campaigns of $20 million or more. Some schools were bringing in individual gifts of $2 million, $5 million, and even $16 million. Girls' schools were also doing better than their peers at getting large numbers of alumnae and parents to support them: Sixty-seven percent of current parents gave to the annual fund drives at girls' schools in 2000–2001, compared to 51 percent at boys' schools and 57 percent at coed schools. The financial gap between girls' schools and onetime boys' schools hasn't yet gone away, but it is slowly starting to narrow.

# 8

# Catholic Schools

*As I worked on this book, I started meeting girls' school administrators from around the country. Several of them gave me the same advice about Julia Morgan:* Be very thoughtful about the culture you set up, because it is really hard to change a school culture once it's established. *This was something that our director, Ann, had realized from the start. Several years later, parents would talk about "that Julia Morgan magic." But it wasn't magic, even though it felt that way. From the very start, Ann set out deliberately to create a certain culture and ethos at the school. It influenced every decision that she made, from hiring teachers to decorating the walls. It took hard work and hard thinking to create that seemingly spontaneous "magic."*

Ann's vision was for a school designed specifically for the needs of middle-school girls. It wouldn't be a miniature, dumbed-down version of high school, which is the fate of too many junior highs. It would build on her own experiences working with middle-school kids and on the growing body of knowledge about girls' development. Through the 1980s and '90s, girls' schools around the country had avidly lapped up new research on girls by people like Carol Gilligan or the American Association of University Women. We at Julia Morgan were in the enviable position of being able to incorporate that research from the ground up. We didn't have to gingerly weave it into an existing school culture that had been established a hundred years ago; we could make it part of the basic fabric of the school from the start.

Ann envisioned a school that would acknowledge the importance of interpersonal relationships to girls. We wouldn't treat the girls' friendships as a distraction from their academic work; we would respect their need for social connections and use those connections to deepen the learning process. We would give them plenty of opportunities for group work. We would promote trusting relationships between girls and teachers. We would provide room for girls to try on new identities and grapple with the important developmental question, "Who am I? Who do I want to be?"

Ann also envisioned a culture that would bolster girls' self-esteem, but not by coddling them. There had been a lot of media attention in the '90s to girls' loss of self-esteem during early adolescence, and many parents responded by trying to shelter their daughters from failure. But Ann believed that self-esteem came from taking risks and overcoming challenges. Julia Morgan would be a place where it was safe for girls to take risks and try new things. It would also be a place that was fun. "Middle school has to be a balance between academic rigor and pure fun," Ann said. "I started that with the faculty. From the beginning, we always had food at meetings and we had lots of parties. If students see the faculty having fun, it's sort of like a family where kids see their parents getting along. They can see there's a time for working really hard and a time for playing really hard."

This awareness of the social and emotional needs of girls infused every decision made by the founding staff. In the weeks before school opened, the teachers decided to have girls call them by their first names in order to foster a culture of trust and honesty. "If this school is about women being real and being honest with each other, we don't need an artificial hierarchy," said Kristen, our sixth-grade social-science and language-arts teacher. They decided against a school uniform because they felt middle-school girls needed the freedom to experiment with new *identities through their clothing. "We are a school for girls, and this is the time when girls are trying things out," Kristen said. "They are experimenting and exploring. To deprive them of that is not right. We can learn so much about who they are. Are they hiding behind big baggy shirts? Are they wearing a little belly shirt?"*

*Ann and the staff created a weeklong orientation program that set the tone for the school. Students and teachers spent the first week together on social activities, creative projects, and trust-building exercises. They swam together in the college pool. Students teamed up in a treasure hunt that forced them to learn about the school and the faculty through clues like "Find a teacher who speaks Russian." By the third day, girls were clambering playfully on their teachers in the pool and sprawling all over each other at lunchtime. Meanwhile, teachers decorated the hallways by painting silhouettes of each student on the walls. Each girl brought in an old wooden chair from home and painted her own colorful designs on it. It remained "her" chair as long as she stayed at Julia Morgan, and the classrooms became a crazy quilt of brightly colored furniture. The goal was to give girls a sense of ownership of the school, a sense that their voices and ideas mattered. The goal was also to immediately lay a foundation of trust, caring, and connection among the students and the teachers. Ann felt that if girls could work through the social anxieties of coming to a new school right away, they would be freed up to zoom ahead in academics. She was right. The girls were hungry to connect with each other. Then, by the end of orientation week, they had started to clamor for schoolwork: "When can we get going with classes?"*

*Ann and the faculty set a conscious tone of inclusivity and egalitarianism from the start. They made room in the curriculum for all kinds of celebrations—Passover, Kwanzaa, Dia de los Muertos, Chinese New Year. They banned portable stereos and other electronic equipment that might identify some girls as "haves" and others as "have-nots." When Halloween drew near, they sensed trouble brewing as some wealthier girls started talking about the elaborate, expensive costumes they planned to wear to school. They nipped that in the bud by starting a tradition of improvised goddess costumes. The sixth-grade curriculum had the girls studying Greek mythology, so the teachers helped the girls dress up in togalike sheets with garlands of tinfoil, paper, pipe cleaners, and other craft supplies. Each girl was a goddess of some-thing—air, water, forests, and so on—and they paraded loudly around the campus to the delight of the college staff.*

*Ann also made a point of reminding the girls from day one that they were pioneers—that launching the school was a "historical mo-ment." The first day of orientation week was a historical moment. The first day of classes was a historical moment. The first soccer game was a historical moment. The first field trip was a historical moment. . . . It became a running joke among students, teachers, and parents that everything was a historical moment for Ann. But it was true. We were all pioneers—the board, the girls, the staff, the parents. The sense of making history gave a sense of even greater import to everything the girls did. It pushed them to be their best selves. "It was like we were all kind of in love—we were all taking this risk together," said Kristen. Ju-lia Morgan started its first year with a shared sense of euphoria among girls and staff. "This is better than my whole summer," one girl de-clared during orientation week. "How am I going to explain this to my friends!" exclaimed another. "Dear Mom: I am so happy here," a third wrote in a note to her mother. "I made the right choice. I love what I am learning, and I have so many friends."*

H oly Names High School sits imposingly on top of a hill in the Rockridge neighborhood of Oakland, a Spanish Gothic stone edifice rising up from a neighborhood of small stucco bungalows. The hillside is covered with trees and bushes that have grown big and full since the school was built in 1931, and near the top a statue of Mary sits serenely in the center of a small flagstone patio. The front doors are heavy oak with leaded-glass windows and luminous stained-glass crosses. Altogether the building and grounds project an aura of solidity and tradition—a silent statement that this school is part of a Church whose history goes back centuries to the great cathedrals of Europe.

Yet when alumnae from the 1940s and '50s trudge up the hill for a board meeting, what often strikes them are the changes in their alma mater. Instead of identical plaid skirts and blazers, students can often be seen in jeans, sweatshirts, and sneakers. Instead of walking silently through the halls in single file, they laugh and shout in clusters by their lockers. Holy Names girls of the 1940s and '50s had to enter school through the back door into the schoolyard, but today's students are free to come and go through the formal front entrance. After school they lounge casually on the front steps, chewing gum, waiting for a ride home, and talking on their cell phones—something that would have been socially as well as technologically inconceivable fifty years ago. Then there are the really big changes. The all-white student body of the '40s and '50s has given way to one that is three-fourths girls of color. And where almost every class used to be taught by a nun, there is only one Holy Names sister teaching at the school today.

While all kinds of girls' schools have seen enormous changes since the 1960s, the changes at Catholic schools like Holy Names have been particularly striking. Not only did they feel the effects of the Vietnam-era counterculture and the 1970s women's movement, but they were also rocked by the Second Vatican Council and the sweeping changes it brought to Catholicism. "It feels like a different school, totally different," mused Lorraine Pagan, who graduated in 1954 but returns often for alumnae events. "I know it's Holy Names, but to me it's different."

## Pioneering Sisters

The oldest girls' school in the U.S. is a Catholic one—the Ursuline Academy, founded in New Orleans in the 1720s by a group of young French nuns who braved a five-month sea voyage to open a convent and school in the New World. But Catholic girls' schools really began spreading in the early 1800s, spurred by waves of German, Irish, and Italian immigration. The public school system hadn't yet been set up, so Catholic schools for girls were part of the burgeoning trend of privately run academies and seminaries—a Catholic parallel to the schools run by women like Emma Willard and Sarah Porter. In 1820 there were ten Catholic academies for girls in the U.S. By 1840 that number had risen to about forty, and by 1860, there were more than two hundred.

The Catholic academies were invariably run by nuns, and typically located alongside or within a convent. Educating girls had been one of the main missions of women's religious orders in Europe, and so when schools were needed in America, it was natural for local bishops to turn to the orders. The sisters who started these early schools—many of them as young as twenty or twenty-one themselves—faced daunting challenges. First, for those coming from Europe there was the arduous journey across the Atlantic. Then there were the primitive living conditions of the frontier. When a group of Carondelet sisters arrived in Chillicothe, Missouri, to open a school in 1871, they found their "convent" was a vacant hotel filled with heaps of debris. They worked until dark to clean the place up, then asked the priest for a lamp and were stunned when he offered them a revolver to protect themselves. More than one group of nuns made the grueling journey to the West, only to find the house that was meant for their convent and school hadn't quite been finished; they undertook the carpentry and painting themselves. Sisters were also often expected to take on housekeeping tasks for local priests, on top of their teaching duties. The priest who started the Sinsinawa Dominican order of nuns in Iowa explained that he needed "some good persons to keep school to the girls of this parish, and to do all the sewing and mending of our house which will be considerable this winter."

Catholic girls' schools grew particularly quickly in the Midwest, where there were few other educational options. Many of the early convent schools attracted Protestant and even Jewish girls as well as Catholic ones. In the frontier environment, convent academies projected an aura of European gentility and aristocratic culture that appealed to upper-class families of all religious backgrounds. They typically emphasized the arts and provided training in piano or harp along with courses in "ornamental" subjects like needlework and painting. In St. Louis, the Sisters of St. Joseph of Carondelet opened a school named St. Joseph's Academy that was more commonly referred to by the French-sounding name of Madame Celestine's School. An 1838 advertisement for Loretto Academy in Kentucky promised instruction in French, painting, music, dancing, reading, writing, grammar, geography, botany, chemistry, history, astronomy, needlework, lace and beadwork, painting on satin and velvet, and "Polite Literature," all aimed at "habituat[ing] the young mind to what is useful, elegant, and proper." In Chicago, a local newspaper waxed enthusiastic about the start of a new Catholic girls' academy in 1846: "What citizen is there who will not hail the coming of these Sisters of Mercy as among the choicest blessings for our city?" Many orders used the fees from running an elite boarding school to subsidize services for the poor, such as free schools for poor girls. They typically needed Protestant families as much as those families needed them—often there weren't enough wealthy Catholics in town to financially support a girls' academy.

The success of these early academies sparked a backlash from some Protestants who feared they were part of a Catholic plot to take over the United States. The United States experienced a general upswelling of nativist sentiment in the mid-1800s, as the number of

*Nuns and students go boating at the Oakland convent school that later became Holy Names High School, 1800s.*

immigrants grew from 150,000 in the 1820s to 1.7 million in the 1840s and 2.3 million in the 1850s. Many of the new arrivals were Catholic, and so fears about immigration often blended with anti-Catholicism. The girls' academies run by Catholic sisters were attacked for promoting a kind of mirror image of the "Republican motherhood" ideal—instead of educating women to be the mothers of good citizens, nativists warned, the academies were training them to breed Catholic subversives. Convent school alumnae "will educate their children for the special service of the Pope of Rome, and their Catholic sons will become our rulers, and our nation a nation of *Roman Catholics*," one magazine warned in the 1830s. This kind of anti-Catholic rhetoric sometimes escalated into actual violence. In Charlestown, Massachusetts, in 1834, a mob of working-class Protestant men burned down an Ursuline convent school that served daughters of the Unitarian elite as well as poor Catholic girls.

In reality, nineteenth-century convent academies walked a fine line in educating their non-Catholic pupils. The academies were first and foremost religious institutions, aimed at inculcating the precepts of Catholicism. "All the chief points necessary for salvation should be taught each year in a manner suited to the age of the students, so that if they leave after that year, they will know enough to save their soul," noted a 1909 teachers' manual for a Sacred Heart school in St. Louis. At the same time, schools were sensitive to nativist accusations and usually refrained from direct efforts to convert their non-Catholic students. Some schools even boasted of their non-Catholic enrollment. In Tucson, the Carondelet sisters placed an ad in the 1881 City Directory saying that "as an indication of the tolerant spirit . . . we will mention the twenty-nine children of Jewish parents" enrolled in the academy.

## Little Novitiates

From their start in the 1800s up though the 1960s, life at a Catholic girls' academy could be an intense and rarified experience. Girls who came to board at these schools were immersed in a highly structured, highly devout world that was even more of a hermetically sealed universe than Protestant boarding schools like Emma Willard's. Girls' daily routines often followed the same patterns and rhythms as the nuns'. They were awakened in the morning with a sprinkle of holy water or the recitation of a prayer; they attended Mass before breakfast and said prayers throughout the day; they wore black chapel veils during the week and white veils on Sunday; they maintained silence in the hallways and, at some schools, during meals. "Until the 1960s, we ran our schools like little novitiates," recalled Sr. Donna Maynard, a Holy Names nun who was principal of the Oakland high school during the early 1970s. There were rules for everything—the proper way to curtsey, the proper way to cross yourself, the proper way to respond to a teacher's reprimand, even in some cases the proper way to sleep. In Antonia White's 1933 novel about a British convent school modeled on the Sacred Heart schools, her nine-year-old heroine is admonished by a nun not to sleep curled up in a ball but on her back with her hands crossed over her breast. "Now, *ma petite*," said the nun. "If the dear Lord were to call you to Himself during the night, you would be ready to meet Him as a Catholic should. Good night, little one, and remember to let the holy Name of Jesus be the last word on your lips."

Newspapers and magazines were often *verboten* at convent schools; popular novels and even fairy tales were also sometimes forbidden. Good behavior was rewarded with colored ribbons or religious medals. To the outside world—and to some students—convent school life could seem like a prison. "We learned to pull our chairs gently from the tables in the students' refectory without scraping the floor, we learned to sit with straight back and uncrossed legs, we learned to speak in clear, well-modulated tones of voice and generally to behave in a manner befitting our station in life—which seemed to me much like Jane Eyre's," wrote V. V. Harrison in her memoir, *Changing Habits,* about her experience at a Sacred Heart boarding school in the 1950s. "Mother Forden's constant message was that our conduct should reflect humility and gratitude at all times. . . . This was not just a strict school—this, I began to realize, was life closely aligned to that in a penal colony."

Yet for all their rules and restrictions, Catholic girls' boarding schools exerted a powerful sway over their students. United by their shared adversity, girls often forged intense friendships. The religious rituals, music, and medals blended with the nuns' visible faith to inspire students. Harrison herself gradually came to understand that the stifling rules were aimed at nothing less than the perfection of her soul. "It was like going through the Crusades together," one classmate of Harrison's recounted, "but after it was over you knew you had something of worth under your belt." Feminist writer Agnes Repplier was a classic rebel as a Sacred Heart student in the 1880s—sneaking cigarettes, drinking medicinal wine, and eventually being expelled—yet she looked back on her time there with nostalgia. "It has been many years since I went to school," she wrote in 1906. "Everything has changed in the Convent that I loved, and I am asked to believe that every change is for the better. I do not believe this at all. I am unmoved by the sight of steam registers and electric lights. I look with disfavour upon luxuries which would have seemed to us like the opulence of Aladdin's palace. . . . Even the iron hand of discipline has been relaxed; for the long line of girls whom I now watch filing sedately in and out of the chapel have been taught to rule themselves, to use their wider liberty with discretion. I wonder how they like it. I wonder if liberty, coupled with discretion, is worth having when one is eleven years old. I wonder if it be the part of wisdom to be wise so soon."

## The Era of Habits and Mystery

As the twentieth century began, some Catholic girls' academies gave birth to women's colleges. Catholics had been even more resistant to college education for women than the general American public. But as young Catholic women started enrolling in secular universities, the Church came under pressure to open its own women's colleges. "Our people cannot much longer be denied equal educational advantages with Protestants. If we don't give them a Catholic Harvard, Girton, or Alexandra [women's colleges in England and Ire-

*Students on an outing at the convent school that later became
Holy Names High School, 1889. One girl is managing to keep
a straight face while "playing" her tennis racquet.*

land], they will go to those places," one Catholic magazine wrote
in 1898.

Some girls' academies evolved into colleges themselves. Others
grew into college-preparatory schools with a full range of math, science, and foreign-language courses. But they often kept parts of
their academy-era culture—such as strong curricula in art and music,
and an emphasis on ladylike etiquette. Pat Murray attended Mt. St.
Mary Academy near Buffalo, New York, in the late 1950s and took
an etiquette class each year that included field trips to a department
store to learn about buying crystal, china, lace, linen, and damask.
"You learned how to eat, how to set a nice table with crystal and
linen, the niceties in life," she recalled. "I remember going home
and showing these things to my mom and she said, 'Ohhh, this is
why we sent you there.'"

Meanwhile, a new kind of Catholic girls' school began to spread in
the early 1900s—four-year high schools run by the local diocese or

parish. Unlike the academies, which could be quite pricey, the diocesan and parish schools were often free and were geared to working-class or middle-class girls. They jumped onto the early twentieth-century bandwagon of vocational education, offering classes in home economics and "female" business skills such as typing and stenography. A 1915 article in the *Catholic Educational Review* summarized the difference between the academies and diocesan high schools: "There are, in fact, two distinct types of secondary schools for girls—the school that aims at culture and distinctly womanly accomplishment, and the school that aims primarily, after religious and moral training, at teaching a girl how readily to earn her own living. Both types are needed—in fact, indispensable, but the second answers better to the general popular demand at present."

The class differences between the academies and the diocesan schools persisted for decades. Judy Williams, who grew up in Queens in the late 1950s, begged her parents to send her to the parish high school instead of The Mary Louis Academy because of its elite reputation. "I didn't want to become snobby," recalled Williams, who despite her protests ended up attending and loving Mary Louis Academy. Rosemary Perry attended a working-class parish high school in St. Louis in the late 1940s and was stunned to see girls from the more elite Villa Duchesne, a Sacred Heart school, begin a basketball match by curtseying to the nuns. "They definitely seemed upper class and snooty," Perry recalled. "We were the peons from the poor section of South St. Louis."

Despite these class differences, the various kinds of Catholic girls' schools had much in common through the 1960s. The biggest common denominator of course was the nuns—in those days bedecked in full habits, cloistered or semicloistered, known only by genderless religious names such as Sr. John Baptist or Sr. Mary Michael, distant and mysterious, scarily all-knowing, sometimes oppressive, sometimes inspiring, women who had renounced all worldly ambitions yet projected a rare vision of female intellect and power.

Nuns have long been the subject of harsh stereotypes and ridicule—a lightning rod for disaffected Catholics' anger with the Church, an easy target of jokes for non-Catholics. Teaching sisters are portrayed in movies and stand-up comedy shticks as rigid and re-pressed, bumbling or cruel. I began my research on Catholic girls' schools expecting to hear scores of horror stories about nuns quash-ing girls' spirits and rapping their knuckles. I was surprised to find that most of the adult women I interviewed had fond memories of the nuns. Certainly there were the occasional mean or inept teachers, but those can be found in any school. When I *did* hear horror stories of bruised knuckles and humiliating punishments, they were mostly from the coed parish elementary schools that these women attended—not, generally, from their all-girl secondary schools.

In Nancy Stricker's coed elementary school in Oakland in the 1960s, the nuns slapped kids' hands with rulers and once tied a pink ribbon in the hair of a first-grade boy for crying too much. That never happened when she moved on to Holy Names High School. In Mary Ellen Welsh's coed elementary school in Milwaukee, one nun would yank Walsh's ponytail back and forth so hard that her eyes would water. That never happened when she moved up to all-girls Divine Savior High School. "The difference between my gram-mar school and the high school was light years," said Marge Gaughan, who attended Preston High School in the Bronx in the early 1960s. "It was the same order of sisters, but I felt the sisters treated us more like adults. There was dialogue, while in grammar school it was 'I'm the boss and that's it.'"

It's easy to speculate about why sisters teaching at the elementary school level may have seemed more abusive. Parish schools histori-cally had as many as sixty or seventy children in a classroom, a daunt-ing number for even the most skilled teacher to control. Half of those sixty would have been boys, many of whom were not developmen-tally ready to sit quietly at a desk all day. The curriculum in most parish schools was conservative, based on rote memorization rather than on activities designed to engage children's interest. Nuns in the pre–Vatican II days were given no choice about their work assign-ments, so some women ended up as teachers even though they had no affinity for young children. And the heavy demand for parish-school teachers meant that young nuns were often sent into the classroom with minimal training. That mix of factors doubtless made for stressed-out teachers who, at their wits' end, would use any available means to maintain order.

By contrast, a girls' secondary school must have been a relatively delightful place for sisters to work. Classes were typically smaller, maybe thirty kids instead of fifty. The absence of boys removed the most loud and flagrant discipline issues. Some nuns probably felt more at home in an environment that, like the convent, was all women. And by high school, girls were mature enough to respond to reason or discussion—to be treated as near-equals. In fact, although few girls recognized it because of the habits, many nuns were just a few years older than the students they taught. "I felt a real change in the relationship from elementary to high school, where it was more of a collegial relationship," said Kate Hartzell, who attended Notre Dame High School in Marysville, California, in the 1960s. "A bonding goes on in an all-female organization like high school that was not there in elementary school. It was easier to relate to these women because they were more relaxed in an environment that was just women."

The sisters nonetheless ran a tight ship. Whether at academies or diocesan schools, they set clear standards for schoolwork and behavior and expected all students to meet those standards. In the pre–Vatican II and pre-Vietnam world, girls had no choice but to accept the nuns as the ultimate authority. "Back then if a sister hit you and you went home and said, 'Sister hit me,' your parents would say: 'What did you do to make Sister hit you?' and you'd be whacked again," recalled Catherine Costello, who attended St. Brendan's High School in Brooklyn in the early 1960s. The nuns magically seemed to know everything that everyone did, particularly if it was against the rules. Pat Newton graduated from Holy Names in Oakland in 1946, when girls either walked to school or took streetcars. She remembers sneaking to the back of a streetcar once with some classmates, horsing around, and "clang-clang-clanging the bell." "The next morning nobody said anything but all our names were on the board," Newton said. "You see, somebody on the streetcar knew the uniform and reported us to the school. And for some reason, the nuns always knew who was on which streetcar. . . . I shined twenty-six pairs of nuns' shoes that afternoon."

The strict rules governing sisters in the pre–Vatican II era effectively required them to distance themselves from students and their families. Until the mid-1960s, nuns wore full habits that covered them from head to toe: It was a matter of great speculation among students whether, under those habits, the nuns were bald or had hair. Most nuns were not allowed to drive cars. Many were not allowed to eat in front of laypeople. They were not supposed to reveal their secular names or any details of their personal lives. Pat Cavagnero, who graduated from Immaculate Conception Academy in San Francisco in 1960, remembers her mother driving two nuns to a continuing-education class across the Golden Gate Bridge. They stopped to get ice cream cones for everyone in the car, including the nuns, but Cavagnero was warned not to look at the sisters eating. "My mom would say, 'Don't turn around. If you turn around, I'll take your ice cream away!'"

The result was that sisters were mysterious, distant figures—probably more distant than some of them would have liked to be. Sr. Margery Smith, who grew up in Cleveland and ultimately joined the Sisters of St. Joseph of Carondelet, recalls offering to share a popcorn ball with her ninth-grade homeroom teacher, who declined and said, "I never eat with laity." Smith was stunned and hurt by her teacher's refusal. "I thought they were strict, conservative," she recalled. "I didn't think they ever laughed. They lived a mysterious life on the other side of the door."

Yet that sense of mystery was also alluring to many girls. Marice Ashe saw Sr. Melanie, her first-grade teacher in Erie, Pennsylvania, as a kind of glamorous princess. Ashe aspired to become a nun herself as a young girl and kept a porcelain statue of a nun with black glasses on her bookshelf. "I loved stories about princesses like Sleeping Beauty, with long dresses and veils, and the nuns were about as close as I could get," she said. "It would be hard for me to separate wanting to be a nun from wanting to be a princess. I was so taken with their clothes. And the nuns were married to Christ, just like a princess gets to marry a king."

Many girls were struck by their teachers' intellect and commitment to their work. "They had been educated far beyond what our mothers had been, and had traveled far more than our mothers," said Carol Tauer, who graduated from St. Joseph's Academy in St. Paul, Minnesota, in 1950. Eileen Flanagan, who graduated from Our Lady of Mercy High School in Rochester, New York, in 1968, remembers her math teacher galloping through the state-mandated material so the class could move on to the parts of math that she thought were really interesting. "The thing that was wonderful was these were some really smart women, who were really into their fields, doing work they liked," Flanagan said. "They were interested and interesting. They liked their students and what they were doing."

## Patent-Leather Shoes and the Chicago Phone Book

Catholic girls' schools typically taught religion in a dogmatic, doctrinaire fashion in the pre–Vatican II days. There was much memorization and little room for questioning. Partly, this was how the Church encouraged all its schools to teach religion. But part was also due to the fact that nuns, unlike priests, were not allowed to enroll at seminaries or schools of theology. Their knowledge of theology was often limited to the rote catechism of their own childhoods. Kathleen Rave, who graduated from Milwaukee's Divine Savior High School in 1965, recalls being told that Catholics were the only true saved people and that other religions had no legitimacy. "There was a lot of memorization, a lot of true-false and multiple-choice tests, not a lot of essays," Rave said. "You were either right or wrong and there was no wiggle room."

Sexuality, dating, and marriage were all approached within the context of Church teachings, which at that time treated divorce, birth control, premarital sex, and even French kissing as mortal sins

*Students mark a feast day at Marymount School
in New York, in the 1920s or 1930s.*

that would earn you an eternity in hell. Some of the instruction about dating and sexuality went beyond conservatism into the absurd. Some nuns truly did tell girls to avoid wearing patent-leather shoes—this is not just an urban legend—because they would "reflect up" and allow boys to see their underwear. Others told girls to take a phone book along on dates for use as a barrier against illicit touching. "They would tell us, 'If you go to a drive-in with a boy, make sure the Chicago Yellow Pages is with you,'" recalled Connie Geraghty, who graduated from Mother McAuley High School in Illinois in 1971. "Not the suburban yellow pages—the Chicago one, because it's thicker." In other dating advice, Geraghty was told to avoid restaurants with white tablecloths because they would make the boy think of sheets. And she was told to fight off sexual urges that might arise at the drive-in in a fairly dramatic fashion. "You have to get on the roof of the car and scream, because the devil is in you," Geraghty said. "You should scream and pray. Can you imagine? You'd never have a date again." Girls were sometimes cautioned not just against boys' advances but against understanding their own bodies. Cynthia Gruszkiewicz, attending a Catholic girls' boarding school in the 1930s, learned to change her clothes without ever leaving a part of her body exposed. Sr. Susan Oeffling, a Sister of St. Joseph of Carondelet, knew a fellow teacher in Minnesota in the early 1960s who advised girls to take a rose into the bathtub with them, so as to distract them from looking at their naked bodies.

Naturally girls didn't swallow all of this hook, line, and sinker. Many—especially the more worldy girls—just raised their eyebrows and snickered at advice about telephone books. Santa Marie Cuddihee, who graduated from Rosata Kain High School in St. Louis in 1961, recalls her Marriage class as one of the first times she questioned authority. "The priest was telling us it was a mortal sin if your husband wants sexual intercourse and you don't give it to him, because you are supposed to obey your husband," Cuddihee said. "We looked at him and said, 'You gotta be kidding. That's not true.' He said, 'Yes it is.' We started saying silly things and asking stuff like, 'What if the woman wants sex and the husband refuses? Is that a mortal sin?' The poor guy didn't know the answer and just stood there blushing."

Some teachers did manage to provide meaningful instruction about sexuality, although it had to be done sub rosa. When Cynthia Gruszkiewicz attended Holy Names High School in the 1930s, she had a life-changing series of sex-education lessons with a nun known as Sister Gertrude Mary who announced, "I am going to teach you everything you can know about your own bodies. I am going to regard whatever I say as confidential in this classroom. You will not discuss it among yourselves outside the classroom. If you have a question, ask me. But this is what I think you need to know." Sister Gertrude Mary told the girls about the menstrual cycle, male and female anatomy, and the mechanics of intercourse. "She said, 'God gave man the ability to procreate and made it pleasurable so he would go forth and multiply,'" Gruszkiewicz recalled. "There was nothing nasty or dirty about intercourse unless people made it so. It was a sublime gift unless it was defiled. I had a whole different view of sex from that time forward. I no longer thought it was disgusting and was afraid of it. . . . I am so grateful to her that I almost don't have any words for it."

But meaningful discussions like Sister Gertrude Mary's were the exception. The best that most Catholic girls' schools did, in the days before Vatican II, was to follow the lead of public schools and avoid all discussion of sexuality. The worst was to inculcate a sense of fear, guilt, and self-loathing among girls about their bodies. "This nun would tell us that we were the temptress and it was all our fault," Mary Ellen Welsh recalled. "I told her that I honestly didn't understand why. I was put out in the hall for trying to raise a ruckus. But I honestly wasn't."

Overall, the future sketched out for young women at Catholic girls' schools in the pre–Vatican II era was a limited one—marry and raise a bevy of children, or become a nun. "They were educating me to be a fine Catholic woman who goes to college, finds a husband— preferably a Catholic—has a lot of kids and makes the husband happy," said Kathy Hume Hanley, who graduated from Marywood High School in southern California in 1968. Schools actively promoted the religious life through annual Vocation Days where girls learned what it was like to be a nun. And taking vows was an attractive option for girls who wanted to do something more with their lives than child rearing. In Pat Murray's class of 1959 at Mt. St. Mary, more than 20 of her 150 classmates became nuns. In Joan McCloskey's class of 1961 at St. Joseph's Academy in St. Paul, about 40 of 100 girls became nuns. "We had a lot of young sisters who were very vivacious, energetic, and enthused," explained McCloskey, who herself wanted to join the convent but was instead sent to college by her father. "A lot of girls were not very wealthy and didn't have college ambitions. This was a good escape for them rather than being a salesclerk."

# Change in the Church

The Second Vatican Council of the early 1960s brought sweeping changes to the Church as a whole, and Catholic girls' schools were no exception. Vatican II defined the Church less as a hierarchy in which the clergy were the aristocracy, and more as a community of spiritual equals where God could act through anyone, even the most lowly peasant. Vatican II also ended the Church's stance of hostility to the modern world, affirming that the Church could and should be affected by the cultures around it. This had numerous repercussions: It launched Catholicism on a new path of ecumenicism, in which the Church acknowledged that other religions could also be following the will of God. It held Catholics responsible for the fate of the world, and for improving life for the poor and oppressed. It revolutionized the liturgy—changing from Latin masses to the vernacular, and turning priests around so they faced their congregations rather than the altar. It offered a wide range of new ways for laypeople to assume spiritual leadership, from helping distribute communion to serving on a committee to plan the liturgy.

For the women's religious orders that ran Catholic girls' schools, Vatican II sparked a series of changes. If the Church were now the "people of God," then sisters needed to seek God among people, not in a cloistered retreat from humanity. Women's orders started questioning the value of the habit and the cloister—were they distancing sisters from the people they aspired to serve? They questioned their traditional vocations—maybe sisters could witness to God by doing community organizing, as well as by teaching and nursing? Perhaps more than any other sector of the Church, nuns took Vatican II's emphasis on social justice to heart. The stereotype of the schoolmarm sister with a ruler ran smack into a new image of the activist nun in the 1980s and '90s—the Maryknoll sisters who were killed by Salvadoran death squads for serving the poor, or Sr. Helen Prejean, the anti-death-penalty activist who was portrayed by Susan Sarandon in the movie *Dead Man Walking*. Many sisters also developed a critical feminist analysis of their own role within the Church. "Sisters are adult women, well-educated and competent counselors of their own sex," wrote Sister Bertrande Meyers in 1965. "Too long have they been regarded as 'innocent minors,' cute little nuns, some of them sheltered from the world and its wounds, ignorant of its urgent needs."

Catholic girls' schools felt the effect of this revolution in a number of ways. Most visibly, many teaching sisters discarded their habits. Some orders made the change gradually, moving from a floor-length full habit to various versions of a knee-length habit, and finally to secular clothes. Others changed overnight. Students greeted the transformation in their teachers' appearance with a mixture of astonishment and welcome. In the all-girls environment, there was also room for humor and some intimate female-to-female advice. At East Orange Catholic High School, the president of the student council played the Motown hit "Devil with a Blue Dress" over the P.A. system when the nuns exchanged their long black habits for knee-length blue dresses. At the Marymount School in Santa Barbara, boarding students loaned the nuns their bobby pins and rollers and warned them that it would take awhile to learn to sleep with rollers. "It was very tender and kind," said Martina Nicholson, a Marymount student at the time. "We weren't laughing at them, or sabotaging them. We were trying to help them. The sisters would talk

*The 1960s brought both modified habits and less formal*
*teaching styles to Holy Names High School.*

about their discussions in the Mother House, about their vocation to bring God into the world, how to become more in the world and vital to the world. It wasn't like religion was something old and stale and useless. It was vital, it was part of why you were doing what you were doing."

The change in dress was accompanied by other changes. Sisters started using their birth names rather than their religious names. They were suddenly freer to share meals with students, or attend nighttime parent meetings, or visit students' homes in various parts of town. Taken together, these changes allowed many sisters a closer relationship with their students than had been possible before. "My mother thought it was the end of the Catholic Church, but I thought it was really positive," said Holy Names alumna Nancy Stricker. "Instead of chairs, we sat in circles on the floor. The sisters were more than happy to join us on the floor now that they had shorter habits."

## Folk Masses and Farmworkers

Through the late 1960s and early '70s, classes in basic Catholic doctrine were supplemented with electives in world religions, or women and spirituality, or ethics in the modern world. More and more, students were encouraged to look within themselves for answers to spiritual questions and to think critically about the world around them. Betsy Reifsnider, who graduated from St. Lucy's Priory in southern California in 1974, remembers debating the morality of the death penalty, whether women should be priests, and Pope Paul VI's encyclical on birth control. "Rather than saying, 'Okay, girls, birth control is bad,' they said, 'Here's this papal encyclical that's a few years old, let's have a debate on it.' Those of us on the side of the encyclical thought, 'Oh, this is an easy grade because the nuns have to support the encyclical.' But it wasn't necessarily so." The horizons of religious observance also opened up, with schools experimenting with folk-music masses and allowing girls to plan their own religious retreats. Jane Levikow was a student at the Convent of the Sacred Heart in El Cajon, California, when the sisters incorporated songs like "Kumbaya" and "Bridge over Troubled Waters" into services. "They had these two young guys come, former seminarians or something, and they would play guitars at Mass, which was a whole new experience of Christianity," Levikow recalled. "We were so excited. It made it more real to me. In high school I definitely established a relationship with God, and that kind of music made it closer."

Many sisters introduced social-justice issues into the curriculum, from racial discrimination to the struggle of farmworkers for decent pay and working conditions. Jane Levikow's school organized a field trip to Tijuana, where the girls saw people living in cardboard boxes. "I was devastated that anyone lived like that," she recalled. "It made me ask questions. They really made the connections between what you do and why you do it." Wendy Walsh showed up at Providence High School in Burbank one day only to find the doors locked and slogans painted on the walls such as "Hate now" and "Don't trust the Establishment." The school had embarked on a daylong simulation game, facilitated by the Black Panthers, to show students the corrosive nature of prejudice. Girls were divided into two groups, the reds and the greens, and were told the goals of the game were the goals of life—get an education, get into college, get a job, buy a house. But each group faced different rules. The red group had to attend "school" in the crowded, smelly locker room, while the green group met in the library with lots of books. Both groups then took a test to get into college and, not surprisingly, more greens succeeded than reds. "By the second hour you had little groups of white kids running to the Panthers and saying, 'This isn't fair!'" Walsh recalled. "It was a lovely experience—kids who'd had no black people in their lives running to these imposing Black Panthers for help. By the end of the day, everyone was very shook-up and changed."

At Holy Names in Oakland, Sr. Donna Maynard was determined to reshape school culture along the open, collegial lines of Vatican II when she became principal in 1969. Until then, faculty meetings had been little more than a string of announcements. Maynard turned them into frank discussions of school issues. She started an innovative "midsession" program, where girls could undertake internships or research projects that were outside the normal curriculum. Holy

Names eliminated its longtime rule of silence in the halls; it eliminated hall monitors; it allowed seniors to leave campus for lunch. The school added a counseling department and started teaching "world cultures" rather than European history. The school's approach to pregnant students also changed. At Holy Names and most Catholic schools before the late '60s, girls had simply "disappeared" once the school found out about their pregnancy. Their classmates were given no explanation; the pregnant girls gave birth invisibly in some distant place and often ended their education forever. "When I was dean, I found out about a girl who had gone through the parish grammar school, through Holy Names, and then her senior year was expelled with no ifs, ands or buts," Maynard recalled. "I remember at the time thinking, 'Something is not right about this.' When I became principal, a student got pregnant and I just put it to the faculty: 'To me, sending her away is not Christian behavior. Kids who have abortions don't get expelled. Here's a girl who is opting to keep her baby, and we expel her?' The faculty was behind me with one voice. We kept her as long as it was safe for her to navigate the school, and then allowed her to come back afterwards. Not one person ever said, 'How could you do this?' I don't know if it was the right moment in time, or if it could have been done earlier, but no one questioned the ruling. And since then, that has been the practice."

## The Vanishing Nuns

Changing habits and folk masses were the most visible ways that Vatican II affected Catholic girls' schools, but it also had another effect that arrived more gradually but was ultimately more significant. Vatican II was the beginning of the end for nuns as teachers in Catholic schools.

Vatican II signaled the start of a long and continuing decline in the number of American nuns. Between 1965 and 2002, the number of sisters fell from 179,954 to 74,177. Nuns left their orders for a variety of reasons. Some felt the reforms had eroded the meaning of being a nun. Others felt the reforms didn't go far enough. Still others took to heart Vatican II's message that laity were people of God, too, and that you could still live a holy life while being married and having a family. While thousands of existing sisters left, women also stopped *entering* the orders. Idealistic young women suddenly had so many options before them—secular service projects like the Peace Corps, professions like medicine and law, or serving as a deacon at their local church. And they could do all these things without renouncing the possibility of marriage and children. While more than 23,000 women entered religious life between 1948 and 1952, only 2,767 entered between the years of 1976 and 1980.

As sisters moved out of teaching or left their orders altogether, Catholic schools of all kinds were forced to rely more and more on lay teachers and administrators. Holy Names High School in Oakland had thirty-four sisters on staff in 1966. Today only three nuns work at the school, and only one is a full-time teacher from the Holy Names community. The convent alongside the school has largely been turned into classrooms and offices. Where twenty or twenty-five sisters used to live, there are now only thirteen, most of whom work outside the school. "This whole place used to be our convent. Now we have this little room," said Sr. Rita Caulfield, eighty-three, meeting a visitor in a small parlor in the convent section of Holy Names. "We're not getting any younger. We don't see people replacing us. So you think, How long is it [the community] going to last?"

The new reliance on lay faculty presented a financial challenge for Catholic schools. Nuns had been willing and able to work for a pittance, but lay teachers required salaries that could support them and their families. Schools had to raise tuition to cover their rising labor costs. Catholic education was still a bargain compared with many other private schools, but it was no longer free or almost free. At Holy Names, salaries mushroomed from 50 percent of the budget in the 1970s to 80 percent in 2002. Tuition rose from about $625 in 1974 to $4,350 in 1994 and $7,995 in 2002.

At the same time, Catholic schools were facing a series of enrollment challenges. The working-class European immigrants who had formed the bulwark of many urban parishes became more middle class in the years after World War II. Many of them joined the white flight to the suburbs. The urban Catholic schools that had been built to serve these communities found it harder and harder to fill their classrooms. Catholic schools as a whole lost half their enrollment between 1965 and 1990, dropping from 5.5 million to 2.5 million students and 13,000 to 9,000 schools. Catholic girls' schools also had to contend with the growing allure of coeducation. Secular schools and colleges were going coed right and left, and the Church's long opposition to coeducation had dissolved in the liberalism of Vatican II. Many Catholic girls and their parents—like their non-Catholic counterparts—wanted to be in school with boys. And now for the first time they had that choice. When dioceses built new Catholic schools in the suburbs, they were often coed or at least "coinstitutional"— boys' and girls' schools located side by side on the same campus. And Vatican II's openness to the modern world removed some of the pressure on Catholic families to attend Church-run schools—it was no longer unthinkable for faithful Catholics to send their children to the local, coed public school.

Under the combined pressure of increased labor costs and dwindling enrollments, many Catholic girls' high schools shut their doors. A few miles from Holy Names, Presentation High School in Berkeley closed down in 1988 after one hundred years of teaching girls. Others merged with boys' schools or went coed. St. Paul, Minnesota, used to have six separate Catholic girls' high schools. Today only one, Convent of the Visitation, continues to exist as an all-girls school.

## New Kinds of Students

Some urban Catholic schools changed along with the neighborhoods around them. As Italian, Irish, and Polish neighborhoods were replaced by African-American or Latino communities, the complexion of students changed. The percentage of minorities enrolled in Catholic schools rose from 10.8 percent in 1970 to 26.1 percent in 2002. Non-Catholic enrollment rose from 2.7 percent to 13.6 percent—a flashback to the nineteenth-century academy days when Catholic girls' schools relied on Protestant girls to fill their desks.

At Holy Names in Oakland, increasing numbers of African-American girls began enrolling in the mid-1960s. Today 35 percent are African-American and a total of 73 percent are girls of color. In an even more dramatic change, about half of today's Holy Names students are non-Catholics who come for the college-preparatory academics, the safe campus, the all-girls environment, the strong arts program—or simply in search of an alternative to the troubled public schools. The non-Catholics generally fit smoothly into the school, which has tried hard to be welcoming while not giving up its Catholic identity. But the integration of non-Catholics can have its ironic moments. At an admissions night, I followed a large group of prospective parents and students as they took a tour of the school. Along one hallway, a girl grabbed her mother's sleeve. "Who's that lady?" she said, pointing to a small statue of a gentle-looking woman nestled in an alcove. Her mother shrugged and gave her an "I have no idea" look. "I think it's the Virgin Mary," I whispered, a Jewish journalist cluing in a Protestant family about the most venerated woman in Catholicism.

From Oakland to Chicago, Catholic girls' schools today share a number of challenges. One is how to preserve their values and mission in an era of dwindling vocations—Catholic schools without sisters. They also share the challenge of how to meet the needs of twenty-first-century girls while remaining faithful to an institutional Church that often denies a voice to women. Despite the blossoming of lay leadership opportunities for women, the most important roles in the institutional Church—priests, bishops, cardinals—remain open only to men. Women still cannot preside at Mass or hear confession. As part of its conservative retrenchment in recent years, the Vatican has directed Catholic institutions to refrain from even *discussing* the possibility of ordaining women as priests. Catholic girls' schools and women's colleges are thus placed in a delicate position. On the one hand, they are dedicated to helping girls become leaders and fulfill their individual potential. Like today's secular girls' schools, they give girls a message that they can be anything they want to be—surgeon, astronaut, president. On the other hand, girls learn that the most important roles in their own Church are off-limits to them. Girls may run the student council, the service club, the athletic association; sisters and laywomen may preside over graduation and lead prayer services. But every time a Catholic girls' school has to import a priest to say Mass, it is giving girls an implicit message that women can *not* in fact do everything—they can not perform the central ritual in their own religion. "Our archbishop says we are not supposed to discuss women priests, but how can you consider yourself an educational institution if you can't discuss certain things?" said a teacher at a longstanding Catholic girls' school in the Midwest.

This contradiction continues in the area of girls' social and sexual lives. The institutional Church continues to prohibit contraception, abortion, and premarital sex. Abstinence is the only officially acceptable behavior for young women. Yet Catholic teenagers, like their non-Catholic counterparts, are in fact embarking on sexual activity at younger and younger ages. Catholic girls face the same health risks as other teenagers—they gamble with the chance of pregnancy or sexually transmitted diseases, they risk date rape, they feel social pressure to engage in casual sex. Girls' schools have an unparalleled opportunity to address these issues frankly with their students, and provide information that will help them remain safe and healthy. They have the potential to help young women grow up feeling positive about their bodies and their sexuality—to help girls avoid the guilt, fear, and passivity that made sex traumatic or alienating for too many women in the past. But Catholic girls' schools' ability to have those frank discussions is constrained by the Church's position.

Some schools avoid any discussion of birth-control options. Others discuss girls' sexuality, but carefully and quietly to stay under the radar of the institutional Church. Sr. Katherine Egan, the principal of Holy Angels in St. Paul in the early 1970s when it was going coed, remembers one sister would let students bring in condoms as part of the discussion. "The diocese didn't know if nobody told, and nobody told, as far as we know," she said. A health teacher at another midwestern girls' school used to invite a local gynecologist to talk about birth control and show examples of condoms and IUDs to the girls. "We currently do not have anyone doing that," she said. "Would I do it again? I don't know, because the Church has become more conservative in our area, and we have a strain of parents who are ultraconservative."

Catholic girls' schools that were founded and run by religious orders rather than by the local diocese often feel a little freer to present topics like birth control that are frowned on by the institutional Church. "If you say you are going to educate young women, you must do that in all areas they are facing," said Celine Curran, dean of students at the High School of the Sacred Heart in San Francisco. "It's so important for them to understand themselves and their own personal health. The Catholic position is always presented through the curriculum, but we have a responsibility to present students with all the information they may need. I don't think by giving them information, you are encouraging them [to engage in sexual activity] in any way, shape or form." But even these schools keep an eye over their shoulders. "Sisters and other folks are constantly making a decision about when to work within the system, and when to move outside the system," said Sr. Susan Oeffling. "What's happening now is the hierarchical Church is taking a much closer look at schools than they did for a number of years. There's more of a sense of scrutiny than there was before. It is true that schools sponsored by religious communities have a little more freedom, but it's also true in canon law that schools are the responsibility of the bishop. So it is walking a tightrope."

Girls' schools walk that tightrope on a range of women's issues. A religion teacher assigns readings about women's ordination, but refrains from holding a class debate on the topic since that might be too flagrant for the local bishop. Or a school allows girls to lead the "call to worship" before Mass officially begins and the priest takes his place at the altar. "We do a lot without priests," said Sr. Pat Coward, a Sister of Mercy at St. Vincent's Academy in Savannah, Georgia. "We had a candlelight penance service with the kids, where we didn't actually *perform* penance—we just had readings, heard stories, and talked about forgiveness. Afterwards we got a letter from some priest saying we couldn't perform the penitential rite. We walk real close to the edge, without breaking the rule. We don't want to set that example."

## Little Teresas of Avila

At Holy Names on a chilly Friday afternoon in November 2002, seventeen girls in jeans and sweatshirts listen quietly while Sister Margaret Kennedy talks about Joan Chittister, a Benedictine sister who has defied Rome with her continuing advocacy of women's ordination. The class is part of their religion requirement, a one-semester-long course for seniors called Women and Spirituality. The girls had been assigned to present oral reports on various religious orders—Franciscans, Dominicans, Sisters of Charity, and so on—but since no one had picked the Benedictines, Kennedy decided to fill that gap with a short description of Chittister, whom she personally admires. She reads from an essay by Chittister about why she chooses to stay in a Church that is "sympathetic only to invisible women." (Chittister compares her role as a feminist within the Church to the irritating grain of sand within an oyster that eventually provokes the oyster to produce a pearl.) Kennedy asks the girls for thoughts or comments, but they have little to say until the lesson moves on to a discussion of what is involved in a monastic life. Earlier in the week Kennedy had asked the class to write down how they imagine she spends her days, and now she teasingly tells the girls that they were way off the mark. "Unfortunately, I don't pray as much as some of you put down here," she says with a smile. "You said one hour in the morning, one hour in the afternoon, plus going to Mass. I don't know how I'd do that! It would be midnight before I was done." Kennedy describes her actual routine—arriving at school at 7 A.M., teaching and attending staff meetings throughout the day, occasionally staying for Mass in the convent at 5 P.M., shopping for groceries on the way home and then taking turns cooking dinner with the two other sisters who share her apartment. The housemates have dinner, pray together, and then spend the remainder of the evening much as anyone else would—reading, watching TV, or working on the computer. It's al-together a much more mundane life than the girls imagined, and their hands shoot up in a frenzy of questions: "I didn't know you were allowed to use computers or cell phones!" "How can you have a cell phone when you take a vow of poverty?" "Where do you buy your clothes?" "Don't you ever want to drive a really fancy car?" "Say your brother was really rich and gave you a Mercedes, could you keep it?" "Suppose the class got together and got you a really nice present like a Louis Vuitton purse, could you keep it?"

Kennedy is the one Holy Names sister still teaching full-time at the school, and very possibly the only nun these girls will have a chance to know in their four years there. She has a calm, even-toned aura about her and a quiet sense of humor that can make her eyes twinkle, and she takes their astonished questions in stride. "Sure, sometimes I'd like to drive a better car," she tells the girls. "But even though I might like it, it's not a high priority to me. I would rather live simply because that is what I professed to do when I took my vows. . . . If my brother got me a Mercedes I'd say, 'Thanks, Tom, but it really wouldn't look good, I've taken a vow of poverty and am trying to live a simple life.'"

Kennedy herself graduated from Holy Names in 1960, when al-most all the teachers were nuns. Now, as one of the few remaining sisters there, Kennedy understands that provoking these kinds of questions is a significant, if unstated, part of her job. Her presence is a constant reminder that it is possible to live life by values other than materialism and individualism. "I think it is important for there to be a Holy Names sister there as long as there can be, for the presence and the witness of the [religious] life," she says after class is over. "It's the simplicity-of-life thing. You could say that my role is being a 'professional religious person,' which sounds crass, but it means witnessing to simplicity of life, to chastity, to community life."

Kennedy, who heads the religion department at Holy Names, tries to use language in school prayers that includes women when-ever possible. This particular week, she was struggling with reword-ing a story about the ten lepers for the Thanksgiving prayer service so the lepers could conceivably be female as well as male. She doesn't hesitate to discuss topics like women's ordination, but she acknowledges that this freedom could diminish if a new bishop is appointed in Oakland. Like Joan Chittister, Kennedy believes in staying within the Church and working to change its approach to women. It's not a banner-waving, bullhorn-blaring approach to change. But it's educating for change nonetheless. "My definition of a feminist is a person who's aware of the injustices and works to change the systems that enhance that," she says thoughtfully, "and yes, that's what we're doing at Holy Names High School." Two thousand miles away in St. Louis, the one remaining nun at 160-year-old St. Joseph's Academy expresses a similar vision but diplomatically couches it in terms of the life of a saint. Teresa of Avila was a sixteenth-century Spanish Carmelite nun who was dismayed by the worldly practices that had taken hold in her order. She braved opposition from Church officials to found a series of new, more simple convents. "We just finished celebrating the feast of St. Teresa of Avila," said Sr. Joan Lampton, president of St. Joseph's, on a November afternoon. "While Martin Luther left the Church, here was a strong woman who faced the Church and made reforms within the Church. I want these women to stay in, make reforms, and make the Church better. I am trying to turn out little Teresas of Avila."

# 9

# The Public School
# Battle

## BECOMING REAL

*The Julia Morgan School started to feel real to me in the spring before
we opened, when I learned that two acquaintances of mine were enrolling their daughters. These weren't people who had been involved in
any of our founding meetings. They weren't people with whom I had
ever discussed the school. Because I knew them only casually through
work, I hadn't even been aware that they had daughters. But here they
were, signing their girls up for this school that I had helped create.
Somehow Julia Morgan had taken on a life of its own. It was a stunning realization.*

*Like the Velveteen Rabbit, we were becoming real. And like the Vel-
veteen Rabbit, we found that the process could be painful as well as exhilarating. In the months before the school's opening, there were
increasing instances of friction between the founding board members
and our director, Ann. We were moving from the stage of abstract ideas
to actually running a school, and that meant more of the decisions belonged to the director. At most independent schools, the board sets general policies and the director implements those policies and runs the*

*school on a daily basis. But those boundaries can be blurry at a start-up school. During their August planning session, Ann and the teachers made the decision that Julia Morgan would not have a uniform, and that students would call teachers by their first names. We were shocked when Ann presented these decisions to us as faits accomplis. We didn't disagree with the actual policies—we would probably all have voted against uniforms and for first names, too—but we felt these issues were central to the school's identity and thus should have been decided by the board. We didn't want to micromanage Ann, but we also wanted to make sure that our vision for Julia Morgan wasn't lost. Meanwhile, Ann chafed at this bevy of amateurs who were constantly telling her things like where to put the furniture.*

*We weren't quite aware of it at the time, but we were evolving from a collective group of activists into a more traditional board of directors. We needed to step back and let Ann run the school. We needed to let go of the little details and focus on the big picture. But if we weren't making all those little decisions, then what were we supposed to do? We weren't sure.*

*The school's opening month was somewhat disorienting for me. My own daughter was five and starting kindergarten, so my attentions were sharply divided. On the first day of school, I wasn't at Julia Morgan—I was across town at my daughter's kindergarten classroom. Other members of our founding group were getting daily reports from their sixth-grade daughters on what life was like at Julia Morgan. I was hearing nothing. After months of constant e-mail discussions, my computer had also fallen strangely silent. It was as if we had spent two years preparing for a rocket launch, I had gripped my seat watching the countdown, and then suddenly the radar and communication went dead. Gradually I got more caught up in the life of Julia Morgan, attending school events and occasionally sitting in on classes. But there was a gap that would remain for me as long as my daughter was too young to attend. I was intimately involved with the school on an administrative level. I knew far more about the school's finances, fundraising, personnel decisions, and lease negotiations than any parent. But I missed the kind of daily details that come home from school with even the most tight-lipped student—those little anecdotes about other* girls in the class, and favorite teachers, and ridiculous assignments, and inspiring field trips.

One of the costs of becoming real was that we could no longer be all things to all people. In the planning stages, it was easy for each of us to imagine the school of her dreams. We could use vague words like rigorous or challenging to avoid coming to terms with the places where we had conflicting visions. Midway through the first year, one of our most dedicated and active founders abruptly pulled her daughter out of Julia Morgan and transferred her to another school. She had been completely committed to the idea of Julia Morgan, but the reality of the school turned out to be a poor match for her daughter's learning style. We worried that her withdrawal would be a major blow to the school's reputation. But fortunately, she and her family left in a principled manner. They didn't badmouth Julia Morgan. They didn't try to sabotage the school. Looking back, I'm struck by the genuinely selfless character of our entire founding group. We may have been bumbling fund-raisers, but we never got into ego battles or personal vendettas. When we disagreed, it was always in a principled way and with the best interests of the school at heart.

Far deeper than the assorted aches and pains of becoming real was an enduring sense of wonder. The school ballooned from a closely held hope within our small founding group to an independent institution with a life of its own. It was like moving from a black-and-white sketch to a brightly colored, three-dimensional mobile that changed with every breeze. The school immediately became more than any of us had imagined. I had vaguely pictured girls doing science, but I hadn't imagined them shrieking with delight as a block of dry ice gave off vapor in front of their eyes. I had hoped they would learn something about money, but I hadn't imagined them learning to short-sell securities as part of a stock market game. The school also grew faster than any of us had imagined. Our initial business plan had projected 20 girls our first year, followed by 55 in our second year, and then 70 in our third year. Instead we opened with 35, grew to 91, and then to 134. By our second year of operation, we had more applicants than we had spaces.

At our opening ceremony, I watched in amazement as the founding class of sixth-grade girls filed in and lined up shoulder to shoulder.

*Some members of the founding class at the Julia Morgan School for Girls*

*Thirty-five girls sounded good on paper, but when you saw them lined up together they were truly impressive. They stretched from one side of the auditorium to the other, a Great Wall of girls, a lineup long enough to lead a suffrage march or return a football kickoff. We had girls from the suburbs and girls from the inner city, tall girls and short girls, funny girls and nervous girls, more students than we had ever imagined, all individuals, each with her own quirks and dreams and stories. Despite all our hours of brainstorming and visioning and philosophizing, we had never managed to picture this.*

Ann Rubenstein was a national correspondent for NBC news who had covered her share of emotional stories—family tragedies, labor strife, lifesaving medical advances. Journalists tend to get inured to the stories they cover: While today's news may be devastating, tomorrow's may be even worse. But something hit home with Rubenstein when she was reporting a story on a Milwaukee high school with a day-care center for teenage moms. She

interviewed one of the young mothers and asked her where she imagined herself in five years. The girl started silently weeping. "She knew
she was doomed," Rubenstein recalled. "She knew she was locked in
a cycle that happens when a teenager has a baby, particularly an un-
derprivileged teenager. She knew, and I knew. That had a profound
impact on me. I knew based on that moment that we were not doing enough. The day-care center wasn't enough. We had to get these
young women on a different path."

Rubenstein carried the image of that teenage mother in her head
for years while she continued her career. Then she met and married
Andrew Tisch, whose family started the Loews hotel chain and built
it into the giant financial conglomerate Loews Corp. Suddenly she
had the resources to do something to help girls like that teen mother.
She came up with the idea of opening a public girls' school in Harlem
that would steer girls away from the dead end of early pregnancy and
toward the bright lights of college.

Tisch knew that her project would be controversial. Title IX of
the Education Amendments of 1972 had been interpreted as prohibiting almost all single-sex public schooling. New York's most
prestigious public high school for girls, Hunter College High School,
had gone coed in 1975 under threat of a lawsuit from some families
of boys. The city's very last single-sex high school went coed in 1985.
Even as Tisch started her organizing, feminists and civil-rights groups
had a high-profile lawsuit pending before the U.S. Supreme Court
to force the Virginia Military Institute to admit women.

Tisch went about her work quietly. She first talked to Diane Ravitch, a prominent historian of education and former assistant secretary of education in the administration of the first President Bush, who
called it a terrific idea. Ravitch introduced her to the chancellor of New
York's public schools, who was also enthusiastic. Tisch hired a lawyer,
who assured her that Title IX would not block her project. She then
spent two years quietly building support for the school—holding
hundreds of meetings and phone conversations with school-board
members, politicians, leaders of the teachers' union, and community
activists from Harlem and the Bronx. "You couldn't do it without
[New York Mayor Rudolph] Giuliani, you couldn't do it without the

chancellor, you couldn't do it without the community school board, you couldn't do it without the United Federation of Teachers," she recalled. The process took so long that Tisch had to deal with two sets of school-board elections, with new members to cultivate each time, plus a new chancellor. Finally, in September 1996, the Young Women's Leadership School was set to open.

News of the school's creation sparked a furor. When the *Daily News* broke the story in July, the New York chapters of the American Civil Liberties Union and the National Organization for Women accused the the city of discrimination against boys. Together with a third group called the New York Civil Rights Coalition, they filed a complaint with the federal government charging that the school violated Title IX. National media like ABC News and *60 Minutes* quickly picked up the story. "Segregation is not the way to achieve equality," NOW's national president, Patricia Ireland, protested in a letter to the *Wall Street Journal.* "No evidence shows that the presence of single-sex schools works to eliminate unequal treatment of girls in education."

Tisch's school indeed proved to be more than a local New York story. The Young Women's Leadership School was part of a new wave of single-sex public education. Some African-American educators had started pushing, unsuccessfully, for all-male public schools in the late 1980s and early '90s. Then in the mid-'90s, in the wake of the AAUW report, dozens of coed public schools from Maine to Arizona started quietly experimenting with single-sex math or science classes for girls. Tisch's was the first school in this wave to successfully open as a fully single-sex institution. But it wasn't the last. Over the next few years, single-sex public schools would sprout up in communities as diverse as Chicago, Albany, Long Beach, and Denver. Law schools and Washington think tanks would start holding seminars on the pros and cons of single-sex public schools. And in 2002, inspired by the Young Women's Leadership School and these other efforts, President George W. Bush would sign bipartisan legislation aimed at eliminating some of the legal barriers to single-sex education. Tisch's long-ago conversation with that teen mother in Milwaukee did more than spark the creation of a new school in New

York—it helped open a new chapter in the history of single-sex public education in the United States.

This was a new chapter—but not the first chapter. Few people are aware of it because coeducation has been so dominant in America, but at one time, single-sex high schools were an accepted part of the public school systems in America's biggest cities.

## The Public Girls' School Tradition

By and large, American public schools have been coed. As public schools first opened in small towns and midwestern cities in the late 1800s, they almost always took in both boys and girls. David Tyack and Elizabeth Hansot, in *Learning Together,* their excellent history of coeducation, give several reasons for this. Americans tended to model their schools on their churches and families, which were coed institutions. Public schools came into being at a time when large numbers of women were entering the teaching profession, and female teachers made families comfortable with sending their daughters into a coed classroom. But mostly, there was economics. In rural areas with dispersed populations, it was hard enough to build one coed school— two single-sex schools would have been prohibitively expensive. Taken together, this all meant that coeducation just seemed natural to most families living outside the big cities of the Northeast. When a Boston school committee wrote a letter to Milwaukee officials inquiring about how coeducation worked there, even the question seemed a little strange to the Milwaukeeians. "Your inquiry strikes a Wisconsin man or woman as would an investigation into the advisability of allowing men and women and boys and girls to occupy the same pews at church," a Milwaukee woman wrote back.

In St. Louis in the 1850s, superintendent William Torrey Harris gradually turned all the grammar schools coeducational. His reasoning was common among nineteenth-century teachers—boys and girls together seemed to moderate each other's behavioral excesses.

Single-sex public schools were more common on the high school level than among elementary schools. But even on the high school

*Some early graduates of the Philadelphia High School for Girls, 1800s*

level, some cities with coed elementary schools still maintained single-sex public high schools. But even on the high school level, coeducation gradually became the order of the day. By 1882, only 19 out of 196 cities surveyed by the federal government reported having any single-sex high schools. By 1900, that number had fallen to 12 cities out of 628. By 1914, there were only 28 all-girl high schools left in the United States.

Single-sex public schools tended to persist in large, older cities like New York, Boston, Baltimore, Philadelphia, and San Francisco. These cities had typically started their public school systems before the Civil War—before coeducation became the dominant model. These cities were also large enough to support multiple high schools, some for boys and some for girls. Two of the first public high schools in what is today New York City were single-sex schools—Girls High School and Boys High School—which opened in Brooklyn in the early 1880s. They remained single sex for nearly a century until they merged into Boys and Girls High in the early 1970s. Similarly, Boston opened the college-preparatory Girls' Latin School in 1877 and maintained it as a female counterpart to all-boys Boston Latin until 1972, when both schools became coed.

There were three kinds of all-girl public schools—general schools that served a whole neighborhood or community, vocational high schools, and academically selective high schools. The vocational schools were mostly started in the early 1900s, when Progressive Era reformers decided that schools should prepare working-class young people for specific trades. Because men and women held different jobs, that meant setting up single-sex schools or single-sex vocational classes within coed schools. Boys were taught things like drafting and mechanical trades; girls were taught needle trades, domestic skills, or clerical skills. Boston opened a trade school for girls that taught subjects such as dressmaking and home economics, as well as a commercial school for girls that trained them to be telephone operators, secretaries, and saleswomen. In New York, middle-class reformers who wanted to help low-income immigrant women opened the Manhattan Trade School for Girls in 1902 with 20 students. In 1910, it was absorbed into the city school system, and by 1919 it had 1,495 students enrolled. Most of the girls were first- and second-generation European immigrants. Their curriculum included dressmaking, lingerie making, glove and straw-hat making, and, by the mid-'20s, manicuring and shampooing.

Progressive Era reformers saw single-sex trade schools as an efficient way to prepare young people for appropriate jobs, but these schools ultimately had the effect of channeling girls into poorly paying, stereotypically female careers. By the late 1960s, New York had thirteen vocational schools for boys but only five vocational schools for girls. In Boston, graduates of girls' trade schools were reportedly earning just 47 percent of what male graduates were making. Meanwhile, single-sex vocational classes within coed high schools placed arbitrary limits on learning that had nothing to do with individual students' interest or aptitude. There were plenty of girls who would have preferred auto mechanics to home economics—and plenty of boys who would have liked to learn how to cook—but they were never given a chance to study those things.

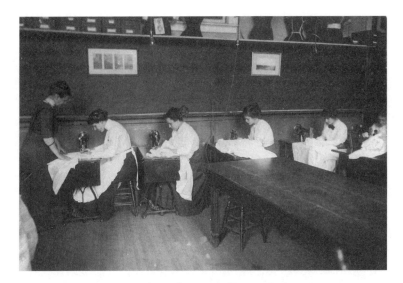

*Dressmaking class at Washington Irving*
*High School in New York*

Beyond the vocational schools, there were other public girls' schools with a more academic focus. Some of these schools had their roots in nineteenth-century teacher-training programs, or "normal schools," as they were called. Boston opened a Girls' High School in 1852 to train teachers for the city's primary schools, and Philadelphia started a teacher-training school in 1848 that became today's Philadelphia High School for Girls. In New York, Hunter College High School got its start in 1869 as the Female Normal and High School. Critics warned that the competitive entrance exam would be too tough for girls' delicate nerves, but more than 1,000 young women took the test to join Hunter's opening class and received scores of 75 percent or higher. The school offered to retest anyone who failed because of nervous problems, but no one took up that offer. The school opened with a whopping 1,095 "teacher-pupils," as they were called.

Girls' public high schools with an academic focus shared some of the same problems as their vocational counterparts—their facilities were often inferior and budgets smaller than those of comparable

boys' high schools. At the same time, they provided girls with attention and leadership opportunities they wouldn't have gotten at coed
schools. Some of the longest-surviving public girls' schools were
ones that were academically selective and attracted sharp, motivated
girls from all parts of their cities. These schools—such as Hunter,
Girls' High in Philadelphia, and Western High School in Baltimore—
were diverse long before diversity was a buzzword. "It took me out
of my neighborhood and I met girls from all over the city, all different classes and races," said Ruth Baum, who graduated from Girls'
High in Philadelphia in 1942. "It opened up a whole different world
for me." As early as 1952, the senior-class president and treasurer at
Girls' High were both African-American. "We had Amish girls, lots
of Jewish girls, and African-American girls," said Deb Rupp, a 1970
graduate of Girls' High. "I took Russian and we had lots of Ukrain-
ian girls who spoke Russian at home. It was the most diverse population I'd ever been in."

Through much of the twentieth century, the selective public
girls' schools offered a heady environment that was dramatically different from both private girls' schools and public coed high schools.
Unlike private girls' schools, they were filled with students from
working-class or middle-class backgrounds who were deeply driven
to achieve. For them, education was a ticket out of poverty, and they
were determined to take advantage of every moment. And unlike
coed public high schools, these schools placed girls at the center of
school life and expected them to be the stars—the valedictorians and
student-council presidents, not the homecoming queens and cheer-
leaders.

## "Feminists Before There Were Feminists"

Audrey Maurer's experience at Hunter in the late 1940s and early
'50s was in many ways typical of students at the selective public girls'
schools. Maurer—who as an adult became a teacher and ran a school
in Africa for twenty years—grew up in a working-class part of

Queens. Few people in her neighborhood had been to college, but from the age of seven she wanted to be a teacher and would play school on the roof of her family's house. She still remembers her excitement the day that her elementary school teacher told her about Hunter—"a school for smart girls in Manhattan." "My eyes popped open," Maurer said. "Then they said, 'Your grades are good enough to take the entrance exam, but you'll never pass it. No one from this school has ever passed it.'"

Maurer's family was skeptical about the idea. Going from Queens into the "big city" of Manhattan was as unimaginable a leap as moving to another country. Maurer took the test and was stumped by the part of it that involved algebra, since her school hadn't taught algebra. But she recouped with the section on English composition. "The only thing I thought would get me into this school with all these smart girls sitting around me was to write something different, like an O. Henry story," she recalled. She wrote a story about a girl who wanted to bring flowers to her teacher, but the flower shop was too expensive, so instead she brought her a pack of seeds. Maurer did indeed get in. "When the letter arrived, I took it in my hand and walked around and around and around the living room. From the time I opened it until orientation, I was sure I'd get a call telling me it was a mistake," she said.

From the day that Maurer arrived at Hunter, she felt like she had stepped through a doorway into a new magical world. There was a level of sophistication she'd never seen before—girls from wealthy Manhattan families were drinking cocktails and smoking cigarettes, while girls like Maurer from Queens were still wearing bobby socks and going to matinees. There were more varied kinds of people than she'd ever encountered—girls from the Philippines, a girl whose family owned a German restaurant, and the first African-American girl that Maurer had ever met, a young woman named Audre Lorde, who went on to become one of America's most prominent poets.

Mostly, though, Hunter was an environment where it was okay—even prestigious—to be smart. Maurer and her friends idolized their teachers, brainy women whom she described as "feminists before there were feminists." "I knew it was going to be a step up, I knew

*Chemistry class at Hunter College High School (N.Y.), 1944–45*

I was going to have to work harder," Maurer recalled. "But Hunter told me that it was okay to be smart. I was part of a community of girls, all of whom wanted to work hard and do well in school. I would not have considered going into class unprepared—not out of fear, but out of respect for the teachers, respect for the system."

On the one hand, Hunter gave students a "sky's the limit" message about their own abilities. On the other hand, it did not directly challenge or address the restrictions that society placed on women's careers in the 1940s and '50s. Some Hunter grads of this era became doctors or engineers, but most ended up entering traditionally female professions like teaching and social work. "It was taken for granted that most of us would become teachers," said Harriet Aufses, a member of the class of 1944, who decades later returned to teach at her alma mater. "Outside Hunter," said Audrey Maurer, "there were pretty much three jobs for women—secretary, nurse, and teacher. The highest of these in my limited view was teacher. That's the one I picked."

Maurer emerged from Hunter with a new self-confidence and a sense of comfort with being a leader. "I went in as a very youthful unformed thirteen-year-old, and I walked out as a seventeen-year-old who could address an assembly of one thousand four hundred girls," she said. Maurer breezed through Queens College, where she was elected president of her class. After a long period living in Africa, she returned to Hunter in 1979 as a French and Latin teacher. She was thrilled to be back at her old school. But by the time she returned, a very big change had taken place at Hunter. It was enrolling boys.

## Title IX and the Demise of Public Girls' Schools

In the second half of the twentieth century, the small number of single-sex public schools gradually dwindled. Then, in the early 1970s, the women's movement and Title IX dealt what seemed to be a final death blow to the idea of public schools for girls or boys.

Title IX prohibited federally funded schools from discriminating against students on the basis of sex, except in limited areas like sex education or gym classes. It was passed for very good reasons. Within higher education, women were often denied admission to graduate programs in fields such as medicine and law, while men were barred from programs in fields like nursing. On the high school level, girls and boys were still being funneled into vocational classes based on their gender rather than their skills or interests. And where separate boys' and girls' public high schools existed, the boys typically had far better resources and faculty. Philadelphia, for instance, had two selective academic high schools for boys and girls that on paper seemed like equal, parallel institutions. But Central High School—the boys' school—had 2.7 times more teachers with Ph.D.s than did Girls' High. Central's campus was almost three times larger. It had twice as many library books and computers as Girls' High, even though it had fewer students. Central offered a wider variety of math courses and about three times as many courses designed for gifted students. Central received about $380,000 over a twelve-year period from a supporting foundation, while Girls' High relied on magazine sales to raise money. Not surprisingly, Central students ended up scoring higher on the SAT exam, getting into college at a higher rate, and receiving $1.2 million in college scholarships compared to $500,000 received by Girls' High students.

During the decade after its passage, Title IX led to sweeping changes in the ways that public schools handled girls' and boys' roles. Schools halted the practice of separating girls and boys for classes such as home economics and shop. They started offering more athletic opportunities to girls. School districts that operated all-boy high schools soon found girls banging on their doors. In Philadelphia, three girls filed suit in 1982 seeking entrance to Central High. They complained about the inferior facilities at Girls' High and an expectation by the school that students would behave like passive, submissive "young ladies." Jessica Bonn, one of the girls who filed the suit, had a sense that the girls' school was second best even before she went there. "When I was in junior high I remember saying to myself, 'If Central took girls, I'd go to Central,'" recalled Bonn. "There was something kind of insulting about going to Girls' High. Think of the name—the boys' school is called 'Central,' but the girls' school is called 'Girls',' like it's a place where the losers who happen to be girls go." Once at Girls' High, she became aware of the disparity in resources. "Central had all kinds of things that Girls' High didn't have," she said. "They had computers, they had Russian, you could skip gym to take more academic classes, they had biochemistry and Girls' High didn't." When a friend told her in tenth grade that she was thinking of filing a lawsuit to enroll in Central, Bonn eagerly joined in.

The girls' lawsuit was extremely controversial. Central's powerful male alumni bitterly opposed the idea of admitting girls. Most teachers and students at Girls' High opposed the lawsuit, too, fearing the court would order a merger of the two schools and they would lose their own autonomy and tradition. But the girls found a sympathetic ear where it counted—in court. "The two schools, and in particular the educational opportunities provided, are materially unequal," wrote Judge William Marutani in 1983. Marutani ordered Central to begin admitting girls.

Most of the Title IX lawsuits aimed at opening up single-sex public schools were targeted at male institutions like Central High, since the boys' schools typically were viewed as higher quality. But Hunter College High School, with its top-notch reputation and its location on Manhattan's wealthy Upper East Side, was also a target. In 1974, two dozen families filed a successful class-action suit seeking admission of their sons to Hunter. The next year, 18 boys entered Hunter's freshman class for the first time. And in 1985, the New York City Board of Education ordered the admission of boys to the city's last single-sex high school—Washington Irving High School, which served a population of about 2,500 African-American and Hispanic girls at its site near Gramercy Park.

By the 1990s, there were only two public girls' schools remaining in the United States—Girls' High in Philadelphia and Western High School in Baltimore, both academically selective schools that drew college-bound students from all over each city. Girls' High and Western each had devoted cadres of teachers and alumnae, but they lived a precarious legal existence. The boys' schools that had been their counterparts had long since gone coed. Everyone acknowledged that Title IX would probably require Western and Girls' High to admit any boys who applied. But the schools did everything they could to keep a low profile and, to their relief, no boys actually tried to test the law.

Western High School today is a loud, bustling community of about one thousand girls. Where once it was filled with daughters of European immigrants, today it is 81 percent African-American, 16 percent white, and 2 percent Asian. Most of the students will be the first generation in their families to attend college—and the school does everything it can to make sure they will in fact attend college. Every student is required to take the SAT exam. Every student takes one semester of Latin. Across the hallway from the principal's office, a long bulletin board is decorated each spring with the names of all the colleges that have accepted Western girls so far that year. The school also posts the total amount of financial aid provided—a total that, in spring 2001, came to $5.2 million.

Girls' voices echo loudly down the long corridors at Western and the lunchroom is a thundering, crowded Babel. Western has cliques and problem kids just like anywhere else, including girls who are teen mothers. "No matter what you try, girls are still going to get pregnant." Eleanor Matthews, an assistant principal and a Western grad, said with a sigh. "Boys can talk them into anything." There's also a large part of the school culture that is focused on fashion, something that bothers some of the more feminist teachers. One of the most prestigious student clubs is called the Fashionettes, and they put on an annual fashion show of increasingly outrageous and skimpy outfits. The show is a major social event in the teen world of urban Baltimore—boys come to check out the girls, girls come to check out what other girls are wearing, and kids from other schools beg their friends at Western to get them tickets. "It's gotten way, way out of control," said Andrew Tomlinson, Western's technology director. "The girls tend to say, 'Oh we're modern now, it's okay for us to succeed in careers and to be at home in our sexuality and beauty.' To me, that's a lot of bunk. All I see is enslavement to fashion, and being sucked in by advertising."

Beyond the fashion show, though, there is a sense of female pride and power at Western. The school's 160-year history is a big part of that. At the annual Unity Day assembly in spring 2001, the student emcee exhorted the crowd that "we are all women, we are all Westernites, we are all one. Cherish yourself and each other." One student group put on a slide show about women's history. Another group called Sisters for Black Awareness matched music and dance from different decades with highlights from Western's history. By the end, all one thousand girls were standing and singing "Lean on Me" along with the performers, waving their arms back and forth in the air and swaying in unison like, indeed, one big sisterhood.

Western students by and large like the single-sex environment. "I don't want to be sitting in class with a bunch of ignorant boys acting stupid to impress the girls—I don't have time for it," said Caryn Hawkins, a junior in 2001 who was both a Fashionette and a member of the National Honor Society. "I like to brag about going to Western," said Dianna Reed, a senior. "I like to see the expression on other females' faces: 'She's smarter, she has a high fashion sense, she knows what she's doing in life, she doesn't let anyone get in her way.'"

Landa McLaurin, principal of Western, is herself a graduate of the school. Since she became principal in 1998, she has been struggling to raise the school's academic standards, which had gradually slipped in recent years. She faces the ongoing challenge of steering the huge bureaucracy that is a large public high school. She also faces some challenges that are unique to a public girls' school under the shadow of Title IX. Western tries to provide a top-notch academic program, while at the same time avoiding any kind of unusual programs that might give boys a reason to seek admission. "We have to convince kids they have the same opportunities here as elsewhere, but be very careful that we don't offer anything at Western that isn't offered elsewhere, because then boys would apply," McLaurin said. It's a frustrating catch-22 for an ambitious educator. Laws that were set up to prevent girls from receiving a second-class education now require this 160-year-old girls' school to stay genteelly in the shadows—purposefully avoiding the cutting-edge technology classes, shiny new science labs, and creative enrichment programs that coed schools routinely strive to create.

## Can Separate Be Equal?

The first attempts to establish new single-sex public schools in the 1980s and early 1990s involved not girls, but boys. Many African-American educators felt that young men in their communities were in deep peril. Young black men were dropping out of school at rates two to three times that of other groups. Many poor black boys were growing up in single-parent families without male role models in their lives. Black males of all classes had to contend with omnipresent racist stereotypes—storekeepers who assumed that every black teenage boy was an incipient criminal, mass media that showed a glamorized image of black men as "gangstas." These educators felt that special attention needed to be paid to the self-esteem and skills of young black men, and they proposed doing that through all-male public schools with an Afrocentric curriculum. Dade County, Florida, set up two all-male kindergarten and first-grade classes geared to African-American boys in 1989. Detroit opened three all-male schools in 1991 called the Marcus Garvey Academy, Paul Robeson Academy, and Malcolm X Academy. Milwaukee approved plans for two schools for African-American boys, with a curriculum built around African-American history and culture.

Opponents generally made two legal arguments against the new single-sex schools—that they violated the Constitution's guarantee of equal protection, and that they violated Title IX. Interestingly, Title IX itself didn't directly prohibit single-sex education at high schools other than vocational schools. But the regulatory guidelines that were adopted to implement Title IX set some very tight criteria for anyone who wanted to try a single-sex approach. The guidelines said that single-sex public schools were permissible if there were comparable facilities and services available to the excluded gender. They also said that single-sex schools were permissible on an affirmative-action kind of basis—if they were designed to overcome conditions that had resulted in boys' or girls' limited participation in a particular subject.

So there was wiggle room in the Title IX guidelines—but none of the Afrocentric boys' schools of the early '90s managed to squeeze through it. The Milwaukee and Florida programs were ordered to admit girls by the Office of Civil Rights, the civil-rights enforcement division of the U.S. Department of Education. The Detroit academies opted to admit girls after a judge issued a preliminary injunction against them in a lawsuit. In New York, school officials considered opening an Afrocentric boys' academy in 1992 but backed down after criticism from civil-rights groups such as the ACLU.

The same pattern held for all-girl classes that started to spring up in the mid-'90s. In the wake of the AAUW report, "How Schools Shortchange Girls," a number of schools around the country had started experimenting with single-gender math or science classes for girls. Some of these efforts were so low-key that they sparked no public criticism. But others were ruled to be in violation of Title IX and were ordered to admit boys. And in 1996, the U.S. Supreme Court issued a ruling in the Virginia Military Institute case that seemed to strengthen the hand of single-sex opponents. VMI was a 157-year-old public college for men that produced many of the business and political leaders of that state. It refused to admit women, saying that women wouldn't be able to handle its "adversative" method of training. It claimed that women could obtain a comparable education through a new state-run program within a nearby private women's college. The VMI case differed in several significant ways from the new wave of single-sex public schools: VMI was a college, not a high school. It was a historic institution that carried a lot of prestige and helped feed the state's "old boys' network." And unlike an all-girls science class or a school for at-risk African-American boys, VMI wasn't trying to remedy the deficits faced by a particular gender.

The Supreme Court's VMI ruling was narrowly focused on the details of that case, and whether the "equal" women's alternative proposed by Virginia really was equal. It was not a blanket edict on all efforts at single-sex education. But the 7–1 decision was still perceived as a major defeat for single-sex education of all kinds. In New York, when Ann Tisch read the front-page headlines about the VMI ruling, her heart sank. It was just three months before the planned opening of the Young Women's Leadership School. "It blew our minds for a day," Tisch said. "There it was on the front page of the *New York Times,* and we had done all this work, we were in our building, we had fifty-six kids enrolled for September. I said, 'Okay, let's calm down, let's get this read and interpret this and see what it means.'" Tisch's lawyers read the opinion and concluded that their situation was sufficiently different enough from VMI. They moved ahead, ready to test on the high school level whether separate could in fact be equal.

Anne Conners, president of the New York chapter of the National Organization for Women, was busy dealing with issues such as the hostile environment for women employees on Wall Street and a series of rapes in Central Park. As she skimmed the newspaper one summer day in 1996, she glanced at a story about a new school for girls that was about to open in East Harlem. She thought little of it and moved on to other things. But later that day, one of her board members called her and asked what NOW was going to do. It was then that the significance of the news item hit Conners. NOW had just finished fighting the battle to open up VMI to women; now here was a single-sex public school being set up in her own backyard. "I realized, 'Oh no, there's public money involved in this,'" Conners recalled.

Conners whipped out a press release opposing the school, which was Ann Tisch's Young Women's Leadership School. Two other organizations also came out in opposition, the New York chapter of the American Civil Liberties Union and a local group called the New York Civil Rights Coalition. The three organizations called on the city to open the new school to boys as well as girls. When the city refused, the groups filed a complaint with the civil-rights division of the U.S. Department of Education, accusing the city of violating Title IX.

The groups' main legal argument was that the Young Women's Leadership School (TYWLS) would provide advantages that were not available at other schools—advantages such as small classes, a project-oriented curriculum, teachers with advanced degrees, and small advising groups with weekly conferences between each student and her advisor. "This is a school that is providing a superior academic environment, and it's only available to girls," said Chris Dunn, one of the ACLU attorneys handling the complaint. "I would hope every child in the city of New York would have an opportunity to go to a school like the Young Women's Leadership School. But they're only making it available to a small number of students on the basis of gender."

The critics also had political worries about TYWLS that were tied in to the broader, highly charged issue of school vouchers. In the mid-'90s, conservative groups around the country were in the middle of a crusade for vouchers that seemed to be picking up steam. Voucher advocates were promising to give parents more choice in schooling by allowing them to use public funds to pay for tuition at private schools. But opponents saw vouchers as more than a simple reform measure—they saw them as a step toward unraveling the country's entire system of public education. And they feared that single-sex public schools were a new ploy of the voucher camp—first you establish that certain groups of students can't be served well in regular public schools, then you make the case that the public should pay for them to attend private schools. It certainly didn't lessen the critics' suspicions to know that one of Ann Tisch's allies in starting the Young Women's Leadership School was the Manhattan Institute, a conservative think tank that had been a strong advocate of vouchers. "We kept arguing, 'This is one way they are going to come at vouchers,'" recalled Conners.

Underneath the legal arguments and political fears, critics of the Young Women's Leadership School had deep concerns about what a revival of single-sex public schooling would mean for the entire landscape of civil rights in America. To them, this battle was over much more than a single school building that would house a couple hundred girls. If all-girl schools were allowed, all-boy schools wouldn't be far behind. Then would come schools that were once again segregated by race, like the academies for African-American boys that had been proposed but shot down in New York and Detroit in the early '90s.

Many of TYWLS's critics had cut their teeth in the civil rights movement of the 1950s and '60s and the long struggle to integrate America's schools. Michael Meyers, head of the New York Civil Rights Coalition, marched on a picket line for desegregation of New York's schools when he was a student at all-black, all-male Frederick Douglass Junior High in Harlem. The disparities between black and white education in the days of segregation were so large—and those days were so recent—that TYWLS critics were skeptical that "separate" could ever be "equal." Even if girls' schools or Afrocentric schools were set up with the best of intentions, critics felt, they would end up with less funding and fewer resources than schools serving more privileged populations. They would return America to the days of second-class schooling for blacks and women. Also, by segregating students according to race or gender, they would undermine the central mission of public schooling in America, which was the creation of a common democratic culture. "I'm in favor of public schools that broaden people's horizons, that seek to extirpate prejudice," said Meyers. "Getting to know each other across race and gender lines is a very important socialization process. A public school system that segregates by race or gender perpetuates discrimination, racial idiocy and gender idiocy. It perpetuates thinking that is parochial and provincial."

## "Slaughtered in the Media"

Anne Conners went into the Young Women's Leadership School fight believing that she and her allies had an open-and-shut case. Instead, she and her allies were stonewalled on the legal front and hammered in the public arena.

The school and its opponents immediately became a hot topic not just in New York but nationally. National news shows, radio talk-show hosts, and newspaper columnists all weighed in. The public response overwhelmingly favored the school. Five years of ripples from the AAUW report had had an effect: People reflexively understood that adolescent girls faced a barrage of challenges ranging from math phobia to accidental pregnancy. It made sense to people to set up a school that would empower girls, especially low-income minority girls, who faced more challenges than just about anyone else. The opposition by NOW, in particular, struck people as rigid and hypo-critical. "Fit the misguided civil libertarians who oppose the school with dunce caps," quipped the *Daily News*. "NOW is evidently more concerned with abstractions than with the lives of actual young women," a *Wall Street Journal* columnist wrote.

Conners was barraged with angry calls from NOW members and other women who felt betrayed by the organization. "Members would call me and say, 'How could you do this? I went to Smith College and it was the best experience I ever had,'" she said. "It was a lot of white liberal guilt, with people feeling, 'I went to a [single-sex] private school, how can I deny this to these poor children in a bad neighborhood.'" Stunned by the public hammering, Conners undertook a bit of personal research into single-sex education. She read whatever research she could find about the effects of single-sex education. She talked to friends who had attended girls' schools. She came out more convinced than ever that single-sex public schools would hurt girls and women: They would divert attention from the broader problem of sexism in coed schools, and would reinforce gender role stereotypes. "I remember talking to a friend from Spence who said, 'My single-sex school didn't produce a lot of scientists and engineers. It produced a lot of art historians,'" Conners said. "Historically single-sex schools don't seem very progressive or dedicated to producing leaders—coming-out parties were more like it. Instead of fighting stereotypes, these schools just enshrine stereotypes."

NOW and the civil-rights groups filed their complaint with the Office of Civil Rights in August 1996, just before the school was scheduled to open. After some months an OCR official telephoned the civil-rights groups and said that the office did have Title IX concerns about the school. Conners and her allies thought that a ruling against the school was set to come out any day. But it didn't. OCR told the civil-rights groups that federal officials felt that the VMI decision required them to analyze the Harlem school in a constitutional framework, not just in terms of Title IX, so they were referring the issue over to the Department of Justice for an opinion. The civil-rights groups kept pressing OCR for a ruling, but nothing came out of the agency. By 1999, they concluded that the Clinton administration was purposefully leaving the complaint in limbo because it didn't want to provoke controversy by killing the school. "Every precedent we could find in OCR was on our side, so someone decided not to decide it," claimed Michael Meyers. Then the presidential election in November 2000 replaced a Democratic administration with a Republican one, which was even less likely to want to enforce Title IX. By June 2001, when the Young Women's Leadership School was getting ready for its first graduation, five years had passed and there was still no word from the federal government on whether the school was in fact legal.

## California's Single-Sex Experiments

The opening of the Young Women's Leadership School lit a national fire for the idea of single-sex public schools—a small fire, a rather sputtering one, but a fire nonetheless. In California, Republican Governor Pete Wilson won national headlines with a plan to open a series of single-sex academies on the sites of traditionally coed middle schools. In Chicago, a group of business and professional women organized a public high school for girls modeled on the Young Women's Leadership School. In Seattle and Denver, individual principals quietly set up single-sex classes within existing elementary schools.

The California program was the broadest single-sex initiative by far, but it was quite different from the New York or Chicago models. California took a top-down approach, with state government dangling grants of $500,000 in front of any school district that wanted to set up single-sex academies. Unlike New York, there were no philanthropists like Ann Tisch beating the bushes to find allies and funding for the California schools. Unlike Chicago, there were no volunteer groups raising money and fleshing out a vision for the schools. While the New York and Chicago schools were founded out of a feminist impulse to assist girls in particular, the California schools came out of a more diffuse desire to provide school choice and eliminate academic "distractions" for both boys and girls.

California's strategy for complying with Title IX was to set up pairs of academies for boys and girls. Each academy was to have comparable programs and facilities so no one could claim discrimination on the basis of gender. In addition, students would choose to attend the academies on a voluntary basis so no one could claim they were being forced to attend a particular program because of their gender. Were those safeguards enough to ensure compliance with Title IX? The question remained unanswered because no one brought a legal challenge—and the academies were only in existence for two short years before they closed down.

In retrospect, the California program had a number of serious flaws from the very start. It began as a rush job, with school districts given just two months to design and submit proposals for single-gender academies. The program set aside funds for ten districts, but only eight applied and only six of those actually received funding. Then the money ran out—Wilson had promised a two-year program but provided money for just one year, and the Democratic legislature derailed efforts to obtain a second year of funding. The districts themselves didn't have a deep commitment to understanding or implementing single-sex education. They saw the program primarily as a way to get extra money to help their lowest-achieving students. As one district administrator said, "Single gender was just another big grant, it's a lot of money." When the money ran out, four of the six academies closed down. Only one still exists today—the 49ers Academy, a one-of-a-kind venture that predated the Wilson initiative and receives financial support from the San Francisco 49ers football team.

Ironically, the largest and most successful single-sex school in California was one that didn't apply for a Wilson grant—Jefferson Leadership Academies in Long Beach. Jefferson was entirely a local initiative, undertaken after a survey of local parents showed that 58 percent would consider sending their children to a single-sex middle school. In 1999, the board voted to turn Jefferson Middle School—an existing school serving a working-class, multiethnic population—into parallel boys' and girl's academies that would have separate classes but shared faculty, facilities, extracurricular activities, and lunch periods. "Single-gender instruction has long been available to families who choose parochial or private schools," the backgrounder paper for the school board said. "We believe that families who choose the public school system are no less deserving than families of parochial and private schools, and we propose to offer them the same opportunity to make a similar choice for their daughters and sons."

The district renovated the Jefferson campus and reopened it in September 1999 as an entirely new school, with a new principal and an almost entirely new staff. It still serves a challengingly diverse population. Most of the students come from the surrounding neighborhood, where stores and businesses routinely print their signs in Spanish, English, and Cambodian. Forty-four percent of Jefferson's

1,100 students are Hispanic; 29 percent are African-American; 18 percent are Cambodian; and 8 percent are white. Eight out of ten are poor enough to be eligible for free lunches.

Jefferson's founding principal, Jill Rojas, was a petite, fashionably dressed woman who radiated a businesslike energy. Rojas had no personal experience with single-sex education before taking on the Jefferson assignment, but was interested in it as an experiment. "I didn't jump on the bandwagon, but I was interested in single-gender and the experience of creating something from nothing," she said. "All of the things don't necessarily work that we try, but we keep trying them."

Rojas was intensely curious about how the single-gender classrooms would affect kids' behavior and performance. The first year, she noticed the biggest changes in the boys. "The boys got so much more out of single-gender than anyone thought," Rojas said. "We saw a lot of boys being less competitive, working in groups, not being so silly about writing poetry, doing plays with a female role and not making it into such a silly thing." The second year, Rojas noticed bigger changes in the girls. Girls started to dominate the student council and the school's community-service group. They also became more assertive in class. "In the classroom, you see much more participation—hands up, becoming more competitive academically," Rojas said. "It seems more widespread this year. Last year a handful of girls assumed that demanding role of 'I want attention from the teachers.' Now it's spread more broadly among all the girls."

Like the academies funded by Wilson, Jefferson created parallel boy-and-girl programs as a defense against Title IX and discrimination charges. That seems to have worked: No one has filed a legal complaint against the school. But the parallel-academies approach dilutes some of the power of a purely all-girl school. At lunch hour at Jefferson, boys monopolize the basketball courts in the schoolyard—of ten pickup basketball games on a typical day, only two involve any girls. And Jefferson shies away from the celebration of female achievement that is common at today's private girls' schools. Marisela Moreno, one of the school's most experienced teachers, was told not to hang any Women in Science posters in her classroom because it would be perceived as discriminatory against boys. (In a small gesture of re-bellion, Moreno stretched the limits by sticking two Powerpuff Girl magnets onto a wall.)

The dual-academy structure has raised some interesting issues for Jefferson around teachers' views and responses to each gender. Faculty members teach the same classes for both boys and girls, which inevitably leads to comparisons as to which gender is tougher to teach. Some teachers—especially the less experienced ones—say it is just too hard to keep order with a roomful of thirty-five twelve-year-old boys and the wide array of digestive noises they can produce at will. Like some of the nineteenth-century advocates of coeducation, they find it easier to handle boys when they are interspersed with girls. One afternoon in late spring 2001, Jefferson biology teacher Lesley Richardson hurled a string of detention threats at her boys' class in an effort to keep order. "AFTER SCHOOL" she wrote on the blackboard, and glared around the room to see whose names to list underneath it. "We can do after-school instruction. I love after-school instruction," she warned. "Five. Four. Three. Two. One. . . ." The room became quiet.

"I adore teaching my girls," Richardson said later. "I just love it. But I can't say the same for them [the boys]. I spend more time just trying to keep them together. Every second I have to be right on them. Girls tend to temper boys' behavior. They're less likely to make body sounds if they're next to a girl. Here, it's just 'Let 'er rip, it's all the funnier.'"

As principal, Rojas worried about a simmering problem of faculty bias against boys. Boys were the subject of more disciplinary write-ups at Jefferson than girls. They received fewer of the school's conduct and citizenship awards. The students themselves were aware of the discrepancy, which was certainly not good for the boys' self-image. But in Rojas's view, the problem wasn't with the boys or with the single-sex classroom. It's with teachers who don't know how to handle that classroom. "Teachers judge our male students more harshly," she said. "They can't separate behavior from the grading process. They think of good students as ones who are polite and nice. The teachers are more physically and emotionally challenged by our male students. Girls aren't any more on-task than the boys are—they're just off-task in a different way, which the teachers tend to accept more. It's one of those gender biases. I'm not even sure how to fix it. I bring it up and talk to teachers about it, but it's in the core of the person."

Clearly, having only boys or only girls changes the social dynamic of a classroom. Problems arise when teachers—invariably trained in coed classrooms—don't know how to handle these new dynamics in a way that goes beyond stereotypes. In 2001, three scholars from the University of California and University of Toronto released a report on the Wilson single-gender academies—the only study done on that project. They gave the academies a mixed review. On the one hand, they said, the single-gender environment allowed students and teachers to have unusually candid discussions about topics like men's and women's roles in life, pregnancy, and dating. They helped students focus on their work, and gave girls more room to be achievers. On the other hand, they sometimes reinforced stereotypes about how boys and girls should behave "Overall, there was little time for deep inquiry about gender among educators, and a general lack of discussion about what it meant to be teaching boys and girls in single-sex classrooms," the academics wrote.

## TYWLS at Six

As Jefferson moved toward the end of its second year, the Young Women's Leadership School in New York was getting ready to graduate its first class of girls in June 2001. All of the thirty-two seniors got into four-year colleges; all were going, except for one who decided to join the Air Force. Eighteen were to receive full-tuition scholarships. Ninety percent would be the first person in their families to go to college.

When it opened, the Young Women's Leadership School ended up in a most unlikely location—the top five floors of an eleven-story commercial building in East Harlem. Students take an elevator up past assorted offices and a video production studio to arrive at school. Once inside, the physical setting feels more like a cramped but afflu-

*A hands-on math lesson at the Young Women's Leadership School in New York*

ent New York private school like Brearley or Spence than a traditional sprawling public school like Western. Girls wear uniforms of navy and ivory. The classes are small—typically sixteen to eighteen students. The chairs are often arranged in a circle rather than in rows. The teachers are young and impassioned.

On one spring day, sixteen ninth-grade girls sat in a circle discussing Herman Hesse's *Siddhartha*. "What does it mean when he says, 'There is no such thing as time?'" teacher Laura Rebell threw out. One girl suggested that it is like your relationship with your mother—she can act mad at you one moment, protective another moment, loving another moment, but she is really all those things at once, without time. On the wall, a poster reminded the students: "I am a girl. . . . I have a body but I am not my body. I have a face but I am not my face . . . I can create. I can make a mistake! I deserve the best. I will give my best."

Most TYWLS students love their school, including the single-sex aspect of it. "It's easier here because it's like you're among friends," said Portia Goodman, a seventh-grader. "It's easier to get along with girls when you're not around boys. The work is not easy, they give you challenges, but there's always someone around to give you help."

Critics of TYWLS don't deny that the school is doing great things for its kids. But they claim it's the small classes and high expectations that make the difference, not the single-sex environment. In reality, it's hard to separate any single part of the school's culture out from the other parts. Certainly, small classes and inspired teachers are a big part of TYWLS's success. But, as both the girls and the teachers attest, there is also something special about the all-girls environment and the focus on women's achievements. "I know if there were boys here, a lot of girls wouldn't be as outgoing," said senior Jessiny Nueces. Several weeks earlier, TYWLS had brought Mae Jemison, the first African-American woman astronaut, to speak to the girls. Meeting Jemison in the all-girl atmosphere of TYWLS affected Nueces on a deeper level than did any guest speakers at her coed junior high. "It was so amazing," she said. "This woman was incredibly smart, and great at math and science. I was like, 'Wait a minute, if she can do it, I can do it too.' And those aren't even my best subjects."

## The Door Cracks Open

By mid-2003, the Department of Education still had not issued a ruling one way or the other on the school's fate. But nationally, the landscape was shifting in a way that would give TYWLS and other public girls' schools a little more legal room to breathe.

Republican Senator John Danforth had proposed legislation in the early 1990s that would have allowed ten schools to carry out single-sex programs on a trial basis. Danforth's legislation died under fire from liberal Democrats, who claimed it would be a first step toward broader racial and gender discrimination. Later in the '90s, similar legislation was introduced by Republican Senator Kay Bailey Hutchison of Texas, but that too died along partisan lines. Then Hutchison got an assist from an unexpected quarter—newly elected Democratic Senator Hillary Rodham Clinton.

Clinton joined Hutchison in 2001 as cosponsor of a bill aimed at making room for single-sex public schools. She cited the success of the Young Women's Leadership School, and said she hoped to see more schools like TYWLS. Another Democrat supporting the bill was California Senator Dianne Feinstein, who herself had graduated from the all-girls Convent of the Sacred Heart High School in San Francisco. "I had the opportunity to go to a Catholic girls' high school which was a very special experience for me, gave me extraordinary benefit," Feinstein said on the floor of the Senate. "Why should not a parent have a choice of whether to send a youngster to a single-sex elementary school if that parent believes that youngster could learn better in that environment? It seems to me to be something that public education ought to offer."

Hillary Clinton's cosponsorship elevated the bill beyond partisan opposition. It passed with unanimous consent and was incorporated into the "No Child Left Behind" education bill signed by President Bush in January 2002.

The Hutchison-Clinton legislation actually included two separate measures. It allowed local school districts to apply for federal funding for single-gender schools and programs. It also required the Department of Education to issue guidelines on how to implement single-sex schools without violating Title IX or the Constitution. The Department put out a request for public comments on how it should draft those guidelines and, in mid-2002, received about 170 responses. Meanwhile, more single-sex classes and schools started springing up. Moten Elementary School in one of the poorest neighborhoods of Washington, D.C., became single sex in 2001, and found that its standardized test scores shot through the roof. A new charter school called Brighter Choice opened parallel boys' and girls' academies under one roof in Albany, New York, and received more than 250 applications for its 90 slots. Cities such as Houston, Cincinnati, and Paducah, Kentucky, opened single-sex programs. By mid-2003, the new federal guidelines had still not been released, and so the legal status of these new efforts remained murky. But there were now nearly fifty public schools around the country offering some kind of single-sex instruction—seventeen schools that were fully single sex, and at least thirty more that offered some single-sex classrooms. There were the historic all-girl schools, Girls' High in Philadelphia and Western High School in Baltimore. There was the new generation of schools like TYWLS that were created to overcome the specific challenges facing girls. And there was the other stream of new schools like Jefferson in Long Beach, where boys' and girls' academies were set up side by side within a single school.

# 10

# What's Best for Girls?

## A Julia Morgan Morning

So this is what we created:

*It's a cool December morning in the Oakland Hills outside the one-time college dormitory that now houses the Julia Morgan School for Girls. A long line of cars inches along the steep, winding road as parents drop off their kids. The girls run inside and cluster in the hallway, greeting each other with hugs. One group of seventh-grade girls in sweatshirts and jeans starts a spontaneous a cappella rendition of "The Raggle Taggle Gypsy-O," a song they are to perform later in the month at a school Renaissance fair. They lean against each other, arms casually draped around each other, except for one girl who is holding a small, wiggly, tan-and-white hamster.*

*The students in this group, and at Julia Morgan generally, are strikingly diverse. Our 140 girls come from over sixty different elementary schools. Over 40 percent are girls of color. Thirty percent receive financial aid—a big commitment for a small, new school but one that we felt was essential to the school's identity.*

*Today this group of seventh-graders is starting their day with lan-*

guage arts, the latest educational buzzword for what used to be called English class. Their teacher, Rebecca Field, asks them to read sonnets they have written as part of their interdisciplinary study of the Renaissance. "Do you have to read it?" one student asks. "No, you can pass," Rebecca says. But thirteen of the fifteen girls choose to read theirs aloud. One girl named Sophie signs her sonnet as "Sophonisba," after the ancient Carthaginian heroine. Their classmates listen attentively and clap after each one is done.

The class moves on to a grammar lesson on the possessive. Rebecca asks the girls to pair up and go over their grammar homework. The room fills with a low, busy burble of voices as girls compare answers. They are brutally honest with themselves: "Okay, that's half credit for me, I did the possessive right but I rewrote the sentence." "Okay, I got one, two, three out of seven." The girls clearly like working together, but there is still an audible sigh of relief when Rebecca tells them it's time to put their possessives away and read the final act of Romeo and Juliet, where Romeo finds Juliet's dead body in the Capulet family tomb. When Rebecca asks for volunteers to read, hands shoot up throughout the room. One girl asks what a tomb looks like. A slim girl with thick, dark hair reads the part of Romeo: "O my love, my wife, Death, that hath suck'd the honey of thy breath," and the room is still. There is not a single giggle. There is not a single fidget. There is none of the elbowing or teasing or snickering that might go hand in hand with a passage like that in a coed classroom.

The seventh-graders move on to music, where they rehearse Renaissance songs and dances. They follow that with math, where teacher Liz Gibbs has them pair up once again to check homework answers. The class is working on equations. Gibbs is trying not just to show them the right answers, but to give them a visceral, hands-on understanding of what an equation is. She invites the girls to crowd around her desk where she has a large drawing of a scale with wooden blocks and a closed bag placed on each side. She talks about equations as a kind of balance like the scale—if a 3-pound block and x (the closed bag) are on one side, and a 5-pound block and y (the other closed bag) are on the other side, and if x weighs four pounds, then what must y be in order to make the

*A seventh-grade science class with teacher Kiyomi Cohn*
*at the Julia Morgan School for Girls*

scale balance? The girls are focused and engaged and speak out. At one point, a tall girl with straight, blond hair exclaims, "Oh! I get it!" and does a little wiggly dance.

Liz, who is passionate about math, has taught at both coed and all-girl independent schools. In her old coed school, she had to institute a no-hairbrushing-during-class rule because the girls were so preoccupied with their appearance. Here at Julia Morgan, she feels she covers more ground because the girls are so focused on the lesson. They're more willing to ask questions. And Liz makes a point of encouraging questions: At the very start of the school year, she emphasized that her classroom was a place where it was okay to make mistakes. Her approach seems to have paid off. When Liz started an after-school Math Club for students who wanted extra challenges, thirty out of fifty-one seventh-graders volunteered to join—a staggering number in any setting, let alone a population of twelve-year-old girls.

*As class ends and the students head outside for lunch, a girl sidles discreetly up to Liz and hands her a piece of paper with a "magic number" problem—brain teasers that students voluntarily invent to challenge each other. Later that week, Liz presents the problem to the class. "It's by a student who wants to remain anonymous," she said. "But I'll tell you—it's a girl." "Ha ha," the class mutters sarcastically, and then digs into solving the problem.*

Six years after it released its influential study on how schools shortchange girls, the American Association of University Women issued another study on girls and education. This one was also picked up by the media, but it didn't get the broad and continuing play that the earlier report did—no special reports on *Dateline*, no spin-off books like *Schoolgirls*, no *Doonesbury* comic strips. It nonetheless landed like a bombshell in one small part of the education world, the world of girls' schools.

The study, called *Separated by Sex*, addressed the question of whether single-sex education was better for girls than coeducation. The answer, according to AAUW officials, was a resounding *no*. REPORT FINDS SEPARATING BY SEX NOT THE SOLUTION TO GENDER INEQUITY IN SCHOOL, proclaimed the headline of the press release issued by the AAUW. "There is no evidence in general that single-sex education works or is better for girls than coeducation," the release went on to say. "There is no escape from sexism in single-sex schools and classes."

Teachers and administrators at girls' schools were taken aback by the report. "We knew they were doing a piece on single-sex education, but we had no idea it would come out and get picked up in the media the way it did," said Whitney Ransome, codirector of the National Coalition of Girls' Schools. But there was more to the report than met the eye—or than was conveyed in the AAUW's press release. The AAUW seemed determined to produce a report that slammed single-sex education, regardless of what the evidence showed. The report was based on a November 1997 symposium of about twenty educators and researchers, not one of whom actually represented or was working at a girls' school. Unlike the 1992 report when the AAUW took pains to bring all interested groups to the table, it did not invite the National Coalition of Girls' Schools to take part in the discussion. And the AAUW's press release was far more harsh in its judgment of single-sex schools than was the actual report. The eighty-four-page report cited numerous studies that found benefits to single-sex schooling, along with other studies that didn't find any benefits. The report included papers from two academics who supported single-sex education for girls, along with two who didn't support it. A more accurate summary of the report might have been "Scholars have reached differing conclusions on whether single-sex education benefits girls," rather than "There is no evidence . . . that single-sex education works."

"I'd characterize their executive summary of the report, particularly their media release, as incorrect," said Cornelius Riordan, a sociologist who is one of the leading American researchers on girls' schools and who took part in the AAUW symposium. "They didn't accurately portray what went on during the day or what the four major [research] papers said. . . . It was a setup. Clearly they wanted to put a stop to it [public support for girls' schools]. But I don't think they were successful."

The AAUW hadn't always been critical of single-sex education. In the wake of the group's 1992 report, "How Schools Shortchange Girls," a number of public schools had started to experiment with all-girl math and science classes. The AAUW had greeted these pilot efforts with cautious praise. "The evidence of the impact of these same-sex classes is still largely anecdotal, but many girls, parents, teachers, and administrators believe they are making a positive difference," the organization wrote in a 1995 report.

But somewhere along the line, the AAUW became worried by the growing interest in single-sex education. "We would get questions from reporters: 'Are you saying that single-sex schools are better for girls?'" recalled Anne Bryant, executive director of the AAUW until 1996. "How could we answer that question? We didn't know." The AAUW feared that single-sex classes would become a quick fix—a substitute for improving the school environment for the vast majority of girls. "What was happening in public schools was that they were setting up a girls' math class and saying, 'That takes care of it,'" said Judy Markoe, the AAUW's communications director until 1997. "Girls were still being discriminated against, and having a class or two wasn't going to solve that problem."

So the AAUW set out to take what it called "a critical look at single-sex education for girls." It compiled a summary of research studies about single-sex education around the world. It convened that daylong symposium. The resulting *Separated by Sex* report—as opposed to the press release—is a useful document. It's a good starting point for anyone interested in learning what kind of research has been done on single-sex schools. It gives a sense of the different academic arguments for and against single-sex education. It explains some of the challenges involved in trying to study single-sex education.

However, it in no way offers a definitive answer to the question on the minds of parents throughout the country—*Are single-sex schools better for girls?* That's a question that has been under discussion for more than a hundred years. It's a question that is heavy with political implications, because of the continuing controversy over whether to allow single-sex public schools. It is also a question that is likely to remain under dispute for quite a while longer.

## From Opinion to Science

The first wave of debate over the merits of single-sex education came in the late 1800s when cities across America were setting up public high schools. Coeducation largely won the day, but the arguments trailed on for several decades as young women increasingly sought out a college education. The *Ladies' Home Journal*, for instance, ran two dueling essays on coeducation for girls in 1911. Hugo Munsterberg, a Harvard psychologist, argued for educating girls and boys separately because their minds worked differently, and they were destined for different roles in life. "A man's college ought, above all, to be a school of manly character and a place of training in manly attitude toward the problems of thought and life," he wrote. "The girls' colleges must stand for an equally characteristic culture for women." The opposing viewpoint was presented by John Dewey, the father of progressive education in America, who claimed that coeducation was essential for teaching men and women how to live and work together. "Co-education . . . is an intellectual and moral necessity in a democracy," Dewey wrote. "Steady, frank, effective cooperation in the many interests men and women have in common . . . cannot be achieved without a sympathetic and practically instinctive understanding by each of the point of view and method of the other. And this is simply impossible of attainment if the sexes have in all the most plastic years of life been kept in a state of artificial isolation."

Such nineteenth- and early-twentieth-century arguments over coeducation typically were based on either personal observation or philosophy. Teachers based their opinions on their own individual classroom observations. Others—like Munsterberg and Dewey—drew their conclusions from a broader personal philosophy about men's and women's roles. Munsterberg believed that men and women had fundamentally different natures, and felt that schools should reinforce those differences. Dewey believed that men and women had more commonalities than differences, and felt that schools should help them learn to work together.

Today's debate over single-sex schooling is different from those earlier ones because of two new developments—the rise of empirical research on education, and a new wave of scientific study of gender and the brain. These developments raise the tantalizing possibility that someone will provide a definitive answer as to whether single-sex or coed schools are better for kids. Some advocates of single-sex education are already claiming that the new wave of brain research "proves" that girls and boys learn better separately. And both fans and foes of single-sex education point to statistical studies of student achievement to back up their point of view. "Girls in single-sex schools perform better than girls in co-ed schools," claims the National Coalition of Girls' Schools. "There is no evidence in general that single-sex education works or is better for girls than coeducation," counters the AAUW. Which one is right? Is either one right? And what the heck do we mean when we say that one kind of education is better for girls? What is "better"? Is good education measured by standardized test scores? College acceptance rates? Number of graduates in *Who's Who*? Number of graduates in math and science careers? How do you factor in the less quantifiable parts of a good education, such as a lifelong love of learning, an ethical and moral compass, a critical mind, or an understanding of how to form healthy relationships? Can we really find an empirical answer to that tantalizing question of whether single-sex or coeducation is "better"?

## Research 'Round the World

The 1980s and '90s gave birth to a growing body of statistical research comparing single-sex and coeducational schools. Many of these studies involved schools outside the United States, in countries such as Australia, Britain, and Thailand that had large numbers of government-sponsored single-sex schools. Despite its wealth of universities and research money, the United States wasn't an easy place to study single-sex education because there was so little of it left. By the 1980s, nearly all the single-sex schools in America were private schools of some sort, either secular or religious. And comparing private schools with public schools is like comparing apples and oranges. While public schools must serve every student in their area, no matter how disadvantaged or unmotivated, private schools can be more selective. Families that attend private school have made an active choice to do so, and thus are likely to offer more academic support to their kids than many public school families. Many private schools cater to well-off, well-educated families whose students enter the classroom with far more advantages than most public school students. The result of all these differences is that you can't do a meaningful direct comparison of American girls' schools and coed public schools. The National Coalition of Girls' Schools claims its graduates have higher SAT scores than the national median, and major in math and science at a higher rate than other girls. These things are true—but the differences don't necessarily have anything to do with a single-gender education. They could be due to the fact that, as private schools, NCGS schools select girls who are smarter and more motivated than the average American student. They could be due to the wealth or educational background of families of private-school students. Or they could be due to the personal attention and small classes that are provided not just by NCGS schools, but by most private schools.

Academic researchers who have looked at single-sex schools around the world have asked a variety of questions. Some try to compare academic performance, as measured by standardized test scores. Others look at more subjective parts of the school experience: How do girls at single-sex and coed schools feel about math and science? How often do they pursue advanced courses in math and science? How high is their self-esteem? And what is the source of their self-esteem—do they feel good about themselves because they're pretty or because they're smart?

Many of the international studies have come up with results favoring girls' schools. For instance:

- A 1985 study of 1,146 high school students in Jamaica found that both boys and girls in single-sex schools outperformed students in coed schools. The students at single-sex schools were also more likely to study subjects that were traditionally popular with the opposite sex.
- A 1989 study of 3,265 eighth graders in Thailand found that test scores for girls in single-sex schools were 40 percent higher than in coed schools. Boys in single-sex schools, however, fared 20 percent worse than their counterparts in coed schools.
- A 2002 study of nearly 3,000 schools in Great Britain concluded that girls in single-sex secondary schools did better academically than girls at coed schools. They were also more likely to take advanced math courses.

The problem is that for almost every international study showing a clear advantage to single-sex schools, there is some other study showing a different or more complicated result. A 1987 study of high school girls in Australia found an advantage to single-sex education in the region of Victoria, but no difference in Queensland. Another Australian study from 1992 concluded that students' performance in physics depended more on their individual socioeconomic background than on the gender composition of their school. It's difficult to make any broad generalization about single-sex education versus coeducation based on such mixed results. In addition, on a personal level as a parent, I found myself questioning the relevance of the international studies because of cultural and socioeconomic differences. It was interesting to know that girls at Nigerian single-sex schools liked math more than their counterparts at coed schools, but I had no idea what Nigerian schools were like or what they taught. Could schools in third-world Nigeria—where only 56 percent of women are literate and only 33 percent of girls are enrolled in elementary school—possibly have anything useful to say about my daughter's educational choices in California?

If the international studies are conflicted and confusing, the empirical studies based in the United States aren't much simpler to understand. To get a sense of just how hard it is to make definitive statistical findings about single-sex education, consider the stories of the two best-known American researchers in this area, Valerie Lee and Cornelius Riordan.

## A $4,000 Gender Question

Valerie Lee had gone into teaching almost by default—seeking a career that would accommodate raising a family, as many young women did in the 1960s. "It was a job to do so I could be a good wife and mother," she said. After a number of years of teaching, she decided she wanted to run a school and thus needed a graduate degree. At forty-two, she entered the master's program at the Harvard Graduate School of Education. One of the courses she was required to take was called Methods of Inquiry, an intensive introduction to statistical research in education. Lee fell in love with the field. She dropped her thoughts of running a school and threw herself into getting a Ph.D. in educational research. "What I found in taking this course was something I was really good at, and I liked it," Lee said. "When you are as old as I am, you know what nose to follow."

Her advisor, Anthony Bryk, was an expert in quantitative methods of research. He had received a small grant to study Catholic schools, using new data that had become available from a 1980 federal study of 58,270 public and private high school students. Lee wasn't particularly interested in Catholic schools. In fact, she looked down on them. But she was amazed by what the federal data showed about Catholic school students. "I was pretty negative about Catholic schools—the notion of all those nuns and repressive education," Lee said. "I was bowled over by what the data showed, which was these really fine places. They showed that *all* kids achieved at a high level, regardless of their social background. That was so intriguing to me, that schools could induce equity and effectiveness simultaneously. I wanted to identify the characteristics that made that happen."

Lee began working with Bryk on crunching the federal data, which came from an unusually rich data set called "High School and Beyond" that looked at students' test scores, academic and social attitudes, course enrollment, future educational aspirations, and self-esteem during their sophomore and senior years. Funding was scarce, but Bryk came across a $4,000 grant for research on gender issues. "Tony said to me, 'Do you have a $4,000 gender question?'" Lee recalled. "We needed something we could solve with $4,000 worth of my time and time on the [mainframe] computer, which cost more than my time." Lee used the grant money to sort the HS&B data by the gender makeup of schools—coeducational versus single sex. That in turn led to one of the landmark pieces of research in the single-sex debate, a 1986 article by Lee and Bryk called "Effect of Single-Sex Secondary Schools on Student Achievement and Attitudes."

Lee and Bryk looked at data on 1,807 students from seventy-five Catholic high schools, forty-five of which were single-sex institutions. Because they were looking just at Catholic schools, they didn't have the apples-and-oranges problem of comparing private and public school populations. They also crunched the data to adjust for students' differences in race, socioeconomic background, and single-parent family background, among other factors. Lee and Bryk found that there might be benefits for boys in single-sex schools, but girls definitely did better in single-sex schools on a number of different fronts. Girls at single-sex schools did more homework than their peers at coed schools, took more math courses, and were more likely to associate with academically oriented peers. They had higher educational aspirations. They were less likely to express stereotyped attitudes about sex roles. In academic achievement, girls at single-sex schools did better than girls at coed schools in reading, writing, science, and math. Lee and Bryk went so far as to estimate that attending a girls' school would give girls the equivalent of an extra year of science knowledge. They were careful to leave room for alternative explanations of the positive findings on girls' schools—for instance, the girls' schools in their study were smaller than the other schools and had lower teacher-student ratios, so perhaps the "magic bullet" was school size rather than gender arrangements. But they ended their paper with a cautious endorsement of single-sex education. "Single-sex secondary schooling may in fact serve to sensitize young women to their occupational and societal potentials in an atmosphere free of some of the social pressures that female adolescents experience in the presence of the opposite sex," they wrote. "If subsequent research supports the positive findings of our investigation . . . then the practical issue is to find ways to preserve existing single-sex schools and to encourage their development in contexts where the option does not currently exist."

Lee's research made her a star in the tiny world of people looking empirically at single-sex education. But one limitation of her work was that it covered only Catholic schools. Lee started getting calls from heads of independent girls' schools, saying, "We're single-sex too, why don't you study us?" It seemed like a reasonable idea to Lee, so she started a new study of single-sex independent schools. She collected data from about sixty independent schools, including SAT scores and questionnaires filled out by their seniors. She and her

associates also made site visits to twenty-one independent schools—
seven coed, seven all-girls, and seven all-boys. But when Lee started
to compile the data, she ran into a serious problem. There was no
pattern showing that either the coed or single-sex schools were better. Coed schools did better on some criteria; single-sex schools did
better on other criteria; and on still other criteria, there was no visible difference. "The findings weren't there," Lee said. "There was
no clear pattern of girls in single-sex schools being favored over coed
schools, and the boys' schools didn't look that good. It really caused
me to have a serious crisis. It's hard to come to any conclusion, because I had two sets of studies with two different sets of findings.
You start to think, 'What did I do wrong?'"

Lee couldn't publish the results of her comparison because there
wasn't anything definitive to say. She had a prestigious grant from the
Rockefeller Foundation to write a book about single-sex schools and
student achievement, but she was unable to complete that either. The
data remained in her files. "For five years I have had an unfulfilled
contract to write a book on this topic," Lee told the AAUW during
its symposium. "I would write this book if I knew what to say."

Lee did manage to use the independent-school data to publish
one paper, on sexism in coed and single-sex schools. As part of her
fieldwork at those twenty-one independent schools, Lee and her as-
sistants had visited classes and taken notes on sexist incidents and incidents that undermined sexism, like when someone challenged a
gender stereotype. Lee's goal was to see whether single-sex schools
offered a less sexist environment than coed schools. Lee concluded
that all three kinds of schools—all-boys, all-girls, and coed—were
guilty of sexism. However, the kind of sexism varied by school type.
At coed schools, the problem lay in classroom dynamics—classes
where teachers overlooked the girls or actively ridiculed girls who
spoke out. Boys' schools showed the most severe forms of sexism—
classrooms decorated with pictures of scantily clad women, a teacher
who addressed her students as "studs," and a discussion of Shakespeare that devolved into talk about "shanky chicks." "That was in
one of the most elite schools," Lee recalled. "My researcher was sitting in the back of room while they were talking about Shakespeare,

when suddenly the boys started talking about women's body parts. She was shocked beyond belief. Then she looked behind her and saw the pictures of women in bikinis on the wall. When the boys walked out [at the end of class], the teacher said, 'Look what I have to deal with.' She wanted to say to him, 'Don't *you* have any role here?'"

Girls' schools offered the most frequent instances of antistereo-typing behavior, Lee said. But they also sometimes displayed their own subtle form of sexism—treating students as if they were helpless children who needed extra support. "We saw instances in which female teachers encouraged girls to engage in dependent or childlike behaviors," she wrote. "In one class, students looked to the female teacher to confirm most of their statements and decisions. . . . [Another] teacher offered to be 'available for major hand-holding for term-paper stuff,' reassuring students about their term-paper assignments before any assistance was requested."*

While intriguing, Lee's paper on sexism didn't address the big question she had initially set out to answer—the question of whether coed or single-sex schools were better for kids. Lee was left frustrated by her inability to come to any consistent conclusions about the effects of single-sex education. She continued to get calls from journalists and researchers asking about her single-sex findings—sometimes up to three calls a week—but she herself moved on to studying other aspects of education. One of Lee's current projects is looking at full-day versus half-day kindergarten programs. Her current recipe for student achievement calls for smaller schools, a limited "core curriculum," a sense of community, a teaching style that

---

*Sexism can be in the eye of the beholder, and Lee may have been too harsh in her judgment of sexism at girls' schools. Some of the incidents of "hand-holding" cited by Lee do indeed seem unnecessarily patronizing. But others of her examples don't necessarily indicate sexism. For instance, Lee criticized a chemistry class where the teacher illustrated a discussion of carbon by pointing to her diamond engagement ring. Was the teacher making a sexist assumption that girls could only understand chemistry through talk of weddings and jewelry, as Lee suggests? Or was the teacher simply using an object from daily life to illustrate her lesson, a technique that she would also have used in a coed class?

encourages students to become actively engaged in their own learning, and a shared belief that all students can learn what they are taught. Single-sex schools are not the answer, Lee now feels, and may even distract educators from working on the more complex changes needed to improve the vast majority of coed American public schools.

## No Axe to Grind

Like Valerie Lee, Cornelius Riordan fell into the study of single-sex schools entirely by accident. A sociologist at Providence College in Rhode Island, Riordan had started examining data in the early 1980s that compared public and Catholic schools. Some of the data was from the same "High School and Beyond" survey used by Lee. Other data came from a different federal survey that looked at 22,652 high school seniors in 1972 and followed up with them periodically through 1986—a nice lengthy period for scholars interested in the long-terms effects of education. At one point Riordan noticed that about half the schools he was studying were single sex, and thought it would be interesting to take a closer look at them. "I had no axe to grind, going in or coming out," Riordan recalled.

Riordan's data crunching turned up little difference in student achievement between coed Catholic schools and public schools. But like Valerie Lee, he found a significant difference between Catholic girls' schools and Catholic coed schools when it came to student achievement—a difference that favored the single-sex schools.

Riordan undertook separate studies of white students and minority students, something Lee hadn't done. He analyzed the data in ways intended to neutralize the effect of students' socioeconomic background and initial ability, so that the results wouldn't be skewed if one type of school happened to attract wealthier or more talented students. He compared seniors' test scores in math, writing, science, and civics and found that white seniors at the all-girl schools ended up scoring half a grade higher than their counterparts at coed schools— as if they'd had an extra semester of study. In science, white students at the all-girl schools scored nearly a full year higher than their coed counterparts. The single-sex advantage for minority girls was even larger. Minority students at all-girl schools scored .8 of a grade higher than their coed counterparts on average. In science they were a year and a half ahead of their coed peers, and in civics they were nearly two years ahead. When he looked at the long-term impact of schooling, he found that girls from single-sex schools maintained an academic advantage for seven years after high school.

Riordan found more ambiguous results among male students. White boys did equally well at single-sex and coed Catholic schools. But minority boys did better at the single-sex schools. Riordan concluded that single-sex schooling was in fact making a difference for many students, with the biggest difference among the least advantaged kids. "Minority females profit the most from single-sex schools, followed by minority males, and then by white females," Riordan wrote.

Why did girls and minorities apparently do better in single-sex Catholic schools, but white boys didn't? And why, in Valerie Lee's work, didn't students at independent girls' schools display the same kind of advantage as those at Catholic girls' schools? Riordan came up with a hypothesis: Single-sex schools don't make a visible statistical difference for middle-class or otherwise advantaged students. But they *can* provide a boost to disadvantaged students from lower-class or minority backgrounds.

Riordan's ideas were in line with research showing that home background has much more to do with students' academic success than the kind of school they attend. That makes sense on an intuitive level—kids raised in homes with plenty of books, educated parents, and high expectations will manage to grow and learn even in a mediocre or crummy school. In Riordan's research, he found that white boys attending Catholic single-sex schools happened to come from more privileged backgrounds than boys at coed Catholic schools— their families were wealthier, they had fewer siblings, and they entered high school with stronger academic skills. These boys were on track already to succeed, Riordan concluded, and so they didn't gain any advantage from attending a single-sex school. Girls and minorities at

Catholic single-sex schools, on the other hand, came from relatively poor families. There was more room for their school to work some kind of "magic" on them—which apparently it did.

Riordan felt confident enough of his findings to do what Lee had been unable to do—write a book about single-sex education. In 1990 he published *Girls and Boys in School: Together or Separate?*, which urged policy makers to consider single-sex education as a useful reform option. "There is at least as much empirical support in favor of single-sex schools (or classes) for girls as there is for magnet schools, smaller schools, or a longer school year," he wrote. Riordan suggested a number of possible reasons for the success of girls' schools—more role models, more leadership opportunities, less gender bias by teachers, smaller school size, a sense of community, and a core curriculum. But the key, in his view, was that single-sex schools provide an environment focused on academics rather than on the adolescent culture of dating, clothes, and cars. When parents and students choose a single-sex school, they are typically choosing a school for academic reasons rather than social reasons. "Single-sex schools are places where students go primarily to learn; not to play, hassle teachers and other students, or simply meet their friends and have fun," Riordan wrote.

Riordan continued to refine his hypothesis through the 1990s and became the country's most prominent academic authority on the effects of single-sex schools. When the AAUW held its 1997 symposium on single-sex education, the guest list included both Riordan and Valerie Lee. Riordan knew he was venturing into hostile territory: The vast majority of people invited to take part in the symposium were critics of single-sex education. "I didn't do it blindfolded," Riordan said. "I knew who they were, and they knew who I was. If nothing else, it was fun debating the issue with forty people who were against me." But the fun stopped for Riordan when the actual AAUW report came out, and he saw it being used as a weapon to beat back the growing public and legislative interest in single-sex schools. Riordan publicly slammed the report as "slanted" and "off the deep end." "The AAUW report claimed that single-sex schools are not a panacea," he said later. "But they set up a straw person. No one claims that single-sex schools are a panacea or silver bullet. But they can contribute, like so many other things, to a positive learning environment."

## Brain Research Enters the Fray

There's another twist to today's debate over single-sex education that's even newer than the kind of empirical studies done by Riordan and Lee—the latest scientific research on gender and the brain. Technology has spurred a whole new wave of investigation of the human brain—what it's made from, how it works, how it develops. Scientists have a sophisticated array of new tools available for brain research, including Positron Emission Tomography (PET scanning) and Magnetic Resonance Imaging (MRI scanning). These tools allow them to analyze the structure of the brain on a much more detailed level than ever before, and to map which parts of the brain are activated by different tasks or experiences. Among the things being documented are a myriad of ways in which female and male brains are different. Some examples:

- Most women use both the right and left halves of their brain for tasks involving language, while most men use only the left hemisphere. Could this be why most girls do better than boys at verbal tasks like reading and writing?
- Men tend to have a proportionally higher volume of white matter, the nerve fibers that connect different regions of the brain. University of Pennsylvania researcher Dr. Ruben Gur found that people who performed the best on spatial tasks were those with the most white matter. Could this be why boys often do better than girls at spatially based tasks like math?
- Women typically have a rate of blood flow in their brains that is 20 percent higher than men. That means their brain tissue gets oxygen and nutrients faster, and rids itself of

waste faster. Could this explain why adult women show less of a decline than men in their attention ability and memory?

- Girls' brains develop at a different rate from boys'. Girls' brains develop myelin—a waxy material that insulates nerve fibers and helps different parts of the brain communicate with each other—at a rate that is three to four years ahead of boys. Girls also seem to integrate the emotional and rational parts of their brain at an earlier age than boys. Could this help explain why girls in a sixth-grade classroom often seem more mature than the boys alongside them?

These kinds of bulletins from the frontiers of neuroscience are fascinating and provocative—great fodder for dinner conversations about whether men really are from Mars and women are from Venus. And some advocates of single-sex education have started using these studies to bolster their case. Leonard Sax, a Maryland physician who in 2001 started a group called the National Association for Single-Sex Public Education, devotes about six pages on his organization's Web site to summarizing the research on gender differences in the human brain. Sax cites several studies that show different rates of development of girls' and boys' brains. "There is no one 'best' way to measure brain development," Sax writes. "But, whichever method you use, the message is the same: Girls develop substantially faster than boys, and boys don't catch up until well after the age of high school graduation. No one would seriously propose putting second-graders and fifth-graders in the same English class with the same curriculum and the same assignments. But when we put a typical eleven-year-old boy and a typical eleven-year-old girl in the same fifth-grade English class, we are essentially doing just that: putting together two children who are at very different maturational levels."

Sax feels that the neuroscientific case for single-sex education is the strongest argument in its favor—much stronger than comparing test scores of students from coed and single-sex schools. Other advocates of girls' schools are also intrigued by the brain data. "It's giving a scientific, physiological underpinning to everything we've known from direct experience—that different teaching approaches for the different genders make a lot of sense," said Whitney Ransome of the National Coalition of Girls' Schools. In coming years, as scientists continue to produce new information about gender and the brain, it's likely that we will hear the neuroscience argument for single-sex schools more and more often.

However, there are good reasons to proceed warily with this particular argument for girls' schools. The saga of Dr. Edward Clarke in the 1870s is a cautionary example of what can happen when people misinterpret the meaning of physiological differences between men and women. Clarke started with indisputable biological differences between the sexes, such as the female menstrual cycle, but then used those differences to argue that adolescent girls were unable to withstand the same kind of rigorous academic study as boys. Other researchers made similarly unwarranted leaps when it came to comparing male and female brains. Nineteenth-century scientists were fascinated by the discovery that women's brains weighed less than men's brains, and interpreted this as proof that women were less intelligent than men. Some even classified women with lower primates like gorillas when it came to intelligence. Nineteenth-century neuroscientist Paul Broca noted, "We might ask if the small size of the female brain depends exclusively on the small size of her body. . . . But we must not forget that women are, on the average, a little less intelligent than men, a difference that we should not exaggerate, but which is nonetheless real."

Today's new wave of brain studies are clearly far more sophisticated than measuring skulls, but their implications for education remain unclear. It is one thing to document that most women use both halves of their brain when doing verbal tasks, but what does that mean for how we should teach girls to read? Even leading neuroscientists shy away from making educational prescriptions based on their research. "I'm not sure the implications are necessarily what a lot of people have taken, which is to support single-sex education," said Gur, one of the most prominent figures in brain and gender research. "The data may be relevant, but the conclusions don't necessarily follow." Richard Haier, a professor of pediatrics at the

University of California at Irvine, puts it even more strongly. "There *are* sex differences in the way the brain works, but the meaning of this is hardly clear," Haier said. "No one knows how to take a fact about a developing brain and turn that into an educational tool of any kind. If someone came to me and said, 'Help us make an argument for single-sex education,' I couldn't make any arguments based on brain research."

There is a variety of reasons why the new brain research doesn't translate into a clear prescription for single-sex classrooms. First, most of the brain-scan studies by people like Gur have been done on adults, not children. "We know how men and women look different as adults, but we don't know at what age they get to look that way," said Gur. For another thing, not all women or men fit neatly into a "male brain" or "female brain" box. Gur estimates that about 15 to 20 percent of men have brains that work in "female" ways, and 5 to 10 percent of women have brains that work in "male" ways. It is probably more useful to train teachers to deal with a variety of learning styles than to lump all girls or all boys together into a single, gender-based category of learner. Finally, the research remains in a very early stage. The real-life meaning of many of these brain differences is simply not clear yet. Some differences may be significant but others may be irrelevant, dwarfed by the similarities in male and female minds. Fascinated by each new report of difference, we risk losing sight of the numerous ways that men and women think alike. And by straining to apply this research to the classroom, we risk misusing it as Clarke did to justify traditional gender stereotypes. "Our brains are basically alike, even if we use them differently," cautions journalist Deborah Blum in *Sex on the Brain*, her thorough book on gender and neuroscience. "If we set the two brains side by side again, they look the same. We have to work hard to find what's different. The contrasts are too tiny, and still far too mysterious, to suggest that these are profoundly different organs. They may do some things in different ways, but the basic repertoire is the same: I can tell you how to get to the library as well as the next guy."

So the neuroscience is still too young and sketchy to use as a solid base for educational prescriptions. The empirical studies of single-sex education are contradictory and less than definitive. But—the AAUW's claims to the contrary—that doesn't mean we should slam the door on single-sex education for girls. As a parent, I didn't get involved in starting the Julia Morgan School because of studies predicting that my daughter's SAT scores would be 10 percent higher. I didn't get involved because of a scientific paper about the myelination of her brain. I got involved because of the very real hurdles I saw facing American girls as they grew up, and because a girls' school seemed a logical way to help them overcome those hurdles. The more I saw of existing girls' schools, the more convinced I became that they were indeed an important option for girls today. Despite the scientific advances of the past century, the strongest case for girls' schools today is not one based on hard science—not a comparison of standardized test scores, and not an analysis of how the brain functions. The best case for girls' schools can be made by looking closely at what these schools are like today—not in the Victorian 1890s, not in the prefeminist 1950s, but *today*—and by listening to the voices of their students and alumnae.

# 11
# Girls' Schools Today

## GRADUATION

*It was another "historical moment." The college theater was filled to overflowing with parents, grandparents, little sisters and brothers. Camera cases rustled and zoom lenses whirred. Wearing long, white academic gowns and carrying single blue irises, the members of the first graduating class of the Julia Morgan School for Girls walked in single file down the aisle to the stage on June 12, 2002. They were poised, almost regal. They seemed so much taller than when they had arrived as nervous sixth-graders three years earlier. They seemed taller than the day before, in fact—possibly because, under the academic gowns, they had all replaced their usual sneakers and sandals with three-inch high heels.*

*Many private girls' schools around the country continue to graduate their students in white dresses with bouquets of flowers, a tradition that goes back to their Victorian roots. Occasionally teachers wonder whether the white dresses are an anachronism, but most students love the dresses in the same way that seniors at Girls Preparatory School cherish their May Day ritual. In our case, we firmly opted for academic*

*Students gather for the first graduation at the
Julia Morgan School for Girls, June 2002.*

*gowns. We wanted our girls to look like accomplished scholars, not brides
or vestal virgins. But we also wanted to celebrate our students' individuality, so over her gown each girl wore a blue sash with her name
and with a colorful swatch of fabric that she had picked out for herself.*

*In keeping with Julia Morgan's determination to foster girls' voices,
not a single adult spoke during the graduation ceremony. I handed out
diplomas. Ann handed out the sashes. Then each girl stepped to the
front of the stage and spoke a couple of sentences about what Julia Morgan had meant to her:*

"Julia Morgan has been like a family."

"I learned that it's okay to be weird and wacky. And that being
weird isn't weird at all."

"I cried when my parent told me I had to come here. Now I'm
crying because I have to leave."

*Parents and board members were sobbing. Because it was our first graduation, it hadn't occurred to us to have Kleenex boxes on hand, so people were stuck with whatever tissues they'd brought in their pockets. This was the culmination of everything we had set out to do. These girls had taken apart computers, built race cars, played marimbas, mastered algebra, dyed Japanese silk scarves, assembled stock portfolios, defined their own Myers-Briggs personality types, practiced yoga, and learned how to spit. They had been admitted to some of the most selective high schools in the Bay Area. Even girls who disliked math had been placed into advanced-level math classes at their new schools. In our mission statement, we had envisioned turning out girls who would be the "confident, capable, creative, and compassionate women of tomorrow." Seeing and listening to them now on the stage, we knew we had succeeded.*

*Almost a year later, I spoke with several of our alumnae about how Julia Morgan looked from the perspective of worldly wise ninth-graders. Some loved their high schools; others were not as happy. But they all looked back at Julia Morgan with a kind of awe and nostalgia. "I can hands-down say it was the best three years of my life," said alumna Rae Draizen.*

*One girl told me she had gotten braver at Julia Morgan, more willing to try new things. Another said she had learned to understand herself, which left her better prepared to deal with the outside world. Several told me that Julia Morgan had turned them from math-phobes into people who, if not loving math, appreciated it and felt competent at it. When I asked them what they liked most about the school, they all mentioned relationships—the trusting friendships they developed with the teachers and with each other.*

*Their words could have been a paraphrase of Ann's when, four years earlier, she crafted a culture for the school. Ann had talked about respecting girls' need for personal connection. She had talked about having the faculty provide a model of friendship and fun. Now, hearing these alumnae sum up their experience, I saw her efforts play out as clearly as if I were watching a football coach's chalkboard arrows turn into action on the field. "The teachers at Julia Morgan were like friends that were helping you learn something, not these foreign adult superiors lecturing to you," said alumna Petra Valoma. "It's not just the girls'-school factor that made it what it was. It was the teachers, the fact that the teachers liked each other and loved to be together. Sometimes I'd stay after school when there was a faculty meeting and I'd hear them laughing and know what a great time they had together. It told me they loved what they were doing. And knowing that, and knowing how much love and energy they put into what they were doing for us, it made us want to put out too. I didn't mind doing homework because I was doing it for a class I loved. I never knew what it felt like to wait for the bell to ring. I never said, 'Oh god, it's math.' I just loved every class."*

*As eighth-graders about to graduate, many girls in our founding class had complained that Julia Morgan was an idealistic "bubble" and voiced a desire to enter the rougher, tougher "real world." "Bubble?" Clare Kelly told me later as a ninth-grader. "That's kind of lame. It is a bubble, but it's a nice bubble. Three years to be in a nice safe place is not your whole life. If you're in a nice bubble, why pop it? I hope a lot of people have the same experience we had."*

M ountain View, California . . . It is the third annual Entrepreneurial Night at the Girls' Middle School. The school has borrowed a meeting room in the Microsoft office complex and turned it into a teenage version of a venture capital conference. Small groups of seventh-grade girls cluster behind booths displaying the products they have developed over the past few months. Each team includes vice presidents of marketing, sales, manufacturing, and finance. The girls have drafted business plans for their products, and later in the evening will pitch them to a panel of real adult venture capitalists. One group hawks little satin pillows; another sells colorful gift boxes that have been made from Chinese takeout containers. Still another is selling wallets made out of duct tape. They project sales of 100 wallets by the end of the year, with revenues of $775 and a net profit of $568. "Our products are made from a long-lasting, good-looking kind of tape—duct tape," student Kersten

Schnurle declares with confidence. "They're good for holding cards and money. Our target market is anyone with a sense of humor, anyone four years old and up, and people who like miscellaneous gifts."

*Charleston, South Carolina* . . . At lunchtime on a spring day, the grassy courtyard at Ashley Hall is alive with spontaneous games of volleyball. Girls' voices echo loudly off the 185-year-old administration building: "Wait for me, y'all!" "Who's got the ball, y'all?" That night, more than two hundred girls and parents jam the auditorium for the annual sports banquet. "We Are the Champions" blares over the sound system, and purple and white balloons festoon the stage with the school colors. The coaches preside over a seemingly endless parade of teams and awards—basketball, soccer, tennis, track, softball, volleyball, felt letters for the junior varsity members, chenille letters for the varsity, awards for the most valuable player, most improved player, most supportive team player . . . One of Ashley Hall's new mottoes is "where girls are champions." And the school has put its money where its mouth is, doubling its athletic staff and investing $1 million in a new outdoor sports complex with a soccer field, softball field, six-lane track, and six tennis courts. This year fifty-two seventh- and eighth-grade girls—more than half their classes—tried out for the volleyball team. Ashley Hall fielded an interscholastic sixth-grade basketball team for the first time in its history. But teachers worry that the competitive fever may be going too far. "There's a tremendous amount of pressure on kids who are sometimes not developmentally ready," muses middle-school director Lois Ruggiero. "Parents want them to become Olympic volleyball players in sixth grade, when they really should be trying a variety of sports."

*East Harlem, New York* . . . Holly Fritz is teaching American history to a class of eleventh-graders at the Young Women's Leadership School. The walls of her classroom encourage girls to speak up, with bumper stickers that say "Speak your mind, even if your voice shakes" and "Well-behaved women rarely make history." The girls are studying World War I through a project that also encourages their individual voices. Fritz has broken them up into small groups, and assigned each group to write letters from the point of view of a conscientious objector or a draft board member. The girls share their writing with the rest of their group; they choose a recorder and a spokesperson; then there is a debate between the spokespeople for the C.O. groups and the draft board groups. The girls are murmuring together eagerly in their clusters; they are focused and clearly enjoy working together with their friends. "Most of the girls in our school, we like to have debates," declares student Stephanie Roman, a senior in 2001. "We don't have lectures. Everyone participates. . . . Girls have a different feeling here. They feel they can do more."

## Warmth and Connection

Those three scenes offer nothing dramatic, nothing tumultuous—just glimpses of life at three very disparate American girls' schools today. All schools are a little different, and every school is a product of its own community and history. But there are also broad commonalities that make it possible to paint a picture of what girls' schools are like at the start of the twenty-first century.

Imagine you're wandering onto the campus of your local girls' school around lunchtime or between classes. Girls might be standing with their arms draped around each other' shoulders, or lying with their heads on each other's laps on a grassy lawn, or even sitting squished together on a single chair staring intently at a computer. There is a sense of physical connection and relaxed warmth. There is also a feeling of *play*. At Ashley Hall, girls give each other piggyback rides up and down the halls. At Girls Preparatory School in Chattanooga, eleventh-graders aren't embarrassed to join in a game of Red Rover on the front lawn. Girls are more willing to abandon the common adolescent mask of cool sophistication and simply have fun. "There was much less of an imperative to be cool, to be self-conscious about what boys would think," said Cate Steane, who graduated from Our Lady of Mercy High School in Rochester in 1976. "It allowed people to be more parts of themselves. We weren't afraid to get into water fights with our lightweight summer uniforms on. We probably wouldn't have wanted to do that if there were guys around."

Walking around the school, you'd notice a lack of self-conscious-

*Wireless laptops help make technology a seamless part of daily life
at Girls Preparatory School in Chattanooga, Tennessee.*

ness among the girls about their bodies. There would be less primp-
ing and preening than at coed schools, less checking of makeup in
mirrors, less constant brushing of hair. At every girls' school I visited, students expressed gratitude and relief at not having to worry
about their looks—they roll out of bed each morning and throw on
a uniform or jeans, without spending time on makeup or a fancy
hairstyle. No one had forced them to wear makeup at their old coed
schools, but they did it anyway. Removing boys from the picture
gave them permission to stop worrying about the way they looked
each day. And when worries about appearance are gone, girls are able
to focus on more important things like academics. "We have a level
of comfort and seriousness that wouldn't be there in a coed group,"
said Georgia Summers, a senior at the Bryn Mawr School in Baltimore in spring 2001. "You come to school in sweatpants or whatever is comfortable. I blow-dry my hair on the weekends, but I don't
have to do it on school days."

As you moved from the hallway into a classroom, you might be struck by how attentive and focused the students seem. Girls tend to have an easier time than boys with transitions, such as settling down after lunch into math class. Especially in elementary school, many girls also find it easier than boys to stay seated and focused for the quiet, small-motor activities that have traditionally been the heart of school. Teachers have less trouble keeping order and moving through their lesson plans in all-girl classes. The advantage of this is obvious— all-girl classes can get more done in a given amount of time. The disadvantage is that it's very easy to slide along as a mediocre or poor teacher in a girls' school. A teacher may not be gripping her students' imaginations, but they're not showing signs of open revolt such as tossing paper wads around the room; they're probably dutifully taking notes and making elaborate doodles in the margins. "As an administrator of an all-girls school you have to be very watchful," said Jessie Lea Abbott, head of the Katherine Delmar Burke School in San Francisco. "You can have a very mediocre teacher and nothing horrible is going to happen. It's critically important to be able to tell the difference between a girl who appears to be thriving, and a girl who really is thriving, because girls know how to 'look good.'"

## Teaching Girls

Today's girls' schools often make the claim "We teach girls in the ways that girls learn best." This isn't quite as straightforward as it sounds. Girls are individuals and learn in a variety of ways—some absorb information easily by listening, others need to see something visually in order to understand it, still others won't really grasp something until they have literally grasped it in their hands. Teachers are individuals, too, and even in a school with a clear philosophy there will be a variety of personal teaching styles. Then there are the differences among schools. Some girls' schools are highly competitive and grade oriented, while others eschew standardized testing and don't assign letter grades. Some structure the day in standard fifty-minute periods, while others opt for more flexible block sched-uling. There isn't any rigid "girls'-school method" of teaching that applies to every classroom like the standardized formula for french fries at a global fast-food chain.

Yet girls' schools today do share a number of common perspectives and approaches to teaching. Virtually every girls' school today is sensitive to areas that have been historic "trouble spots" for girls, such as math, science, and technology, and they put special attention into teaching these subjects. Girls' schools typically view their mission as extending beyond academics to address the social and emotional challenges facing girls, such as issues of self-esteem, body image, and sexuality. They are committed to including female role models and voices within the curriculum.

Moving from classroom to classroom on your school visit, you'd be likely to see group work going on—students gathered in clusters of three or four, cooperating on a project like those World War I draft letters at the Young Women's Leadership School. "Collaborative learning," as this kind of group work is called, has been taken up by all kinds of schools during the past decade. But it's particularly common at girls' schools because girls tend to enjoy group work and do it well. Some girls' schools have deliberately shaped their curriculum and even their facilities to allow for group work. When the Marlborough School in Los Angeles renovated its science center in the late 1990s, it chose round lab tables rather than the traditional long narrow ones so that girls could work together easily. The Young Women's Leadership School made similar decisions when it set up its classrooms. "One of the theories is that girls are more social—they're social learners," said TYWLS guidance counselor Chris Farmer. "So there are no desks at this school. All learning is done at tables with groups of four to six students. Working together keeps all the girls engaged. There are no passive learners here."

Girls' schools are particularly likely to use hands-on approaches to abstract subjects like mathematics. Girls tend to lag behind boys in the kind of spatial understanding that is the basis for subjects like math and physics. Experts are still debating over whether this is due to innate brain differences, less time spent playing with blocks and Legos, or some combination of both—but regardless of cause, teachers have found that hands-on activities are a good way to close that gap. At Ashley Hall, math teacher Betsy Sellers makes her seventh-grade students fold and tape paper cutouts into three-dimensional solids such as pyramids and cubes. When the girls are done, they open up one side of their solids and fill them with M&M's to learn about the concept of volume. "Girls are much more visual and more hands-on—they don't like to learn formulas," said Sellers. "This lets them learn in a hands-on way."

There are other teaching techniques that are popular today at girls' schools—things like incorporating writing into the teaching of math, or "wait time," in which the teacher pauses for a few seconds after asking a question to include students who need time to reflect before answering. It remains to be seen which of these techniques will persist and which will fade away with the next new trend. The important thing is not so much the particular technique, but how girls' schools are thinking about teaching. Like other schools, they keep an eye out for new ideas that can improve teaching in general or can help them reach particular kinds of students. But they also keep alert for ideas that might meet the unique needs of girls. When they see something that seems likely to work for girls, they're free to try it without worrying about whether it's good for the boys. Especially in fields like math, technology, and financial education, they are real-life laboratories for new ways to teach girls.

## Facing Girls' Real Lives

Today's girls' schools are reaping the benefits of the investments they've made in science and athletic programs over the past twenty years. They've by and large overcome their history of benign neglect of science and sports, and often provide state-of-the-art athletic complexes and labs. Many independent girls' schools are on the leading edge nationally when it comes to teaching students about financial literacy. They're aware of how financial ignorance has left generations of adult women vulnerable and victimized, and they're putting girls through the paces of stock market games, "Green Power" seminars, and projects aimed at teaching them household budgeting or the dangers of credit card debt.

Today's girls' schools continue the mission they embraced in the 1970s and '80s of presenting girls with female role models and an understanding of women's experiences. Classroom walls feature posters of women achievers like computer scientist Grace Hopper and anti-lynching activist Ida B. Wells, not just the Einsteins and Martin Luther Kings common at coed schools. At Western High School in Baltimore, an alumna describes her work as a lobbyist for the recording industry while the girls pepper her with questions: "What was your starting salary?" "What's the worst part of your job?" At the Atlanta Girls' School, students trade opinions about the business and professional women they have recently been assigned as mentors. "My mentor's sweet as anything, but I never see her because I have so many extracurricular activities and an hour of homework every night," complains one seventh-grader.

Some schools remain in an initial 1970s-feminist phase of exhorting girls that they can succeed in any endeavor, and that the sky's the limit. Others are groping for a way to prepare girls for the complex trade-offs in women's lives when it comes to having both a career and a family. At the Spence School on New York's wealthy Upper East Side, teachers no longer feel a pressing need to explain to girls that they can be surgeons or investment bankers. Many of their students have mothers who are themselves surgeons and bankers and who have been pushing their children since kindergarten to prepare for high-powered careers. "This is not a group that needs 'Take Your Daughters to Work' so much. This is a group that needs, 'Let Your Daughter Relax,'" quipped Arlene Gibson, head of Spence. Foxcroft head Mary Lou Leipheimer tries to tell her students that life is not linear and there is no single unswerving path to success. "Girls tell me, 'What a glamorous life you have with all that travel,'" Leipheimer said. "I sit down and tell them, 'Yes, I was in Saudi Arabia. And yes, I missed my son's Parents' Weekend. And it broke my heart. . . .' I don't want to set kids up for depression and for disap-

*Seniors at the Agnes Irwin School in sweatshirts
of the colleges they will attend, spring 2003*

pointment in themselves. So we tell them that they can go anywhere,
they can do anything—and that it is going to be tough sometimes."

Girls' schools also continue the work they began in the 1980s
and '90s of confronting the social and emotional challenges facing
young women. The days are gone when girls' schools kept a genteel,
repressive silence about issues such as anorexia and pregnancy. Stroll
around a girls' school and you'll likely pass a bulletin board devoted
to female body image, with a collage of magazine pictures assembled
by students as a critical examination of the supermodel ideal. Schools
regularly offer speakers and curricula on sexuality, eating disorders,
and drugs and alcohol. Girls' schools are far from immune to any of
these problems: At a National Coalition of Girls' Schools conference
in 2000, heads from around the country anxiously queried each
other for ways to counter the pressure on girls to provide boys with
casual oral sex. But the single-sex environment allows girls' schools

to address these issues directly with a minimum of giggling or embarrassment. The most thoughtful girls' schools have developed curricula that address a wide range of social issues in an open, honest manner. When the Julia Morgan School was putting together its program for girls' social and emotional growth, we found a model in a comprehensive twelve-year curriculum for "women's life studies" that had been developed during the 1990s by the Kent Place School in Summit, New Jersey. Some of the Kent Place curriculum covers health topics that would be addressed at any school, such as a first-grade lesson on "How I take care of myself" that includes brushing teeth and wearing seat belts. But other topics are targeted specifically at girls. The fourth-grade curriculum starts with a discussion of body types, and compares the bodies shown in advertisements with the range of bodies that exist in the real world. Students are asked to define the words *real* and *fantasy*, and are given homework of looking for pictures of girls in magazines, and discussing with their parents whether each picture is real or fantasy. By high school, Kent Place students have talked about friendship, assertive communication, and how to make tough decisions where you may have to go against peer pressure. In tenth grade, they examine sex-role stereotyping and sexism. They learn to do breast self-exams. They talk about AIDS, the history of abortion, abusive relationships, date rape, and eating disorders. At Julia Morgan, the Kent Place curriculum was incorporated into twice-weekly advising groups that quickly became the favorite part of school for many girls. These were not perfunctory check-in sessions with announcements of the week's schedule, but deep dialogues where girls talked about everything from menstruation to tensions at home during a painful divorce. "The sex-education part was really helpful for me because it wasn't just the basics," said Rae Draizen, a member of the first class at Julia Morgan. "Since it was in little groups with people we felt comfortable with, we were able to ask more personal questions. We talked about getting our periods. We asked questions about blow jobs, making out, all kinds of things that would actually happen in life. We even asked our teacher what it tasted like to give a blow job. We talked about what age we thought sexual relationships were appropriate." Draizen turned to her advising group for help when she was worried about a friend with an eating disorder. Even now, in her coed high school, those old advising discussions continue to provide a kind of personal compass. "I know I'm not not going to be pressured into doing anything, because I'm more comfortable with myself," she said.

## Why a Girls' School?

When I think about the benefits of a girls' school, I draw upon these kinds of stories and images from the daily life of schools rather than upon statistical data or neuroscientific theories. The attention to the intellectual and social challenges facing girls . . . the atmosphere of connection and warmth where girls feel free to be themselves . . . the commitment to helping girls become leaders in a world that still doesn't always welcome female leadership. . . . For me, these are the defining characteristics of contemporary girls' schools. And they feed into the reasons for choosing a girls' school today:

*Girls play all the roles.* It's a cliche, but a true one. At girls' schools, girls play all the roles—the math whiz, the student council president, the class clown, the star athlete. They are forced by necessity to learn skills and take on responsibilities that in a coed environment would typically devolve to boys. Girls push the grand piano onto the auditorium stage without a second thought; they call on each other for help when they have a computer problem. "The mere fact there were no boys there meant that girls were the ones running student government and organizing clubs," said Alyson Kozma, who graduated from Good Counsel Academy High School in White Plains, New York, in 1994. "We were able to do things we never would have done in a coed environment." The result? Some girls find a lifelong interest in fields like physics or engineering that they would probably not have discovered in a coed setting. And all girls absorb the implicit message that it's normal for women to play all kinds of roles—it's natural for a woman to be a leader or an inventor or even U.S. president. "I never had any idea of gender inequality or that because I was female, there were things I couldn't do," said Betsy Reifsnider, who graduated from St. Lucy's Priory in 1974.

*Girls are freed from the constant pressure to please boys.* The pressure on teens to be popular with the other sex can be overwhelming. For girls that often means pressure not to look too smart, too capable, or too ambitious. Walking a tightrope between fear of looking dumb and fear of looking too smart, many girls silence themselves in coed classrooms. Taking boys out of the picture allows girls to stop second-guessing themselves during the school day—making it easier to speak up, take risks, and be themselves. Rocky Rothenberg, a sixth-grader at the new Atlanta Girls' School in 2001, said she didn't feel compelled to "watch her language" as much in her all-girls classroom. "At my old school, the boys could find hidden meaning in every other word. The boys could have won a Nobel Prize in finding hidden meanings," Rothenberg said. Her schoolmate, eighth-grader Lauren Gluck, agreed. "At my old school I didn't want to stick myself out in classes," Gluck said. "I was kind of passive. Here I talk more."

*Girls are valued for brains and heart, not just looks.* Without boys to worry about, girls can concentrate on more important things than their appearance. Girls are valued for their brains, basketball skills, humor, or kindness. "I loved the way I didn't have to worry about what I wore," said Alice Rivlin, a Madeira graduate from 1948 who became director of the White House Office of Management and Budget under President Clinton. "I wasn't competing with girls for the best sweater, which had been part of the public school environment. . . . You didn't have to be embarrassed to be brainy, which was the case at public school." Girls' schools aren't free from the ubiquitous social pressures about girls' looks. They have their share of anorexics and clotheshorses. But for many girls, they offer a healthy oasis where brains and character are what counts. "At a regular school you got praised for popularity or how you looked," said JoAnn Spadafora Vallese, who graduated from the Baldwin School in Philadelphia in 1988. "At Baldwin, the points shifted and it was all about what you thought and how you performed academically."

*Girls' schools allow their students to stay girls a little longer.* The absence of boys allows girls to be silly—to play Red Rover like those GPS eleventh-graders, to wear a wacky hat to school, to retain the playful parts of their childhood just a little longer. Barraged by mass media, American children seem to grow up faster every year. In an era when six-year-olds listen to Britney Spears and twelve-year-olds feel pressure to have oral sex, allowing our daughters a little more time to be girls can be a particularly precious gift.

*Teachers can focus on the specific educational needs of girls.* Many individual teachers at coed schools are committed to helping girls succeed in traditionally male subjects like physics or computer science. But it is typically an individual commitment and can vanish when that individual teacher retires or is reassigned: Mr. Smith may beat the bushes urging girls to sign up for his computer science elective, but when he leaves, his successor may not maintain that effort. At girls' schools, on the other hand, the focus on girls is institutional and permanent. Girls' schools are able to marshal their resources and focus their attention on how to improve girls' learning. Heads of girls' schools spend time on all the usual administrative issues—budgets, hiring, college admissions—but they also spend a good deal of time thinking about how to prepare young women for a world of changing gender roles. Girls' schools are unrecognized "think tanks" on raising and educating girls.

*Girls' schools tend to include more girls and women in their curriculum.* Teachers in coed schools should include women in the curriculum, too, and these days many do. But a teacher whose American history class is made up solely of girls is more likely to go the extra mile to dig up some readings on the Lowell mill girls or on the role of women in the abolitionist movement. At the Julia Morgan School, seventh-graders cap their study of Renaissance Europe with a fair in which each girl takes on the persona of a famous person from that period. The assignments include all the usual male figures— Michelangelo, Machiavelli, Galileo—but they also include a score of lesser-known women, such as Lucrezia Borgia, Artemisia Gentileschi, and Hildegard of Bingen. The point isn't to blindly cheerlead for one's own gender. It's to give girls a personal connection with history, as well as some tools to understand how women's roles have changed over time. "It's about having your own voice," said Sharlim Pagan, a tenth-grader in 2001 at the Young Women's Leadership School in Harlem. "We learn about women's history, how women are depicted, and how we can make a change. We learn how to express ourselves in a certain way so we can stand out, so when we face the world after college we know how to stand in a crowd of a thousand and be an individual."

*Girls' schools can directly address the most difficult social issues facing young women.* Girls' schools can discuss tough issues like sexuality in an atmosphere of trust and caring rather than embarrassed giggling. They can't shield their students from pressures about things like drugs, alcohol, or sex. But at their best, they can give girls the information and confidence they need to make healthy choices. They can foster a peer culture that supports those healthy choices. And they can give young women a reassuring sense that they are not alone: *You're not the only girl in the world who feels bad because she doesn't look like a supermodel. You're not the only girl who is scared about getting her period for the first time. You're not the only girl who feels conflicted over how to handle dating and sexuality.*

*Girls can build strong female friendships, free from competition over boys.* Many girls and alumnae told me they found their female friendships easier, deeper, and less fraught with competition than at their previous coed schools. These close school friendships set the stage for girls to relate collegially and supportively to other women throughout their adult lives. "I value female friendships very highly, maybe because I had more time to forge those friendships," said Sara Klein, who graduated from Forest Ridge School of the Sacred Heart near Seattle in 1981. "I saw I *could* have very close female friendships, which was not an experience familiar to me from junior high."

## Trade-offs and Pitfalls

There are of course pitfalls and trade-offs in a girls' school education. Some schools still carry cultural legacies from their past that are at cross-purposes with their goal of preparing girls for a twenty-first-century world. Sexism and stereotyping can wend their way into girls' schools, just as they permeate the rest of society. The emotional intensity of adolescent girls can turn a school into an unhealthy hothouse of angst and intrigue if administrators aren't careful. And there is, of course, the question of boys. "What's the best thing about a girls' school? The absence of boys," several alumnae told me. "What's the worst thing?" they continued. "The absence of boys."

Among the pitfalls that can beset contemporary girls' schools are:

*Ghosts of the past.* We are long past the era of finishing schools and polite accomplishments. Nearly all girls' schools today are trying to turn out smart, capable young women who have the confidence to be leaders. Yet some schools—especially those in more conservative sections of the country—continue to give girls a mixed message about whether they should be "ladylike" or strong. At Ashley Hall, for instance, the buzzwords are *girl power* and *where girls are champions*. But on a spring day near the end of the school year, a group of seniors meet with their old first-grade teacher and get some advice that could have come straight from the prefeminist 1950s. As part of a pregraduation ritual, the girls return to their first-grade classroom, sit in a circle on the floor, and look through an old steamer trunk that has their names written inside in the awkward printing of six-year-olds. Their first-grade teacher, now retired, dispenses purple lollipops and bits of life wisdom. "Don't be afraid to change your mind," she tells them. "I'm glad we're ladies, because they give us that prerogative for changing our minds." Students sense the contradictions within the school's culture. "They want the image of a traditional conservative school for young ladies, but they also want Girl Power, to be feminist and on the cutting edge," complained Erin Stevens, a senior in 2001.

*The danger of coddling.* One hundred twenty years ago, Dr. Clarke warned Americans not to work their daughters too hard intellectually, and some schools responded by lightening the workload or excusing girls with "delicate health." Schools today no longer think of girls' bodies as frail flowers that will wither on the vine from too much algebra, but they sometimes slip into a similar kind of coddling under the new banner of self-esteem. The AAUW report,

*Reviving Ophelia,* and similar books justifiably raised a red flag about the erosion of self-confidence among girls during early adolescence. But some parents and teachers took those warnings to mean that girls' psyches were as fragile as Clarke's description of their bodies. The smallest word of reprimand, a D on a report card, or failure to be chosen for the varsity basketball team—any of these, they worried, could send a girl spiraling into a bottomless abyss of negative self-image. Under pressure from parents, girls' schools occasionally go too far in trying to protect girls from failure. Some teachers handle girls with kid gloves, afraid of provoking tears. They forget girls' resilience, and the fact that challenges and failure are necessary for learning. "In all the girls' schools I've worked in, I see a tremendous desire to protect girls from the consequences of what they've done," said Sandra Theunick, head of the Chapin School in New York City. "If an eight-year-old boy beats someone up on the playground, he has to stand up and take his punishment 'like a man.' With a little girl, we say, 'Oh, that punishment is too harsh for her, she didn't mean it.' But if you want girls to be strong and insightful, with really high self-esteem, you can't rescue them from life. We've got to get beyond the culture of protection if we want girls to learn to be leaders."

*Girls' schools run a risk of becoming hothouses of emotion.* Adolescent girls tend to spend a lot of time and energy on their relationships with each other. They're verbal. They're not shy about showing emotion. They care about winning teachers' approval and doing perfect work. These traits can all lead to positive outcomes—deep friendships, a sense of the school as one big family, high academic achievement, and cooperative work in the classroom. But if handled badly, they can turn a girls' school into a kind of Peyton Place. Girls can spread news—or rumors—at rates close to warp speed. They can work each other up into a frenzy over grades, or a nasty comment, or over whether to hold graduation indoors or outdoors. At coed schools, boys often provide a counterbalancing attitude of "aww, that's no big deal"—a nonchalance that can be harder to find at a girls' school. Fran Scoble, head of the Westridge School in Pasadena, sees part of her job as defusing the level of emotions at school. When girls are wringing their hands in despair over schoolwork, she tries to

play a "snap out of it" role: "There's a lot of dysfunction and emo-
tionalism that goes on when there are no boys around to say 'shape
up,'" Scoble said. "I say to the girls, 'Let's break this down into man-
ageable components. Which part of your assignment is due when?' I
try to get them to be more analytical rather than emotional."

*Boys.* Probably the most common charge against girls' schools is
that they stunt girls' social development. Without boys around, this
argument goes, girls won't know how to function in the "real world."
Girls will hit college or the workplace and find themselves hopelessly
at sea—insecure about dating, intimidated by male colleagues, unable to relate to men as co-workers and friends.

Certainly some young women have had this experience, particularly in earlier generations when girls' schools were more hermetically sealed communities. Pat Greenwald, one of the first women to
break into the executive ranks in the advertising industry, went to
the Dalton School in New York City when it was all-girls in the
1940s. She then went overboard in dating when she finally made it
to college. "I chose a school with the most men I could find, which
was Case Western Reserve with a ratio of seventeen men to every
woman," Greenwald said. "I didn't know how to sit in class with
men, study with men, walk to class with men. My first year I had a
straight-D average since I was going out with every man around. I
had dates, but I never learned how to live with men. All these other
students from small towns seemed very comfortable with men. I was
very uncomfortable, very shy, very scared." Tori Williams, who graduated from Miss Porter's in 1972, felt similarly at sea with male-
female relationships when she went to college. "I went from no
contact with guys to sleeping with them in about a day," Williams
said. "I felt like I was in a game, but I had no idea what the rules
were or the consequences if I didn't follow the rules. One guy gave
me a bottle of perfume. I said, 'My God, I can't accept this. Then I'll
have to sleep with him!' My roommate said, 'No, you don't. Just accept the perfume.'"

On the other hand, many girls' school graduates *didn't* feel hampered socially by their single-sex experience. Or they felt that any social gap was more than offset by the confidence and self-knowledge

they had gained. "I don't think Hamlin retarded my social growth—
it gave me time to think through how I wanted to behave with boys,"
said Sue Davenport, who graduated from the Hamlin School in San
Francisco in 1971. "You can catch up with lapses in how to talk with
boys and play the game," said Emily Webber Palmer Brown, who
graduated from Westover in 1984. "I don't know if you can catch up
with finding yourself."

Clearly, one of the challenges facing girls' schools is ensuring that
their students gain enough familiarity with boys to have a smooth social transition into coed colleges and workplaces. Many girls' schools
are trying to do this in more thoughtful ways than in the past, such
as partnering with other nearby schools to sponsor coed theater productions or community-service projects. Others aren't doing much.
Their efforts are limited to hosting a handful of Friday-night dances—
stilted, sexually charged encounters that are probably the least healthy
way to get to know the opposite sex. In either case, parents also face
a responsibility. If parents are sending their daughter to a single-sex
school for more than a couple of years, they should make sure she
has opportunities to be friends with boys outside of school. That can
happen through a religious youth group, after-school clubs, summer
camp, or simply through time spent hanging out with brothers or
cousins. The point isn't to ensure that girls are dating furiously by
the age of sixteen—it's to ensure that they are comfortable with boys
as friends and colleagues.

Rarely does any school meet all the academic and social needs of
a child. Parents are used to looking beyond school for piano lessons,
swimming lessons, or religious instruction. At coed schools, some
parents make an effort to arrange single-sex extracurricular activities
like Girl Scouts or an all-girl summer camp. At girls' schools, parents
can stave off any potential "boy problem" by doing the reverse and
arranging some coed extracurricular activities for their daughter. In
today's world—unlike fifty years ago—there are plenty of such opportunities. If schools and parents do their jobs, no girl today should
emerge from a girls' school feeling unprepared for the coed world.

## Life Lessons of Girls' Schools

Girls carry the lessons learned at school into adulthood in ways that are not easily measurable through questionnaires or test scores. There is something about a girls' school that leaves many women more confident of themselves and more willing to speak their minds—more prepared, in short, to become leaders. Michelle Matz, who graduated from Foxcroft in 2000, found her school experience made her more outspoken at home. "When we go home and have family discussions, all my cousins are just sitting there but I'm arguing and arguing," Matz said. Many girls' school alumnae told me how surprised they were, upon arriving at college, to see how much more often they spoke out in class than other women. It had simply never occurred to them to censor themselves, or to defer to the men. "At college, some of my women friends couldn't believe how much I put my hand up in class and argued with the teacher," said Tori Williams, the Miss Porter's grad. "My response was, 'Why shouldn't I? We're paying all this money, why shouldn't I ask questions?'" Similarly, Rose Bright, a 1990 graduate of Holy Names High School in Oakland, would jump into heated college debates with men while her female classmates watched silently. "We weren't combative at Holy Names, but if you had an opinion you stuck by it," Bright said. "We got used to sticking up for our opinions. So I'd jump right in."

Many alumnae told me how the confidence and self-knowledge acquired at school helped them build successful lives and careers as adults. Pat Greenwald may have gone "boy crazy" in college, but later her single-sex experience helped her succeed in the corporate world. "I thought a lot about my high school education when I got into business," Greenwald said. "I was one of the first women to be a senior officer of a multinational corporation in advertising. The area I excelled at in business was typically a masculine area, 'pitching'— getting up, making a presentation, selling the agency, bringing in new business. I feel, as I look back on it, that my years at Dalton made me a much more competitive female than if I'd been at a coed school. At a coed school, I would have been competing on a sexual level. Here I was competing on all those other levels that you have to function in—being bright, being Miss Personality who is liked by the other girls, being honest, being a good person. I was competing with other girls but not on a sexual level. When I got into the business world, I was able to compete like a man—and men don't compete for the prettiest shirt or suit."

Other alumnae told me how, when they hit rough spots in life, it was their girls' school experience that inspired them to persevere. Certainly many coed schools inspire their students, too, but there was something special about the female-centered nature of these schools. Elizabeth Pitt, who graduated from the Brearley School in 1947, remembers thinking at difficult moments in her life, "I'm a Brearley girl, I can do this." "It gave you a sense that you were equipped to face life," said Pitt, who went on to become a teacher, homemaker, and volunteer. "Whatever life dealt you, you could do it. Brearley gave you the confidence and the equipment." Vanessa George's life has been quite different from Pitt's—an African-American member of the class of 1983 at Emma Willard, she became a highly driven marketing executive for Silicon Valley technology companies. But her words are eerily similar. "When I am confronted with a challenge these days," George said, " I don't think, 'I'm a Stanford grad, so I should be able to accomplish this.' I don't think, 'I have a Georgetown M.B.A., so I should be able to do that.' I think about Emma Willard and the legacy of Emma Willard. I think about what women are capable of, and how I have a responsibility of fulfilling that potential. I remember hearing over and over again, 'You can do anything you want to.' All of the teachers believed it, all of the administrators believed it, every authority figure in that school really believed that girls were capable of achieving anything they wanted. . . . When I am having doubts or questions, that is the well I go back to."

For me, stories like George's show in a way that goes deeper than any statistical research how the benefits of a good girls' school far outweigh the drawbacks. That self-confidence—that well of inspiration remaining with a girl throughout life—was what I vaguely hoped for when we first started imagining the Julia Morgan School. But there turned out to be something else, which I would not have been able to articulate when we first began talking about launching a girls' school. That has to do with the small bit of alternative reality created within a girls' school—the countercultural nature of girls' schools today.

*Countercultural* seems like a strange word to describe institutions that are often more than a hundred years old, that cling tenaciously to traditions like ring ceremonies and white graduation dresses, that often serve daughters of the elite, that strive to get their charges into Harvard and Yale. And girls' schools are *not* countercultural, if countercultural means that teachers and students must be running around in tie-dyed shirts and love beads, or black leather jackets and nose rings.

But today's girls' schools are genuinely countercultural in their opposition to society's expectations for teenage girls. From sports to careers, the world has opened up to girls and women in unprecedented ways over the past thirty-five years. But girls also face an unprecedented level of pressure to shape themselves in harmful ways—to become sexually active at earlier and earlier ages, to be pathologically skinny, to define themselves in terms of their looks and sexuality. Watch the music videos on MTV. Read the body language of Ralph Lauren fashion ads. Follow the laugh tracks on TV sitcoms, where every second joke is about sex. From before they even know how to read, girls are confronted with cultural images that tell them that the most important parts of them are their breasts, their lips, their skinny waists.

Girls' schools are an antidote to the dominant culture that treats young women as sex objects, that says success means being thin and having nice clothes and a cool boyfriend. Girls' schools create a small culture-within-the-culture where the things that matter are brains, talents, and hearts—where girls can be themselves, for themselves, rather than constantly looking over their shoulder to see how they appear to boys. This underlies the comments I heard from girl after girl about what a relief it was not to have to worry about dressing up for boys at school. Yes, there is the immediate relief of not having to put on eyeshadow at 7:30 every morning. But there is also a deeper, psychic relief of spending the day at a place where you are not constantly having to evaluate your every comment or action in light of how it looks to boys. "At Hunter you could be whoever you were, and no one told you you were being 'like a boy,'" said Judy Kunofsky, who graduated from Hunter College High School in 1963. "It was a great relief to go through so much of adolescence not worrying so much about the outside, just saying what you had to say."

Critics of single-sex schools often say, "Yes, there are terrible sexual pressures on girls these days. But we should fight these pressures rather than run away from them. We should focus on helping girls in coed schools resist the pressure to define themselves sexually." The two approaches are not mutually exclusive. We should challenge the media's portrayal of girls and women, and we should help kids in coed schools look past gender stereotypes. But we should also support the existence of girls' schools because they are countercultural— even subversive—in a way that cannot be duplicated in a coed school.

There's more to the girls' school counterculture than just building self-esteem, teaching calculus, or turning out basketball stars. Girls' schools and women's colleges turn the world on its head. In this one very small place and time, women are the center. This is a world where the pronoun of default is *she*, not *he*. It's a world where the president is a woman, the editor is a woman, the team captain is a woman. It's a world where female friendships are valued and important. This is all profoundly different from everyday life in the rest of America. Shana Penn, who graduated from Western High School in Baltimore in 1973, described it as "like going to another country." Alexandra Johnson, who graduated from Crystal Springs Uplands School in California in 1967, described it as "an alternate possibility of narrative in your life, of how the world could be and you could be."

Spending even a short amount of time in this "other country" of an all-female institution can profoundly change the way you view the rest of the world. It is like going to the Third World for the first time, coming home, and suddenly being aware of luxuries like flush toilets, paved streets, and the boundless surplus of the local supermarket. This can happen in small, subtle ways. One girl finds herself questioning why the women in her family are so silent during family discussions. Another girls' school graduate arrives at college and finds it curious that "the Game"—a men's football match—receives so much more attention than other sports events.

Shana Penn credits her time at Western High School with giving her a vivid awareness of women's lives that continued through her adult life as a journalist and publicist. Penn ended up researching and writing about the unheralded role of women in the Solidarity movement in Poland, something she might not even have thought about without her Western roots. "When I actually started school, I walked in and saw lots of girls everywhere, all sizes and shapes and colors, even different stages of pregnancy," Penn recalled. "I was blown away. It was so visceral for me. You could feel the female energy. . . . It opened my eyes in a way. Even in women's groups at college, you felt like a group on the margins. At Western, you never felt on the margins."

Meredith May, a reporter at the *San Francisco Chronicle*, went to a women's college, not a girls' school. But she came out of Mills College with a similar ability to draw upon an alternative, female-centered perspective. "Being in a single-sex setting showed me thousands of examples of smart, funny, unique women and gave me the impression that I could be that too," May said. "And secondly, it created a terrific sexism barometer for later in life. Now, when I hear a comment that I think is offensive, etc., I know it's offensive because I know that at Mills such a comment never would have been uttered. I have something to bounce the 'real world' off of. Because I've been in a place where women are respected I can immediately spot when they are being slighted. I'm not sure I would be as able to do that if I had stayed in coed settings all my life."

At their best, girls' schools turn out young women with self-esteem, intelligence, and character—and also an inner, guiding vision of what a society would look like that truly respected and valued women. They can then go on and help turn that vision into reality. The girls' schools of today aren't cloisters or cozy homes aimed at keeping girls away from the world. They're training grounds for future leaders, places where girls have room to grow, to develop their talents, and then emerge to shape a better world.

## Best Selves

When I started work on this book, I wanted to know about the white-gloves, finishing-school image of girls' schools. How much was stereotype, and how much was reality? Was there any connection between those nineteenth-century schools for young ladies and what we were hoping to accomplish at the Julia Morgan School? What I discovered was a mixed history. There were times and places where the finishing-school stereotype held true—where schools valued the superficial over the substantive, where they focused on polite accomplishments, where they took the boundless potential of young women and channeled it, trimmed it, corseted it to fit society's narrow definition of what women should be and do. There were schools that were little more than holding stations on the road to a respectable marriage. There were schools that were elitist, racist, and anti-Semitic. There remain schools today that give girls a mixed message, caught in a transitional phase between the old and the new, the demure and the assertive.

But there were many other instances when girls' schools played a radical role in challenging society's limits on women, and in giving girls the skills and confidence to transcend those limits. There have also always been a few brave schools that believed in educating all girls, regardless of class or racial boundaries—think of Emma Willard extending personal loans to poor girls who wanted to become teachers, the nineteenth-century nuns who used private academies to subsidize free schools for the poor, or women like Myrtilla Miner and the Oblate sisters who dedicated their lives to educating African-American girls.

I gradually came to feel a sense of kinship and indebtedness to the women who ran all these schools. I started to feel that Emma Willard was as much a guiding light for the Julia Morgan School as was our actual namesake, Julia Morgan. When running into tough problems in work or in life, I found myself muttering the watchwords of Lucy Madeira: "Function in disaster, finish in style." When talking to my daughter about the importance of standing up against injustice, I recounted the story of Prudence Crandall. When I imagined a new and permanent home for the Julia Morgan School, I pictured a big plaque in the entryway with the words of Mary McLeod Bethune: "God give us girls—the times demand strong girls, good girls, true girls with willing hands, girls whom the world's gold cannot buy. . . ."

Girls' schools have made a real, positive difference in the lives of hundreds of thousands of women. But their history shows us that there were certain times when they made a bigger difference than others—when they were their best selves, when they most fulfilled their potential. These were the times when girls' schools were most conscious of the societal barriers facing women, and made overcoming those barriers a central part of their mission and identity. One such moment was the early 1800s, when America did not provide any organized kind of schooling for women, and people like Emma Willard set out to create strong, solid schools for girls that were the equal of the best boys' schools. The next such moment was the late 1800s, when college was a new and controversial option for young women, and schools like Bryn Mawr and Brearley were founded specifically to give girls a college-preparatory education. The third such moment is our era today. Women no longer face the institutional barriers to education that they faced in the past. Emma Willard or M. Carey Thomas would be stunned and delighted to see the wide array of schools, colleges, and graduate programs open to women in the twenty-first century. But girls face another, more subtle set of challenges today in retaining their confidence, wholeness, and sense of self. Girls' schools have a clear view of these challenges and have stepped forward to meet them, much as Willard or Thomas stepped forward to meet girls' needs in their own eras.

What the best girls' schools from these three periods have in common is that they haven't run on autopilot. They haven't done things a particular way because "we've always done them like this." They haven't been content to follow along with whatever the rest of society is doing. They haven't accepted the common stereotypes of their day about what women are or aren't capable of accomplishing. They have been innovative, risk-taking, and most of all, they've held fast to a vision of girls as full human beings, equal with boys, with minds and voices that deserve to be challenged and taken seriously. They have been deeply feminist institutions, even if they would not have applied that label to themselves.

Those first and second waves of girls' schools were so successful that their innovations became commonplace, the norm. Forty years after Emma Willard opened the Troy Female Seminary, girls were routinely studying geometry and geography in public schools across America. Forty years after M. Carey Thomas started the Bryn Mawr School, public high schools were routinely preparing girls for college alongside boys. Today, it's unclear what lessons the rest of the educational system will learn from the current generation of girls' schools—how the vision behind today's girls' schools might spill over into the largely coed system of American education. We may see the opening of more public girls' schools like the Young Women's Leadership School in Harlem. We may see the creation of more all-girl classes within coed public schools. We will probably see the rise of a few more new independent girls' schools like Julia Morgan. If they choose to actively reach out, girls' schools can also provide models for use in coed schools and classrooms. Some schools have already begun doing this. The National Coalition of Girls' Schools, for instance, has published pamphlets on techniques for teaching science and technology to girls. But by and large, the experience of a girls' school can't be duplicated in a coed environment. Coed schools can incorporate hands-on math techniques or a curriculum about body image, but they can't re-create the "alternate reality" quality of girls' schools in which, for just one small moment, girls and women are the center of the universe.

When I started researching this book, I kept my eyes peeled for archival material from the very early histories of schools—letters from the founders, journals by the girls, articles that described a typical school day in 1827 or 1853. I became highly appreciative of schools that kept good archives, and I started viewing every piece of paper that came out of Julia Morgan as potential archival material. "Someday there may be a researcher who is profoundly grateful that I saved my notes about our discussion of frogs!" I would tell myself with a smile. But somehow, the permanence of what we were doing didn't really register. It was enough of a challenge to make it through opening week, the first semester, the first year. Any moment, it seemed, everything could irretrievably fall apart. But by year four, we had started thinking about a permanent site and talking in terms of twenty-five-year leases or thirty-year mortgages. It stunned me to realize that we were planning for a future that would extend long past the time my daughter would attend the school, long past the time I would be actively involved—long past any horizon I could reasonably imagine. We were assuming that the Julia Morgan School would still be going strong when Hillary Clinton and Condoleezza Rice would be distant historical names, when kids piercing their nostrils would seem like a quaint and old-fashioned gesture, when it might be routine and ho-hum to have women as presidents of the United States.

Will we still need girls' schools in that undefined future? There will clearly be a place for girls' schools as long as our culture undermines the wholeness and capabilities of women. As long as boys set the tone in coed classrooms, as long as music videos and fashion magazines reduce girls to sexual objects, as long as women face glass ceilings at work and unachievable expectations at home, we will need places where young women can listen to their own voices and develop strong, undauntable senses of identity. Perhaps we will be living in some kind of nonsexist utopia twenty-five years from now, but I doubt it. Changes in gender roles happen very slowly, and backlash is as likely as continued progress. We may elect a woman president, but average girls and women are likely to continue facing many of the same issues they face today. "We need schools that place girls at the center, and that need isn't going to change any time soon," said Jean Norris, head of Miss Hall's School in Massachusetts. "I'd like to wake up tomorrow and find that all girls have broad affirmation, but I'm afraid we will still need these schools."

Even in a world that fully valued girls and women, there would be a place for single-sex schooling. The need would not be as urgent; it would not be a question of saving girls' selves and lives. It would instead be a question of deepening girls' understanding of themselves and what it means to be female. Many traditional cultures used to set aside time when women and men would separate themselves for storytelling, seasonal rituals, or coming-of-age ceremonies. Girls' schools and women's colleges could become that kind of an institution—a place where young women would go to listen to themselves, learn from older women, and then return to the coed world with a heightened appreciation both of their female identity and of the commonalities between men and women. "I believe that every girl—and probably every boy—needs a single-gender experience of some sort for some period of time," said Robin Robertson, a former head of the Emma Willard School. "How much time? It depends on the girl. What kind of experience? It depends on the girl. It enables girls to breathe deeply in a place where people are like themselves."

## A WORK IN PROGRESS

*As I condensed the story of starting Julia Morgan into little episodes for this book, it occurred to me that I was creating a false illusion of neatness. Episode one: Our group comes together. Episode two: We learn to raise money. Episode three: We struggle over a curriculum. . . . In reality, all these things occurred in a gradual and indistinct way over extended periods of time. We weren't sure how anything would turn out. We wandered down our share of dead ends. We saw the tasks on our immediate to-do lists—*get tax-exempt status, hold a yard sale, tape up leaflets—*but didn't see how we were growing and changing as an institution. Writing about it now, it appears that each step was part of a logical and orderly process leading to the grand opening of the school, but at the time it didn't feel that way at all.*

*Books have endings. It would be nice to have a definite ending to this process, a point at which I could take a deep breath and relax and say, "Okay, Julia Morgan is done," as a cake or a book or a homework assignment is done. When we opened the school, several of our founders felt they had completed their mission and stepped off the board. Another founder left when her daughter graduated in our first class of alumnae. I felt compelled to stay on, both because the school had become a big part of my life and because it would be another three years until my own daughter was old enough for Julia Morgan. I wanted the school to be around when she was ready. It didn't yet feel secure to me. I wasn't sure when it would feel secure—when we had a building of our own? when we started an endowment?—but it sure didn't feel that way yet. Every day our teachers were changing girls' lives, but inside me, I still felt as if we were balanced on a very thin thread that could snap at any moment.*

*Just before our first graduation, some intriguing news came our way. Mills College—the women's college we had unsuccessfully pursued in our site-search days—was now apparently interested in giving us a home. There was a beautiful 1920s building on campus that had been designed by none other than Julia Morgan. Built as an orphanage for Chinese girls, it offered ample classroom space plus a beautiful court-yard that looked out onto the women's soccer field. Mills currently used the building as a conference center, but if we could match their conference revenue, they would consider renting it to us on a long-term basis.*

*We walked through the building. The possibilities were tremendous. There was enough space to expand to 180 girls, a large and sunny meeting room that opened onto the courtyard through Venetian glass doors, and a cottage in back that would be a perfect art room or science lab. It occupied its own little corner of the Mills campus, so it would really feel like "our" space. There were infinite opportunities for partnering with Mills's faculty and staff. Mills in fact had started out as a girls' school—a seminary—in 1852. Together we could become a real community resource offering programs and conferences on girls' education and development. We would have long-term security through a twenty-five-year lease. And the Julia Morgan School would be in a genuine Julia Morgan building. Standing in the courtyard, imagining girls' voices echoing off the walls, we felt shivers of excitement.*

*There was one catch—money. We estimated that it would cost about $2.5 million to do the earthquake retrofitting, disability accommodations, and other renovations necessary to turn the building into a school. The figure terrified me more than any other challenge in the history of* the school. *Two million dollars might be chump change for established schools with long lists of alumnae, but the most Julia Morgan had ever raised in one year was about $200,000. How would we reach $2 million? I made lists in my head of everyone I knew and came nowhere close to $2 million. I woke up at night worrying about it. I walked around with a sick feeling in my stomach.*

*The time came for a board vote on whether to proceed with the Mills deal. Ann wanted to move ahead. She believed the site—the building itself, the Mills partnership, the Julia Morgan connection—would be compelling to donors. I was torn. I felt the magic. I saw the possibilities. But I was terrified of the cost, terrified in the same way that Ann had been back in the days when she worked alone in her closet with only a tote bag to show that the Julia Morgan School was real. "It's a good thing we each felt that terror at different points," Ann mused later, "because if we had all felt it at the same time, the school never would have been started."*

*As I thought about it, though, I realized that the Mills lease was more than a financial decision and more than a real estate decision. It was a covenant with ourselves. This lease would last twenty-five years! By the time it expired, our founding class of girls would be almost forty years old. My own daughter would be in her thirties, perhaps a mother herself. I would be seventy. With this lease, we were making a promise to ourselves that Julia Morgan was not just a fad or a flash or a brief spurt of good intentions. No matter how tenuous the school's existence might feel to me, this was a promise that the thread would not snap. This school would be around for a very long time.*

*Someday, indeed, researchers might come to pore over our archives the way I had pored over those nineteenth-century diaries and composition books at the Emma Willard School and Miss Porter's.*

*I took a breath, raised my hand, and leaped on for another wild ride.*

# Appendix A: Number of Girls' Private Schools in the United States

| | 1899–00 | 1900–10 | 1919–20 | 1929–30 | 1932–33 | 1940–41 | 1947–48 | 1960–61 | 1965–66 | 1978–79* | 1999–2000* |
|---|---|---|---|---|---|---|---|---|---|---|---|
| **PRIVATE SECONDARY SCHOOLS** | | | | | | | | | | | |
| Total | 1,978 | 1,781 | 2,093 | 2,760 | 2,600 | 2,997 | 3,053 | 4,053 | 4,606 | 5,766 | 10,694 |
| Boys only | 327 | 348 | 385 | 504 | 484 | 557 | 558 | 808 | 961 | 499 | 562 |
| Girls only | 530 | 511 | 728 | 873 | 783 | 941 | 965 | 844 | 1,132 | 551 | 470 |
| Percent girls only | 27% | 29% | 35% | 32% | 30% | 31% | 32% | 21% | 25% | 10% | 4% |
| Percent boys only | 17% | 20% | 18% | 18% | 19% | 19% | 18% | 20% | 21% | 9% | 5% |
| **TOTAL PRIVATE SCHOOLS** | | | | | | | | | | | 27,223 |
| Boys only | | | | | | | | | | | 667 |
| Girls only | | | | | | | | | | | 528 |
| Percent girls only | | | | | | | | | | | 2% |
| Percent boys only | | | | | | | | | | | 2% |

These figures cover both religious and nonreligious private schools.

Data from different periods are not strictly comparable because different survey methods were used, but this gives a relative sense of the scope of single-sex schooling within American private education.

Sources: U.S. Dept. of Education, *Biennial Survey of Education, 1946–48*, Table 2. ("Number of schools, staff, pupils, and graduates in nonpublic secondary schools from 1889–90 to 1947–48.")

National Center for Education Statistics, *Private Schools in American Education*, Table E-1. ("Number of private schools by affiliation, type of facility, and sex of student, and by type of school: U.S., 1976 to 1978.") 1981.

National Center for Education Statistics, *Statistics of Nonprofit Elementary and Secondary Schools*, Table D. ("Historical statistics of nonpublic elementary and secondary schools in the U.S., 1899–1900 to 1965–66.") 1968.

Number of Private Schools, by level of school and sex of student body, 1999–2000, unpublished data from NCES.

*Data from these years include schools that serve both elementary and secondary students.

# Appendix B:

# Prominent Alumnae of Girls' Schools

While biographies of prominent people often mention where they went to college, they rarely mention where they went to high school or elementary school. Yet high school and childhood education often do more to shape someone's identity than their college years. The following list includes some of the prominent and high-achieving women who attended all-girl elementary or secondary schools. It is by no means a complete list.

ABRAHAMSON, SHIRLEY—first woman member and chief justice of the Wisconsin Supreme Court. Hunter College High School (N.Y.), 1950.

ADAMS, ALICE—short story writer and novelist, *Superior Women*. St. Catherine's School (Va.), 1943.

ALLRED, GLORIA—feminist attorney. Philadelphia High School for Girls (Pa.), 1959.

ALSOP, MARIN—principal conductor for the Bournemouth Symphony Orchestra. Masters School (N.Y.), 1972.

ALVAREZ, JULIA—novelist, *How the Garcia Girls Lost Their Accents*. Abbot Academy (Mass.), 1967.

AMATO, ERIKA—lead singer for Velvet Chain rock band. Kent Place School (N.J.), 1987.

ARCHER, ANNE—actress, *Fatal Attraction*. Marlborough School (Calif.), 1965.

ARMSTRONG, ANNE—former ambassador to Great Britain. First woman to chair the President's Foreign Intelligence Advisory Board. Foxcroft School (Va.), 1945.

ARTHUR, BEA—actress, *Maude*. Linden Hall School (Pa.), 1941.

ASTOR, NANCY—first female member of Parliament in Great Britain. St. Catherine's School (Va.), 1898.

AUCHINCLOSS, EVA SEED—former head of the Women's Sports Foundation. Miss Hall's School (Mass.), 1951.

BABBITT, NATALIE MOORE—novelist, *Tuck Everlasting*. Laurel School (Ohio), 1950.

BABCOCK, BARBARA—Emmy Award–winning actress, *Hill Street Blues*. Miss Porter's School (Conn.), 1955.

BALDRIGE, LETITIA—White House social secretary for Kennedy administration and authority on manners. Miss Porter's School (Conn.), 1943.

BAETJER, KATHARINE—curator, Deptartment of European Paintings, Metropolitan Museum of Art. Miss Hall's School (Mass.), 1963.

BARNES, FLORENCE LOWE "PANCHO"—pioneering aviator and stunt pilot; confidante to test pilots including Chuck Yeager. Westridge School (Calif.), 1919.

BECK, PHYLLIS—first woman to serve on Pennsylvania Supreme Court. Hunter College High School (N.Y.), 1945.

BERRESFORD, SUSAN—president of the Ford Foundation. Brearley School (N.Y.), 1961.

BLUME, JUDY—children's author, *Are You There God? It's Me Margaret*. Battin High School (N.J.), 1956.

BOGAEV, BARBARA—National Public Radio talk show host. Baldwin School (Pa.), 1979.

BOLSHOI, ALISON BUCKLEY—opera singer, soloist with Wagner Festival Orchestra of New York. Ursuline School (N.Y.), 1983.

BOSTON, RACHEL—actress, NBC drama *American Dreams*. Girls Preparatory School (Tenn.), 2000.

BROWN, ELAINE—first woman to head the Black Panther Party. Philadelphia High School for Girls (Pa.), 1961.

BROWN, KATHLEEN—California state treasurer. Santa Catalina School (Calif.), 1963.

BURNS, BEVERLY—first female captain of a Boeing 747 on a cross-country flight. Western High School (Md.), 1967.

BURROS, MARIAN FOX—*New York Times* food writer. Rosemary Hall (Conn.), 1950.

BUSH, BARBARA—First Lady, married to President George Herbert Walker Bush. Ashley Hall (S.C.), 1943.

BUTTNER, JEAN BERNHARD—CEO of Value Line. Emma Willard School (N.Y.) and Rosemary Hall (Conn.), 1953.

BYRON, BEVERLY BUTCHER—congresswoman from Maryland, 1978–1993. National Cathedral School (Wash., D.C.), 1950.

CALISHER, HORTENSE—novelist, *Sunday Jews*. Hunter College High School (N.Y.), 1928.

CAMPBELL, BEBE MOORE—novelist, *Brothers and Sisters*. Philadelphia High School for Girls (Pa.), 1967.

CANNON, SARAH—comidienne. Inducted into Country Music Hall of Fame for her character Minnie Pearl. Harpeth Hall School (Tenn.), 1932.

CARMODY, CAROL JONES—member of the National Transportation Safety Board, former U.S. representative to the International Civil Aviation Organization. Louise S. McGehee School (La.), 1960.

CHANNING, STOCKARD—actress. Chapin School (N.Y.), 1961.

CHOPIN, KATE—novelist, *The Awakening*. Academy of the Sacred Heart (Mo.), 1868.

CHOW, AMY—Olympic gymnast, 1996 gold and silver medals. Castilleja School (Calif.), 1996.

CLAYBROOK, JOAN—president of Public Citizen, former head of National Highway Traffic Safety Administration. Roland Park Country School (Md.), 1955.

CLAYTON, CONSTANCE—first female and first African-American superintendant of schools in Philadelphia. Philadelphia High School for Girls (Pa.), 1951.

CLOSE, GLENN—actress. Rosemary Hall (Conn.), 1965.

CURTIS, CHARLOTTE—former op-ed page editor of the *New York Times*; first woman to be listed on the masthead of the *Times*. Columbus School for Girls (Ohio), 1946.

CURTIS, LUCILLE ATCHERSON—first female foreign service officer in 1922. Columbus School for Girls (Ohio), 1909.

DAUGHTREY, MARTHA CRAIG KERKOW—first woman on Tennessee Supreme Court. National Cathedral School (Wash., D.C.), 1960.

DAWIDOWICZ, LUCY—historian, *The War Against the Jews 1933–1945*. Hunter College High School (N.Y.), 1932.

DEE, RUBY—actress and civil rights activist. Hunter College High School (N.Y.), 1939.

DEFOREST, MARIAN—journalist, founded Zonta Club for businesswomen which grew into Zonta International with 1,200 chapters in 67 countries. Buffalo Seminary (N.Y.), 1884.

DENNERY, LINDA LIEBERMAN—publisher of the *Newark Star-Ledger.* Philadelphia High School for Girls (Pa.), 1965.

D'HARNONCOURT, ANNE—director of the Philadelphia Museum of Art. Brearley School (N.Y.), 1961.

DODGE, GRACE HOADLEY—founded Columbia University Teachers' College. Miss Porter's School (Conn.), 1873.

DOERR, HARRIET—novelist, *Stones for Ibarra.* Westridge School (Calif.), 1927.

EDWARD, ANNIE—first female postmaster in the U.S., in Rockford, Ill. Abbot Academy (Mass.), 1855.

ELIOT, MARTHA MAY—child-health expert, first woman admitted into the American Pediatric Society and first woman elected president of the American Public Health Association. Winsor School (Mass.), 1909.

ELSTNER, ANNE—actress who played "Stella Dallas" on the radio. Mt. de Chantal Visitation Academy (W. Va.), 1918.

EUSTIS, DOROTHY HARRISON—founded the Seeing Eye, the first guide dog facility in the United States. Agnes Irwin School (Pa.), 1904.

FADIMAN, ANNE—journalist, editor of *The American Scholar.* Marlborough School (Calif.), 1970.

FANNING, KATHERINE WOODRUFF—editor of the *Christian Science Monitor,* first female president of the American Society of Newspaper Editors. Westover School (Conn.), 1945.

FAUSET, JESSIE REDMON—Harlem Renaissance novelist and poet, literary editor of W.E.B. DeBois's magazine, *The Crisis.* Philadelphia High School for Girls (Pa.), 1900.

FEINSTEIN, DIANNE—U.S. Senator from California. Convent High School of the Sacred Heart (Calif.), 1951.

FENWICK, MILLICENT HAMMOND—congresswoman from New Jersey, 1975–83. Model for the fictional Lacey Davenport in *Doonesbury.* Nightingale-Bamford School (N.Y.), 1920–24, and Foxcroft (Va.), 1925.

FERRARO, GERALDINE—first woman to run for vice president of the United States. Marymount School (N.Y.), 1952.

FITZGERALD, FRANCES—journalist. Won 1973 Pulitzer Prize for *Fire in the Lake.* Foxcroft (Va.), 1958.

FITZHUGH, LOUISE—author of *Harriet the Spy.* Hutchison School (Tenn.), 1946.

FONDA, JANE—actress, political activist. Emma Willard School (N.Y.), 1955.

FORE, HENRIETTA—director of the U.S. Mint. Baldwin School (Pa.), 1966.

FORT, CORNELIA—first woman pilot to give her life in service of the U.S. military. Harpeth Hall School (Tenn.), 1936.

FOUT, NINA—equestrian who won 2000 Olympic bronze medal. Foxcroft (Va.), 1977.

FRANKLIN, SHIRLEY CLARKE—first female mayor of Atlanta. Philadelphia High School for Girls (Pa.), 1963.

GATES, MELINDA FRENCH—cofounder, Bill & Melinda Gates Foundation. Ursuline Academy (Tex.), 1982.

GELLHORN, EDNA—cofounder of the League of Women Voters. Baldwin School (Pa.), 1896.

GIBSON, MARGARET—poet, professor at University of Connecticut, finalist for National Book Award in 1993. St. Catherine's School (Va.), 1962.

GLESS, SHARON—Emmy Award–winning actress, *Cagney and Lacey*. Marlborough School (Calif.) and Santa Catalina School (Calif.), 1961.

GOODALL, JANE—anthropologist, leading expert on chimpanizees. Oldfields School (Md.), 1944.

GRANT, AMY—singer. Winner of five Grammy awards. Harpeth Hall School (Tenn.), 1978.

GRAYBIEL, ANN M.—neuroscientist, first woman to win National Medal of Science. National Cathedral School (Wash., D.C.), 1959.

GUETTEL, MARY RODGERS—composer and playwright, *Once Upon a Mattress*. Brearley School (N.Y.), 1948.

GULKIS, SUSAN—principal violist, Seattle Symphony. Westridge School (Calif.), 1984.

GUTHRIE, JANET—first woman to race in Indianapolis 500. Miss Harris's Florida School for Girls, 1955.

HALL, VIRGINIA—O.S.S. operative in World War II. Organized three battalions of French Resistance forces in occupied France. Only civilian woman in World War II to receive the Distinguished Service Cross. Roland Park Country School (Md.), 1924.

HAMILTON, ALICE—founder of field of industrial medicine. First woman faculty member at Harvard University Medical School. Miss Porter's School (Conn.), 1888.

HAMILTON, ANN—sculptor, MacArthur genius award recipient. Columbus School for Girls (Ohio), 1974.

HAMILTON, EDITH—classical scholar, author of *The Greek Way*. Miss Porter's School (Conn.), 1886.

HAMPL, PATRICIA—author of *I Could Tell You Stories* and other works; Pushcart Prize winner. Convent of the Visitation School (Minn.), 1964.

HANCOCK, ELLEN MOONEY—first female vice president at IBM. Ursuline School (N.Y.), 1961.

HANDLER, EVELYN—first woman president of the University of New Hampshire and Brandeis University. Hunter College High School (N.Y.), 1950.

HANDY, PATRICIA—associate conductor with Greenwich Symphony Orchestra; first American woman to receive a conducting fellowship to the Tanglewood Music Center. Roland Park Country School (Md.), 1961.

HANFF, HELENE—author, *84 Charing Cross Road*. Philadelphia High School for Girls (Pa.), 1933.

HARRIS, REV. BARBARA—first female bishop in the Episcopal Church in America. Philadelphia High School for Girls (Pa.), 1948.

HARVEY, REBECCA MILLER—cofounder of Crabtree & Evelyn, Ltd. Miss Porter's School (Conn.), 1959.

HEALY, BERNADINE—cardiologist, first woman to head the National Institutes of Health; CEO of American Red Cross at time of 9/11 attacks. Hunter College High School (N.Y.), 1962.

HEARNE, SHELLEY—executive director of the Trust for America's Health, a nationwide nonprofit public-health advocacy group. Board chair of the American Public Health Association. Stuart Country Day School of the Sacred Heart (N.J.), 1979.

HENDRIX, LEE—Curator of Drawings, the Getty Museum. Hutchison School (Tenn.), 1971.

HEWITT, SARAH COOPER—founded the Museum of Fine Arts at Cooper Union. Miss Porter's School (Conn.), 1876.

HILLS, CARLA—U.S. Trade Representative in first Bush administration. Marlborough School (Calif.), 1951.

HOWE, FLORENCE—founder of the Feminist Press, first woman president of the Modern Language Association. Hunter College High School (N.Y.), 1946.

HUGHES, SARAH TILGHMAN—first female federal district judge in Texas. Administered presidential oath of office to Lyndon Johnson after Kennedy assassination. Western High School (Md.), 1913.

JACOBSEN, JOSEPHINE—poet. Consultant in Poetry to the Library of Congress, 1971–73. Roland Park Country School (Md.), 1926.

JONES, JANIS—mayor of Las Vegas, 1991–99. Marlborough School (Calif.), 1967.

KAEL, PAULINE—film critic. Girls' High School (Calif.), 1930s.

KANTER, MARTHA—president of De Anza College. Winsor School (Mass.), 1966.

KELLY, KATE—CBS news anchor. San Domenico School (Calif.), 1975.

KELLY, MARGUERITE—syndicated columnist on parenting issues, author of *Family Almanac.* Georgetown Visitation Preparatory School (Wash., D.C.), 1950.

KOBAK, HOPE MCELDOWNEY—cofounder of *Kirkus Reviews.* Emma Willard School (N.Y.), 1940.

KOLLAR-KOTELLY, COLLEEN—federal judge who presided over the Microsoft antitrust case. Georgetown Visitation Preparatory School (Wash., D.C.), 1961.

KOPPEL, ANDREA—journalist, CNN. Stone Ridge School of the Sacred Heart (Md.), 1981.

KOVEL, TERRY—antiques expert. Laurel School (Ohio), 1946.

KURSINSKI, ANNE—equestrian, Olympic silver medalist in 1988, 1996. Westridge School (Calif.), 1976.

LANE, PINKIE GORDON—first African-American poet laureate of Louisiana. Philadelphia High School for Girls (Pa.), 1940.

LEBENTHAL, ALEXANDRA—CEO of Lebenthal & Co. brokerage firm. Nightingale-Bamford School (N.Y.), 1982.

LEE, ANDREA—writer, *Sarah Phillips.* Baldwin School (Pa.), 1970.

L'ENGLE, MADELEINE—author of *A Wrinkle in Time.* Ashley Hall (S.C.), 1937.

LEONI, TEA—actress. Brearley School (N.Y.), 1984.

LEWIS, CARLA—senior director of investor relations for Microsoft. Forest Ridge School of the Sacred Heart (Wash.), 1975.

LINDBERGH, ANNE MORROW—writer, *Gift from the Sea.* Chapin School (N.Y.), 1924.

LIPPARD, LUCY—cultural critic, feminist activist. Abbot Academy (Mass.), 1954.

LLOYD, KATE RAND—editor in chief, *Working Woman.* Westover School (Conn.), 1941.

LORDE, AUDRE—poet and feminist. Hunter College High School (N.Y.), 1951.

LUZZATTO, TAMARA STANTON—chief of staff for Senator Hillary Rodham Clinton. Brearley School (N.Y.), 1975.

MARLIN, ALICE TEPPER—founder and executive director of the Council on Economic Priorities, nonprofit that promotes corporate social responsibility. Baldwin School (Pa.), 1962.

MARSHALL, CAPRICIA—White House social secretary for President Bill Clinton. Beaumont School (Ohio), 1982.

MATHEWS, JESSICA TUCHMAN—president of Carnegie Endowment for International Peace. Brearley School (N.Y.), 1963.

MAXMAN, SUSAN—first female president of the American Institute of Architects. Columbus School for Girls (Ohio), 1954.

MCCORMICK, ANNE O'HARE—*New York Times* foreign correspondent. In 1937 was first woman to win a Pulitzer Prize in journalism. St. Mary of the Springs Academy (Ohio), 1898.

MCCORMICK, RUTH HANNA—first woman to run for the U.S. Senate. Miss Porter's School (Conn.), 1897.

MCEVOY, NAN—former owner of the *San Francisco Chronicle*. San Domenico School (Calif.), 1937.

MCMORROW, MARY ANN—first woman chief justice on Illinois Supreme Court. Immaculata High School (Ill.), 1948.

MCPHERSON, MARY PATTERSON—president of Bryn Mawr College from 1978 to 1997. Agnes Irwin School (Pa.), 1953.

MERLINO, NELL—designed and produced Take Your Daughters to Work Day for the Ms. Foundation for Women. Stuart Country Day School of the Sacred Heart (N.J.), 1971.

MESSINGER, RUTH—executive director of American Jewish World Service, former borough president of Manhattan. Brearley School (N.Y.), 1958.

METHVIN, STACY PERPER—vice president of transportation for Shell Oil Products U.S. and former CEO of fifth-largest oil refinery in the U.S. Springside School (Pa.), 1975.

MILLER, EMILY—First female department chair at the Virginia Military Institute. St. Catherine's School (Va.), 1971.

MILLER, INGER—runner, 1996 Olympic gold medalist. Westridge School (Calif.), 1990.

MONROE, HARRIET—poet and critic, founded *Poetry* magazine in 1912. Georgetown Visitation Preparatory School (Wash., D.C.), 1879.

MORRIS, SARAH—actress in *Felicity*. Hutchison School (Tenn.), 1996.

MUNSON, EDITH CUMMINGS—1923 national golf champion, first woman on the cover of *Time* magazine. Westover School (Conn.), 1917.

MUELLER, CATE TINKLER—head of the U.S. Navy's News Desk at the Pentagon. Girls Preparatory School (Tenn.), 1983.

NAKASONE, MARIKO—cohost of PBS children's show *DragonflyTV*. Convent of the Visitation School (Minn.), 2002.

NUSSBAUM, MARTHA—professor of ethics, University of Chicago Law School. Baldwin School (Pa.), 1964.

O'HEILL, ANNE CUNNINGHAM—director of public relations for the United Nations. Hutchison School (Tenn.), 1966.

O'KEEFFE, GEORGIA—painter. Chatham Hall School (Va.), 1905.

ONASSIS, JACQUELINE BOUVIER KENNEDY—First Lady married to President John F. Kennedy. Chapin School (N.Y.) and Miss Porter's School (Conn.), 1947.

OZICK, CYNTHIA—author, *The Puttermesser Papers*. Hunter College High School (N.Y.), 1946.

PALTROW, GWYNETH—actress. Spence School (N.Y.), 1990.

PARKER, DOROTHY—writer. Miss Dana's School (N.J.), 1911.

PARKS, ROSA—civil rights activist. Montgomery Industrial School for Girls (Ala.), 1920s.

PERT, FLORENCE—first woman ordained as a Collegiate Church minister. Harpeth Hall (Tenn.), 1949.

PETERS, ELLEN—first female member and chief justice of the Connecticut Supreme Court. Hunter College High School (N.Y.), 1947.

PILOT, ANN HOBSON—principal harpist, Boston Symphony Orchestra. Philadelphia High School for Girls (Pa.), 1961.

PHILLIPS, TERESA LAWRENCE—first woman to coach a Divison 1 men's basketball team, as Tennessee State athletic director. Girls Preparatory School (Tenn.), 1976.

POST, EMILY—authority on etiquette. Miss Graham's School (N.Y.), 1891.

POST, MARJORIE MERRIWEATHER—philanthropist. Mt. Vernon Seminary (Wash., D.C.), 1904.

PRITZKER, PENNY—president of Pritzker Realty Group, chairman of Classic Residency by Hyatt. Castilleja School (Calif.), 1977.

RAISER, MOLLY—Chief of Protocol for U.S. State Department, 1993–97. Buffalo Seminary (N.Y.), 1960.

RASIN, MARTHA—former chief judge of the District Court of Maryland. St. Margaret's School (Va.), 1965.

READY, STEPHANIE—first woman to assistant coach a men's pro basketball team, the Greenville Groove. National Cathedral School (Wash., D.C.), 1993.

REAGAN, NANCY—First Lady, married to President Ronald Reagan. Chicago Latin School for Girls (Ill.), 1939.

REES, MINA—mathematician, first female president of the American Association for the Advancement of Science. Hunter College High School (N.Y.), 1919.

RICE, CONDOLEEZZA—national security adviser to President George W. Bush. St. Mary's Academy (Colo.), 1971.

RICH, ADRIENNE—poet, winner of National Book Award. Roland Park Country School (Md.), 1947.

RICHARDSON, SALLY—director of federal Medicaid program in Clinton administration. Baldwin School (Pa.), 1950.

RIDDLE, THEODATE POPE—architect. Miss Porter's School (Conn.), 1888.

RIDE, SALLY—astronaut. Westlake School for Girls (Calif.), 1968.

RIPLEY, ALEXANDRA BRAID—author of *Scarlett: The Sequel to Gone with the Wind*. Ashley Hall (S.C.), 1951.

RIPLEY, ROSEMARY—vice president for corporate development, Philip Morris Company. Miss Porter's School (Conn.), 1972.

RIVLIN, ALICE—economist, director of the White House Office of Management and Budget under President Clinton. Madeira School (Va.), 1948.

ROBERTS, COKIE—journalist, ABC-TV. Stone Ridge School of the Sacred Heart (Md.), 1960.

ROBERTSON, DONNA—dean of College of Architecture, Illinois Institute of Technology. St. Margaret's School (Va.), 1970.

RODIN, JUDITH SEITZ—first female president of the University of Pennsylvania. Philadelphia High School for Girls (Pa.), 1962.

ROGERS, EDITH NOURSE—congresswoman from Massachusetts from 1925 through 1960. Rogers Hall School (Mass.), 1890s.

SERETEAN, TRACY—won 2001 Oscar for Best Documentary Film Short. Girls Preparatory School (Tenn.), 1977.

SEXTON, ANNE—poet. Rogers Hall (Mass.), 1947.

SHEPARD, MOLLY—chair, president, and cofounder of Manchester Inc., an outplacement and career management company. Miss Hall's School (Mass.), 1964.

SHRIVER, MARIA—journalist, NBC-TV. Stone Ridge School of the Sacred Heart (Md.), 1973.

SIMMONS, ADELE—president of Hampshire College and of the John D. and Catherine T. MacArthur Foundation. Garrison Forest School (Md.), 1959.

SIMPSON, WALLIS WARFIELD—wife of Edward, Duke of Windsor, for whom he abdicated the British throne. Oldfields School (Md.), 1914.

SINKLER, REBECCA PEPPER—former editor of *New York Times Book Review*. Springside School (Pa.), 1955.

SKINNER, CORNELIA OTIS—actress and writer, *Our Hearts Were Young and Gay*. Baldwin School (Pa.), 1918.

SLICK, GRACE—lead singer for rock group Jefferson Airplane. Castilleja School (Calif.), 1957.

SMITH, ANNA DEVEARE—actress and playwright. Western High School (Md.), 1967.

SMITH, MARY OATES SKINNER—vice president of the World Bank. Springside School (Pa.), 1959.

SMITH, ROBIN—chair and former CEO of Publishers Clearing House. Baldwin School (Pa.), 1957.

SORENSON, ALEXANDRA—MSNBC anchor and correspondent. Marlborough School (Calif.), 1978.

STAHLMAN, MILDRED—pediatric neonatologist who developed the first modern neonatal intensive-care unit in the world. Harpeth Hall School (Tenn.), 1940.

STANTON, ELIZABETH CADY—suffrage leader. Troy Female Seminary/ Emma Willard School (N.Y.), 1837.

STARK, MELISSA—sports reporter for ABC's *Monday Night Football*. Roland Park Country School (Md.), 1991.

STEARNS, KENDRA—first female head of Phillips Exeter Academy. Emma Willard School (N.Y.), 1960.

STOCKWELL, TRACY CAULKINS—swimmer with three Olympic gold medals. Harpeth Hall School (Tenn.), 1981.

SWADOS, ELIZABETH—playwright and musician, winner of three Obie Awards and five Tony Award nominations. Buffalo Seminary (N.Y.), 1968.

SZOLD, HENRIETTA—founder of Hadassah, the national organization of Jewish women. Western High School (Md.), 1877.

TAYLOR, MELANIE SMITH—Olympic gold medal equestrian. Hutchison School (Tenn.), 1967.

TAYLOR, PEGGY—president of PeopleSoft Investments, Inc., a subsidiary of PeopleSoft. Forest Ridge School of the Sacred Heart (Wash.), 1968.

THIELEN, CYNTHIA—congresswoman from Hawaii. Marlborough School (Calif.), 1951.

TOWNSEND, KATHLEEN KENNEDY—lt. governor of Maryland. Stone Ridge School of the Sacred Heart (Md.), 1969.

TYSON, NORA WINGFIELD—first woman to head a navy aviation operational squadron. Second in command of the USS *Bataan*. St. Mary's Episcopal School (Tenn.), 1975.

TIERNEY, GENE—actress. Miss Porter's School (Conn.), 1938.

URBAN, AMANDA—cohead of New York office of International Creative Management. Kent Place School (N.J.), 1964.

VANDEN HEUVEL, KATRINA—editor in chief of the *Nation*. Brearley School (N.Y.), 1977.

VANDERVEER, TARA—coach of gold-medal-winning U.S. women's basketball team in 1996 Olympics. Buffalo Seminary (N.Y.), 1971.

VAN LENGEN, KAREN—dean of the University of Virginia's architecture school. Stoneleigh-Burnham School (Mass.), 1969.

VIEIRA, MEREDITH—television host, *The View*. Lincoln School (R.I.), 1971.

VON STADE, FREDERICA—opera singer. Stone Ridge School of the Sacred Heart (Md.), 1963.

WALSH, DIANA CHAPMAN—president of Wellesley College. Springside School (Pa.), 1962.

WALTHER, BEVERLY RAYBURN—first female tenured professor at the Kellogg School of Business at Northwestern University. Hutchison School (Tenn.), 1987.

WASSERSTEIN, WENDY—playwright, *The Heidi Chronicles*. Calhoun School (N.Y.), 1967.

WEAVER, SIGOURNEY—actress. Chapin School (N.Y.), 1967.

WHITE, KATHERINE SERGEANT—first fiction editor of *The New Yorker*. Winsor School (Mass.), 1909.

WHITMAN, CHRISTINE TODD—governor of New Jersey, EPA secretary for President George W. Bush. Chapin School (N.Y.), 1964.

WILLIAMS, MARY ALICE—journalist, founder of CNN, won Emmy as anchor of NBC *Nightly News*. Convent of the Visitation School (Minn.), 1967.

WITHERSPOON, REESE—actress. Harpeth Hall (Tenn.), 1994.

WRIGHT, LANA DUPONT—equestrian. At 1964 Olympics was first woman to compete in equestrian sport of eventing. Oldfields School (Md.), 1957.

(Note: Dates listed are for graduation, or in cases where a student attended but did not graduate, the year she would have graduated.)

# Acknowledgments

This book grew out of my experience helping start the Julia Morgan School for Girls. So first of all I need to thank the other founders of the school—founding board members Cynthia Ashley, Barry Epstein, Laurel Hulley, Judy Levin, Barbara Maco, Deborah Valoma, Laurie Werbner, and Irene Yen. Without our visionary director, Ann Clarke, there would have been no school at all. Our pioneering teachers, girls, and parents also made the school happen and thus made this book happen.

Edna Mitchell and the Women's Leadership Institute of Mills College offered me an institutional home when I began working on this book. They made the leap from a secure newspaper job to the uncertainties of book writing much less lonely and scary. Several friends and colleagues took the time to critique sections of the book—Bil Banks, Sr. Mary Oates, Sharon Chipman, Sharon Sprowls, Sam Schuchat, and Deb DeBare. Their expertise and suggestions were invaluable. Of course, I alone am responsible for any errors or omissions in the book.

The National Coalition of Girls' Schools was supportive of this project from the very start. Meg Moulton and Whitney Ransome shared their insights, experience, and organizational files with me, and helped put me in contact with their member schools. Sr. Mary Tracy of the National Catholic

Educational Association also provided her encouragement. Many, many schools sent me their histories and other written materials. Many heads of school, teachers, and students shared their personal stories and perspectives. I was unfortunately able to visit only a handful of schools in person. I thank these schools for graciously opening their classrooms or archives: Ashley Hall, Atlanta Girls' School, Bais Rivka, Brearley School, Bryn Mawr School, Castilleja School, Schools of the Convent of the Sacred Heart (San Francisco), Emma Willard School, 49ers Academy, Foxcroft School, Holton-Arms School, Girls' Middle School, Girls Preparatory School, Hamlin School, Holy Names High School, Immaculate Conception Academy, Jefferson Leadership Academies, Katherine Delmar Burke School, Madeira School, Manhattan High School for Girls, Marin Academy, Marymount School (New York), Miss Porter's School, Mother Caroline Academy, Nightingale-Bamford School, Phillips Academy, Spence School, Western High School, and the Young Women's Leadership School. I am particularly appreciative of the superb nineteenth-century archives at Emma Willard and Miss Porter's.

David Tyack offered encouragement when I was just getting started on this project. Kate Rousmaniere shared her unpublished work on several girls' schools. Eric Eisenstadt and Fay Rosenfeld opened their home when research took my family to New York for a month. Megan Elcea helped with the laborious task of tracking down names of prominent girls' school alumnae for the appendix. My neighbor Leslie Laurien became my Scanning Guru when it was time to collect photographs. Michael Franko came out of retirement to help me obtain photos of Western High School. Karen Stabiner shared valuable publishing advice based on her experience with her own book about girls' schools, *All Girls*.

More than two hundred alumnae of girls' schools took the time to share their school memories—sometimes wonderful, sometimes painful. Not every story made it into the book, but I learned things from every single conversation or commentary. I felt privileged to share people's life stories in this intimate way. I hope each alumna knows that she helped shape the themes and ideas in this book, even if her individual comments don't appear in print. Thank you so much to Fran Abramowitz, Adelaide Adams, Mitzi Alper, Sharman Anderson, Elizabeth Antonia, Marice Ashe, Sr. Rosario Maria Asturias, Harriet Aufses, Gina Banzon, Ellen Barry, Ruth Baum, Emelia Benjamin, Nancy Birdwell, Doreen Boatswain, Mary Mueller Boenke, Brita Bonechi, Jessica Bonn, Katherine Boyer, Karen Brailsford, Rachel Hammond Breck, Rose Bright, Emily Webber Palmer Brown, Dorothy Cantwell, Pat Cavagnero, Catherine Cavanagh, Cathy Chapman,

Susan Chehak, Garry Clifford, Alison Cobb, Catherine Colinvaux, Barbara Cortese, Catherine Costello, Joanna Crews, Betty Cummings, Kathy Dalton, Priscilla Danforth, Yvonne Daniel, CeCe Davenport, Sue Davenport, Jara Dean-Coffey, Karen DeAngelis, Mary DeBare, Vicki Della Joio, Lisa Diethelm, Nancy Downey, Martha Dudman, Donna Duhe, Jeanne Eaton, Cecile Miller Eistrup, Mary Helen Ellet, Jaime English, Gina Espinal, Reese Fernandes, Ann Fishel, Elizabeth Fishel, Ann FitzGerald, Frances FitzGerald, Eileen Flanagan, Rebecca Fox, Pat Fry, Jane Futcher, Tracy Gary, Marge Gaughan, Vanessa George, Connie Geraghty, Amy Glenn, Lisa Goddard, Marjorie Goldsmith, Maisie Grace, Pat Greenwald, Mary Gregory, Cynthia Gruszkiewicz, Marny Hall, Monica Simmons Hammonds, Kathy Hume Hanley, Marjorie Hargrave, Lorraine Harper, Kate Hartzell, Molly Hathaway, Anne Herlick, Chelsea Hoffman, Veda Howell, Beppie Huidekoper, Eun-Mee Jeong, Alexandra Johnson, Sr. Emily Mary Kemppi, Kath Kettmann, Alice King, Sr. Bernice Kita, Susan Klaus, Sara Klein, Alison Kliegman, Claire Klinge, Amanda Kovattana, Alyson Kozma, Judy Kunofsky, Patricia Labalme, Stephanie Lamonaca, Courtney Lamontagne, Joan Lane, Millie Lang, Flora Lazar, Martha Lee, Libby Lepow, Jane Levikow, Dana Lobell, Karen Lynn-Dyson, Sally MacNichol, Racheline Maltese, Marianne Manley, Sr. Mary Mardel, Camille Marlow, Katherine Matheson, Audrey Maurer, Audrey Maynard, Joan McCloskey, Shenequa McLeod, Marion McNeely, Betty Merck, Josie Merck, Tanisha Mojica, Sally Montgomery, Pat Murray, Elizabeth Newberg, Sarah Newman, Pat Newton, Margaret Nichols, Martina Nicholson, Jennie Orvino, Lorraine Pagan, Judith Palfrey, Louisa Palmer, Mae Parker, Julie Pell, Shana Penn, Rosemary Perry, Mary Pat Pfeil, Linnie Pickering, Meeghan Piemonte, Ellen Pinderhughes, Elizabeth Pitt, Judith Plank, Carolyn Poe, Lois Poinier, Milbry Polk, Renee Rausin, Kathleen Rave, Vicki Marie Rector, Ellen Reeder, Betsy Reifsnider, Carolyn Rhodes, Esther Ridder, Emily Ridgway, Alice Rivlin, Beth Rogers, Nancy Rollins, Susan Rosenthal, Mary Ellen Ross, Merry Ross, Helen Rossi, Deb Rupp, Ellen Rutt, Kumea Shorter-Gooden, Catherine Skinner, Sr. Margery Smith, Pat Talbert Smith, Trish Campbell Smith, Starr Snead, Nicole Sotelo, Clare Springs, Lee Steadman, Cate Steane, Mary Stephens, Catherine Stern, Peggy Stern, Louise Stevenson, the late Hellie Stowell, Jenepher Stowell, Lally Stowell, Nancy Stricker, Susan Sweitzer, Betty Symington, Susan Tague, Marjo Talbott, Page Talbott, Carol Tauer, Jane Taylor, Juliet Teixeira, Sr. Mary Anne Thatcher, Elizabeth Thomson, Sr. Ethel Tinnemann, Ann Tompkins, Olivia Tsosie, Carol Valladao, JoAnn Vallese, Wendy Vella, Anita Waldron, Belinda Walker, Wendy Walsh, Wendy Wasserstein, Mary Ellen Welsh, Tensie Whelan, Gina Wickwire, Judy

Williams, Tori Williams, Mary-Sherman Willis, Anne Woolf, Francene Young, Lucinda Ziesing, and several women who asked to remain anonymous. If I have inadvertently omitted others who shared stories about their school days, I deeply apologize.

I also feel a debt of gratitude to the many scholars who have written about American women's history over the past 25 years. When I was an undergraduate at Harvard in the late 1970s, there was practically nothing in the curriculum about the lives and work of women. We petitioned the university in vain to establish a women's studies program; we organized independent study seminars to try to fill the void. Returning to women's history twenty-five years later, I was awestruck by how much information had become available. There were journal articles like Anne Firor Scott's study of the lives of nineteenth-century Troy Female Seminary alumnae; there were unpublished dissertations like Lynne Templeton Brickley's excellent work on Sarah Pierce's Litchfield Academy; there were books like Eileen Brewer's *Nuns and the Education of American Catholic Women, 1860–1920.* I often felt I was standing on the shoulders of these scholars. Certainly many gaps remain, and I hope that some graduate students somewhere are inspired to tackle the many unanswered questions about girls' schools and their impact. But writing this book showed me firsthand what a difference has been made by the women's movement and by the field of women's studies. They have shone a light on an entire slice of American experience—girls' education—that would have remained dark and neglected if things had been left to the traditional priorities of mostly male history departments.

Finally, I must thank my agent, Elizabeth Kaplan, and my editor, Sara Carder, who made my maiden voyage into the sea of book publishing a smooth and happy one. Neither Elizabeth nor Sara went to a girls' school, but from the very first minute they "got" what girls' schools were all about and why they were important. Their suggestions made this a better book.

My parents, Charles and Nancy DeBare, and my stepmother, Mary DeBare, have always supported all my writing endeavors, including this one. My husband, Sam Schuchat, provided boundless encouragement and four years of patience while I sat in bed at midnight obsessively reading obscure histories of Miss So-and-so's School for Girls. And last but not least, I thank Rebecca Schuchat, who was two when we started organizing the Julia Morgan School and who is now ten and is really what started this whole ball rolling.

# Notes

INTRODUCTION: THE LAPTOP AND THE MAYPOLE

6    *Declining number of schools*   "Table D: Historical Statistics of Non-public Elementary and Secondary Schools," in *Statistics of Nonpublic Elementary and Secondary Schools, 1965–66*, National Center for Education Statistics, U.S. Dept. of Education, 1968. See also "Table E-1: Number of Private Schools," in *Private Schools in American Education*, National Center for Education Statistics, 1981.

1. RADICAL ROOTS

16    *"All a young lady ..."*   Anne Firor Scott, "The Ever-Widening Circle: The Diffusion of Feminist Values from the Troy Female Seminary, 1822–72," in *Making the Invisible Woman Visible* (Urbana, Ill.: University of Illinois Press, 1984.)

16    *"I had rather ..."*   Nancy Cott, *The Bonds of Womanhood: "Woman's Sphere" in New England, 1780–1835* (New Haven: Yale University Press, 1997), 111.

16    *"man is, in general ..."*   Thomas Woody, *A History of Women's Ed-*

*ucation in the United States* (New York and Lancaster, Pa.: The Science Press, 1929), 40.

17    *42 percent*    Ibid., 159.

17    *"dame schools"*    Lucy Larcom, a shopkeeper's daughter who worked in the Lowell mills before becoming a teacher and poet, described her experience in a dame school in her memoir *A New England Girlhood*. (Boston: Houghton Mifflin, 1890). "I began to go to school when I was about two years old, as other children about us did. The mothers of those large families had to resort to some means of keeping their little ones out of mischief, while they attended to their domestic duties. Not much more than that sort of temporary guardianship was expected of the good dame who had us in charge. But I learned my letters in a few days, standing at Aunt Hannah's knee while she pointed them out in the spelling-book with a pin. . . ."

17    *two hundred New England towns*    Woody, 142.

17    *"The sons shall . . ."*    Ibid., 144. Some New England town schools started allowing girls to attend on a limited basis in the 1700s—around the edges of the boys' class schedules. The town of Medford, Massachusetts, for instance, told its schoolmaster in 1766 that he could teach girls for two hours each day after the boys' lessons were done. In 1787, the town said that girls could attend school for one hour in the morning and one hour in the afternoon for four months of the year. In 1790, it allowed girls to attend during the summer, when boys were typically out working in the fields. It wasn't until 1834 that girls were allowed to attend the Medford town school year-round.

18    *"As we have had . . ."*    Cott, 40.

18    *"You boast . . ."*    *Lady's Magazine*, August 1892, 121–23, cited in Linda Kerber, *Women of the Republic: Intellect and Ideology in Revolutionary America* (Chapel Hill: University of North Carolina Press, 1980), 203.

19    *"Academies"*    Some late-eighteenth-century academies for girls cited by Thomas Woody were Timothy Dwight's school in Greenfield, Connecticut, in 1785; an academy in Medford, Massachusetts, which opened in 1789 and ran for about seven years; and William Woodbridge's school in New Haven, which opened in 1790. Early-nineteenth-century academies included schools for girls run by Joseph Emerson, Catherine Fiske, and Zilpah Grant. In Philadelphia, John Poor started a female academy in Philadelphia in the 1780s and

a Quaker named Anne Parrish opened a school for poor girls in 1796.

19    *Young Ladies Academy*    Ann D. Gordon, "The Young Ladies Academy of Philadelphia," in *Women of America: A History,* eds. Carol Ruth Berkin and Mary Beth Norton (Boston: Houghton Mifflin, 1979), 79. See also Marion B. Savin and Harold J. Abrahams, "The Young Ladies Academy of Philadelphia," *History of Education Journal* 8, no. 2 (winter 1957).

19    *"Female academies...*    Judith Sargent Murray, *Excerpts from The Gleaner* (Schenectady, N.Y.: Union College Press, 1992), 703.

19    *Sarah Callister*    Kerber, *Women of the Republic,* 202.

20    *"I left school..."*    Cott, 115.

20    *I have brought*    *Godey's Lady's Book* 46 (May 1853): 457, as cited in Bernard Wishy, *The Child and the Republic* (Philadelphia: University of Pennsylvania Press, 1968), 14.

21    *Catherine Beecher*    Catherine Beecher, *Suggestions Respecting Improvements in Female Education,* 1829, cited in Woody, 352–53.

22    *"The enterprizing [sic] turn..."*    Letter from Samuel Hart to John Willard Esq., 8 October 1809, in Emma Willard School archives.

23    *"When it was so cold..."*    Alma Lutz, *Emma Willard: Pioneer Educator of American Women* (Boston: Beacon Press, 1964), 15.

23    *Middlebury College*    Henry Fowler, "Educational Services of Mrs. Emma Willard," in *Memoirs of Teachers and Educators,* ed. Henry Barnard (New York: Arno Press, 1969), 133. See also Lutz, 23.

23    *"... regarded as visionary..."*    Ibid., 134.

24    *"In those great republics..."*    Emma Willard, "A Plan for Improving Female Education" (Marietta, Ga.: Larlin Corp., 1987), 32, 37.

25    *"republican motherhood"*    For excellent discussions of republican motherhood and women's roles in early-nineteenth-century America, see Linda Kerber's *Women of the Republic* and Nancy Cott's *The Bonds of Womanhood.*

25    *"Institutions for young gentlemen..."*    Willard, *Plan,* 10–11, 14.

26    *"To have had it..."*    Fowler, 145.

28    *Troy trustees*    A.J. Weise, *History of the City of Troy* (William H. Young: Troy, 1876). Samual Reznick, *Profiles out of the Past of Troy, New York, Since 1789* (Troy: Greater Troy Chamber of Commerce, 1970).

29    *A typical day*    Lutz, 42.

29    *Tabor, Clark*    Emma Willard School archives.

30    *"Truly in the midst..."*    Carolina Eliza Wills diary, Emma Willard

School archives. A headmistress's perspective on revivals can be found in *Thornton Hall*, a didactic 1872 novel about life at a girls' school, by Phebe McKeen, the head of Abbot Academy.

30    *The curriculum*    Historian Thomas Woody tracked the subjects offered at 162 female seminaries between 1742 and 1871. The most common were academic subjects such as English grammar (offered at 139 schools), arithmetic (132 schools), natural philosophy (123 schools), and rhetoric (121 schools). By contrast, just 37 schools offered ornamental needlework, 29 offered plain needlework, and 20 offered embroidery. Among the subjects that wouldn't be seen today, two schools offered classes in "Conversation" and four offered classes in "Politeness." Woody, 563–65.

31    *"Some said . . ."*    Fowler, 147. See also "Emma Willard the Pioneer in the Higher Education of Women," by Elizabeth Cady Stanton, read before the Emma Willard Association at the World's Congress on Education, 19 July 1893. Emma Willard School archives.

31    *"The exercise . . ."*    Letter from Emily F. Smith to Almira McQueen, 28 September 1865, Emma Willard School archives.

32    *"Mr. Brace exceeded . . ."*    Emily Noyes Vanderpoel, *Chronicles of a Pioneer School From 1792 to 1833, Being the History of Miss Sarah Pierce and Her Litchfield School* (Cambridge, Mass.: University Press, 1903), 181.

32    *Abbot student*    Susan McIntosh Lloyd, *A Singular School: Abbot Academy 1828–1973* (Hanover, N.H.: Phillips Andover Academy, distributed by University Press of New England, 1979), 51. Sara Willis, a student at the Hartford Female Seminary in 1829, also fell in love with math at school. She wrote, "At last [I] became so deeply imbued with the spirit of arithmetic that even my language took coloring from it. . . . I rose in the morning to make my toilet when, to my great consternation, my hair, instead of forming itself as usual into flaxen circles, very deliberately erected itself into triangles, angles, and parallelograms all over my head. . . ." (Sophia Smith collection at Smith College).

33    *"Mr. Brace gave . . ."*    Lynne Templeton Brickley, "Sarah Pierce's Litchfield Academy, 1792–1833" (Ed.D. dissertation, Harvard University, 1985), 273.

33    *"Females . . ."*    Willard, *Plan*, 21, 34.

33    *"From the bursting . . ."*    Ibid., 21.

35    *"seem[ed] peculiarly . . ."*    Cited in Sarah Elizabeth Buckley, "The Bodying Forth of a Long-Loved Idea: Emma Willard's Reformula-

tion of School, Family, and Nation" (thesis, Harvard College, 9 March 1994), 41.

35    *"To be a political . . ."*   Letter to newspaper by Emma Willard dated 5 July 1816, Emma Willard School archives.

36    *"No—my dear . . ."*   Lutz, 72.

36    *"Shame on the woman . . ."*   Emma Willard, "Places of Education," *The Ladies' Magazine and Literary Gazette* 6 (September 1833): 387. Willard was conservative on some other issues as well as women's role in the family. Her position on slavery is appalling to modern eyes. In an 1862 essay called "Via Media," Willard called on Americans to avoid civil war by replacing slavery with a "regulated servitude" in which white masters would own slaves but not abuse them. She attacked those who suggested equality for blacks and said that God had meant for white men to rule the country. "Were a grand family procession to set forth in the order appointed by Providence, the white men would go first, the white women with their children second, and next the colored servants," she wrote. "We know by the ten commandments that the servant's place in the family is sanctioned by God; and who knows that in forming the negro He has not had it in view to create a race with a mission to serve the white women, and add strength to their physical weakness?"

36    *"Must you keep . . ."*   Emma Willard, letter to Mr. B. Mumford, 28 June 1823, Emma Willard School archives.

37    *"She was always robed . . ."*   Lutz, 87.

37    *"Let it be borne . . ."*   *American Ladies' Magazine* 6 (1833): 405.

38    *"Go, in the name . . ."*   Scott, "The Ever-Widening Circle," 72.

38    *loans*   Lord, 136.

39    *"Such a sentence . . ."*   Ibid., 117.

39    *"My first feeling . . ."*   Celia Burleigh, "Mrs. Emma Willard on the Woman Question," *The Woman's Journal* (1 April 1871), Emma Willard School archives.

41    *"To none of the heroes . . ."*   Stanton, "Emma Willard the Pioneer in the Higher Education of Women," Emma Willard School archives.


## 2. ELITE ENCLAVES

45    *Abbot founding*   Lloyd, 5.

46    *Abbot enrollment*   Ibid., 22, 39, 72, 77, 101, 185. She writes that after the coed high school opened, "there were to be far fewer efforts to accommodate the Academy to the local clientele and fewer brakes

applied to tuition raises. The advent of Andover's first public high school pushed Abbot to take its own more independent course as a boarding school."

48  *Spread of public schools*  Woody, 544–45.

49  *Louisville spending*  David Tyack and Elizabeth Hansot, *Learning Together: A History of Coeducation in American Public Schools* (New Haven: Yale University Press, 1990), 130.

49  *"Only by having . . ."*  Ibid., 116.

49  *"The rudeness . . ."*  William Torrey Harris, *St. Louis Report for 1870,* in Tyack and Hansot, 102.

49  *"radical and fundamental . . ."*  John D. Philbrick, "Coeducation of the Sexes," American Institute of Instruction, *Lectures and Proceedings,* 1880, 122, 124, in Tyack and Hansot, 99.

50  *"parents have objections . . ."*  *San Francisco Report for 1868,* 33–34, in Tyack and Hansot, 95.

50  *"for there the conditions . . ."*  *Majority and Minority Reports of the Boston School Committee on the Subject of Coeducation of the Sexes* (Boston: Blackwell and Churchill, 1890), 60, in Tyack and Hansot, 95.

50  *"As God made us . . ."*  Tyack and Hansot, 134.

50  *single-sex data*  U.S. Bureau of Education, "Coeducation of the Sexes in Public Schools of the United States," *Circular of Information No. 2,* and *U.S. Commissioner of Education Report for 1900–1901,* in Tyack and Hansot, 114.

51  *academies becoming college-prep*  Lawrence Benedict Fuller offers a good description of how academies redefined themselves as college-preparatory schools in an unpublished dissertation, "Education for Leadership: The Emergence of the College Preparatory School" (Baltimore: Johns Hopkins University, 1974).

51  *private school data*  U.S. Department of Education, *Education Report, 1919,* Table 127, 1168. There are no data on the number of single-sex private schools before 1899–1900.

52  *"In choosing a school . . ."*  Margaret E. Sangster, "A School for the Girl of Thirteen," *Harper's Bazar* 33 (9 June 1900): 375.

52  *"Often these men . . ."*  Camille R. Kraeplin, ed., *Of Hearts and Minds: The Hockaday Experience, 1913–1988* (Dallas: The Hockaday School, 1988), 26.

53  *Spence's youth*  Mary Dillon Edmondson, *Profiles in Leadership: A History of the Spence School, 1892–1992* (West Kennebunk: Phoenix Publishing, 1991), 1–11.

54  *Victorian values*  Ibid., 25–26.

55    *Spence's adoptions*  Ibid., 17, 41, 52–56. Historian Alan Siroky
      points out that Clara Spence was not the only girls' school principal
      to adopt children as a single mother. Caroline Ruutz-Rees, head-
      mistress of Rosemary Hall, adopted an orphaned baby boy in 1909
      and named him after her deceased brother. Alice Howland and
      Eleanor Brownell, who became heads of the Shipley School in
      Philadelphia in 1916, each adopted a baby girl. The two girls grew
      up as sisters and shared the last name of Shipley. See Alan Siroky,
      "Progressive Era Reform and Private Secondary Schools for Women,
      1890–1920" (Ph.D. dissertation, City University of New York,
      1996), 306–7.

56    *"Industry and finance . . ."*  Edmondson, 57.

57    *"I began the first year . . ."*  Lucy Madeira Wing, 1956 commence-
      ment speech. In the Kathleen Galvin Johnson '53 Archives of the
      Madeira School.

58    *post office encounter*  Madeira School archives.

58    *"One thing I appreciated . . ."*  Ibid.

58    *"You should have heard . . ."*  Ibid.

59    *"She told us directly . . ."*  Ibid.

59    *watchwords*  "Miss Madeira's School: A Portrait," *Madeira Today*
      (fall 1981): no. 117, 2. Also see chapel talk by Allegra Maynard on
      Lucy Madeira's life, in the Madeira School archives.

59    *Katharine Graham recalls*  Katharine Graham, *Personal History*
      (New York: Knopf, 1997), 44.

59    *Astor at Madeira*  Brooke Astor, *Patchwork Child: Early Memories*
      (New York: Harper & Row, 1993), 232.

61    *"Well-to-do families . . ."*  Porter Sargent guidebook for 1935–36.

62    *"When they hit . . ."*  Mary Custis Lee deButts and Rosalie Noland
      Woodland, *Charlotte Haxall Noland, 1883–1969* (Foxcroft School,
      1971), 40.

63    *"It is the ideal training . . ."*  Ibid., 42, 80.

63    *"Girls! Off with . . ."*  Ibid., 74.

64    *"O my girls . . ."*  Sermon by Charlotte Haxall Noland, 6 June
      1937, in the Foxcroft archives.

64    *"always a 'doer' . . ."*  DeButts and Woodland, 86.

65    *"There is this essential irony . . ."*  "Miss Chapin's, Miss Walker's,
      Foxcroft, Farmington," *Fortune* (August 1931): 38.

65    *"Selfishness is a* hedious *[sic] sin . . ."*  Mary Deming Shipman, who
      attended from 1884 to 1886 and wrote her reminiscences in 1943.
      In Miss Porter's School archives.

66 *Noland and trunks . . ."* DeButts and Woodland, 31
66 *"If any arrived . . ."* Abby Farwell Ferry, *When I Was at Farming-ton* (Chicago: Ralph Fletchers Seymour, 1931), 177. In Miss Porter's School archives.
66 *"Now, at this stage . . ."* Charlotte Porter, "Physical Hindrances to Teaching Girls," *Forum* (September 1891): 42.
67 *"Miss Winsor's School . . ."* Porter E. Sargent, *A Handbook of the Best Private Schools of the United States and Canada* (Boston: Porter E. Sargent, 1915), 107, 120, 128, 141.
68 *schools for Jewish girls* Ibid., 1935–36, 826. However, Porter Sargent's listing of schools accepting Jewish students is probably incomplete. For instance, the Brearley School in New York accepted Jewish pupils from the start but was not included in Porter Sargent's list.
68 *"What did matter . . ."* Edmondson, 45
69 *Bryn Mawr School* Rosmond Randall Beirne, *Let's Pick the Daisies: The History of the Bryn Mawr School, 1885–1967* (Baltimore: Bryn Mawr School, 1970), 29. Also see Andrea Dale Hamilton, "A Vision for Girls: A Story of Gender, Education, and the Bryn Mawr School," (Ph.D. dissertation, Tulane University, 1987), 65–66. For more on how Bryn Mawr's founders clashed over admitting Jewish students, see Helen Lefkowitz Horowitz, *The Power and Passion of M. Carey Thomas* (New York: Knopf, 1994), 231–32, 267.
69 *"The Bryn Mawr School is seventy-six . . ."* Letter from Judith Sullivan (Palfrey) to Mrs. M. Lawrence Millspaugh, 23 September 1961, in the Bryn Mawr School archives.
70 *"People will accept . . ."* Phyllis LaFarge, "A Warm-Hearted Guide to Certain Girls' Schools," *Harpers* (April 1963): 77.
70 *Abbot integration* Lloyd, 293–94.

### 3. FINISHING AND FITTING

76 *"finishing schools for young ladies . . ."* Fuller, "Education for Leadership," 131.
77 *"December 16, 1853 . . ."* Sarah Porter journal entry for 16 December 1853, cited in Louise Stevenson, *Miss Porter's School—A History in Documents, 1847–1948* (New York: Garland, 1987).
78 *"As to the woman . . ."* Porter, letter to Annie B. Jennings, 1 March 1894. Cited in Stevenson, 84.
78 *"I do not want . . ."* Nancy Davis and Barbara Donahue, *Miss*

*Porter's School—A History* (Farmington, Conn.: Miss Porter's School, 1992), 21.

78    *"The Wellesley girl..."*   Stevenson, unnumbered page in her introduction.

79    *The brouhaha began*   Tyack and Hansot, 151. Rosalind Rosenberg, *Beyond Separate Spheres: Intellectual Roots of Modern Feminism* (New Haven: Yale University Press, 1982), 5.

80    *"Not a great while..."*   Edward H. Clarke, *Sex in Education; or, A Fair Chance for the Girls* (Boston: James R. Osgood & Co., 1873), 102.

80    *"the young girls..."*   Rosenberg, 10.

81    *"It is a fact..."*   Anna C. Brackett, *The Education of American Girls. Considered in a Series of Essays* (New York: Putnam, 1874), 312.

81    *"No one dares deny..."*   "Shall Our Daughters be Liberally Educated," *The Tilden Enterprise* 3, no. 2 (January 1873). In the Sophia Smith Collection at Smith College.

82    *"studies will be remitted..."*   *The Year-Book of Brearley School,* 1892–93, 7. In the Brearley School archives.

82    *"Girls seem to me..."*   Charlotte Porter, "Physical Hindrances to Teaching Girls," *Forum* (September 1891): 47.

83    *conservative Baltimore*   Beirne, 1–3. Hamilton, 32. See also M. Carey Thomas, *A Brief Account of the Founding and Early Years of the Bryn Mawr School,* 1931.

84    *"we'll never consent..."*   Hamilton, 39.

84    *"The winged Victory..."*   Mary H. Cadwalader, "No Carpet and No Red Door," *Baltimore Evening Sun,* 1971, Bryn Mawr School archives.

85    *Bryn Mawr enrollment struggles*   Hamilton, 32, 52, 84.

85    *"The school is offering..."*   Ibid., 74.

85    *physical-culture program*   Ibid., 52–55.

85    *"Don't allow..."*   Ibid., 42.

86    *Baldwin tracks*   Heather Neal and Judith L. Hammerschmidt, *A Preposterous Extravagance: The Centennial History of the Baldwin School, 1888–1988* (Bryn Mawr, Pa.: Baldwin School, 1988).

87    *"... really what I learned..."*   Davis and Donahue, 18.

89    *"Dr. King felt very strongly..."*   Lydia Chapin Kirk, *Schooldays, Farmington 1911–1913,* in the Miss Porter's School archives.

89    *"Miss Palliser marshaled..."*   Ibid.

90    *"Ladies do not drink..."*   *The Way of a School: Columbus School for Girls, 1898–1989,* brochure published by the school, 15.

92      *"The queen was . . ."* Christie Anne Farnham, *The Education of the Southern Belle: Higher Education and Student Socialization in the Antebellum South* (New York: New York University Press, 1994), 169.

93      *"help girls realize . . ."* Lloyd, 228.

93      *"One of my general observations . . ."* Headmistresses Association of the East, Fall Meeting, Nov. 9 and 10, 1923. In the Sophia Smith collection of Smith College.

95      *1932 curriculum study* Sue Cleveland Hamilton, "Programs of Studies of Private Secondary Schools for Girls" (master's dissertation, University of Chicago: 1932), 32–34.

96      *"We do still quite positively . . ."* Sarah Porter, Letter to "Ethel," March 1896, in Stevenson, 85.

98      *". . . residual fear . . ."* Anna Seaton Huntington, "All Sugar and Competitive Spice," *New York Times,* May 17, 1998.

## 4. SINGLE-SEX SCHOOLS FOR GIRLS OF COLOR

103     *"rests upon the type"* Mary McLeod Bethune, "A Philosophy of Education for Negro Girls," in *Mary McLeod Bethune, Building a Better World: Essays and Selected Documents,* ed. Audrey Thomas McCluskey and Elaine M. Smith (Bloomington: Indiana University Press, 1999), 84.

104     *Crandall* My account of Prudence Crandall is based primarily on three books about her: Susan Strane, *A Whole-Souled Woman: Prudence Crandall and the Education of Black Women* (New York: Norton, 1990); Edmund Fuller, *Prudence Crandall: An Incident of Racism in Nineteenth-Century Connecticut* (Middletown, Conn.: Wesleyan University Press, 1971); and Philip S. Foner and Josephine F. Pacheco, *Three Who Dared: Prudence Crandall, Margaret Douglass, Myrtilla Miner—Champions of Antebellum Black Education* (Westport, Conn.: Greenwood Press, 1984). Strane's book is not only the most recent but the most comprehensive.

104     *abolition in Connecticut* Connecticut banned the import of slaves in 1774. In 1784, it mandated that all slaves born after March 1, 1784, be freed at age twenty-five. In 1797, it lowered the age of freedom to twenty-one. Slavery was not entirely abolished in the state until 1848.

104     *"My feelings began . . ."* Foner and Pacheco, 8.

105     *"We are not merely opposed . . ."* Fuller, 30–31.

106    *Burleigh*  More than thirty years later, William H. Burleigh married Celia Burr Burleigh, the friend of Emma Willard who helped reshape her thinking about women's suffrage. William Burleigh wrote a poem in honor of Willard's eightieth birthday ("For noble was thy work and nobly done . . .") that was included in an anthology of his writings. Willard herself must have been aware in 1833 of the controversy over Crandall's school, especially given her own roots in Connecticut. But there is no evidence that Willard took a stand in support of Crandall, and her writings on race suggest that she would not have approved of Crandall's crusade to educate young black women. In an interesting historical twist, Celia Burleigh was chosen in 1870 to be pastor of the Unitarian church that was once led by May—the first woman to be ordained a Unitarian minister.

106    *"break down the barriers . . ."*  Reprinted in *The Liberator*, 6 April 1833, cited in Foner and Pacheco, 19.

107    *"My ride from Hartford . . ."*  *The Liberator*, 22 June 1833, cited in Dorothy Sterling, ed., *We Are Your Sisters: Black Women in the Nineteenth Century* (New York: Norton, 1984), 181.

108    *Twain correspondence*  Strane, 220–21.

108    *"receive young females . . ."*  Foner and Pacheco, 32.

109    *"Alas, for the . . ."*  *The Emancipator*, 20 July 1833, cited in Marie J. Lindhorst, "Sarah Mapps Douglass: The Emergence of an African American Educator/Activist in Nineteenth Century Philadelphia" (Ph.D. dissertation, Pennsylvania State University, 1995), 81. Lindhorst notes that one of Douglass's cousins was reportedly a student of Crandall's.

109    *New York move*  Lindhorst, 82.

109    *"She evidently treats . . ."*  Sterling, 128.

110    *Oblates*  Grace Sherwood, *The Oblates' Hundred and One Years* (New York: Macmillan, 1931), 7–8, 35. The ninth woman to join the new Oblate order was Marie Becraft, who at the age of fifteen had started a well-regarded school for African-American girls in Georgetown. Becraft's school had the active support of white nuns from the Visitation convent in Georgetown. See Barbara Miner, *"Highly Respected and Accomplished Ladies": Catholic Women Religious in America, 1790–1850* (New York: Garland, 1988), 204.

110    *"When we hear you . . ."*  Sterling, 182.

111    *aspiring to be "ladies"*  African-Americans weren't the only people of color who aspired to seminary training for their daughters. In

1851, the Cherokee Nation Council opened the Cherokee Female Seminary in Tahlequah, Oklahoma. Modeled on Mt. Holyoke, the Cherokee Female Seminary offered subjects such as geometry, Greek history, Latin, and vocal music. Students referred to themselves as "rosebuds" and aspired to play the same inspirational role in Native households that white women were supposed to play in white homes. For a detailed history of the Cherokee Female Seminary, see Devon A. Mihesuah, *Cultivating the Rosebuds: The Education of Women at the Cherokee Female Seminary, 1851–1909* (Urbana: University of Illinois Press, 1993), 31, 37.

112    *"It was a whole . . ."* James D. Anderson, *The Education of Blacks in the South, 1860–1935* (Chapel Hill: University of North Carolina Press, 1988), 5–6.

112    *975 schools* Ronald E. Butchart, *Northern Schools, Southern Blacks, and Reconstruction: Freedmen's Education, 1862–1875* (Westport, Conn.: Greenwood Press, 1980), 4.

112    *"To these groups"* Ibid., 21.

113    *schools for young women of color* Another African-American girls' school started by church groups was Mary Holmes Seminary in Jackson, Mississippi. Today a coed junior college, the school was started in 1892 by the Presbyterian church to teach domestic skills and Christian values to the daughters of former slaves.

113    *"What I learned . . ."* Rosa Parks and Jim Haskins, *Rosa Parks: My Story* (New York: Dial, 1992), 43, 48.

114    *"We are not going . . ."* Foner and Pacheco, 122–24, 138.

114    *"Miss Miner if you . . ."* Ibid., 189.

114    *"I have thought . . ."* Sterling, 190, 201.

115    *"literally children . . ."* *Ramona Days*, no. 2, (1 July 1887). In the Sophia Smith collection of Smith College.

117    *Bethune's childhood* Audrey Thomas McCluskey, "Mary McLeod Bethune and the Education of Black Girls in the South, 1904–1923" (Ph.D. dissertation, Indiana University, 1991), 43–46.

117    *"Something happened . . ."* Ibid., 49.

117    *Scotia Seminary* Ibid., 53–59.

118    *"I was the prize . . ."* Ibid., 59.

118    *"We burned logs . . ."* Gerda Lerner, *Black Women in White America*, cited in McCluskey, 170.

120    *"Girls who came . . ."* McCluskey, 174–76, 178, 181.

120    *"I called you . . ."* Ibid., 188.

120    *"God give us girls . . ."* Ibid., 227.

121 *"With Mrs. Bethune . . ."* Interview with Lucy Miller Mitchell, 22 August 1977, from Elizabeth H. Ihle, ed., *Black Women in Higher Education* (New York: Garland, 1992), 91.

121 *Burroughs's youth* Traki Lynn Taylor, "God's School on the Hill: Nannie Helen Burroughs and the National Training School for Women and Girls, 1901–1961" (Ph.D. dissertation, University of Illinois-Champaign, 1998), 8–19.

122 *"What every woman . . ."* Evelyn Brooks Barnett, "Nannie Burroughs and the Education of Black Women," in *The Afro-American Woman; Struggles and Images,* ed. Sharon Harley and Rosalyn Terborg-Penn (Port Washington, N.Y.: Kennikat Press, 1978), 106.

122 *"to prepare leaders . . ."* Taylor, 33.

122 *"For [girls'] proper . . ."* Ibid., 26.

123 *"Woodson said . . ."* Opal V. Easter, *Nannie Helen Burroughs* (New York: Garland, 1995), 70.

124 *As historian Audrey McCluskey* For an excellent comparison of Bethune and Burroughs's schools with the recent movement for Afrocentric boys' academies, see Audrey McCluskey, "The Historical Context of the Single-Sex Schooling Debate Among African Americans," *The Western Journal of Black Studies* 17:4 (1993): 193–201.

## 5. SMASHES, CRUSHES, AND FEMALE FRIENDSHIPS

130 *"I feel perfectly . . ."* Diary of Elizabeth Failing Conner, 1 February 1888, in Stevenson, 253–54.

132 *"Hattie is in love . . ."* Farnham, 156. Farnham has a good chapter on women's romantic relationships at southern schools.

132 *"There seems to . . ."* *The Snooper,* 9 March 1927, in the Foxcroft School archives.

132 *Victorian relationships* For an excellent presentation of nineteenth-century intimate female friendships, see Lillian Faderman, *Surpassing the Love of Men: Romantic Friendship and Love Between Women from the Renaissance to the Present* (New York: Morrow, 1981).

133 *Duryee diary* Susan Duryee diary, 9 July 1883 and 21 July 1882, in Stevenson, 220–23, 245–46.

135 *Thomas at school* Horowitz, *The Power and Passion of M. Carey Thomas,* 45–46.

135 *Molly and Helena* Carroll Smith-Rosenberg, "The Female World of

Love and Ritual: Relations between Women in Nineteenth-Century America," *Signs* 1:1 (Autumn 1975): 5–8.

137 *"I hope the ball . . ."* Horowitz, *The Power and Passion of M. Carey Thomas,* 46.

137 *"Her innocent admirers . . ."* *The Snooper,* 9 March 1927, in the Foxcroft School archives.

138 *"What a pest . . ."* Helen Lefkowitz Horowitz, *Alma Mater* (New York: Knopf, 1984), 65–66.

138 *"Cousin Julia says . . ."* Phebe McKeen, *Thornton Hall; or, Old Questions in Young Lives* (New York: Anson D. Randolph & Co., 1872), 67.

138 *"Warm affection . . ."* Havelock Ellis, "Sexual Inversion in Women," in *Studies in the Psychology of Sex,* vol. 1 (New York: Random House, 1942), 219.

139 *"a wicked, bawdy . . ."* Ibid., xvii.

139 *"We had never . . ."* Farmington Society of Washington, D.C., *When I Was at Farmington,* typewritten manuscript in the Miss Porter's School archives.

139 *Ellis on school friendships* Ellis, "The School-Friendships of Girls," in *Studies,* 369.

140 *HAE meeting* Annual Meeting of the Headmistresses Association of the East, 12 and 13 November 1920. In the Sophia Smith Collection of Smith College.

140 *"Years afterward . . ."* Oral history of Eleanor Brewster, recorded in 1984, in Miss Porter's School archives.

141 *"Today six of our . . ."* *The Chatham Hall Storybook: The First 100 Years* (Chatham, Virginia: Chatham Hall, 1994), 17.

141 *GPS advice column* *Static* no. 3 (2 June 1931) and later issues, in the archives of Girls Preparatory School.

## 6. "THE WORLD WAS BREAKING OPEN"

158 *Foxcroft and Madeira admissions* "The Young Ladies Buckle Down to Work," *Newsweek,* 9 February 1959.

158 *"The main point . . ."* Ibid.

172 *Concord Academy* Philip McFarland, *A History of Concord Academy: The First Half Century* (Concord, Mass.: Concord Academy, 1986), 212–13, 218, 226.

172 *dwindling numbers* U.S. Department of Education, National

Center for Education Statistics, *Private Schools in American Education,* Table E-1 ("Number of private schools, by affiliation, type of
facility, and sex of student, and by type of school: U.S., 1976 to
1978"), January 1981. And *Statistics of Nonpublic Elementary and
Secondary Schools, 1965–66,* Table D ("Historical statistics of nonpublic elementary and secondary schools in the U.S., 1899–1900
to 1965–66"), 1968. This includes all private schools, both religious
and nondenominational.

173    *"Attracting boys . . ."* "Evaluation of Strategies," 12–13. Typed
manuscript in the archives of the Sisters of the Presentation of the
Blessed Virgin Mary, San Francisco.

175    *"You're going to merge . . ."* Lloyd, 370.

175    *Male faculty outnumbered female* Kathleen M. Dalton, *A Portrait
of a School: Coeducation at Andover* (New York: Phillips Academy/
toExcel, 1999), 16–17.

175    *"The Board* [sic] *would accept . . ."* Lloyd, 438, 440.

176    *"Andover is still . . ."* Dalton, 15, 21.

177    *"There is a discrepancy . . ."* Elizabeth Edmonds, "On Your Knees,
Eleanor Roosevelts," *The Phillipian,* 3 November 2000, A7.

## 7. REVIVAL

187    *demographic problem* National Center for Education Statistics,
*Digest of Education Statistics, 2001,* Chapter 2, Table 56, "Enrollment in grades 9 to 12 in public and private schools compared with
population 14 to 17 years of age: 1889–90 to fall 2000."

194    *increase in girls in sports* U.S. Department of Education, *Title IX:
25 Years of Progress—June 1997,* June 1997. See *http://www.ed.gov/
pubs/TitleIX/.*

200    *"Seeing themselves seen . . ."* Lyn Mikel Brown and Carol Gilligan,
*Meeting at the Crossroads: Women's Psychology and Girls' Develop-
ment* (Cambridge, Mass.: Harvard University Press, 1992), 164.
See also Carol Gilligan, Nona P. Lyons, and Trudy J. Hanmer, eds.,
*Making Connections: The Relational World of Girls at the Emma
Willard School* (Cambridge, Mass.: Harvard University Press,
1990).

201    *"It was first . . ."* Brown and Gilligan, 221.

203    *"On the surface . . ."* Myra and David Sadker, *Failing at Fairness:
How Our Schools Cheat Girls* (New York: Simon & Schuster,
1994), 44.

206     *"At first blush . . ."*   Mary Pipher, *Reviving Ophelia: Saving the Selves of Adolescent Girls* (New York: Ballantine, 1994), 12.

206     *"Something dramatic*   Ibid., 19.

209     *endowment data*   The 2002 survey data is from the National Association of Independent Schools' endowment survey for the 2001–2002 school year. Among 691 coed independent schools that responded to the survey, the average endowment was $13.1 million, lower than both the boys' and girls' schools. A separate 2002 survey of a smaller group of about 200 independent schools by the Council for Aid to Education, a division of the Rand Corporation, showed coed schools with an average endowment of $39.2 million, boys' schools with $34.3 million, and girls' schools with $24.3 million. The discrepancy between the NAIS and CAE data may come from the fact that the CAE survey included responses from a smaller number of schools, which tended to be the larger and better-funded schools. Figures cited for individual school endowments come from the CAE survey, except for Ursuline and Jesuit, which came from the schools themselves.

210     *$1,000 more in tuition*   "The Young Ladies Buckle Down to Work", *Newsweek*, 9 February 1959.

212     *Enrollment rose*   The National Coalition of Girls' Schools, *Statistical Profile of NCGS Schools, Fall 2000*.

213     *annual fund drives*   Annual giving data is from the National Association of Independent Schools' survey of annual giving for the year 2000–2001. Twenty-eight percent of girls' school alumnae gave to their schools' annual fund drives that year, compared with 25 percent of boys' school alumni and 16 percent of coed school alumni. The average total amount raised in annual giving was $863,049 among boys' schools, $804,833 among girls' schools, and $560,030 among coed schools.


## 8. CATHOLIC SCHOOLS

218     *spread of academies*   Eileen Mary Brewer, *Nuns and the Education of American Catholic Women, 1860–1920* (Chicago: Loyola University Press, 1987), 15. See also Mary J. Oates, "Catholic Female Academies on the Frontier," *U.S. Catholic Historian,* 12:4 (fall 1994): 122; and Carol K. Coburn and Martha Smith, *Spirited Lives: How Nuns Shaped Catholic Culture and American Life, 1836–1920* (Chapel Hill: University of North Carolina Press, 1999). For a general history of Catholic education that includes the

girls' academies, see Harold A. Buetow, *Of Singular Benefit: The Story of Catholic Education in the United States* (New York: Macmillan, 1970).

219   *Chillicothe*   Coburn and Smith, 173.

219   *"some good persons . . ."*   Brewer, 31. See also James K. Keneally, *The History of American Catholic Women* (New York: Crossroad Publishing, 1990), 15.

220   *Madame Celestine's*   Coburn and Smith, 164.

220   *"habituat[ing] the young . . ."*   J. A. Burns, *The Catholic School System in the United States: Its Principles, Origin and Establishment* (New York: Benziger Bros., 1908), 381.

220   *"What citizen . . ."*   Oates, 123.

221   *"will educate their children . . ."*   Coburn and Smith, 171.

221   *Charlestown convent*   For an in-depth study of the Charlestown convent burning, see Nancy Lusignan Schultz, *Fire & Roses: The Burning of the Charlestown Convent, 1834* (Boston: Northeastern University Press, 2000).

221   *"All the chief . . ."*   Brewer, 46.

221   *"as an indication . . ."*   Coburn and Smith, 171.

222   *"Now, ma petite"*   Antonia White, *Frost in May* (New York: Dial, 1933), 35.

222   *"We learned . . ."*   V. V. Harrison, *Changing Habits: A Memoir of the Society of the Sacred Heart* (New York: Doubleday, 1988), 24–25.

223   *"It was like . . ."*   Ibid., 181.

223   *"It has been many . . ."*   Agnes Repplier, *In Our Convent Days* (Boston: Houghton Mifflin, 1906), vii–viii. One sign of the intensity of the convent school experience is that it inspired a whole minigenre of memoirs—Repplier's, Harrison's, White's, as well as George Sand's *My Convent Life* about her education in a French convent school. Mary McCarthy includes her time at a Catholic girls' school in her *Memories of a Catholic Girlhood,* although it is not the focus of her book.

223   *"Our people . . ."*   Thomas M. Landy, "The Colleges in Context," in *Catholic Women's Colleges in America,* ed. Tracy Schier and Cynthia Russett (Baltimore: Johns Hopkins University Press, 2002), 61. In addition, women's religious orders felt an increasing need to provide college classes for their own sisters as states started demanding a college degree for teachers in the public schools.

225   *"There are, in fact..."*   Buetow, 448. See also J. A. Burns, *Growth and Development of the Catholic School System in the United States* (New York: Benziger, 1912), 369.

234   *"Too long..."*   Bertrande Meyers, *Sisters for the 21st Century* (New York: Shed and Ward, 1965), 259.

237   *dwindling vocations*   The number of American nuns fell from 179,954 to 135,225 in 1975, 115,386 in 1985, 90,809 in 1995, and 79,814 in 2000, according to the Center for Applied Research on the Apostolate at Georgetown University. The number of nuns fell much more dramatically than the number of priests or brothers. This was at a time when the overall Catholic population of the United States grew, from 41.5 million in 1965 to 60.8 million in 2000.

238   *dwindling enrollment*   Anthony S. Bryk, Valerie E. Lee, and Peter B. Holland, *Catholic Schools and the Common Good* (Cambridge, Mass.: Harvard University Press, 1993), 33.

239   *Presentation closure*   Archives of the Sisters of the Presentation BVM, San Francisco. Administrators at Presentation started sensing trouble in the 1970s. A report from the mid-70s cited "problem areas" such as declining enrollments at parish schools that fed into Presentation, and rising costs due to increased lay faculty. Each lay teacher increased the school's expenses by $4,000, at a time when tuition was only about $400.

239   *The percentage of minorities*   National Catholic Educational Association, data for 2001–2002 school year.

## 9. THE PUBLIC SCHOOL BATTLE

251   *"No evidence shows..."*   Patricia Ireland, "Wrong Lessons at Girls' Schools," *Wall Street Journal,* 3 September 1997, A21.

252   *"Your inquiry..."*   Tyack and Hansot, *Learning Together,* 98.

252   *number of single-sex high schools*   Ibid., 114.

254   *vocational schools*   John L. Rury, *Education and Women's Work: Female Schooling and the Division of Labor in Urban America, 1870–1930* (Albany: State University of New York Press, 1991), 152, 161. Jane Bernard Powers, *The "Girl Question" in Education: Vocational Education for Young Women in the Progressive Era* (London: The Falmer Press, 1992), 29, 104–5.

254   *gender stereotyping in vocational schools*   Tyack and Hansot, 185, 211, 265.

255     *Hunter entrance exam*    "Hunter College High School: A Chro-
        nology," in *Hunter College High School Alumnae/i Association Di-
        rectory 1993* (White Plains, New York: Bernard C. Harris
        Publishing Company, 1993), v.

259     *disparity between Central and Girls' High*    These data are from the
        late 1970s and early 1980s, and are included in the judge's ruling
        in 1983 that required Central High School to admit girls. See *Eliz-
        abeth Newberg et al.* v *Board of Public Education et al.*, 9 Phila 556,
        565–66.

261     *Washington Irving*    Larry Rohter, "Order to Add Boys Upsets
        City High School for Girls," *New York Times,* 2 July 1985, B3. See
        also Eleanor Blue, "An Era Ends at Girls' School," *New York Times,*
        17 August 1986.

268     *"Fit the misguided . . ."*    "Uncivil Rights," *Daily News,* 9 February
        1998.

268     *"NOW is evidently . . ."*    Christine B. Whelan, "NOW Isn't Pro-
        Choice on Education," *Wall Street Journal,* 19 August 1997, A18.

270     *California program*    Amanda Datnow, Lea Hubbard, and Elisa-
        beth Woody, "Is Single Gender Schooling Viable in the Public Sector?
        Lessons from California's Pilot Program." *http://www.oise.utoronto.
        ca/depts/tpsadatnow/final.pdf* [20 May 2001].

271     *"Single-gender instruction . . ."*    Memo on "The Thomas Jefferson
        Academy," Board of Education, Long Beach Unified School Dis-
        trict, 2 March 1999.

274     *"Overall, there was . . ."*    Datnow et al., 44.

## 10. WHAT'S BEST FOR GIRLS?

283     *"The evidence of the impact . . ."*    "Growing Smart: What's Work-
        ing for Girls in School," Executive Summary, American Asssocia-
        tion of University Women, 1995, 10.

284     *Munsterberg and Dewey*    Hugo Munsterberg, "Is Co-Education
        Wise for Girls?" *Ladies Home Journal 27,* 15 May 1991, 16, 32,
        and John Dewey, "Is Co-Education Injurious to Girls?" *Ladies
        Home Journal 28,* 11 June 1911, 22, 60–61. Although Dewey sup-
        ported coeducation in general, he added that there would always be
        room within American education for at least some single-sex insti-
        tutions. "Society is very complex," he wrote. "There will long be
        room for separate institutions—just as the rise of women's colleges
        has not driven out 'finishing schools.'"

288    *international studies*  For a summary of some of the international research on single-sex schools, see Pamela Haag, "Single-Sex Education in Grades K–12: What Does the Research Tell Us?" in *Separated by Sex: A Critical Look at Single-Sex Education for Girls* (Washington, D.C.: American Association of University Women Education Foundation, 1998). See also Mary Moore, Valerie Piper, and Elizabeth Schaefer, *Single-Sex Schooling and Educational Effectiveness: A Research Overview,* submitted by Mathematica Policy Research, Inc., to the U.S. Department of Education, 24 July 1992. A more recent summary of the research can be found in Rosemary Salamone's *Same, Different, Equal: Rethinking Single-Sex Schooling* (New Haven: Yale University Press, 2003).

289    *Lee and Bryk Study*  Valerie E. Lee and Anthony S. Bryk, "Effects of Single-Sex Secondary Schools on Student Achievement and Attitudes," *Journal of Educational Psychology* 78, no. 5, 381–95.

291    *Lee's independent school study*  Valerie E. Lee, Helen M. Marks, and Tina Byrd, "Sexism in Single-Sex and Coeducational Independent Secondary School Classrooms," *Sociology of Education* 67 (April 1994), 92–120.

295    *"There is at least . . ."*  Cornelius Riordan, *Girls and Boys in School: Together or Separate?* (New York: Teachers College Press, 1990), 150.

295    *"Single-sex schools are places . . ."*  Cornelius Riordan, "The Future of Single-Sex Schools," in *Separated by Sex: A Critical Look at Single-Sex Education for Girls* (Washington: AAUW, 1998), 56.

295    *"slanted"*  Nick Anderson, "One-Sex Schools Don't Escape Bias, Study Says," *Los Angeles Times,* 12 March 1998, A-1.

298    *"We might ask . . ."*  Cited in Deborah Blum, *Sex on the Brain: The Biological Differences Between Men and Women* (New York: Viking Penguin, 1997), 38, 63. See also Anne Moir and David Jessel, *Brain Sex: The Real Difference Between Men and Women* (New York: Lyle Stuart, 1991), 11.

299    *"If we set . . ."*  Ibid., 49.

# Selected Bibliography

For a more comprehensive bibliography, see *www.wheregirlscomefirst.com*.

Alexander, Sara Colclough. *The Open Door: Celebrating the First Hundred Years of the Holton-Arms School*. Louisville: Harmony House, 1999.

American Association of University Women Educational Foundation. *How Schools Shortchange Girls: The AAUW Report*. New York: Marlowe & Co., 1995.

———. *Separated by Sex: A Critical Look at Single-Sex Education for Girls*. Washington, D.C.: AAUW, 1998.

Arnold, Winifred. "The Girl in Boarding School." *Harper's Bazar*, April and September 1908, 387–89 and 878–80.

Barnett, Evelyn Brooks. "Nannie Burroughs and the Education of Black Women." In *The Afro-American Woman: Struggles and Images*, edited by Sharon Harley and Rosalyn Terborg-Penn. Port Washington, N.Y.: Kennikat Press, 1978.

Beadie, Nancy, and Kim Tolley, eds. *Chartered Schools: Two Hundred Years of Independent Academies in the United States, 1727–1925*. New York: Routledge Falmer, 2002.

Beirne, Rosamond Randall. *Let's Pick the Daisies: The History of the Bryn Mawr School, 1885–1967*. Baltimore: The Bryn Mawr School, 1970.

Bishop, Susan O. "Where Have All the Headmistresses Gone?" *Independent School Bulletin*, October 1974, 22–24.

Bortz, Ave Marie DeVanon. *Mayfield: The Early Years, 1931–1950*. Pasadena: Mayfield Senior School, 2000.

"Boys & Girls/Together and Apart." *Independent School* 52 (fall 1992).

Brackett, Anna C., ed. *The Education of American Girls*. New York: G.P. Putnam's Sons, 1874.

Bready, Mary H. *Through All Our Days: A History of St. Paul's School for Girls*. Brooklandville, Md.: St. Paul's School for Girls, 1999.

Brewer, Eileen Mary. *Nuns and the Education of American Catholic Women, 1860–1920*. Chicago: Loyola University Press, 1987.

Brickley, Lynne Templeton. "Sarah Pierce's Litchfield Academy, 1792–1833." Ed.D. diss., Harvard University, 1985.

Brittain, Kilbee Cormach, Valerie Weiss Newman, and Cecil Carnes, eds. *Leaves from a Marlborough Diary, 1888–1938*. Los Angeles: Marlborough School, 1987.

Brown, Lynn Mikel, and Carol Gilligan. *Meeting at the Crossroads: Women's Psychology and Girls' Development*. Cambridge, Mass.: Harvard University Press, 1992.

Bryk, Anthony S., Valerie E. Lee, and Peter B. Holland. *Catholic Schools and the Common Good*. Cambridge, Mass.: Harvard University Press, 1993.

*Buffalo Seminary, The: 125 Years*. Buffalo: Buffalo Seminary, n.d.

Clarke, Edward H. *Sex in Education; or, A Fair Chance for the Girls*. 1873. Reprint, New York: Arno Press and The New York Times, 1972.

Coburn, Carol K, and Martha Smith. *Spirited Lives: How Nuns Shaped Catholic Culture and American Life, 1836–1920*. Chapel Hill: University of North Carolina Press, 1999.

Cochran, Heather, ed. *Celebrating Milestones: The Life and Legacy of the Harpeth Hall School*. Nashville: Harpeth Hall, 2001.

Cookson, Peter W., Jr., and Caroline Hodges Persell. *Preparing for Power: America's Elite Boarding Schools*. New York: Basic Books, 1985.

Cott, Nancy. *The Bonds of Womanhood: "Woman's Sphere" in New England, 1780–1835*. New Haven: Yale University Press, 1997.

Dalton, Kathleen M. *A Portrait of a School: Coeducation at Andover*. New York: toExcel, 1996.

Datnow, Amanda, and Lea Hubbard. "Gender in Policy and Practice: Perspectives on Single-Sex and Coeducational Schooling." New York: RoutledgeFalmer, 2002.

Datnow, Amanda, Lea Hubbard, and Elisabeth Woody. "Is Single Gender Schooling Viable in the Public Sector? Lessons from California's Pilot Program," 20 May 2001. *http://www.oise.utoronto.ca/depts/tps/adatnow/final.pdf.*

Davis, Nancy, and Barbara Donahue. *Miss Porter's School—A History.* Farmington, Conn.: Miss Porter's School, 1992.

Davis, Mary M. *A Remarkable Journey: The Story of St. Mary's Episcopal School.* Little Rock: August House, 1998.

Dawson, Virginia P. *Learning for Life: The First 50 Years of Hathaway Brown School: 1876 to 1926* Cleveland: Hathaway Brown School, 1996.

DeButts, Mary Custis Lee, and Rosalie Noland Woodland, eds. *Charlotte Haxall Noland, 1883–1969.* Middleburg, Va.: Foxcroft School, 1971.

Dewey, John. "Is Co-Education Injurious to Girls?" *Ladies Home Journal,* 11 June 1911, 22, 60–61.

Easter, Opal V. *Nannie Helen Burroughs.* New York: Garland, 1995.

Edmondson, Mary Dillon. *Profiles in Leadership: A History of the Spence School, 1892–1992.* West Kennebunk, Maine: Phoenix Publishing, 1991.

Elliott, Mary. "School Days at the Sacred Heart." *Putnam's Magazine,* March 1870, 275–86.

*Emma Willard and her Pupils, or Fifty Years of Troy Female Seminary, 1822–1872.* New York: Mrs. Russell Sage, 1898.

Everett, Carole. *The Nightingale-Bamford School: 75 Years of Excellence.* New York: Nightingale-Bamford School, 1996.

Farnham, Christie Anne. *The Education of the Southern Belle: Higher Education and Student Socialization in the Antebellum South.* New York: New York University Press, 1994.

Ferry, Abby Farwell. *When I Was at Farmington.* Chicago: Ralph Fletchers Seymour, 1931.

Foner, Philip S., and Josephine F. Pacheco. *Three Who Dared: Prudence Crandall, Margaret Douglass, Myrtilla Miner—Champions of Antebellum Black Education.* Westport, Conn.: Greenwood Press, 1984.

Fowler, Henry. "Educational Services of Mrs. Emma Willard." In *Memoirs of Teachers and Educators,* edited by Hennry Barnard. New York: Arno Press, 1969.

Fuller, Edmund. "Prudence Crandall: An Incident of Racism in Nineteenth-Century Connecticut." Middletown, Conn.: Wesleyan University Press, 1971.

Fuller, Lawrence Benedict. "Education for Leadership: The Emergence of the College Preparatory School." Ph.D. diss., Johns Hopkins University, 1974.

Generous, Tom. *Choate Rosemary Hall: A History of the School.* Wallingford, Conn.: Choate Rosemary Hall, 1997.

Gifford, Dorothy W. *Lincoln School: The First Century.* Providence, R.I.: Lincoln School, 1984.

Gilligan, Carol, Nona P. Lyons, and Trudy J. Hanmer, eds. *Making Connections: The Relational World of Girls at the Emma Willard School.* Cambridge, Mass.: Harvard University Press, 1990.

*Gone Away.* Middleburg, Va.: Foxcroft School, 1989.

Gordon, Ann D. "The Young Ladies Academy of Philadelphia." In *Women of America: A History,* edited by Carol Ruth Berkin and Mary Beth Norton. Boston: Houghton Mifflin, 1979.

Green, Nancy. "Female Education and School Competition: 1820–1850." *History of Education Quarterly* 18 (summer 1978): 129–39.

Griffin, Frances. *Less Time for Meddling: A History of Salem Academy and College, 1772–1866.* Winston-Salem, N.C.: John F. Blair, 1979.

Hamilton, Andrea Dale. "A Vision for Girls: A Story of Gender, Education, and the Bryn Mawr School." Ph.D. diss., Tulane University, 1997.

Hamilton, Sue Cleveland. "Programs of Studies of Private Secondary Schools for Girls," Master's thesis, University of Chicago, 1932.

Handler, Bonnie Silver. *Linden Hall: Enduring Values, Changing Times.* Lititz, Penn.: Sutter House, 1997.

Harris, Jean S. "Let's Hear It for Coeducation, Folks." *Independent School Bulletin,* December 1973, 5–7.

Harrison, V. V. *Changing Habits: A Memoir of the Society of the Sacred Heart.* New York: Doubleday, 1988.

Headmistresses Association of the East. Papers. Sophia Smith Collection of Smith College.

Howe, Julia Ward. *Sex and Education: A Reply to Dr. E. H. Clarke's "Sex in Education."* Boston: Roberts Brothers, 1874.

"Hunter College High School: A Chronology." In *Hunter College High School Alumnae/i Association Directory 1993.* White Plains, N.Y.: Bernard C. Harris Publishing Co., 1993.

Hunter, Judith A. *A Centennial History of Kent Place School, 1894–1994.* Summit, N.J.: Kent Place School, Photocopy.

Johnson, Karen A. *Uplifting the Women and the Race: The Educational Philosophies and Social Activism of Anna Julia Cooper and Nannie Helen Burroughs.* New York: Garland, 2000.

Jost, Kenneth. "Single-Sex Education." *The CQ Researcher* 12 (12 July 2002): 569–92.

Kaminer, Wendy. "The Trouble with Single-Sex Schools." *Atlantic Monthly,* April 1998, 22–36.

Keneally, James K. *The History of American Catholic Women.* New York: Crossroad Publishing, 1990.

Kerber, Linda K. *Women of the Republic: Intellect and Ideology in Revolutionary America.* Chapel Hill: University of North Carolina Press, 1980.

Klaus, Susan L., and Mary Porter Johns Martin. *A Part of Us Forever: A Centennial History of St. Catherine's School, 1890–1990.* Richmond, Va.: St. Catherine's School, 1989.

Kraeplin, Camille R., ed. *Of Hearts and Minds: The Hockaday Experience, 1913–1988.* Dallas: The Hockaday School, 1988.

Kraushaar, Otto F. *American Nonpublic Schools: Patterns of Diversity.* Baltimore: Johns Hopkins University Press, 1972.

———. *Private Schools: From the Puritans to the Present.* Bloomington, Ind.: Phi Delta Kappa Educational Foundation, 1976.

Labouchere, Albert E., ed. *The Chatham Hall Storybook.* Chatham, Va.: Chatham Hall, 1994.

LaFarge, Phyllis. "A Warm-Hearted Guide to Certain Girls' Schools." *Harpers,* April 1963, 73–79.

Lee, Valerie E., and Anthony S. Bryk. "Effects of Single-Sex Secondary Schools on Student Achievement and Attitudes." *Journal of Educational Psychology* 78 (1986): 381–95.

Lee, Valerie E., and Helen M. Marks. "Sustained Effects of the Single-Sex Secondary School Experience on Attitudes, Behaviors, and Values in College." *Journal of Educational Psychology* 82 (1990): 578–92.

———. "Who Goes Where? Choice of Single-Sex and Coeducational Independent Secondary Schools." *Sociology of Education* 65 (1992): 226–53.

Lee, Valerie E., Helen M., Marks, and Tina Byrd. "Sexism in Single-Sex and Coeducational Independent Secondary School Classrooms." *Sociology of Education* 67 (1994): 92–120.

Lindhorst, Marie J. "Sarah Mapps Douglass: The Emergence of an African American Educator/Activist in Nineteenth Century Philadelphia." Ph.D. diss., Pennsylvania State University, 1995.

Lloyd, Susan McIntosh. *A Singular School: Abbot Academy 1828–1973.* Hanover, N.H.: University Press of New England, 1979.

Lord, John. *The Life of Emma Willard.* New York: D. Appleton & Co., 1873.

Lutyens, Elizabeth. *So Grows the Tree: The Brooks School of Concord, Nashoba Country Day School, Nashoba Brooks School.* Concord, Mass.: Nashoba Brooks School, 2001.

Lutz, Alma. *Emma Willard: Pioneer Educator of American Women.* Boston: Beacon Press, 1964.

McCallie, Eleanor Grace. *Don't Say "You," Say "We": The Founding of Girls' Preparatory School, 1906–1918.* Chattanooga: Bruiser Press, 1982.

McCarthy, Marina Chukayeff. "The Anchor and the Wind: A Profile of Sacred Heart Schools in the U.S." Ph.D. diss., Harvard University, 1990.

McCluskey, Audrey Thomas. "The Historical Context of the Single-Sex Schooling Debate Among African Americans." *The Western Journal of Black Studies* 17 (1993): 193–201.

———. "Mary McLeod Bethune and the Education of Black Girls in the South, 1904–1923." Ph.D. diss., Indiana University, 1991.

McCluskey, Audrey Thomas, and Elaine M. Smith, eds. *Mary McLeod Bethune: Building a Better World.* Bloomington: Indiana University Press, 1999.

McKeen, Phebe. *Thornton Hall; or, Old Questions in Young Lives.* New York: Anson D. Randolph & Co., 1872.

McLachlan, James. *American Boarding Schools: A Historical Study.* New York: Scribner's, 1970.

Melder, Keith. "Mask of Oppression: The Female Seminary Movement in the United States." *New York History* 55 (1974): 260–79.

Mihesuah, Devon A. *Cultivating the Rosebuds: The Education of Women at the Cherokee Female Seminary, 1851–1909.* Urbana, Ill.: University of Illinois Press, 1993.

"Miss Chapin's, Miss Walker's, Foxcroft, Farmington." *Fortune,* August 1931, 38–44, 84–86.

"Miss Madeira's School: A Portrait, 1906–1981." In *Madeira Today,* fall 1981.

Moore, Mary, Valerie Piper, and Elizabeth Schaefer. *Single-Sex Schooling Educational Effectiveness: A Research Overview.* Washington, D.C.: Mathematica Policy Research, 1992.

Morrison, Louise Douglas. *A Voyage of Faith: The Story of Harpeth Hall.* Nashville: Harpeth Hall School, 1980.

Morrow, Diane Batts. *Persons of Color and Religious at the Same Time: The Oblate Sisters of Providence, 1828–1860.* Chapel Hill: University of North Carolina Press, 2002.

*Mount de Chantal Centenary, 1848–1948.* Wheeling, W.Va.: Sisters of the Visitation, n.d.

Munsterberg, Hugo. "Is Co-Education Wise for Girls?" *Ladies Home Journal,* 15 May 1991, 16, 32.

Murphy, Hope Ford. *Educating the Independent Mind: The First Hundred Years of Laurel School.* Shaker Heights, Ohio: Laurel School, 1998.

Neal, Heather, and Judith Hammerschmidt. *A Preposterous Extravagance: The Centennial History of the Baldwin School, 1888–1988.* Bryn Mawr, Pa.: The Baldwin School, 1988.

Neel, Joanne. *Miss Irwin's of Philadelphia: A History of the Agnes Irwin School*. Wynnewood, Pa.: Livingston Publishing Company, 1969.

Noerdlinger, Charlotte Johnson. *And Cheer for the Green and Gold: An Anecdotal History of the Chapin School*. New York: The Chapin School, 2000.

Oates, Mary J. "Catholic Female Academies on the Frontier." *U.S. Catholic Historian* 12 (fall 1994): 121–36.

Perkins, Linda M. "The Impact of the 'Cult of True Womanhood' on the Education of Black Women." *Journal of Social Issues* 39, no. 3 (1983): 17–28.

Peyster, Deborah, and Roberta Tenney. *The National Association of Principals of Schools for Girls: A Celebration of 75 Years*. National Association of Principals of Schools for Girls, 1995.

*Philadelphia High Schools for Girls: 150 Years, A Beginning*. Video. Philadelphia High School for Girls Alumnae Association.

Pinckney, Josephine. Call Back Yesterday: The First Twenty-Five Years of Ashley Hall. Charleston, S.C.: Quin Press. In the Ashley Hall archives.

Post, Winifred Lowry. *Purpose and Personality: The Story of Dana Hall*. Wellesley, Mass.: Dana Hall School, 1978.

Potwine, Elizabeth B. *Faithfully Yours, Eliza Kellas*. Troy, N.Y.: Emma Willard School, 1960.

Powell, Arthur G. *Lessons From Privilege: The American Prep School Tradition*. Cambridge, Mass.: Harvard University Press, 1996.

Powers, Jane Bernard. *The "Girl Question" In Education: Vocational Education for Young Women in the Progressive Era*. London: Falmer Press, 1992.

Pratt, Constance Ballou, ed. *Sharing*. National Association of Principals of Schools for Girls, 1974.

Ravitch, Diane. "All-Girls School: A Blessing or a Bias?" *New York Daily News*, 10 July 2001.

Reid, Doris Fielding. *Edith Hamilton: An Intimate Portrait*. New York: Norton, 1967.

Repplier, Agnes. *In Our Convent Days*. Boston: Houghton Mifflin, 1906.

Riordan, Cornelius. *Girls and Boys in School: Together or Separate?* New York: Teachers College Press, 1990.

Rury, John L. *Education and Women's Work: Female Schooling and the Division of Labor in Urban America, 1870–1930*. Albany: State University of New York Press, 1991.

Safian, Joanne. *Educating the Heart and Mind: A History of Marymount School, 1926–2001*. New York: Marymount School, 2002.

Sahli, Nancy. "Smashing: Women's Relationships Before the Fall." *Chrysalis* 8 (summer 1979): 17–27.

Salamone, Rosemary C. *Same, Different, Equal: Rethinking Single-Sex Schooling*. New Haven: Yale University Press, 2003.

———. "Single-Sex-Schooling: Law, Policy, and Research." In *Brookings Papers on Education Policy: 1999*. Washington D.C.: Brookings Institution, 1999.

Savin, Marion B., and Harold J. Abrahams. "The Young Ladies Academy of Philadelphia." *History of Education Journal* 8 (winter 1957).

Schier, Tracy, and Cynthia Russett, eds. *Catholic Women's Colleges in America*. Baltimore: Johns Hopkins University Press, 2002.

Schultz, Nancy Lusignan. *Fire and Roses: The Burning of the Charlestown Convent, 1834*. Boston: Northeastern University Press, 2000.

Scott, Anne Firor. "The Ever-Widening Circle: The Diffusion of Feminist Values from the Troy Female Seminary, 1822–72." In *Making the Invisible Woman Visible*. Urbana: University of Illinois Press, 1984.

———. "What, Then, Is the American: This New Woman?" In *Making the Invisible Woman Visible*. Urbana: University of Illinois Press, 1984.

*Seventy-Five Years of Excellence: The Ellis School, 1916–1991*. Pittsburgh: The Ellis School, 1991.

Sherwood, Grace H. *The Oblates' Hundred and One Years*. New York: Macmillan, 1931.

Shmurak, Carole. *Voices of Hope: Adolescent Girls at Single Sex and Coeducational Schools*. New York: Peter Lang, 1998.

Siroky, Allen. "Progressive Era Reform and Private Secondary Schools for Women, 1890–1920." Ph.D. diss., City University of New York, 1996.

Sizer, Theodore. *The Age of the Academies*. New York: Teachers College, 1964.

Sklar, Kathryn Kish. "The Founding of Mount Holyoke College." In *Women of America: A History*. Edited by Carol Ruth Berkin and Mary Beth Norton. Boston: Houghton Mifflin, 1979.

Smith-Rosenberg, Carroll. "The Female World of Love and Ritual: Relations between Women in Nineteenth-Century America." *Signs: Journal of Women in Culture and Society* 1 (1975): 1–29.

Solomon, Barbara Miller. *In the Company of Educated Women*. New Haven: Yale University Press, 1986.

*Springside School 1879–1979: One Hundred Years of Tradition and Change*. Philadelphia: Springside School, n.d.

Spykman, Elizabeth Choate. *Westover*. Middlebury, Conn.: Westover School, 1959.

Stabiner, Karen. *All Girls: Single-Sex Education and Why It Matters*. New York: Riverhead, 2002.

Sterling, Dorothy, ed. *We Are Your Sisters: Black Women in the Nineteenth Century.* New York: Norton, 1984.

Stevenson, Louise. *Miss Porter's School—A History in Documents, 1847–1948.* New York: Garland, 1987.

————. "Sarah Porter Educates Useful Ladies, 1847–1900." *Winterthur Portfolio* 18 (1983): 39–59.

Strane, Susan. *A Whole-Souled Woman: Prudence Crandall and the Education of Black Women.* New York: Norton, 1990.

Streitmatter, Janice L. *For Girls Only: Making a Case for Single-Sex Schooling.* Albany: State University of New York Press, 1999.

Taylor, Traki Lynn. "God's School on the Hill: Nannie Helen Burroughs and the National Training School for Women and Girls, 1901–1961." Ph.D. diss., University of Illinois-Champaign, 1998.

Tyack, David and Elisabeth Hansot. *Learning Together: A History of Coeducation in American Schools.* New Haven: Yale University Press, 1990.

U.S. General Accounting Office. *Public Education: Issues Involving Single-Gender Schools and Programs.* May 1996.

Vanderpoel, Emily Noyes. *Chronicles of a Pioneer School From 1792 to 1833, Being the History of Miss Sarah Pierce and Her Litchfield School.* Cambridge, Mass.: Harvard University Press, 1903.

*The Way of a School: Columbus School for Girls, 1898–1989.* Columbus, Ohio: Columbus School for Girls, 1989.

White, Antonia. *Frost in May.* New York: Dial, 1933.

Whitney, Catherine. *The Calling: A Year in the Life of an Order of Nuns.* New York: Crown, 1999.

Willard, Emma. Papers. "A Plan for Improving Female Education." Reprint. Marietta, Georgia: Larlin Corp., 1987.

Woody, Thomas. *A History of Women's Education in the United States.* New York: Science Press, 1929.

Yenne, Bill. *The Lions by the Golden Gate: Sarah Dix Hamlin and the History of San Francisco's Hamlin School.* San Francisco: The Hamlin School, 1990.

"The Young Ladies Buckle Down to Work," *Newsweek,* 9 Feburary 1959, 53–56.

# Photo Credits

1. Painting by Joseph Alexander Ames, Emma Willard School Archives.
2. Martha Decker Memorial Archive, Albany Academy for Girls; The Harpeth Hall School, Nashville, Tennessee; The Hamlin School.
3. Phillips Academy Andover Archive.
4. The Spence School.
5. Kathleen Galvin Johnson '53 Archives of The Madeira School.
6. The Foxcroft School, Middleburg, Virginia.
7. The Buffalo Seminary.
8. Choate Rosemary Hall Foundation, Inc.
9. Lake Forest Academy-Ferry Hall Archives.
10. Chatham Hall.
11. Archive of Schools of the Sacred Heart, San Francisco.
12. Archives of the Agnes Irwin School.
13. Collection of The Chapin School archives.
14. Florida State Archives.
15. Florida State Archives.
16. Miss Porter's School.
17. Miss Porter's School.
18. Archives of the Agnes Irwin School.

19. Western High School.
20. Roland Park Country School, Baltimore, Maryland.
21. Lake Forest Academy-Ferry Hall Archives.
22. Reprinted from *Educating the Heart and Mind: A History of Marymount School, 1926–2001* by Joanne Safian, RSHM.
23. The Laurel School Archives, Shaker Heights, Ohio.
24. Our Lady of the Sacred Heart Convent School, Sisters of the Holy Names, California Provincial Archives.
25. Our Lady of the Sacred Heart Convent School, Sisters of the Holy Names, California Provincial Archives.
26. Reprinted from *Educating the Heart and Mind: A History of Marymount School, 1926–2001* by Joanne Safian, RSHM.
27. Archives of Holy Names High School, Oakland, California.
28. The Julia Morgan School for Girls, Oakland, California.
29. Marilyn Newby Cooper Archives, Philadelphia High School for Girls.
30. Collections of the Library of Congress.
31. Hunter College High School Alumnae Association.
32. Courtesy of Andrew Spreitzer.
33. The Julia Morgan School for Girls, Oakland, California.
34. The Julia Morgan School for Girls, Oakland, California.
35. Girls Preparatory School, Chattanooga, Tennessee.
36. Archives of the Agnes Irwin School.

# Index